WITHDRAWN

JOYCE AND REALITY

Irish Studies
James MacKillop, *Series Editor*

Other titles in Irish Studies

Family Secrets: William Butler Yeats and His Relatives. William M. Murphy

Writing Irish: Interviews with Irish Writers from The Irish Literary Supplement.
    James P. Myers, Jr., ed.

An Anglo-Irish Dialect Glossary for Joyce's Works. Richard Wall

The Anti-Modernism of Joyce's "A Portrait of the Artist as a Young Man." Weldon Thornton

Children's Lore in "Finnegans Wake." Grace Eckley

Crimes Against Fecundity: Joyce and Population Control. Mary Lowe-Evans

Dreamscheme: Narrative and Voice in "Finnegans Wake." Michael Begnal

The Economy of "Ulysses": Making Both Ends Meet. Mark Osteen

"Finnegans Wake": A Plot Summary. John Gordon

Fionn mac Cumhaill: Celtic Myth in English Literature. James MacKillop

Flann O'Brien, Bakhtin, and Menippean Satire. M. Keith Booker

Gender and History in Yeats's Love Poetry. Elizabeth Butler Cullingford

Irish Poetry after Joyce. Dillon Johnston

James Joyce: The Augmented Ninth. Bernard Benstock, ed.

Reading "Dubliners" Again: A Lacanian Perspective. Garry Leonard

Seamus Heaney, Poet of Contrary Progressions. Henry Hart

"Ulysses" as a Comic Novel. Zack Bowen

Yeats and Postmodernism. Leonard Orr, ed.

Yeats and the Beginning of the Irish Renaissance. Phillip L. Marcus

Myself, My Muse: Irish Women Poets Reflect on Life and Art. Patricia Boyle Haberstroh, ed.

Reading Roddy Doyle. Caramine White

Yeats and Artistic Power. Phillip L. Marcus

JOYCE AND REALITY

The Empirical Strikes Back

JOHN GORDON

SYRACUSE UNIVERSITY PRESS

First Edition 2004
04   05   06   07   08   09   6   5   4   3   2   1

The paper used in this publication meets the minimum requirements
of American National Standard for Information Sciences—
Permanence of Paper for Printed Library Materials, ANSI
Z39.48–1984.∞™

Library of Congress Cataloging-in-Publication Data

Gordon, John, 1945–
Joyce and reality : the empirical strikes back / John Gordon.— 1st ed.
p. cm.—(Irish studies)
Includes bibliographical references and index.
ISBN 0–8156–3019–0 (cl. : alk. paper)
1. Joyce, James, 1882–1941. Ulysses. 2. Bloom, Leopold (Fictitious character)
3. Bloom, Molly (Fictitious character) 4. Dublin (Ireland)—In literature.
5. Empiricism in literature. 6. Reality in literature. I. Title. II. Series.
PR6019.O9U63 2004
823'.912—dc22
2004001993

To the memory of Father Robert Boyle, S.J.

JOHN GORDON is professor of English at Connecticut College. He is the author of *James Joyce's Metamorphoses*; *"Finnegans Wake": A Plot Summary*; *Physiology and the Literary Imagination*, and many articles on modern literature.

Contents

Illustrations

Introduction

—The question is, I said, is literature to be fact or is it to be an art?
—It should be life, Joyce replied, and one of the things I could never get accustomed
to in my youth was the difference I found between life and literature.
                                    —Arthur Power, *Conversations with James Joyce*

THIS BOOK is what Hollywood would call a prequel to my earlier *"Finnegans Wake": A Plot Summary*. There, I set out to show that for all its verbal arabesque, Joyce's most perplexing work nonetheless maintained its author's lifelong commitment to his own brand of realism, to the mimetic rendering of a world in which real things happen, in chronological succession, according to laws of cause and effect. That phrase "his own brand of realism" requires some explaining, which is where this book comes in. I am undertaking to explore, through Joyce's work leading up to *Finnegans Wake*, the evolution of Joycean reality and the Joycean strategies for expressing and dramatizing it.

The premises remain the same. They are:

1. Joyce was a realist, aggressively, always. From the beginning his deepest disdain was for writers who fudged or muddled the truth. His commitment to calling a spade a spade was pursued with enough determination and virtuosity to change American constitutional history, among other things. ("I made them take it!" someone heard him yelling out, after a night of drinking.) This commitment did not fade. It is in evidence, in overplus, during the writing of *Ulysses*, for instance in his letters back to Dublin soliciting details about this or that locale. It most certainly did not cease with the composition of *Finnegans Wake*. In the year he began on that book, Joyce was aligning himself with Ernest Hemingway, for having "reduced the veil between literature and life, which is what every writer tries to do." He wrote, again, to Ireland for details about his new book's site, in this case Chapelizod, and had a journalist interview his father for memories of that site. In 1933 he sent Frank Budgen to Ireland to interview the proprietors of the Chapelizod inn at the center of the action, had him

do a sketch of the relevant surroundings, and quizzed him about what he had found out.[1] Because this Chapelizod saga was also a dream-book, he studied dreams and dream literature. He enjoyed pointing out the generally expressive and specifically onomatopoetic effects with which the book was chocked. He believed—"Anna Livia Plurabelle" is built on this belief—that river names transmitted river nature mediated by human nature, because the people living on rivers would absorb their sounds and come up with names like "Mississippi" and "Minnehaha." We may today feel ourselves in a position to dismiss such a mimetic enterprise as having been a snare and a delusion, because everyone knows or else should know that bees go buzz in one language and hum in another, that Eskimos have fourteen words for snow and we don't, that Max Müller was wrong and Saussure was right. That may all be true (actually, it isn't, about the Eskimos, anyway) but it doesn't matter. What matters is what, from the evidence, textual evidence most of all, Joyce thought he could do and tried to do.

2. Joyce's brand of realism was different from ours. That is because his idea of reality was different. In particular, he believed in or entertained beliefs in all sorts of occult and pseudoscientific ideas, combined with other ideas held over from his religious phase or maintained, Yeats-like, in general resistance to the encroachments of positivism. When, in the "Sirens" episode, Leopold Bloom's watch stops in synchronization with his wife's sexual betrayal of him, it does not mean that *Ulysses* has jettisoned its claims to credibility. It means that *Ulysses* is grounded in a real world in which such things can, under the right conditions, really happen, and that those conditions are now in place. This added potentiality has the effect of licensing effects—telepathy, ghost-visitation, metempsychosis—extending Joyce's writings beyond what is generally meant by naturalism without thereby transgressing the boundaries of the Joycean real. Taking my cue from Joyce's notes, I have adopted the term "Orphic" for this dimension. It has, like everything else real, its own protocols, its own rules of possible and impossible, which I have undertaken to describe and summarize. That watch, for instance, would not have stopped in any of the episodes before "Sirens."

3. In the process, I have operated from the assumption that ideas current in Joyce's period are probably more useful guides to what is going on in his writings than ideas around in other periods, including our own. I think that too much has been made of the antennae-of-the-race notion that Joyce and a few others were clairvoyant forecasters of what we in this our own more illuminated age are now able to see plain. Joyce certainly considered himself an ad-

vanced writer if ever a writer did, but the avant-garde of his time was the avant-garde of his time. Those "Orphic" effects of his, for instance, which tend to get ignored today because foreign to current ideas of what serious fiction is, were familiar literary properties taken quite seriously indeed in the age of James, Conrad, Lawrence, Yeats, Doyle, Wells, and Kipling. The psychologies on display in his books owe something to Freud, as much to the Gestaltists, more to the pre-Freud generations (John Stuart Mill, Alexander Bain, William James, Wilhelm Wundt, Gustav Fechner, Charles Sherrington) that had worked to map the mechanisms of associationism and the mechanics of the neural synapse, and probably something to Jung, but little if anything to anyone later. In the matter of myth Joyce was a prestructuralist, not a poststructuralist: he understood the Troy cycle to have been the retroactive mythification of a sordid trade war but still believed that this mythification had something permanent to say about any given present. His philology is fundamentally late-nineteenth and turn-of-the-century philology, of, in the terminology of the time, the nativist camp tracing back to Wilhelm von Humboldt rather than the empiricist camp stretching forward to Derrida, much concerned with questions of sound symbolism, linguistic archaeology, meaning-by-analogy, and the perhaps recoverable memory of a common language: Stephen Dedalus may be taken seriously when he hypothesizes that all poetry began with "the simplest verbal gesture of an instant of emotion," of laborers shouting to encourage one another; much the same idea, this time around inflected with the gestural linguistics of Joyce's contemporary Marcel Jousse, is prominent in *Finnegans Wake,* one of whose tutelary spirits, Giambattista Vico, taught that language embodies the history of humanity. *Finnegans Wake* itself testifies throughout to the enduring appeal of the monogenetic theory of language origins still being advanced in its time, most conspicuously by Alfredo Trombetti, and every one of Joyce's major works, in tune with the philology of the age and the age before, attends studiously to the ways of etymology and folk-etymology,[2] to the sometimes linguistically structured generation of meanings out of prior meanings according to rules implicitly universal in scope. Interested in such evolutionary issues, Joyce was like the rest of his generation deeply influenced by Darwinian developmentalism, including the theorizings about race and genetics advanced by some of Darwin's more dubious epigones, and, at least at times, adhered to the totalizing version of universal process synthesized from Darwin by, notably, Herbert Spencer, a figure as fashionable in his time as he is unfashionable in ours. As Harry Levin pointed out long ago, in his aesthetic program Joyce positioned himself between the twin inheritances of late-nineteenth-century naturalism and late-nineteenth-century *symbolisme*—Zola and Mallarmé, objective truth and subjective truth—and looked for guidance to those writers, especially Flaubert and Ibsen, whom he believed had brought the two together with some success.

4. Yes, yes: "objective truth and subjective truth," and there's the rub. But Joyce's realism was the opposite of naïve. He carried in his epistemological bones the problematics of representationalism that had vexed the sophisticated literature of the West for two hundred years and more. Like others before him, he understood that the desert-island outcast imports his culture in his head, that the poet turning to nature for pure unmediated experience is like the tourist trying to drive to some place where there are no cars. "And what," asks the Shaun of *Finnegans Wake,* addressing a gang of schoolgirls, "do ye want trippings for when you've Paris inspire your hat?" (*FW* 453.25–26). It is a question, here by way of answer to the classic scene of Huysman's *A Rebours* in which a Parisian aesthete aborts his trip to London because nothing could equal the city he imagined while awaiting the train, never completely out of the Joycean picture. Solipsism lurks. His characters dream, get things wrong, hallucinate, and so on, taking the diegesis along with them, and it can often be difficult to disentangle the actual from the projected. Any reader inclined to emulate the Chinese emperor who dreamt he was a golden butterfly and could never thereafter be sure that it was not the other way around has a friend in Joyce's court. But the reader who wants to draw the line somewhere before that while still reserving the prerogatives of free-floating relativism is going to be given a harder time. He or she is going to have to decide just where that line should be drawn. Time and again Joyce challenges his readers to reevaluate some preliminary percept, to get it right or righter on a second or third look, and time and again there is such a thing as passing the test, and such a thing as not passing the test. That readerly operation, of dead-reckoning, like Odysseus, into near and then nearer approximation of the right place, is a major consequence—I would say a major purpose—of Joyce's puzzle-palaces. And the results are important, because they add up and interlock into composites of extraordinary complexity and internal consistency, to miss which is to be, increasingly, out of things.

The criteria by which these judgments are made to stand or not stand are in the main the usual ones of observation, evidence, relative probability, and process of elimination. (Joyce was a contemporary of Sherlock Holmes, too.) *Pale Fire, The Turn of the Screw, The Good Soldier, La Jalousie, In the Name of the Rose*—these are distinguished examples of the kind of hall-of-mirrors fiction that Joyce did not write. On the contrary: in Joyce's books, the Paris of

Huysman's non-tourist, though doubtless seen differently by different people, remains importantly a real place not to be confused with other places, for instance Dublin. That, in fact, is the real reason that Shaun, afraid that it might teach them a thing or two, does not want the girls to go there.

The following book consists of twenty chapters, some of them new, some of them coming out of previous essays and notes, conference presentations and panels, Internet list-group exchanges (especially in the j-joyce and fwake-l groups), and private e-mail and snail-mail—all herein revised and redistributed into what I hope will be a clear if sometimes multi-track argument, which goes as follows. (In the following summary and thereafter, I have adopted the convention of referring to the divisions of *Ulysses* as episodes, the divisions of this book as chapters.) Chapters 1 and 2 propose a foundational, essentially late-nineteenth-century cosmology underlying Joyce's view of things, as evidenced in *A Portrait of the Artist as a Young Man* and the *Dubliners'* story "A Little Cloud." Chapter 3 suggests further applications of this cosmology to the later work, especially *Ulysses,* and argues for an understanding of Joycean character formation and identity along its lines. Chapter 4, concentrating on the "Sirens" episode, explains how some of the transformations just described may be further explained by reference to Joyce's belief in "Orphic" reality—that is, occult phenomena put on a scientific basis. Chapter 5 tracks these Orphic effects into the lair of Joycean eroticism, concentrating on the presentation of Gerty Mac-Dowell in "Nausicaa," and chapter 6 extends that discussion into the area of Leopold Bloom's relationship with the two main women in his life, Molly and Martha Clifford. Chapters 7 through 12 all deal with what, based on the preceding, really happens in "Oxen of the Sun," from the point of view of this book's thesis one of the two most challenging episodes of *Ulysses.* Chapter 7 gives an overview of the essential processes at work in that episode; chapter 8, by way of illustration, focuses on one particularly knotty section; chapter 9 works to explain why one cue—the sound of a bell—has the effect that it does on the episode's action; chapter 10, in covering the more general subject of Joyce's attention to Bloomsday's sun, moon, and stars, extends the reading earlier given in chapter 8; chapter 11, also based on that reading, applies the astronomical (and astrological) material just considered to propose a date for Bloom's birthday; chapter 12 returns to a final survey of the episode as a whole, specifically in light of the cosmology originally described in chapter 1. Chapters 13 through 17 then address "Circe," along with "Oxen of the Sun" the other episode that, for my realist approach, requires the most explaining. Chapter 13 argues that Stephen's and Bloom's hallucinations in that episode are mainly traceable to parallel spells of disorientation induced respectively by absinthe and the condition known at the time as twilight-state epilepsy; in that light, chapter 14 surveys a number of passages in which "Circe" has been taken as opting for *différance*-generating textuality and makes the case for realist readings instead; chapter 15 shows how such a reading can account for the action of the episode's climax; chapter 16 explores a sidelight of the absinthe hypothesis introduced earlier. Chapter 17 analyzes the tenor and techniques of the final three episodes, especially "Ithaca," as psychologically determined effects—mainly, aftermath—of the action just reviewed. Chapter 18 concentrates on the juncture between "Ithaca" and "Penelope" to suggest a possible future change in the lives of Leopold and Molly Bloom, in that real world of theirs, after *Ulysses* ends. Chapter 19, drawing on all of *Ulysses*, will try to convince you that the man in the macintosh is really someone real. Chapter 20, something of an *envoi*, returns briefly to the subject and thesis of *"Finnegans Wake": A Plot Summary*, finding at the formal center of *Finnegans Wake* an all-too-real point-by-point reenactment, literally graphic, of one of Joyce's eye operations. There will be a good deal of cross-referencing along the way, but the hope is that the whole will build and follow its own momentum, like a Slinky going downstairs.

The book's title was suggested by the title of John Romano's excellent *Dickens and Reality*. The subtitle is a meretricious bid to lure the cultural studies crowd. The people whose commentaries and communications have helped me along really are too numerous to mention. Anyway, the mistakes are mine. My word processor's search function informs me that I have now used some form of the word "real" twenty-four times. It is just the beginning.

Abbreviations

REFERENCES TO JOYCE'S WRITINGS are abbreviated and cited parenthetically. *Ulysses* is cited by chapter and line numbers, separated by a period. *Finnegans Wake* is cited by page and line numbers, separated by a period. Standard editions used are listed as primary sources in the references. Abbreviations to standard editions are as follows.

CP	*Collected Poems*
CW	*The Critical Writings of James Joyce*
D	*"Dubliners": Text, Criticism, and Notes*
E	*Exiles*
FW	*Finnegans Wake*
JJ	*James Joyce* (Ellmann)
JJP	*James Joyce in Padua*
L1	*Letters of James Joyce* Vol. 1
L2, L3	*Letters of James Joyce* Vol. 2, 3
P	*A Portrait of the Artist as a Young Man*
SH	*Stephen Hero*
SL	*Selected Letters of James Joyce*
U	*Ulysses: A Critical and Synoptic Edition*

JOYCE AND REALITY

1

A Portrait of the Artist

A Domino Theory

1

MOLLY AND LEOPOLD BLOOM come fatefully together in a game of musical chairs; Maria in "Clay" learns her future in a fortune-telling game; in *Finnegans Wake* a chess game's checkmate is also the mating of lovers. In James Joyce's books, the games people play tell you something about the lives they are leading. In the concluding chapter of *A Portrait of the Artist as a Young Man*, there is a handball game going on as Stephen conducts his own back-and-forth contest of wits, and a chess problem, which never gets beyond "Pawn to king's fourth," punctuating the last colloquy before his departure. "Pawn to king's fourth" is of course a standard first move, therefore the right move for a young man setting out, especially one determined to "go forth" (*P* 159). When the same young man returns in *Ulysses*, first to occupy and then to be locked out of a tower, he will have been in chess terms first promoted to a "crown," like a pawn who has made it to the last—tower's—rank, and then mated, as his opposite makes the move of "king to tower" (*U* 14.1538–40). Since this opposite is Mulligan and since Mulligan's move involves an alliance with the English occupier, it is worth noting that in Dublin the English center of authority was called the Castle, and that this move of Mulligan's is known as castling.[1]

At the other end of *Portrait*, three games put in an appearance—football, hacking chestnuts, and dominoes. As elsewhere in Joyce, football pretty much stands for the worst features of red-blooded male culture. So does the chestnut game, which amounts to seeing whether your entry can smash the other fellow's. Because if it does it will assume, cannibal-king-like, the conquests of every chestnut its rival smashed and the chestnuts they smashed and so on, it is an instructive game for a boy learning not only about power (on the football field) but also about power's permutations, about for instance how many magistrates equal a marshal.

Which leaves the third game, dominoes. Like the others, it appears when it does because Stephen is ready to notice it. Football, a violent sport Joyce disliked, got noticed when Stephen was feeling unhappy and put-upon; cricket, a summer game Joyce liked, will later get noticed when Stephen is feeling buoyant. So with dominoes: when he observes it (P 13–14), Stephen is indoors, in a noisy room, about to come down with the collywobbles and struggling to "hear for an instant the little song of the gas" (P 14), that is, to apprehend one distinctive rhythmic strain from out of the din of general background commotion "which," as his older self will put it, "is not it" (P 212). The phrase comes from his formulation of the stages of apprehension later given in his aesthetic theory, which also begins with the question of what gets noticed and how. What gets noticed by the timorous boy during the football game, for instance, are the boots and legs of the players otherwise blurred into a swarm, plus the ball they are kicking, and the reasons are obvious: the six-year-old Stephen is shorter than the others; the eye follows a moving object; he is mainly interested in not being kicked, therefore in those feet and legs.

Such initial perceptions are generated out of contrasts, usually figure-ground contrasts: near against far, moving against static, what matters against what does not. The forging of such contrasts is the essential operation through which Stephen processes the binary divisions defining this phase of his growth. "The little silk badge with the red rose on it looked very rich *because* he had a blue sailor top on" (my italics)—that is, its perceptual saliency arises from the contrast with the blue field against which it is set (P 12). That red rose in turn is accented by its contrast to the white rose, as are York against Lancaster and Stephen against Jack Lawton, the one prevailing over the other or not in perpetual oscillation of perspective. Irish politics is a composition of green for Parnell and maroon for Davitt, and so is the green earth in its maroon clouds (P 15). (So Ireland, as Joyce was to spend the rest of his life showing, equals the world in microcosm.) The train Stephen remembers in his dream is colored chocolate "with cream facings" and staffed by guards dressed in blue and silver, locking and unlocking, locking and unlocking the doors as their whistles go "click, click: click, click" (the colon tells when to start a new bar of paired notes); it takes him to a home of "holly and ivy, green and red" (P 20).

Hence the first reason those dominoes register in Stephen's vision, at a particularly dizzying moment when he is struggling to make sense of things: with their distinctive white-dots-on-black-field design, they epitomize just the kind of external fact that he looks for and holds to. That green-and-maroon picture of the world was done with a schoolboy's box of crayons, and these first pages, this first of the book's synoptic pictures of the real world through Stephen's eyes, are crayon-like too, mainly primary colors and simple masses set off in strongly distinguished shapes: green circle on maroon page; white circles on black rectangle.

As many, beginning with Hugh Kenner, have observed, these pages are also the basis from which everything in Joyce's labyrinthine book will grow. Wet, cold, "suck," "eyes," and so on are not just words; they are themes for later orchestration. And those dominoes Stephen notices are especially instructive as to how that orchestration happens. The game not only attracts Stephen's pattern-finding consciousness; it illustrates it. You play dominoes by matching. The total number of dots on one of your tile's two squares must match those on the square of a tile already played. If it does not, it doesn't count. And in young Stephen's mind, matching is also the name of the game he plays in order to encounter the reality of Clongowes. "Go and fight your match. Give Cecil Thunder a belt" (P 9)—so one boy to another, having himself been matched into memory by that word "belt," from the belt of Stephen's suit. Such connections, of matching like to like, constitute the second essential stage in Stephen's project of making sense of this new, bewildering world, "swarming with boys" all with "different clothes and voices," each with "a different way of walking" (P 13). Having dialectically distinguished what features are to be noticed from the background of everything else—having isolated out and counted the white domino dots, for instance—he automatically seeks a match with some other recognizably similar pattern, similarly generated. It is his main way of making categories out of chaos, and not surprisingly the main kind of action he notices around himself as well: matched chestnuts hacking one another, one set of lips pressed to another in that strange business called "kissing," "Hayfoot! Strawfoot!", rhymes and riddles and puns and wordplay ("How we wobble when we have the collywobbles!"; "What's up? The sky is up"), canker and cancer, the equations of sums, the pairing of infirmary beds, the gushing of paired hot and cold faucets.

The world is thus made to come approachably together through the isolation, pairing, and congruence of foregrounded similarities—through, that is, the forging of analogies. The word most instrumental to this operation is "like." It occurs thirty-one times in the second section's nineteen pages, more frequently than for instance "with" or "is" or for that matter "Stephen," at a rate above that for any other section and about twice that for the book as a whole.[2]

Its first appearance, in the section's opening, is instructive: "The wide playgrounds were swarming with boys. All were shouting and the prefects urged them on with strong cries. The evening air was pale and chilly and after every charge and thud of the footballers the greasy leather orb flew like a heavy bird through the grey light" (*P* 8). Against pluralized and generalized—therefore backgrounded—boys and prefects, shoutings and cryings, chargings and thuddings, the eye, following a moving object, isolates one distinctive thing and, via "like," matches it with a more familiar distinctive thing, earlier inscribed in Stephen's memory. (In the first section he already knew what an eagle was, therefore what birds were.) Near the section's end, when this experience returns in memory, the "like" will have dropped away (he recalls, simply, "a heavy bird flying low through the grey light"), to take its place in his permanent repertoire of images.

The process is one of psychic assimilation, of familiarizing the new by finding matching alliances between uncoordinated outside and established inside, thus making the world a friendlier place. Dependent as it is on selection, the process necessarily involves exclusion. Snug in bed, Stephen shuts in his warmth by shutting out the cold (*P* 17), as he installs birds within his field of personal symbols by dislodging footballs. Then he shuts his eyes.

Earlier, in that disorienting room where he noticed the dominoes, feeling sick and bewildered by "All the boys" with all their different attributes, he made himself feel better by rhythmically shutting and opening the flaps of his ears. This action accomplishes three things. It cuts the total aural input in half, automatically making it more manageable. It gives it a pattern: roar—stop; roar—stop. And, by way of the indispensable "like," it makes that pattern recognizable, therefore familiar, therefore comforting: "It made a roar like a train at night. And when he closed the flaps the roar was shut off like a train going into a tunnel. That night at Dalkey the train had roared like that and then, when it went into the tunnel, the roar stopped. He closed his eyes and the train went on, roaring and then stopping; roaring again, stopping. It was nice to hear it roar and stop and then roar out of the tunnel again and then stop" (*P* 13). It is "nice" because it now has a comprehensible shape, established by a match to a memory drawn from happier and less confusing days. Chaos has been matched away into the equivalent of an old familiar tune. Likewise the "little song of the gas" he listens for, whose great charm is that it is, like God (*P* 16), "always the same" (*P* 11), always like itself, therefore the latest version of what the previous section calls simply "his song."

And so, too, with the game of dominoes Stephen watches while hearing that song: not only the kind of thing that he notices, it is also the kind of thing, seeking matchings, that he likes to notice, first because it makes for a simple, familiar pattern, and second because in so doing it confirms his working assumption that things make sense by matching up.

And also because, though he does not yet know it, that pattern, like the song, is "his." His name is Dedalus; Daedalus was the maze-maker; the shape of a game of dominoes is the shape of a maze. As a game progresses the matchings shoot off rows of tiles that double back at right angles, growing into the kind of pattern, of right-angled branchings doubling back and intersecting other branchings, found in the mazes through which experimental psychologists were soon to start running laboratory rats. The maze theme will be sounded repeatedly from now on, but this is its first appearance in the book, and the important point to note is that, like a dominoes layout, it does not spring but grows into existence as a result of mental acts. It is not something in which, Theseus-like, Stephen is plunked down; it is something which, Daedalus-like, is generated out of a mind—his mind, at work as we have seen, generating its mental materials and making them match up, in an action that expands into increasingly intricate shapes: a labyrinth, growing.

2

That the mind was a labyrinth had become a commonplace by Joyce's day, inspired in part by surgery's exposure of the brain's "convolutions" and the microscope's detection of the tree-like ("dendrite," "cortex") branchings of its nerves. There was nothing particularly surprising about a one-time medical student like Joyce adopting such a model, which also attracted such different sorts as Hart Crane and Paul Valéry, George Eliot and T. S. Eliot. What does set him apart is his attention to and demonstration of its dynamics, of how it grows into being. This distinction will continue to mark his work from now on, in books of which it is frequently said that they take on mental lives of their own. From its beginning, *A Portrait of the Artist as a Young Man* establishes the mechanism which makes this internal dynamism possible. It is primarily a psychological study whose psychology is primarily developmental, following laws of growth that the age would have called evolutionary. Stephen Dedalus, maze-making prodigy, agent of a mind forever ramifying through the cumulative trial-and-error processing of external environment just described, is, for an age preoccupied with such things, someone eminently worth studying.

An example of someone who is not is his companion Lynch, for reasons that become clear in a moment of phrenology-influenced scrutiny: "The long slender flattened skull beneath the long pointed cap brought before Stephen's mind the image of a hooded reptile. The eyes, too, were reptilelike in glint and gaze. Yet at that instant, humbled and alert in their look, they were lit by one tiny human point, the window of a shrivelled soul, poignant and selfembittered" (*P* 205–6). This is a picture of someone who will never grow, whose "portrait" will always be the same. Lynch's soul is tiny and ingrown ("selfembittered") because seated in a brain locked into a narrow skull; its owner is reptile-like because consequently lower on the evolutionary scale, in that limbic region down by the brain stem; that his skull should be "flattened" may recall that for Darwin and his followers a smooth, relatively unconvoluted brain surface—*lissencephaly* came to be the clinical term—was evidence of retardation.[3]

Smoothness equaled retardation because developmental progress was marked by the record of how many branchings the organism had taken, by how convoluted the inner labyrinth had become. We never really find out how Stephen looks from the outside, but his inside is consistently represented as a field of gathering changes, of a scope and intricacy far beyond the likes of Lynch. For instance: "The dull light fell more faintly upon the page whereon another equation began to unfold itself slowly and to spread abroad its widening tail. It was his own soul going forth to experience, unfolding itself sin by sin, spreading abroad the balefire of its burning stars and folding back upon itself, fading slowly, quenching its own lights and fire" (*P* 103). It can do that sort of thing, expand outward to absorb "experience" that it then folds into itself before resuming, because unlike Lynch's brain it is not shut up in some hardened container. On the contrary, a soul like this, forever unfolding to "spread abroad" and incorporate new experience across some transfusive membrane through which it can at other times send "a vital wave . . . out of itself and back again" (*P* 103), might if anything be visualized as protean, even amoeboid. The mergings and mutations that typify Stephen's crucial encounters with experience are of that sort, a business less of penetration than of interpenetration, dynamically managed through variously permeable surfaces.[4]

And the soul's movement is driven by that living labyrinth inside, by its drive to ramify endlessly by assimilating ever more of the outer environment. Stanislaus Joyce recorded that his brother's initial conception for *Portrait* was to show that a man's "character, like his body, develops from an embryo" (Stanislaus Joyce 1950, 17); it remained a goal of the finished product, too. For Stephen in *Portrait* that conception is the fundamental principle behind the growth of mind and soul, of body (cells), of math equations (see above), of music, and of the cosmic processes that compose and decompose stars: "The vast cycle of starry life bore his weary mind outward to its verge and inward to its centre . . . The stars began to crumble and a cloud of fine stardust fell through space" (*P* 103).

All of which can certainly sound like metaphysical mumbo-jumbo. But it would not likely have seemed that way to the Joyce who was to go on to write *Finnegans Wake*, or, before that, the "Oxen of the Sun" episode of *Ulysses*, which like *Portrait* also embraces and coordinates, among other things, cytology and astronomy.

To explain that last: I once did a study of "Oxen of the Sun" (the basis for chapter 12 of this book) that turned up more than I had bargained on. The point I had set out to demonstrate was that the episode coordinated not only the histories of English prose and embryological development familiar from Joyce's account (*L1* 139), but a number of other staged chronologies as well—of an individual male life, of a nation's rise and fall, of the biblical narrative of mankind's progress. All this, I thought, made theoretical sense according to premises known to be around in Joyce's time, in particular the biogenetic law formulated by Ernst Haeckel. If phylogeny recapitulated ontogeny, then so might any other organic cycle. If the developmental stages of the embryo reenacted the evolution of the species, then so, conceivably, might the life of the individual who emerged from the embryo and the history of the tribe or nation composed of many such individuals; in fact just such a concatenation of correlations might explain how the development of a nation's literature, itself the expression of many related individuals all part of one common destiny, could evolve in tandem with a representative fetus of that nation. Organic life was organic life, went the formula: all growth followed the same narrative, on different scales.

What set me back was the discovery that this narrative also seemed to apply to phenomena that were not organic—to the geologic ages of the earth, for instance, or, weirdest of all, to a tour of the solar system. "Oxen of the Sun," so help me, among many other things enacts a journey from the sun outward, taking note in its passage of each of the planets in their proper order and then heading out toward the Milky Way.

Which enactment is, face it, not to be explained as a function of embryology. The apparent anomaly leaves, I think, two possible explanations. One, Joyce was fooling around. Probably a history of kitchen sinks is somewhere in there too. Or, two, he had in mind a unified-field theory of everything, of which embryology was but one part—something that could embrace cells, continental drift, constellations, history, music, mind, whatever. In which case, Stephen's likening of his math-solving mind to the mechanics of star formation is not just self-aggrandizing afflatus. He may be onto something.

I believe the second explanation to be the correct one. Stephen really is onto something—to a version of the most influential non-Marxist Theory of Everything being advanced in his day, one that Joyce himself went on to embroider but not abandon, even as it was falling from favor. Its most recognizable components come from Darwin, but Darwin cosmologized, made into a theory not just of life but of the inorganic raw material from which life arose, at one end, and, at the other, of art, politics, and all the refinements of human organization.

Of the many people working the applied-Darwinism vein during the years in which Joyce was coming into his own, the best known was Herbert Spencer. He seems an unlikely influence. The Joyce who sometimes did not seem to think very highly even of Darwin himself would not, you would think, take warmly to his main champion, nor to the racial boosterism and progress-at-any-price shibboleths connected with Spencer's name. Still, Joyce did tell his biographer Herbert Gorman, apparently without condescension, that he had read Spencer, along with other advanced thinkers of the time (*JJ* 142). And there were reasons that he might have found Spencer, if not congenial, pertinent. First, Joyce was manifestly interested in the issues of evolutionary genetics, including racial genetics. He read the pseudoscientific genetic theorists Cesare Lombroso, Allen Upward, Louis Berman, and Otto Weininger with enthusiasm and at times apparent approval,[5] wrote breezily about the "anabolism" of one institution (*SH* 147) and of another's natural tendency to "degenerate" from "creative force" to "frenetic sensationalism" (*JJP* 21), and wondered whether the most famous "degenerate" of his time, Oscar Wilde, was the victim of "heredity and the epileptic tendency of his nervous system" (*CP* 203). In general he thought less in terms of the Irish nation than of the "race," a race whose peasantry the Stephen of *Stephen Hero* calls "almost Mongolian" (*SH* 244) and whose patricians the Stephen of *Portrait* hopes to improve through Darwinian or Lamarckian eugenics (see *P* 238). He entertained similar ideas throughout *Ulysses* and *Finnegans Wake,* with what degree of irony it is difficult to determine. In any case, he was always concerned with what he once called the "prehuman" (*L1* 180) elements composing human nature. This bent, most fully on display in the metamorphic effects of *Finnegans Wake,* where variously humanoid figures split and couple like cells, is present as early as *Stephen Hero,* in which Catholicism is in Stephen's conceit a matter of "amoeboid" "primal cells," expanding and contracting its "elastic body" and consuming by absorption (*SH* 123).

So Joyce was at least interested in many of the same things that engaged Spencer, whose writings would have been the natural first place to turn. Spencer's standing at the time was incomparably higher than now. Turn-of-the-century academics ranked him among the greatest thinkers ever. And in fact he was a cogent if long-winded exponent of some of the main ideas around, which he coordinated into the cosmological theory laid out in a series of volumes beginning with the synoptic *First Principles.*

The theory goes like this: In the beginning there was chaos, a scattering through all space of random bits of matter. Eventually, due to gravity, they began clumping together. In doing so they followed what is known as the "nebular hypothesis," which had been formulated by Pierre Laplace (and anticipated separately by William Herschel and Immanuel Kant) in order to explain this odd fact about the solar system, that all the planets circle the sun in the same direction, in the same approximate plane. Laplace's explanation was that as the bits of cosmic dust came together all of the resulting "nebulae" would be emitting radiation—their fusion generating energy, spreading outward—and that all or almost all would be rotating. According to the laws of physics, a body doing both will accelerate its rotation for as long as the radiation goes on. Because of its spin, it will also flatten out, becoming not a sphere but what the popular public scientist Sir James Hopwood Jeans, like Leopold Bloom's favorite astronomer Sir Robert Ball a Laplace adherent,[6] called a "slightly flattened oblate spheroid . . . an orange-shaped figure."[7] (Compare Stephen, in *Ulysses,* calling the earth an "oblate orange" (*U* 15.4427); surely Jeans is his source.) At high velocities of rotation, before, like the present earth, it has mostly finished cooling down, it will seek equilibrium by throwing off quantities of matter from around its equator, matter that in its turn will also clump, heat up, radiate, spin off, dim, and cool. That is how the planets were created and why they all rotate on the same plane in the same direction.

For many theorists of Joyce's time, the elaboration of the planets out of the sun's molten mass prefigured all later evolutions, and its basic shape is the seen-sideways shape of Saturn, the Milky Way,[8] the solar system, and, probably, the atom, according to the theorizings of among others Niels Bohr and Ernest Rutherford, who in 1912 introduced the term "nucleus," drawing an implicit analogy with cell's center and planet's core. Spencer saw the generation of the solar system as the starting point of evolution: "Evolution, under its primary aspect, is illustrated most simply and clearly by this passage of the Solar System from a diffused incoherent state to a consolidated coherent state" (Spencer 1916, 281), the change being always "consequent on the dissipation of motion and integration of matter" (Spencer 1916, 299). All existence, not just life, is a matter of process, not stasis, which because of what he calls the inherent instability of all "homogeneous" systems must become increasingly heterogeneous. For Spencer, joining Darwin with a tradition incorporating Goethe, Comte, and George Henry Lewes, evolution is a universally applicable process leading to increasing concentration, differentiation, and specialization in everything that changes (which is everything), and as such the force behind, in the words of Jonathan H. Turner's study of Spencer, "the building of solar systems, the creation of chemical compounds, the emergence of new species, the elaboration of cognitive complexity, and the growing complexity of . . . social systems" (Turner 1985, 36). The "elaboration" of the planets out of the sun's molten mass prefigures all later evolutions.

Which would explain what the planets are doing in "Oxen of the Sun," parallel to an embryo's evolution. They too are being evolved, out of a half-nebular, half-molten proto-sun whose linguistic signature, following an opening invocation to go "sunward," is the garrulously hypotactic diction of the first pages, into the more distinctive presences that emerge later in the episode as the styles correspondingly become more particularized (see chapter 12). Planets aside, such a cosmology would supply a rationale for Joyce's application, in that episode, of the principles of embryology to virtually any kind of change.

It would also explain what Stephen has in mind in *Portrait,* comparing the growth of his soul to that of a galaxy. In general, in fact, it would account for his peculiarly dynamic psychology, a psychology passing through stages that are at all points also compared to various other kinds of development. And here, it is time to acknowledge my indebtedness to Sidney Feshbach, whose essay "A Slow and Dark Birth: A Study of the Organization," taking off from Richard Ellmann's suggestion that the book represents the "gestation of a soul" (*JJ,* 297), brilliantly demonstrates that *Portrait*'s five chapters enact a five-stage spiritual phylogeny, from "plant or vegetative" to animal to "human or rational" to "angelic or intellectual" to "divine or imaginative." Thus Stephen shakes like "a loose leaf" in the first chapter, moans like a "beast" in the second, is scared (and reasoned) out of his body in the third, devotes himself to an "angel of mortal youth and beauty" in the fourth, and in the last chapter creates his first imaginative work, out of a vision of "seraphic life" (Feshbach 1998, 130–42).

Feshbach identifies Aristotle, Aquinas, and the Neoplatonists as among the sources, as no doubt they are.[9] But Joyce's notes and charts for "Oxen of the Sun" show that the modern science of embryology was much in his mind too. Looking to find in embryology a universal principle—one encompassing

Aquinas and Plotinus, for instance—he would certainly have considered, if not Spencer himself, then the body of contemporary post-Darwinian thought that Spencer synthesized.

In this body of thought, he would have found the basis for the project with which the prototype of *Portrait* began, the realization of his subject's "individuating rhythm."[10] The aesthetic announced with that phrase is mimetically expressive: the form of the artifact should follow the inherent individuating movement of its human subject. It seems to me a limitation of Feshbach's thesis that it does not allow *Portrait* really to do that. The stages of development derived from Aristotle, etc., apply equally to all souls that reach maturity. But surely one striking fact about the structure of the book as Feshbach has described it is that it is a complex of analogies, and the forging of analogies is, as I have tried to show, a distinctive activity of Stephen's mind. At one point, Feshbach in effect agrees: "the novel's emphasis on the technique of analogy corresponds to the way Stephen's spirit functions," he says, and goes on to cite examples of "Stephen's habit of analogization of himself and his landscape" (Feshbach 1998, 139). However, his assumption apparently remains that Stephen's labyrinthine matchmaking is a function of the novel's formal properties: Joyce has constructed a manifold of analogies, and so the central figure embedded within them must out of formal consistency replicate the operation that brought it into existence, somewhat as, for instance, an author who views the world sentimentally might produce sentimental characters. But Stephen is not just a character, he is *the* character—the artist—whose engagement of reality, generations of readers have sensed, determines more than follows the book's formal development: when the temper of the book changes, it is always to some extent because he changes.

So it is not mainly, I suggest, that Stephen's habit of analogization exemplifies an artifact built up of analogies. The reciprocal applies at least as forcefully. Not that all the analogies detectable in the text are Stephen's own; there is also, as usual in Joyce, the consubstantial narrator, who can share the protagonist's cast of mind while extending it into new territory. Nor does it mean that *Portrait* is dismissibly solipsistic—though the book does tend that way periodically and perhaps warns us of the fact at the outset, where Mr. Dedalus looks "through a glass" in language reminiscent of Paul's metaphor for the clouded vision of youth,[11] commencing a chapter much of which will come to us through a youth's uncorrected presbyopia. Still, there really is a young man here whose impositions on the world we can, more or less, gauge and evaluate, and there seems no reason to reject the correspondences that Feshbach demonstrates, especially since Joyce was to return to them later.

Stephen's mind, that is, is fitted, more or less adequately, to a world, itself largely a matter of matching entities, from which it draws its own recognitions. Stephen's thinking corresponds to the reality of analogies as his vision, however distorted at times, corresponds to the reality of light. It is similarly a product of evolution, with the difference that it not only registers but reenacts the phenomenon that brought it into being: the universe makes him up out of a complex of correspondences (giving him the body of a boy like other boys, the name of a Christian martyr and Greek inventor), and he returns the favor. The process of evolution is extended by way of his brain and then detected: Feshbach's five-stage phylogenetic continuum is, if not something Stephen directly perceives, the sort of thing someone like him, sooner or later, would look for. And that cast of mind, again, is given to drawing connections between itself and areas vaster even than life, in its own individual way.

Hence the "individuating rhythm" desiderated by the young Joyce, in a phrase reminiscent of neo-Darwinian psychology. Evolution works through the development of the human mind, according to Spencer and others as it works through atom, cell, and galaxy, as the engine of increased concentration, differentiation, and specialization—that is, individuation. According to evolutionary psychology, Stephen's five organic stages of development, even while following a standard pattern, should make him increasingly sui generis, because increasingly adapted to his unique niche, following the same laws by which crocodiles and marigolds have evolved from cell colonies. Or, indeed, from single cells: "All writers who have devoted themselves . . . to the study of unicellar organisms," wrote Alfred Binet in 1894, "have attributed to these beings most of the psychological properties which M. Romanes reserves for this or that higher-class animal" (Binet 1894, v). The climate of opinion that, from one end of the continuum, licensed Stephen to speak of human institutions in terms of "amoeboid" operations was, from the other end, one in which it was possible to speak of the psychology of cells.

Cells were like minds because they wanted to go forth to encounter reality, by selectively meeting and absorbing the material around them, in the process becoming more and more themselves. They did this through a three-stage operation of (1) coming in contact with the environment, (2) distinguishing what was ingestible from what was not, and (3) ingesting the former. The second of these stages, wrote Binet, shows that a cell "in some manner or other knows how to choose and distinguish alimentary substances from inert particles of sand" (Binet 1894, 41). He might have added that it is essentially a business of matching, of recognizing in the exterior environment an organic substance akin to that already in the interior.

The mental equivalent of these three stages was outlined by, among others, Theodule Ribot, an influential turn-of-the-century psychologist in the Darwin tradition whose developmental approach made him an advocate of Vico's theory of historical cycles (Ribot 1906, 174–75). Ribot drew on the work of Spencer along with near-contemporaries Alexander Bain and Georg Heinrich Schneider in analyzing all thought on whatever level into two activities, differentiation (the "limitation . . . of the field of consciousness" in focusing on one object or field of objects) and recognition of resemblances ("associating, combining, unifying"),[12] which second activity was facilitated by a third, the retention of what had been previously internalized mentally through the first two. Memory, in short. So, to return to our original example, Stephen (1) differentiates the moving football from its environment, (2) combines it with his internal image of a bird, from a previous recognition, and (3) retains what is now a new memory, for future matchings with future differentiated input. All this traces back to a sequence that began, as all consciousness begins—as, according to Spencer, all creation begins—with disruption, with a change from the homogeneous to the heterogeneous. As Ribot puts it: "A homogeneous or continuous state of consciousness is an impossibility . . . Nevertheless a succession of change does not suffice to constitute consciousness. This succession must be regular. Changes form only the raw material of consciousness; it is necessary in addition that they be organized, that is to say, classed according to resemblances and differences" (Ribot 1873, 184). Consider, for instance, the organization of resemblances and differences in the opening lines of *Portrait:* "Once upon a and a very good time it was there was a moocow coming down along the road and this moocow that was coming down along the road met a nicens little boy named baby tuckoo. . . . His father told him that story: his father looked at him through a glass: he had a hairy face. He was baby tuckoo" (*P* 7). Tracking psychological development, Joyce begins not with Stephen's birth but with the dawning of his consciousness, which comes into being with the emergence of a salient singularity, one time ("Once") being distinguished from other times, in turn immediately matched with the category "good time." Building on this base, the sequence of matchings rhymes us toward Stephen's first distinct awareness of himself: from time to good time, good time to good time with moocow on the road, moocow on the road to story of moocow on the road, story of moocow on the road to father telling story of moocow on the road, father telling story to the hairy face that distinguishes him from the other parent (the one with the "nicer smell"), parents to their child, their baby—him, baby tuckoo.

This is all, of course, in the tradition of associationism, but an associationism inflected with the dialectic,[13] especially as recast by Darwin. It is not a matter of one percept randomly triggering another; rather the links proceed according to the "regular," "organized" progression of "resemblances and differences" that Ribot describes, moving geometrically outward, building their expanding labyrinth, each new complex incorporating all those that have been forged earlier. Spencer and Ribot both emphasize that the alternating current of mental growth comes from the nature of evolutionary development, as manifest, for instance, in the two afferent and efferent conductions of the nervous tissue, or the two "antagonistic processes" of differentiation by oxygen and integration of nutrition that power all cells (Ribot 1873, 185), or all the other exhaust-and-replenish pulsings of life. This alternating current occurs on a multitude of micro-- and macro-levels, with a corresponding range of durations, extending, in history, to the rise and fall of dynasties. On the level of individual psychology, it applies, according to Spencer, to the rhythms of creation and infatuation:

> If we contemplate mental actions as extending over hours and days, we discover equilibrations analogous to those hourly and daily established among the bodily functions. This is seen in the daily alternation of mental activity and mental rest—the forces expended during the one being compensated by the forces acquired during the other. It is also seen in the recurring rise and fall of each desire. Each desire reaching a certain intensity, is equilibrated either by expenditure of the energy it embodies in the desired actions, or, less completely, in the imagination of such actions: the process ending in that satiety, or that comparative quiescence, forming the opposite limit of the rhythm. And it is further manifest under a two-fold form on occasions of intense joy or grief. Each paroxysm, expressing itself in violent actions and loud sounds, presently reaches an extreme whence the counteracting forces produce return to a condition of moderate excitement; and the successive paroxysms, finally diminishing in intensity, end in a mental equilibrium. (Spencer 1916, 404)

Those "loud sounds" accompanying the extremes of cyclical "paroxysm" may elucidate Feshbach's observation that each of the five stages of *Portrait* climaxes in "a cry in Stephen's mind," a vocal release of "increased pressure" (Feshbach 1998, 131). Such releases are periodic. Given the cumulatively maze-making nature of evolutionary psychology, it is inevitable that things pile up inside. This is all the more the case because, following cell biology, the neo-Darwinians also followed Rudolph Virchow's doctrine of *omnis cellula e cellula*, that each cell is an outgrowth of a long succession of predecessors whose genetic inheritance it encodes; that was why the biogenetic law made sense. So we all come extensively networked to begin with, in addition to which the more evolutionarily

advanced of us—artists, for instance—continue to go on enacting and extending the essential vital processes, forming "sub-classes and sub-sub-classes,"
building up one "vast structure" within after another (Spencer 1916, 307).

The logic behind this progression is, again, Darwinian. The reason it con-
duces to evolutionary success is that the more detailed and nuanced one's reading of the environment, the better one's chances of surviving in it: a
color-sensitive cat has an adaptive edge over a color-blind cat. Theoretically,
then, it might be expected that evolution, driving us teleologically toward "the
establishment of a correspondence between relations among our ideas and relations in the external world" (Spencer 1916, 465), would eventually produce an
organism ideally interactive with its environment, one in which every external
blip called up each its proper neuronal twitch. There are two reasons that will
never happen. The first is that things change, so that successful adaptation to
one environment can unfit an organism for the next. (The Stephen Dedalus of
chapter 1 who learned how to prevail in a Jesuit environment by playing one
priest against the other is mostly an encumbrance to the Stephen of chapter 2,
removed from Clongowes.)

The second reason comes rather unexpectedly from a school often associated with onward-and-upward progressivism. Spencer, again, defined evolution as "a change from a less coherent form to a more coherent form, consequent
on the dissipation of motion and integration of matter." "Dissipation," written
at a time when "dissipated" commonly meant effete and overbred, signifies the
evolutionary price to be paid, as the energy that drives the process of individuation thereby brings about its own dispersion. The nebular hypothesis, after all,
requires from the outset that its coalescing systems be simultaneously radiating
energy, in other words cooling or running down. As Turner summarizes, "the
very process in integration creates a decrease in the vital forces . . . For example,
as the masses that constitute a solar system become integrated, they also begin
the long process of decay. Or as diverse populations of people become organized politically, much of the vitality and force that prompted such organization
in the first place can be lost" (Turner 1985, 38). Likewise with psychology: intellectual refinement is the result of growth, and growth, in multiplying the internal correlates to external reality, diminishes the power of each, to the point
where the whole may in Turner's words become "stagnant" and dissolve
(Turner 1985, 38). By the same token, an ambitious musical-celestial composition begun in the heat of inspiration can "crumble" into a "cloud of stardust" (P
103), and a Daedalus can become lost in the labyrinth of his own creation, or
simply lost.

3

I propose that the stages of *Portrait*'s five chapters occur according to this logic, as successive acts of psychological adaptation to changing environments by a dynamic organism best thought of as a protoplasmic vessel, following evolutionary principles, implicitly applicable to all other developments, which are self-limiting in the way described above. Richard Ellmann was the first to point out that Stephen's insides are often represented as some kind of liquid in some way identified with life processes.[14] I would add that these liquids can congeal and vaporize, and that in any state they behave in certain consistently hydrodynamic ways. First, they seek expansion through proliferation. Second, they are enclosed, usually under pressure, and their release or failure to be released is always a big deal. Inner tides surge and blood flushes cheeks; tears burst forth or, distressingly, dry up and fail to burst forth; an attack of conscience induces a spasm of vomiting and later a confession that oozes and trickles out; thoughts "condense" in the head or send out "fumes" from the heart. The question of the relative occlusiveness or penetrability of the membrane separating liquid interior from exterior, itself often also figured as liquid, is one that constantly concerns Stephen when contemplating his identity and its frontiers: "He had tried to build a breakwater of order and elegance against the sordid tide of life without him and to dam up, by rules of conduct and active interests and new filial relations, the powerful recurrence of the tides within him. Useless. From without as from within the water had flowed over his barriers: their tides began once more to jostle fiercely above the crumbled mole" (*P* 98). As usual, this way of looking at his body and at its connection with the environment gets elaborated by the narrator, sometimes in ways past Stephen's ken.[15] The six-or-so-year-old contemplating the word "suck" cannot, probably, appreciate the innuendo that has raised generations of eyebrows—"To remember that and the white look of the lavatory made him feel cold and then hot. There were two cocks that you turned and water came out: cold and hot. He felt cold and then a little hot: and he could see the names printed on the cocks. That was a very queer thing" (*P* 11)—even though he has recently observed that the water coming out of his own as yet unnamed spigot can make the bed warm, then cold (*P* 7). But the connection marked here between Stephen and cold and hot faucets will soon carry over into illness experienced as "cold slimy water," later into the "scalding" tears that gush from his eyes, then, in the chapter's last line, into contentment experienced as a "brimming bowl." In the sexual sequences to follow, it will be useful to remember that Joyce has early taught us to think of Stephen's "cock" not as a rooster but as a faucet, as something that can release pressure from a brimming reservoir.

Inner distress equals inner turgidity. Father Arnall's sermon, a "withering" "simoom" (P 108) blown into Stephen's "burning" (P 115) ear, heats his interior into magma: "His blood began to murmur in his veins, murmuring like a sinful city summoned from its sleep to hear its doom. Little flakes of fire fell and powdery ashes fell softly, alighting on the houses of men. They stirred, waking from sleep, troubled by the heated air" (P 142).

This passage may owe something to the fire and brimstone visited on the Cities of the Plain, but more, surely, to the fire and ashes that, in the version made popular by Bulwer Lytton, fall on sinful Pompeii, erupting from what are sometimes called the earth's underground veins, sometimes its entrails[16]— which may help account for the curious fact that Stephen's later vomiting is said to come not from his gorge but from his clogged and revolted "entrails" (P 138). The logic is chemically geothermal, on a Miltonic scale: Hot blasts of wind vaporizing, melting, and expanding earth's innards into eruptions of lava, dispersing as flakes of fire and ash. In Stephen's imagination, Father Arnall's wind, funneled into his insides, has volatized a largely liquid explosion upward and outward.[17] The conceit completes the most vivid imagery of the sermon, that of souls constricted and writhing in the fire at earth's exact red-hot center ("four thousand miles thick" in either direction [P 119], which equals the planet's eight-thousand-mile diameter), therefore at maximum pressure for eruption. "Entrails" are the right locus for sin envisioned as inner liquidity swelling with its own putridity.

This way of envisioning his innards has been with Stephen since at least his first visit to the red light district, that "maze" calling to mind "an obscene scrawl . . . on the oozing wall of a urinal" (P 100). The word that most sums up his sense of oozing self-pollution is "filth," introduced to describe the cow pies of the farmyard (whose milk cans [P 64] show up in the "battered canisters" [P 137] in Stephen's nightmare of an excremental hell, also inspired by Arnall's sermon), magnified in Arnall's evocation of an infernal cistern. "Like a beast in its lair his soul had lain down in its own filth" (P 115), goes one of his assents to the sermon's diagnosis, and everything that follows confirms the picture, a picture of suffocation in distinctively viscous filth. An erection is "fattening on the slime of lust," like his soul's "fattening and congealing into a gross grease" (P 111, 140), clogged by the relentless process of inner accumulation mapped out in Arnall's image of the multiplying mountain of sand, or in Stephen's own derivative vision of an exponentially multiplying labyrinth of streets (P 139).

It is fitting that such mathematically conceived versions of maximum density emerge under the influence of the priest who taught Stephen to do sums. About to meet him again, meditating on his next meal's "fat" and "thick" and "flourfattened" consistency as a symbol of how his repetitions of sin have "multiplied his guilt and punishment," Stephen discerns yet another symbol of the same thing in his lesson's fattening equation, an equation that he could not now perform had he not learned the rudiments from his "old master": "The equation on the page of his scribbler began to spread out a widening tail, and starred like a peacock's; and, when the eyes and stars of its indices had been eliminated, began slowly to fold itself together again" (*P* 103).

This equation gives us, in essence, the shape of the nebular hypothesis. It may be the *Portrait*'s shape as well. Hans Walter Gabler has argued for the book's "chiastic" structure—chapters 1 and 5, 2 and 4 balancing off one another, with chapter 3 set like a stone in the center of the ring (Gabler 1998. See also Hart 2002 for a similarly chiastic pattern in "Oxen of the Sun"). Michael Levinson has further proposed, quite persuasively, that the book's fringes, of prologue at one end and diary at the other, constitute mirror images of one another (Levinson 1998). Add to these observations the common perception that Arnall's sermon, occupying the middle of the middle chapter and imaginatively situated, for much of its length, at earth's core, is the book's heaviest, most oppressive stretch, even perhaps that at the center of that sermon and of the book occurs *the* paragraph of absolute ultimates.[18] The possibility arises that, formally, *Portrait* has the symmetrical shape of that equation, which is the shape of Rutherfordian atom, cell, galaxy, solar system, and spiral nebula, and that the book too can be thought of as growing up and out through processes of association, concentration, accumulating articulation, and centrifugal dispersion, with its center therefore logically the point of greatest density.

Stephen's feeling of mounting internal coagulation in chapter 3 is an extreme case, but of a pattern found throughout. The hot tears that "burst" out of him in chapter 1 have likewise been building up for a long time, and were so to speak precipitated by the preceding section, the Christmas dinner scene. Categorically, some such sense of accumulating inner pressure comes over him in each phase of his development, and it is always intellectual as well as emotional. The pattern of mental pressure, then release, applies from the beginning, as when trying to imagine his way out to the edge of the universe makes Stephen "feel his head very big" (*P* 16). Not just feeling, he is learning too, which is to say retaining what he has felt and working it into the scheme made of earlier impressions deposited, mainly, during the recent past, in his increas-

ingly "big head." Over and over, the pattern is for such accretions of encountered reality to accumulate, ramify, knit, and thicken to a maximum of eventually unsustainable intricacy and density, at which point either or both of two
things ensue—the whole complex, having expanded beyond the capacity of its
finite store of energy, dissipates in the way Spencer described, or it finds an outlet and vents, seeking release into what always turns out to be yet another vessel, with which the operation begins again.

We can witness both processes at work early in chapter 2. Stephen's triumph
at the end of chapter 1 has produced a stasis of ideal plenitude—that "brimming bowl." The pages that follow give a picture of exhaustion, of stale habit
(the defining word is "would": the dilapidated Mike Flynn "would be found,"
"would stand," and "would make his comments," "uncle Charles would often
pay a visit," "the boys would take turns," and so forth), of decrepitude (Flynn,
Uncle Charles, Mr. Dedalus), of the disintegration of what was earlier whole
and sufficient. Although influenced by the decline in family fortunes, Stephen's
noticing of such things as usual also reflects an internal collapse of the stasis he
had recently achieved. Later in the chapter his earlier brave appeal to Father
Conmee will have become routinized—he will become the one the other students send to the priests in order "to beg them off" (P 84)—not to mention trivi-
alized by his family (P 72), but well before that his sense of earned heroism has
been translated, through his reading, into flimsy fantasy, courtesy of the cave
remembered from *The Count of Monte Cristo*, of "transfers and paper flowers
and coloured tissue paper and strips of the silver and golden paper," all easily
broken up (P 62).

Along with this dispersal of the previous chapter's focal fusion of self-
defining energy, there is also displacement, that principle of physics recently
adapted by Freud to his version of psychic kinetics. In Stephen's mind such exchanges are often intensely physical, characteristic of a cytoplasmic body expanding and eventually dividing. All of the crucial changes of his life are
accompanied with a "trembling" or "tremor" that typically invests his whole
self, and he is several times given to envisioning such changes in terms of total-
ized metamorphosis, of one organism emerging as a completely different and
separate organism. In chapter 2, the process, though not so dramatic, is still a
transformation of vital interiority from one vessel into another. Stephen is attracted to the Monte Cristo story, as he will be later to the Claude Melnotte
story,[19] because its revenge narrative sustains his new-minted (in chapter 1)
sense of himself as a triumphant vindicator while at the same time supplying a
flattering way of understanding how such a figure could have ended up in his

current degraded state (betrayal, and the envy of inferiors: that's how). At the same time it also, through the story's Mercedes component, gives the betrayed-hero narrative an erotic side, newly pertinent to this newly adolescent male. *The Count of Monte Cristo,* in seizing and then loosing Stephen's imagination, in matching its narrative shape to the new outline of Stephen's inner life, helps mediate one kind of master fantasy into another.

That is, the dissipation of Stephen's previous complex is also the occasion for a rechanneling toward the formation of another. The principles at work are physics-text physical, beginning with fluid mechanics: as the contours of one network weaken, opportunities for new connections open up. The labyrinthine walls of the weakening vessel become more and more permeable; the pipes spring leaks; the emerging lines of directed energy seek their paths of least resistance until, in some other place, the countervailing force of mutual attraction begins drawing some of them together into a new complex.

And then the nebular hypothesis takes over. On the biological, including the cellular, level, the word for the initial act by which fluid breaks through vessel wall toward eventual fusion with another vessel, is *anastamosis,*[20] a term familiar to readers of *Ulysses* (*U* 14.300) and *Finnegans Wake* (*FW* 583.22–23, 615.05), in both of which it signifies a new juncture between internal conduits (umbilical, genital, "adomic") in the process of generating a new organism from haploids of the old order. The word could apply to *Portrait* as well. The Stephen quoted above worrying about how "tide" without and "tides" within are about to overflow the "crumbling mole" between them is contemplating an anastamosis he does not desire. Here, on the other hand, is how it is experienced when such a breach, as usual seen as a physiologically psychological one, is coveted, as a transition from old stage to new:

> The verses passed from his lips and the inarticulate cries and the unspoken brutal words rushed forth from his brain to force a passage. His blood was in revolt. He wandered up and down the dark slimy streets peering into the gloom of lanes and doorways, listening eagerly for any sound. . . . He wanted to sin with another of his kind, to force another being to sin with him and to exult with her in sin. He felt some dark presence moving irresistibly upon him from the darkness, a presence subtle and murmurous as a flood filling him wholly with itself. Its murmur besieged his ears like the murmur of some multitude in sleep; its subtle streams penetrated his being. His hands clenched convulsively and his teeth set together as he suffered the agony of its penetration. He stretched out his arms in the street to hold fast the frail swooning form that eluded him and incited him:

and the cry that he had strangled for so long in his throat issued from his lips.
(*P* 100)

Forget, for a minute, that this is supposed to be a featherless biped in a state of excruciating sexual arousal, and a picture that might emerge, I suggest, is of an encysted protoplasm seeking conjunction with another, through anastamosis. It seeks such conjunction as a release from the pressure of a liquescent inner substance that must "force a passage" out, a pressure in turn augmented by the flooding of its "being" by liquids that have forced a similar passage inward. Weeping and ejaculating, according to this picture, are not distinctly delegated functions of an articulated organism; they are, rather, pretty much interchangeable manifestations of any pressurized container's action of seeking a weak point and punching through it to the outside, through what Stephen habitually envisions as, and sometimes calls, an "outlet" (*P* 64, 77, 151). What makes the process distinctively biological is the requirement that the anastamosis be an act of matching, one performed with "another of his kind." (And this creature of his kind should acknowledge, and "exult" in, their sin, should be like-minded as well as like-bodied.) That Stephen thinks he will "force" this on her, after all, makes little sense as a description of the actual sexual transaction—he is not contemplating rape—but may convey that when the two are together yet another "passage" will "force" its way through. The passage or passages will be two-way, interpenetration not penetration, less like a picture of heterosexual copulation than like a picture of amoeboidal interfusion, extending both ways from both vessels. Seldom can the "inter" of "intercourse" have been taken so literally.

To write of someone in such a way is to envision him as an agent of some life force or élan vital. Stephen, who is being at least partly serious in *Ulysses* when he has nature determining the generative "ends" for which he and his randy friends are "means" (*U* 14.227–28), almost never chooses on his own, is almost always propelled by some version of the "dark presence" driving him "irresistibly" to sin or whatever, toward "the end he had been born to serve yet did not see," reached by "escape by an unseen path" toward some new path, now "opened" (*P* 165). And when, in the latter pages of the book, he contemplates such forces at work in himself and tries introspectively to determine their governing laws, what he finds is some phase of the nebular hypothesis: "A dim antagonism gathered force within him and darkened his mind as a cloud against her disloyalty: and when it passed, cloud-like, leaving his mind serene and dutiful towards her again, he was made aware dimly and without regret of a first noiseless sundering of their lives" (*P* 164). Initially "dim" elements converge by mutual attraction, thicken and thus darken, in the process achieving a peak of emotional energy ("antagonism" at "her disloyalty") too intense to sustain; the energy accordingly disperses, the cloud thins and dims again, and the final effect is one of disintegration.

Throughout his career, Joyce was given to similar accounts of his and others' thought processes. Beginning to write *Finnegans Wake*, he was to have this to say about the act of composition: "I work as much as I can because these are not fragments but active elements and when they are more and a little older they will begin to fuse of themselves" (*L1* 205)—in other words at a certain point will reach what a later age would call critical mass and begin gathering, out of mutual attraction, into clusters. The Joyce-ish, Stephen-ish Richard Rowan of *Exiles*, on the subject of his own next book, speaks of "some new thing . . . gathering in my brain" (*E* 19). *Finnegans Wake* contains many variants on the theme, including an apparition of Issy as "nibulissa," a "little cloud" (*FW* 256.32),[21] hovering over her brothers, like one of those so-called thought-balloons that cartoonists were beginning to distinguish from their regular conversation balloons by fluffing them into cloudlets. As we will see in the next chapter, in the story "A Little Cloud," written a few years before *Portrait*, a character's thoughts about his life can gather, coalesce, distill, and precipitate strictly according to standard weather-report principles.

To an extent, doubtless, Joyce at such times is drawing on conventional talk about sunny dispositions and stormy moods. But at least in "A Little Cloud," he takes it past casual metaphor: he sticks with it, keeping it in play and fore-grounding it with title and climax. For the length of that story, anyway, nebular dynamics have as much to teach us about Little Chandler's story as the *Odyssey* has to contribute on the subject of Leopold Bloom. And although *Portrait* is certainly a more heterogeneous production, during its last third or so those are the dynamics that Stephen discovers when he looks within—thoughts typically gathering together into thickening nebulae from out of the particles of previous, now-dispersed aggregates, to culminate, distill, and disperse in turn.

The climactic "swooning" at the end of chapter 4 illustrates the process, amidst a suitable setting: without are "slowdrifting clouds," "veiled sunlight," a "hazewrapped city," and "drifting" "seatangle" under "dim waves"; within is "nebulous music." In another anastamosis, atypically painless, Stephen's inner state blends with the environing haziness: "So timeless seemed the grey warm air, so fluid and impersonal his own mood, that all ages were as one to him" (*P* 167). Coming out of what he calls the "mists" of his life, he becomes at one with nebulous air, water, and under-water; their laws become his laws. One such law is that new elements entering his system commingle catalytically, blending with and changing one another along with their medium, like grit in an oyster or dust in a cloud. His last name, called out to him, engenders, in a mind brooding on antiquity, his own legendary namesake, then couples with the new impression of "swordlike pain" of pity penetrating him to conjure up the analogous forger Siegfried, "forging anew in his workshop out of the sluggish matter of the earth a new soaring impalpable imperishable being"—the sword of destiny.[22] This self-crystallization prepares him to meet his Brünhilde, the goddess-girl who, as many have pointed out, distills in her person all the iconic female figures he has known or imagined up to now. She can do that because the myth-making, identity-forging intelligence turned on her is at maximum pitch, overheated like Stephen's cheeks and body, "aflame" and "aglow." When that faculty in that body then turns its attention back to the sky "traversed by cloudy shapes and beings" (P 172)—not just clouds now but clouds worked into recognizable if fantastic figures by Stephen's aroused imaginative energy—it is as if that energy, at red-hot pitch, finally expended itself utterly in imposing on the firmament its color and its innermost vision of the symmetrical sublime: "Glimmering and trembling, trembling and unfolding, a breaking light, an opening flower, it spread in endless succession to itself, breaking in full crimson and unfolding and fading to palest rose, leaf by leaf and wave of light by wave of light, flooding all the heavens with its soft flushes, every flush deeper than other" (P 172).

Thus does the nebular mass find and forge its glowing center, and then radiate out from its nucleus. The multifarious shapelessness—the nebulousness—of the initial experience is essential: it is in the matching of analogies out of disparate material (girl—bird; drawers—feathers; seaweed—Hermetic emerald sign) that the energy is generated. A few pages into the next chapter Stephen will represent his thinking as "a dusk of doubt and selfmistrust lit up at moments by the lightnings of intuition" (P 177), having already learned that the two go together, that the greater the obscurity, the brighter the lightning. He has learned as well, through introspection, how involuted the process can be, to what extent such fusions draw on earlier fusions retained in the memory. His vision of that girl on the beach was such a composite, of Eileen and Virgin Mary and prostitute and so on, and if he did not realize it then he certainly does by the time, late in the next chapter, when he composes his villanelle and recognizes in his memories of various females the "fragments" and "distorted reflections" of the one "fair image" he is trying to in all senses compose on paper (P 220).

In fact the introspection (or "intuition") that prevails throughout his aesthetic phase can have the paradoxical effect of taking him not so much into as back through himself, to scrutinizing the "reflections" appearing from his past and the hidden "chemistry" that selects and assembles them. Why (he asks himself) does his mind, specifically his image-forging faculty, by generating its picture of Cranly's disconnected head, signal that it wants Cranly to be John the Baptist? (see *P* 178, 248). An easy question: So Stephen can play Jesus. Why (he also asks himself) does the same faculty, by giving a "freckled and strong" hand to its apparition of a guilty couple, show that it wants to impute incest to the blameless Davin? (see *P* 228). A difficult question, never really answered. And why, exactly, is this same faculty so hard on the dean of studies, on the evidence's showing a worthy and well-meaning fellow, "courteous and vigilant" (*P* 189) in dispute, in his way as much a spiritual exile as Stephen? Introspecting, Stephen tries to figure out the answer to that as well, this time with uncertain results.

The difficulty of the question is an index of how much more complicated has become his picture of his own inner workings during the course of one chapter. In the parallel scene of chapter 4, presenting Stephen's encounter with "the director," one has only to recognize in "the swish of a soutane" that begins the meeting (*P* 154) the dread leitmotif established by Father Dolan ("the swish of the sleeve of the soutane as the pandybat was lifted to strike" [*P* 50] to understand why things then go as they do,[23] why on once being jump-started by this remembered sound Stephen's mythopoeic motors should immediately start generating hangman's noose and skull and "crossblind" out of cord and head and windowshade, and why the director's appeal will never have a chance. But how, exactly, does the Stephen of chapter 5 come to conceive of the dean of studies as "an unlit lamp or a reflector hung in a false focus" (*P* 187)? The answer, this time around, is more tangled.

As a start, there are the usual stage effects, here casting their conventional gloom: a gray light coming through a dusty window, an emptied room, a solitary man in black standing beside a cold hearth. By now Stephen has acquired enough self-knowledge to know that he is responding to these effects in conjuring the conceit of the "unlit" lamp, and presumably knows as well that his picture of a "lamp" with a "reflector" has been prompted by the dean's story of how Epictetus, having had his "lamp" stolen, "reflected" on what to do. But he apparently has not yet realized, as he will have by the time of *Ulysses*, that the sight of the dean "crouching" before the fireplace has reminded him of the same attitude being assumed by chapter 1's Brother Michael (*U* 17.135–47), whose perceived pathos (he is a "brother," lower than a "father": "Was he not holy enough or why could he not catch up on the others?" [P 23]) seems here to have resurfaced, displaced, in Stephen's otherwise puzzling conviction that he will never call this "faithful servingman" (bending down to the hearth, Brother Michael reminded Stephen of a "tramhorse" [P 23]), "this halfbrother of the clergy," "his ghostly father" (P 190). ("Halfbrother"? The dean belongs to the Jesuits, renowned for not doing things by halves.) He seems unaware as well of how the dean's name, revealed in *Ulysses* as "Father Butt" (U 17.145; see Gottfried 2002, 40), has combined with the unlit "candlebutts" in his pocket (P 185) to make him over into the unlit candle stuck in the reflector's holder, or of how the ludicrously lowly associations of the name may have influenced Stephen's picture of him as clerical dogsbody. Had the dean been named, say, Father Ambrose, would the narrative still have him resting on his "hunkers"?

The thought may occur that it is Stephen, more than the dean, whose "reflector" is out of focus here—seems indeed to be occurring to Stephen himself when he hits on the metaphor. A reflector is, essentially, a concave mirror,[24] designed to capture and concentrate a room's lights. A mental reflector, if trying to make things cohere but not quite succeeding, could be expected to come through as something like this: "A smell of molten tallow came up from the dean's candle-butts and fused itself in Stephen's consciousness with the jingle of the words, bucket and lamp and lamp and bucket. The priest's voice too had a hard jingling tone. Stephen's mind halted by instinct, checked by the strange tone and the imagery and by the priest's face which seemed like an unlit lamp or a reflector hung in a false focus. What lay behind it or within it?" (P 187–88).

Stephen may not know the answers to such questions by this point but remains reasonably clear on the mental operation by which they are to be pursued. It is to be by the reflector's optical equivalent of the nebular hypothesis, the fusing together of cloudily dispersed memories and impressions in the "consciousness," conjoining them into a concentrated whole that will not be in "false focus."

This version of his mental chemistry, implicit throughout, becomes explicit in his last and longest exercise of sustained imaginative generation, the writing of the villanelle. Most commentators have felt that the finished poem is derivative and artificial and just not very good, and the poet of *Chamber Music* would probably have concurred. In fact, to some extent that is the point: the sequence is all about trying to recapture the fine flush of inspiration now forepassed and failing in the attempt. That inspiration has been an "instant of enchantment," an enactment of the "enchantment of the heart," which Stephen, drawing on Luigi

Galvani's account of the electrification (the "galvanizing") of a frog's heart, had the day before used in describing the "mysterious instant" of perfect aesthetic apprehension (*P* 217, 213). By contrast the moment's "afterglow" into which Stephen wakes is, in a word, nebulous: "The instant of inspiration seemed now to be reflected from all sides at once from a multitude of cloudy circumstance of what had happened or of what might have happened. The instant flashed forth like a point of light and now from cloud on cloud of vague circumstance confused form was veiling softly its afterglow" (*P* 217). Throughout the section, these two states, hard gemlike point of perfect concentration and aftermath's diffusions of "cloudy circumstance," divide experience between them. Stephen's whole purpose is to reconstitute the former out of the conditions of the latter.[25]

It will take, in more senses than one, concentration—or, to use a near-synonym, distillation. Stephen wakes from the quintessential moment bathed in "dew," all "dewy wet" (*P* 217), and given the passage of "cloudy circumstance" that follows halfway down the page it seems pertinent to recall that dew is distilled mist.

Before pursuing this avenue further, I wish to consider one other of that word's likely significances. I am persuaded by Hugh Kenner that the "enchantment" from which Stephen awakes has been a wet dream (Kenner 1956, 123). It seems to me a decisively corroborating detail that in *Ulysses* the word *dew* reappears, with similarly rhapsodic iteration (*U* 13.740–41), at the moment when Bloom ejaculates. As to why Joyce chose this particular form of precipitation, it is a perhaps a clue that elsewhere in *Ulysses* we are informed that semen is formed through "distillation" (*U* 17.2224). Indeed, Molly thinks of semen as "like gruel or the dew" (*U* 18.1355), and the prolifically procreative Theodore Purefoy will be compared to the Gideon whose fleece was drenched with dew.

Kenner's reading has the virtue of supplying an explanation for the evolution of Stephen's mood during this section, specifically for the way that it goes from lassitude to increasing excitement. The reason for the former may be summed up in the phrase "post-orgasmic"; the reason for the ensuing change may be explained by the fact that our hero is a twenty-year-old male of demonstrated ardency, lying in bed and thinking prolonged thoughts about the woman he most desires. Time, in other words, passes, enough so that by the end of the sequence that began with visions of virgins and seraphim we find him in the company of a "lavish-limbed" "temptress" responding to a "glow of desire [which] kindled again his soul and fired and fulfilled all his body" (*P* 223). (Note: kindled *again*.) With this culmination the moment has come, once the villanelle is set down for good, to drop the curtain whose raising introduced Stephen in his state of dewy afterglow, and for much the same seemly reason. The temptress in question is still a cloud, but one trembling ("again") on the verge of distillation: "Her nakedness yielded to him, radiant, warm, odorous and lavish-limbed, enfolded him like a shining cloud, enfolded him like water with a liquid life: and like a cloud of vapour or like waters circumfluent in space the liquid letters of speech, symbols of the element of mystery, flowed forth over his brain" (*P* 223). So the immediate forecast is for yet more dreamy wetness.[26]

One reason for the distillation of this "cloud of vapour" is that it has "enfolded" a solid object, Stephen's body (brain very much included), around which water forms and flows for the same reason that the Andes and Rockies tend to be rainy on their seaward sides. Just before and just after either end of the villanelle sequence there occurs a focus of concentration—the same one, actually: Stephen evokes his "temptress" at the end by remembering her from the beginning, speculating about whether she might have been psychically attuned to the moment "his soul had passed from ecstasy to languor," and thanks to Kenner we know what *that* means—which also, as a center of distillation, begins the process toward dissolution. In between is a spell of dispersed nebulosity, charged with receding "afterglow" and the intermittent flashes of stray thoughts.

In the generation of those flashes, Stephen's principle of ideation sounds as if it were inspired by a contemporary invention, still being perfected in his day, known as the cloud chamber. This device, "originally developed between 1896 and 1912 by the Scottish physicist C.T.R. Wilson . . . has as the detecting medium a supersaturated vapour that condenses to tiny liquid droplets around ions produced by the passage of energetic charged particles, such as alpha particles, beta particles, or protons."[27] Today, a more common term for those charged particles is "cosmic rays." Given that the first occurrence of that phrase listed in the *OED* dates from several years after *Portrait* was published, it may be just a weird Joycean coincidence that the inspirational "point of light" that darts from heaven into the "cloud"-suffused medium of a "chamber" should emerge as flashing "rays" which "burned up the world"—that sounding like the kind of thing it would take a "cosmic" ray to do.[28] It may even be, the close proximity of "cloud," chamber," and "rays" notwithstanding, that as of his book's publication in 1916 Joyce had not heard of Wilson's device, which as far as I can determine had not made it into the 1911 *Encyclopedia Britannica*. In any case, Wilson himself had made it there, under several entries, along with various forerunners of his invention, demonstrating the process of condensation around ionized nuclei in the kind of medium he was at work perfecting. And if Joyce had not heard of the cloud chamber itself, I can only say that the resemblance of its operation to Stephen's mental processes in this section is uncanny:

> The instant flashed forth like a point of light and now from cloud on cloud of vague circumstance confused form was veiling softly its afterglow. O! In the virgin womb of the imagination the word was made flesh. Gabriel the seraph had come to the virgin's chamber. An afterglow deepened within his spirit, whence the white flame had passed, deepening to a rose and ardent light. That rose and ardent light was her strange wilful heart, strange that no man had known or would know, wilful from before the beginning of the world: and lured by that ardent roselike glow the choirs of the seraphim were falling from heaven. (*P* 217)

The point of (mobile) light has "passed" through Stephen's clouded mind, leaving the track of its afterglow. That light's energy has been electric, originating in an act of "enchantment" induced, it will be recalled, by galvanization: the "ions" whose passage condenses the cloud chamber's rays are electrically charged molecules.[29] Its mark is like the inspirational "word" glowing in the imagination, like the divine Word growing in Mary's womb, the Annunciation's traditional beam of light here rendered as a pentecostal "white flame" shooting down from above. (These sources are otherworldly, therefore, in one sense of the word anyway, cosmic.) Image of white flame traced against rose-red field (the "overblown scarlet flowers" of this "chamber" 's wallpaper [*P* 221–22; Gottfried 2002, 70]) then fades into its semi-eidetic reversed-color after-image: the flame continues burning—it is still *ardens*, "ardent," but now rose-colored. Which, by way of the remembered print, on his girlfriend's sideboard, of the Sacred Heart (*P* 219)—customarily red, customarily shown shooting out rays of light—returns the picture to one of "seraphim" falling to earth from their cosmic heights. (See also Nugel 2001–2002, 52.) In fact those seraphim are "lured" by the track of that burning red mark to follow in its path, down into the chamber, where they duly track their own paths of light. They thus become "rays," in their apocalyptic descent burning up world and men's hearts. Setting everything "ablaze," they also supply the next rhyme, generate the next tercet, and move the poem along.

But not indefinitely: apocalyptic longings or no, Stephen's fervor continues its downward, post-"enchantment" slide. The blaze of the second verse snuffs to "smoke" in the third, as the images summoned by Stephen's increasingly lax free-association sink from the liturgical ("ball of incense," remembered from his days of religious devotion) to the ludicrous ("ellipsoidal ball," remembered from a lackluster science lecture, where it became a joke-word for testicle). With which the composition fizzles out—"the heart's cry is broken." Although this may just be a self-important way of saying that things have gotten too silly for poetry of the elevated sort this aspires to, "broken" turns out to be the operative word for the spell of wool-gathering that makes up the section's middle passage. Stephen's environment reasserts itself in all its grungy particularity as, within his mind, various (broken) bits of memory are shunted about by various (broken) fits of mood. A few lines from the section's word-count midpoint, a self-induced gust of anger "routed the last lingering instant of ecstasy" and "broke up violently" the "image" at the center of his poem, dispersing its "fragments" as "distorted reflections." The reflector's mirror is broken into shiny splinters; the "cloudy circumstances" that at the outset were still holding the lingering "afterglow" of the focal vision have dispersed, apparently taking the last light with them.

Then, duly following the script of, sure enough, the nebular hypothesis, stray remnants of the old composite start to draw together into a new one and to generate their own energy. Like many a young creative writer since, Stephen makes a poem about his inability to make a poem, about how his effort at a hymn of praise has been "broken." So "broken" returns, in the pivotal line (tenth of nineteen), "united" and remade "unbroken" by "the radiant image of the eucharist" (salvaged from the preceding wreck of unhappy thoughts about the woman, about her consorting with priests, about priests), into a verse whose reviving beat promotes the gratifyingly show-offily polysyllabic "eucharistic." And with that, some highly recognizable nineties conventions can begin to rally round. Christ and Eros, high-mass ritual and high-art poetics converge as our reviving poet, his mind newly "suffused," literally heats himself up by "making a cowl of the blanket" (another retrieved fragment: two pages earlier he was fancying himself a "monk"), wrapping himself up in it in order to renew the "warmth" of the "scarlet glow," slowly achieving "a gradual warmth" of accumulating reflected body heat—that is, doing with heat what the reflector does with light. It is, we may remember, what he did in chapter 1, wrapping the sheets around himself to compose, against the new cold disorienting strangeness without, a self-warmed revivification of homey memories (P 19–21).

And he did the same in chapter 3 when, battling the nebular forces working "to scatter his thoughts and overcloud his conscience" (P 136–37), he tried "wrapping the blankets closely about him" only thereby to concentrate, from out of his most disagreeable memories, his most vivid picture of damnation. That there might be something inverted in the technique—in this instance, after all, a prologue to masturbation—seems clear. Still, in its own terms it works: there will be some more ups and downs and the usual complications, but by next page, just before the final, complete version of the villanelle rounds off this sequence, a "glow of desire," counterpointed to the "afterglow" with which this poetry writing started, has been "kindled again."

In sum: whatever its merits as a poem, Stephen's villanelle repays attention as a record of what the Joyce of the original "Portrait of the Artist" called "the curve of an emotion" (Joyce, "A Portrait of the Artist, P 258). Its development tracks, verse by verse, the course of the loss and then the retrieval of the power that, in Stephen's mind, is needed to fuse and to energize the creative act. (The creative act can produce bad poems too.) That power is essentially the heat-generating gravitational attraction that according to the nebular hypothesis determines the course of all growth at all levels, including the growth of a poet's mind. It is essentially the same power that Stephen sensed when he envisioned his soul "going forth to experience, unfolding itself sin by sin, spreading abroad the balefire of its burning stars and folding back upon itself, fading slowly, quenching its own lights and fires" (P 103), which sends him forth on the last page to "forge" something new, from "experience," for the millionth time, and which in the first chapter started him matching up his data to build his mazes from the inside out. Its invariable dynamic is toward greater and greater concentration around a central point, resulting in a widening reach of attraction into the nebular expanses beyond, coupled with an increasing degree of articulation throughout the system as a whole, until it all overextends and breaks down—in Bloom's words, the "whole ghesabo" stops "bit by bit" (U 13.990)—and begins again.

In the case of the villanelle's composition, in fact, the gravitational reach may be said to go beyond the surrounding "circumstances" into most of Stephen's preceding life.[30] Its poetic ideal of "ardent roselike glow" seems clearly influenced by a desire to recapture the transcendent rose-vision (P 172) achieved at the end of chapter 4. The poem itself seems calculated to test the hypotheses of the aesthetic theory, as laid out earlier in the chapter. Like the vision of the girl on the beach, it also combines various versions of womanhood recognizably drawn from Stephen's earlier experiences and imaginings, especially in chapters 2 and 3; in the process the story of fall (with the prostitute) and salvation (by way of the Virgin Mary) are revisited. There are other echoes. All in all this antepenultimate section of the book may represent one last ambitious effort to refuse the fragments of Stephen's life into one hot glowing articulated whole. That it should be followed by a spell of increasing dissolution—a desultory stroll with Stephen's one remaining companion, soon to be discarded; the diminuendo of the diary—simply reiterates, one last time, the terminal stage of a process that has been governing the book throughout.

4

The terminal stage, that is, of *Portrait*, but not of its operation throughout whatever of Stephen's life may remain, or of the lives of other Joycean characters. As Levinson has shown, that diary also allusively recapitulates the book as a whole—haphazardly for the most part, but toward the end, as the prologue's opening notes start sounding in reverse order (Levinson 1998, 41–45), beginning to gather to a point. The evolutionary assumption continues that the mind, to stay alive, must keep growing forward, building new and then newer systems from combinations of fresh data mixed together with unextinguished, redistributed material of systems past.

The alternative is regression, in a reversed-direction relinquishment of personal evolution. Such a prospect was a major concern of the school I have been describing. Theodule Ribot was able to draw on an immense body of research and anecdote from nineteenth-century mental science in affirming that what he called the "progressive amnesia" accompanying various neurocerebral crises invariably begins with the most recent memories and acquisitions and proceeds backwards (Ribot 1977, 30–31). In one book he relates, for instance, the story of a Dr. Scandella, a native-speaking Italian living in America who had later learned French and, still later, English: "In the beginning of the yellow fever . . . he spoke English only; in the middle of the disease, he spoke French only; but, on the day of his death, he spoke only in the language of his native country" (Ribot 1977, 182). In another study, he relates the case of the young man who, on suffering "a violent attack of hystero-epilepsy," is observed to regress through six separate stages, back to the point of childhood illiteracy, each stage shorn of the memory of everything following it, each separately recoverable by examiners employing "physical methods of transference (steel, soft iron, magnet, electricity)" (Ribot 1977, 75–80). It sounds like the step-by-step winding down of Hal in *2001:* turn another key and talk to another self, one rung lower down the scale. It sounds, too, like the scrutiny of the incumbent Shaun in *Finnegans Wake* 3.3, which is also conducted by a team of examiners, who also apply various materials and agents to Shaun's person and also succeed in drilling through what one of them calls the "tissue of improbable liyers" (*FW* 499.19)—layers of selfhood, all lying—down to preliterate and then preverbal infancy.[31]

This theme of regression by degrees was established in Joyce's first work of published fiction, "The Sisters," the story of an old priest, once intellectually vigorous enough to have made his way from the Dublin slums of Irishtown to the elite Irish College in cosmopolitan Rome, but now reduced by a series of strokes to infantile dependence on the semiliterate sisters with whom he grew up, his last coherent wish having been that they all take a trip to their old home. Before that— somewhere, probably, between strokes two and three—he had initiated with the story's young narrator a facsimile of the catechism (*D* 13) that began his own ascent from Irishtown to Irish College. Those strokes have been the agents of a staged regression, a scaled unbuilding of something worked out painstakingly over his young years. The ominous "Paralysis" introduced on the first page as diagnosis for Flynn—and not Flynn alone—has resulted from developmental regression in the form of successive loss of memory: Ribot's "progressive amnesia." (Joyce elsewhere described the condition as "hemiplegia"—partial paralysis, of the kind that Flynn must have experienced.) And that, too, is a condition that is general all over the Ireland of *Dubliners,* narrated by a succession of voices rendering characters almost all of whom seem to have a piece missing—a "gnomon"—in some crucial part of themselves. Which is perhaps why, like the Shakespeare described by the Stephen Dedalus of *Ulysses,* they turn "backward," like "an old dog licking an old sore" (*U* 9.472, 475–76), their stories the record of a search expedition for that missing datum; perhaps their failure in that mission explains their inability to grow any more—in other words their (partial) paralysis.

It is not, in the end, a condition afflicting the Stephen of *Portrait;* nor, sundry supernumerary sad cases notwithstanding, is it the general condition of *Ulysses.* Like *Portrait, Ulysses* is a book with a memory, one that stays in force throughout its length and grows and adjusts as the raw material piles up. Each episode represents a new systematic articulation of memory's new, newly augmented landscape; and, as many have pointed out, those episodes accordingly tend to get longer, denser, and more complicated as the book proceeds. The culmination of the progression is of course "Circe," which in terms of the nebular hypothesis is the stage of maximum articulated extension, a comprehensive drawing together of all the elements within the book's memory's range before the dissipation of the next stage, "Eumaeus." In the course of this chapter I have tried to indicate something of the scope of the universal dynamics therein illustrated, prominently including a physiologically-grounded psychology of the kind widely taught in Joyce's youth. The next chapter considers a more localized application from *Dubliners.*

2

"A Little Cloud"

A Nebular Hypothesis

"A LITTLE CLOUD" would seem to advertise its investment in nebular phenomena. It is, after all, a largely internal record of its central character's
thoughts, and much of the time those thoughts could well be called cloudy.
Plus, it's called "A Little Cloud." Still, critical opinion on the apparently giveaway title has been conflicted, dividing into two camps. The first holds that the
title in some way refers to the main character, whose repeated nickname "Little
Chandler," applied to someone who sees himself as diminutive and insubstantial, certainly sounds meant to signal some kind of connection. The second is
that it is an allusion, of the sort that Chandler imagines putting in his poetry (D
74), to the "little cloud out of the sea, like a man's hand" summoned by Elijah in
I Kings 18:44. Here again, the nature of the connection seems vague, but some
have found an Elijah-like spirit of denunciation running through *Dubliners,* and
the story does end wetly and noisily. Perhaps because Elijah and Little Chandler are so utterly dissimilar, no one has yet made a sustained effort at reconcil-
ing these two interpretations.[1]

Here goes.

To begin with the first camp, let us take the hint and consider the possibility
that Little Chandler might actually *be* a little cloud, on something close to a literal level. That may sound farfetched, but the story is after all the work of the
same author whose only epigraph came from Ovid's *Metamorphoses,* and who
in *Finnegans Wake* was to have Issy repeatedly shape-change into a wispy or
drifting or hovering or weeping or silver-lined cloud. Keeping her in mind, consider Little Chandler's introduction: "His hands were white and small, his
frame was fragile, his voice was quiet and his manners were refined. He took
the greatest care of his fair silken hair and moustache and used perfume dis-
creetly on his handkerchief. The half-moons of his nails were perfect and when
he smiled you caught a glimpse of a row of childish white teeth" (D 70). The

"white small hands" here may recall Elijah's cloud the size of a man's hand, and certainly much of the rest fits the cloud picture: white, fragile, quiet and (a cloud is refined seawater) "refined." There is the fair hair of the wispiest texture, the glimpse of a doubtless white handkerchief wafting its cloud of scent, yet another "glimpse" of white in the teeth, even the white half-moons, up there in the sky.

And, thus nebulized, Chandler proceeds to behave like a cloud, being blown over the landscape. Like Issy he is seen to "gaze" (D 71) down—at least in one sense—on those beneath him, whether the Dubliners beyond and possibly below his office window or the urchins to whom he finds himself feeling "superior" as he looks "down the river" (D 73).[2] At the outset he espouses a philosophy of drift, of not "struggl[ing] against fortune" (D 71), and envisions himself a poet whose "wistful" verse would identify him with the famously misty "Celtic school." On his eastward passage to Corliss's, as night is falling and the winds therefore likely blowing east, toward the sea,[3] he wanders lonely as a cloud and, head in the clouds, in "revery" (D 74), initially drifts past the entrance.[4] The main points of this itinerary are a river, a drinking establishment, and a room in which he stands accused of—speaking of drinking—having missed tea and forgotten coffee, and of causing the baby to burst into tears, soon matched by his own. Before that, in Corliss's, he is with a man who has gotten "a little gray" atop his "heavy, pale" face (D 74, 75), who proceeds to fill him up with liquid, with water mixed with (watered) whisky ("water of life" in Gaelic): "Water? Say when."

Against serious competition, "A Little Cloud" at this point becomes among the wettest of Dubliners stories, full of drinking and references to drinking. And there is another indulgence introduced in Corliss's as well, occasioning the passage where "A Little Cloud" seems most aware of its title: "I'll tell you my opinion, said Ignatius Gallaher, emerging after some time from the clouds of smoke in which he had taken refuge" (D 78). Which tells us that Chandler, also smoking a cigar, is similarly enveloped, in clouds of a darker and heavier cast than have attended him up to now. And he himself, under influence of cigar and drink, has become, literally, darker and heavier in the face, blushing repeatedly until he feels the "blush . . . establishing itself" (D 80), his "colour . . . heightened" (D 81), the pale skin that distinguished him on the first page now darkened by congestion of blood.

The meeting, he tells himself, has "upset the equipoise of his sensitive nature." "Equipoise" is not a bad word to describe the nature of that diffused suspension of water droplets in process of condensing from gas to liquid that we call a cloud. When a cloud's equipoise is "upset," when its droplets reach too high a level of relative density (particulate "nuclei of condensation"—from cigar smoke, say—will help facilitate the process;[5] that is how cloud-seeding is supposed to work), it darkens and produces rain.[6]

"A Little Cloud" ends as follows: "Little Chandler felt his cheeks suffused with shame and he stood back out of the lamplight. He listened while the paroxysm of the child's sobbing grew less and less; and tears of remorse started to his eyes" (D 85). So, finally, does the story's gathering storm break. Little Chandler cries because overcharged with the accumulating impulses that in earlier stages of congestion have suffused and congested his cheeks. (Meanwhile his child is, as they say, crying himself out.) His weeping is a culmination, as a cloudburst is the culmination, of accumulated density. Like Stephen's villanelle, Chandler's story has traced the mounting trajectory of his emotion, from inception to discharge, and its governing conceit has been that emotions like clouds can begin inconspicuously, gather mass until they become oppressively heavy, and dissolve in sudden acts of release, thus, as the saying goes, clearing the air.

The title of "A Little Cloud," then, enjoins attending to a process rather than to any one point of correspondence—to the succession of stages by which the fragile and apprehensive happiness described on the first page drifts, wavers, thickens, darkens, and breaks down into the tempest of the last page. Once that fact is understood, we can I think understand as well the relevance of the title's biblical allusion, which should properly be taken as referring not to one verse but to three, I Kings 18:43 through 45:

> 43 And he [Elijah] said to his servant, Go up now, look toward the sea. And he went up, and looked, and said, There is nothing. And he said, Go again seven times.
>
> 44 And it came to pass at the seventh time, that he said, Behold, there ariseth a little cloud out of the sea, like a man's hand. And he said, Go up, say unto Ahab, Prepare thy chariot, and get thee down, that the rain stop thee not.
>
> 45 And it came to pass in the mean while, that the heaven was black with clouds and wind, and there was a great rain.

Seen thus in context, the words "a little cloud . . . like a man's hand" pretty obviously emphasize the cloud's contrasting relation to what went before (invisibility) and what came after (a great rain). They function to specify a point in a process, the point just after something has come into noticeable existence and begun its development into something momentous. My primary authority here is Stephen Dedalus, who in *Ulysses* uses a version of the same words in exactly this sense when he relates how "a matutinal cloud . . . at first no bigger than a woman's hand" had by evening swollen into a thunderstorm big and loud enough to make him faint with fear (*U* 17.36–41).

Once we recognize that its title directs our attention to questions of developmental process, of growth from near-nullity to dissolving consummation, we may come to notice to what extent "A Little Cloud" is concerned with establishing events as stages in a temporal continuum of just that sort. Little Chandler and narrator alike are much given to looking before and after. The story begins with the words "Eight years before" (by way of relating what Gallaher has made of himself in the intervening time) and ends (by way of relating what Chandler has come to in a comparable period) in a room of furniture bought "on the hire system" (*D* 83), with the wife (in both before and after version—picture and person) of a year-and-a-half-old marriage beginning to fray badly and a no-longer-newborn starting to get on the nerves, whose presence is the last straw because it simultaneously embodies to Chandler both what he has done with his life so far and what it will be from now on. The honeymoon is over, the bloom is off the rose, he has made his bed. For Chandler, the meaning of his home is of things ending (badly) and beginning (worse), of an ongoing developmental continuum suddenly seen as intolerable rather than generative, to which the most elemental of responses is the one word he yells at the baby: "Stop!"

In other words, "A Little Cloud" enacts Chandler's growing perception of what he, contrasted with Gallaher, is coming to, over time, and the commonplace but by no means self-evident assumption behind that perception is that life is a testing-ground of coming-into-being, of inception leading to growth leading or not leading to certain culminative fulfillments by which all that has gone before may be judged. So: "His temperament might be said to be just at the point of maturity" (*D* 73). Behind that statement is a kind of theory of life, among other things.

Among those other things is a poetics. In the course of the story Chandler finds himself wanting to be a poet of a certain type, which can be described with some precision because "A Little Cloud" acts it out. From Chandler's point of view, in fact, were he allowed to complete the story whose hero he would be, the main narrative thread would probably be about the poem not written, the poem that in the course of the evening was conceived, pondered, nurtured, matured, brought to the verge of fulfillment, then cruelly aborted in the glare and blare of his home. Considering the similarities in their respective compositions, real and envisioned, this poem might have resembled Stephen's villanelle (although it would probably have soft-pedaled the eroticism). It would have been the work of a "sensitive nature" (*D* 80) whose finely-balanced "equipoise" registered fleeting sensations and transfused them into an inner repository that then imbued them, over time, with the gentle melancholy of its native spirit. (We may glimpse, behind this portrait, the James Joyce of *Dubliners,* balefully surveying the James Joyce of *Chamber Music.)*[7] It would have been all Symons and *Silverpoints* and Whistler nocturnes, wispy *aperçus* swathed in glimmery-shimmery mist, casting a (cloudy) "shower of kindly golden dust" (*D* 71) on the locals to transform them, with perhaps a piquant touch of irony, into "cavaliers" and "alarmed Atalantas" (*D* 72).[8]

Implicit to this school is the principle that such moments must come unbidden. Like the Symbolistes and the Romantics before them, Chandler in his poetic role values vagrancy, the aleatory over the ordained, drift over directedness, neither the cosmopolitan observer holding the mirror up to nature nor the questing spirit seeking out truth in its lair but rather the trembling, sensitively receptive soul waiting to be "touched" by the "poetic moment" (*D* 73) as it comes. It is fitting that there should be a suggestion of *sortes Virgiliniae* in the way Chandler allows his undirected left hand to open the volume of Byron that "lay before him on the table" and reads the first poem it lights on, a lament for a dead lover, which one would think could have little to say to a man one of whose perceived problems at the moment is an all-too-lively wife, but to which he nonetheless responds as to the call of his lost self (*D* 84).

Small wonder that someone with a poetic program of this sort, a program of undirected responses to "different moods and impressions" (*D* 73), should be "disillusioned" with the Gallaher whose literary code is one of "Always hurry and scurry, looking for copy and sometimes not finding it" (*D* 76, 75). Looking and finding is exactly what the Chandlerian poet does not do. Such a poet is a sensitive vessel whose function is to receive, nourish, bear, and bring to term whatever poetic matter chance may grant it. The metaphor of gestation is explicit: "the thought that a poetic moment had touched him took life within him like an infant hope" (*D* 73). Crystallization might also serve as a metaphor for the process, a suggestion perhaps implicit in Thomas B. O'Grady's description (1991, 400–401) of Chandler's scene with his child as "the crystallizing point of the story," the baby functioning as a "desperate compression" embodying Chandler's "accumulated frustrations" and in the process displacing and obliterating the story's other baby, "the infant hope" of the earlier "poetic moment."

In line with the nebular principles described earlier, I would however argue

that the most adequate figure for the process is that specialty of clouds, distillation. Rather than being consumed or enwombed, the moods and impressions
that make their way into Chandler's poetic interior are absorbed, randomly,
through a permeable surface akin to Stephen's, to accumulate and combine
with other such gatherings until they coalesce into quintessence that can then
be, in Chandler's term for poetic production, "expressed" outward. Like—two
other resident analogies—the "drum of his ear" "pierced" by his child's wail or
the room in which the story ends, Chandler's poetic vessel has "thin walls,"
easily perfused, through which impressions pass to be gathered and "echoed"
(D 84).

Imagine such a vessel set adrift, like a cloud, and you have, I think, the essential character of Chandler's poetic progress during the story, which can be
tracked, meteorologically, as a progressive sequence of points of absorption,
condensation, and distillation. The first point would probably be the new feeling of superiority that comes over him as he passes through the "dull inele-
gance of Capel Street" with his head full of his friend the Great Gallaher (D 73).
Still under the influence of that feeling, he then pities "the poor stunted houses"
that appear to his sight as he crosses Grattan Bridge. Out of this mingling of
inner mood and outer impression is engendered his imaginative vision, instantly antiqued with infusions of early-middle-Yeatsian diction (the archaic
patina has apparently long come naturally to him: eight years ago he wished his
friend "godspeed"), anthropomorphizing the houses as huddled tramps waiting for night to "bid them arise, shake themselves and begone." It is Chandler's
"poetic moment," and its sensed presence yields an "infant hope" taking "life
within him," which so suffuses his soul that "a light began to tremble on the
horizon of his mind" (D 73), and which by the time he reaches Corliss's has by
condensing around the conjured image of Gallaher's triumph grown heavy
enough—"moods" overbalancing "sensations"—to screen out the exterior
world.

That world returns in full force when Chandler enters the assaultive "light
and noise" of the bar and spends a prolonged period in the presence of what the
weather report of *Finnegans Wake*, forecasting "lucal drizzles," calls "A sotten
retch of low pleasure" (*FW* 324.32)—a sodden wretch (and wretched sot) given
to low pleasures, a sudden reach of low pressure (invariably precipitation-
producing), sodden with humidity. Under the influence of Gallaher and his natural environment, through the absorption of water and whiskey, smoke and
noise, hot air and low talk, Chandler's cloud, at the eye of the story's storm,
thickens and darkens toward what fancifully inclined weather reporters have

long described as the "brooding" or "ponderous" state that will emerge in the concluding section. Large and lowering, "disillusioned" and disengaged from the major mass of nuclei of condensation embodied in Gallaher, its temperature dropping to dew point as it moves from the "warm and excited" (D 80) atmosphere of Corliss's to the chilliness of home ("He looked coldly into the eyes of the photograph and they answered coldly" [D 83]), this cloud, in order to erupt, requires only one last center of condensation around which it can gather. At the end it is as if Chandler, supersaturated with the day's accumulated occasions of grief, were looking, from the volume of Byron to the furniture to the photograph, for such a center of condensation—for, as the saying goes, something to cry about. He is looking, that is, for something to concentrate on. The child supplies it.

As much as the composition of Stephen's villanelle, the progress of "A Little Cloud" is an exercise in tracking what Joyce had two years earlier called "the curve of an emotion." The curve of Little Chandler's emotion is plotted scientifically, meteorologically, following processes like those governing the cloud chamber of Stephen's villanelle. It also forecasts the work of a writer who will hereafter make it his practice to connect his narratives to the endogenous rhythms and cycles of his human subjects as they absorb or fail to absorb the outer world through nebular media of varying permeability (Gabriel's window, Duffy's wall), whether that connection be to the curves of mounting rage and sexual release in "Cyclops" or "Nausicaa" respectively or to the larger individuating rhythms involved in gestation, lifetime, or day's passage. A self-proclaimed Aristotelian by way of Aquinas, Joyce seems determined from the beginning not only to observe the unities within each story or episode but to extend them, to the rendering of inner space and its evolving interaction with outer. The nebular processes of motion, absorption, distillation, reflection, "expression," and discharge, which the title of "A Little Cloud" alerts us to recognize in the consciousness of its subject as he engages his environment, will henceforth return in different combinations as regular features of Joyce's supple and meteorically mercurial brand of *style indirect libre*.

3

Distillates, Counterparts

"IT IS," concedes *Finnegans Wake* early on, "nebuless an autodidact fact" that "the shape of the average human cloudyphiz," "given the wet and low visibility" of "slopperish" conditions, can be hard to "idendifine" (*FW* 51.5). Nevertheless—"nebuless"—everyone in it keeps trying, along the lines we have been reviewing. Like Stephen or Chandler, they work at epitomizing or crystallizing or—again, the main conceit—distilling one another out of the cloudy circumstances environing everything.

At one point, for example, the character Shaun is being interviewed by a reporter who wants to know who he is and what he's about. Hoping to cut a respectable figure, Shaun adopts the pose of a pious civil servant, a mailman attending mass, while also coaxing that mailman's nemesis the household dog: " 'Ghee up, ye dog, for your daggily broth, etc., Happy Maria and Glorious Patrick, etc., etc. In fact, always, have I believe. Greedo! Her's me hongue!' " " 'And it is the fullsoot of a tarabred,' " responds his interrogator, half convinced, " 'Yet one's minutes observation, dear dogmestic Shaun, as we point out how you have while away painted our town a wearing greenridinghued." To which Shaun, caught out but up to the game: " 'O murder mere, how did you hear? . . . Well, so be it! The gloom has rays, her lump is love. And I will confess to have, yes. Your diogneses is anonest man's' " (*FW* 411.18–29).

By "Greedo! Her's me hongue!" Shaun means, mainly, "Credo! Here's my tongue"—the communicant sticking out his tongue to receive the host after reciting the creed. But in the context established by his talk about dogs, Shaun's interviewer frames a different tongue-extended scene, that of an entry at a thoroughbred dog show being inspected by one of the judges. And not just thoroughbred but "tarabred"—"Tara" or Irish-bred—a reading perhaps influenced by Shaun's invocation of Ireland's patron saint, and clinched by, again, that extended tongue, which in heraldic iconography is the one token distinguishing a wolf from a dog (see, for instance, Franklyn 1967, 102–3, 109–10). Shaun's tongue, given that context, changes his outline enough to make him a wolf, or more accurately a wolfhound. And (as affirmed in "Cyclops") the wolfhound is the Irish dog par excellence. So, with tongue extended, Shaun, back at the dog show, becomes "tarabred," and his full suit is "fullsoot," bringing with it the Gaelic *"faolchu,"* wolf (see *FW* 480.4), and he is said to have painted the town not English red but Irish green.[1] Or, rather, "a wearing greenridinghued," since by his change to a wolf, outwardly innocent, going his rounds, he fits easily into the role of the "Little Red Riding Hood" wolf. (He is also a reformed "wolf" in the sense of lecherous male—a usage dating from the mid-nineteenth century—confessing to having painted the town red in his wild pre-reformed youth.) Which explains his reply of "O murder mere, how did you hear?": O grandmother, what big ears you have; all the better to hear you with—joined with hints about a murdered mother-figure (again, Little Red Riding Hood's), cloaked in a prayerful invocation to a sainted mother, to the tune of the patriotic Irish song "The Wearing of the Green" ("O Paddy dear, and did you hear . . .").

This passage typifies how characters in *Finnegans Wake* are generated and presented, as discernible figures distilling, typically around some salient detail such as Shaun's extended tongue, from out of a shifting field of contextual variants, after the manner of those atmospheric precipitations reviewed in the previous two chapters. The point being emphasized here, one earlier learned by Stephen and Little Chandler, is that characters thus engendered can influence but not control the process. It is within Shaun's power to adopt a certain posture, and even to put in circulation hints ("Credo!") about how the resulting configuration should be read. But past that point other elements enter the equation, converging on a whole of which Shaun's contribution is only a part. So "Credo" becomes "Greedo," and "dogmatic" (and "domestic") "dogmestic," canine and lupine readings that Shaun, even if it forces him to concede that his interlocutor's diagnosis is an honest one, then rather desperately tries to turn back to his own use by casting himself as "diogneses," that is as someone who like Diogenes the Cynic is dog-like, literally "cynical," only in homely bluntness.

In this chapter I will consider the ways in which similar effects operate on the characters of Joyce's pre-*Wake* fiction.[2] In particular I will consider how such effects relate to, sometimes clash with, the efforts of Joyce's characters to determine how they see themselves and are seen. In terms of the two preceding chapters, we will be observing how such moments of presentation/self-presentation distill at certain focal points, points of the type of Stephen's rays, Chandler's Byron book, and Shaun's tongue. And since, as Derek Bickerton first remarked (1968, 33–46) and John Paul Riquelme has shown in detail,[3] a character's self-presentation is generally infused into the narrative voice, I will also be considering interpretation, the reader's integration of the elements presented.

Interpretation, and especially misinterpretation. I think that Joyce's readers tend to get things wrong in the same ways that his characters do, and from the same causes. We, also, like to see things distilled. (Consider the legacy of the "epiphany," a word that Joyce employed only once in his published work, and then in mockery.) There is a continuity between the way the perceiving self imposes heraldic patterns on dog-plus-tongue to frame a wolf, the way the judging self imposes moral patterns on a companion caught red-handed to identify an outcast, and the way the reading self imposes patterns on a character caught in some unflattering pose to conjure a villain.

Still, a crucial point: to say that they and we often get things wrong is to admit the possibility of getting them right, or at least more right. The idea may be not to equate and dismiss all versions but instead to notice more and take more into account, so as to come closer to the mark the next time. The process enacted reflects less on the problematics of constituted identity than on the observer's integration of that identity into the pattern or patterns he or she selects, in short on how successfully the reader reads what is there.

In such successive approximations of the features and figures of his texts, a Joyce reader will, as in other ways, often be extending the mentality of the narrative's main character. Thus the first story of *Dubliners*, "The Sisters," is an act of re-vision by a narrator returning to an old subject in the hopes of getting it more right the second time around, and taking the reader with him. The process is repeated in the conclusion of "The Dead," in each succeeding chapter of *Portrait*, and in the last episodes of *Ulysses*. It is as much a sign of moral seriousness for Joyce's as for Henry James's characters that, like Gabriel in the hotel room, they be willing to reevaluate what has been. It is also the mark of the serious reader, for whom, as Clive Hart has documented (Hart 1974, 181–216), all manner of traps may be set to snare the unwary and impatient, the jumpers-to-conclusions. Like some others before me, I believe that wily, much-tried Odysseus is Joyce's model for the reader of *Ulysses*, and that Joyce devotes much effort to bringing his readers up to that standard. He wants to make us smarter. That means getting us to notice the kinds of things we are prone to miss.

To begin with, he is one of those authors who likes to reintroduce figures from earlier works—the easiest way of inducing a second look. The Corley who, juxtaposed with the sycophantic Lenehan, seems so menacing in "Two Gallants," is merely pathetic when juxtaposed with an indifferent Stephen in

"Eumaeus," where the same "gallantry" that led him to cajole a servant girl into getting him one gold coin (a coin dramatically highlighted in the story's concluding vignette, with Corley's hand extended forward into close-up focus, light beamed onto palm, reader meanwhile set up to draw a pejorative comparison between disk of money and disk of moon, romantically highlighted earlier) constrains him from letting Stephen give him more than one silver coin (this coin, by contrast, rendered generic, blurred, and in shadow, to the point that Stephen cannot tell the difference between a penny and a half crown). The Hynes whose loyalty to Parnellite nationalism makes him a poignant champion in "Ivy Day in the Committee Room" is, from the same cause, thoroughly unpleasant in "Cyclops," partly because sentiments touching in individuals can be ugly in groups, partly because in "Cyclops" Bloom is present to notice, as the narrator of the story did not, that Hynes is a deadbeat.

Or consider Mrs. Kearney. Almost everyone finishes "A Mother" convinced that she is a harridan who has ruined her daughter's professional prospects.[4] But by *Ulysses* that daughter is attracting the professional envy of a rival, Molly Bloom,[5] and we pick up enough about the crew that occasioned Mrs. Kearney's scene to wonder whether her suspicions may have been well-founded after all.[6] Indeed, rereading her from the perspective of the later book, we may come to recognize in her story a situation that all of us have experienced, the one in which you are being fleeced, and know it, and know that your fleecer knows that you know it and is counting on your sense of decorum, for which he or she feels contempt, to make you keep quiet about it. Do you go along, feeling used, or throw a show?

Mrs. Kearney throws a show: "This is four shillings short." Now, two points here. On the one hand, there is no way to deliver that line without sounding piggy. On the other hand, it *is* four shillings short.[7] As her antagonists charge, Mrs. Kearney is acting unlike a lady—but then her author, himself sometimes called a cad for negotiating maneuvers at least as rough, was no great admirer of ladies. Mrs. Kearney is certainly disagreeable here, partly because she just is, partly because she has been given a choice between being a shrew and being a chump, but she is also right. The narrator of "A Mother" foregrounds the disagreeableness and backgrounds the rightness; the retrospective prompted by *Ulysses* permits us to reverse the process and, this time equipped with a suppler, more cosmopolitan sensibility, a reader's eye more awake to and tolerant of anomaly, complexity, and extra-conventional composites, to see her again, as a strong-willed woman with an unlovely strain of tenacity that can be admirable or insufferable or a mixture of both, depending on circumstances.

Such a reevaluation ought to be further encouraged if we go on to consider the extent to which our original judgment was elicited by a narrative that mimics Mrs. Kearney's idiom, in particular the cattiness that is her least attractive feature, and then reflect that to accept its judgment of her is to share the one thing about her that we like least. Revisited, "A Mother" brings readers up against a *tu quoque*. "Catty" is a catty word. To condemn Mrs. Kearney outright is to be ungenerous ourselves, with less excuse. If Mrs. Kearney winds up judged by an observer who to some extent originates, ironically, in her own consciousness, the irony waits to recoil on anyone who, joining with that judge, joins with her.

That is the kind of trick Joyce likes to play on readers given to the broad stroke and the nutshell summary. All summings-up in his work after the unpublished *Stephen Hero* are subject to supersession by new data or a different angle. They come to the reader as provisional arrangements of highlighted material from out of the blooming, buzzing confusion of something among other things that happened somewhere to someone among other people, a vast virtual reservoir that we can never grasp completely but can always know better than before.

And it is, again, probably always and certainly usually true that a major but never sufficient determinant of what gets noticed and how it gets arranged is the way the character at the center of things wants to be viewed.[8] As it is true of Shaun so it is true of Mrs. Kearney (and, come to that, of her daughter, whose name has facilitated her pose as a musical nationalist, a card she is still playing in *Ulysses* [*U* 18.375–79]) that the character's self-image and with it her way of putting things, though finally not enough to control her story, can certainly influence it. The same holds true in *Ulysses*. As it reminds us with the odd reference to a Mrs. Sinico or Gretta Conroy, *Ulysses* encompasses a crowd of individuals each of whom would have a story to tell if given center stage. Thus one of the striking things about it: pitiless anatomization though it may be, it is also a book full of heroes—of different kinds, certainly, but recognizable all the same. "He's a hero" (*U* 10.492), says Lenehan of Tom Rochford, truthfully enough, in my book anyway: Rochford has risked his own life to save others. The same goes for Buck Mulligan: "You saved men from drowning. I'm not a hero, however" (*U* 1.62–63)—so Stephen, despite his disclaimer recognizably related to the Stephen Hero of the earlier work of that name. Stephen, averse to water, could not be Mulligan's kind of hero. So he has selected from the cultural inventory a different kind of story prizing a different kind of prowess, that of the mental fight of the "cold steel pen" (*U* 1.359). His kind, in short.

That is, like Joyce characters in general, he became practiced in viewing the world from the one perspective, selecting the one arrangement of available data most calculated to set him off to advantage when permitted to congregate about its proper center of focus. His voice, full of literary allusions in language out of the reach of the people by whom he feels least appreciated, is among other things the fitting narrative accompaniment for that arrangement. In their instinctive selection of the most theatrically gratifying interior narrative, Joyce's characters are in the tradition of Madame Bovary (*pace* McGee 1988, 87), living their lives as the heroes of fictions, defined as critical convergences of certain given facts, classifiable according to the kind of personality they foreground and render heroic, chosen from among those the culture makes available, usually distilled from one salient fact or feature. We can catch Tom Kernan in the act as he looks in a mirror, remarks the reflection of his objectively unprepossessing self, takes in the red face that testifies to his weakness for drink, the flashy secondhand coat that testifies to shabby-genteel shoneen affectations, the gouty movements and gray hair, and, after rummaging for the most flattering of plausible foci, comes up with this: "High colour, of course. Grizzled moustache. Returned Indian officer. Bravely he bore his stumpy body forward on spatted feet, squaring his shoulders" (*U* 10.755–57). (The moustache is probably the detail that does the trick here, the point of distillation.) The last sentence's silent shift to third-person narrative is instructive. Joyce's Dubliners do that kind of thing habitually, supplying a bridge between interior monologue and melodrama, between for instance Kernan's inner landscape and for instance the fantasy landscape of "Nausicaa," in which a lame woman imaginatively places herself in a scene composed on the premise that immobility equals sublimity. Having had years to work it up, she has a more elaborate story than Kernan's, but the process has been much the same.

It is perhaps inevitable, then, that by its second half *Ulysses* should become an anthology of literary styles. The panoramic rendering of characters goes with the panoramic rendering of fictions, to the point that in some cases certain identified cultural models can seem to be controlling the narrative through characters as much mediums as agents.[9] As Florence Walzl has shown, Eveline displays on her wall a picture representing an analogue, perhaps origin, of the story she is acting out (1982, 120). The aloof Mr. Duffy has on his shelf a copy of Nietzsche, mythographer to the insufferably unclubbable. Gabriel Conroy identifies himself as an admirer of Robert Browning, a similarly cerebral sort famously over the heads of much of his audience but humanized by his marriage to a woman of simpler and purer expression. (Treating Gretta like the invalid

Elizabeth Barrett, he insists that she wear galoshes.) Father Conmee is writing a book in which a Conmee-style priest is the privileged bearer of noble secrets. The interior monologue of Gerty MacDowell is almost indistinguishable from the sentimental fiction that she likes to read.

And there are others whose derivative interior drama, though not specified, is easy to guess. Blazes Boylan, "conquering hero" (*U* 11.340), is the Don Giovanni whose duet with Zerlina he will perform with Molly. Haines is a cultural emissary, bringing the sweetness and light of his and Matthew Arnold's Oxford (*U* 1.173) to the "wild Irish" (*U* 1.937), recording Ireland's native woodnotes for academic posterity. Mr. Deasy is the last of the just, like Stockmann in *An Enemy of the People* trying to waken the benighted. These figures are all the heroes of their own stories, and their heroism is the art of selecting, presenting, and distilling an inherent identity from among their culture's usable types. Its virtuosos are those who are especially good at playing up certain features.

Playing up certain features, and also playing down others, those least compatible with the chosen role. Well before *Finnegans Wake* and its Shem-Shaun play of coinciding contraries, of "polar andthisishis" (*FW* 177.33), Joyce was dealing in characters who "idendifine" (*FW* 51.06) themselves in a mental act inseparable from defining and shunning an opposite, or rather that part of themselves which their adopted role requires them to treat as an opposite. Self-definition equals self-negation, to the point where sustaining one's identity involves constant suppression, constant struggle between self chosen and self rejected. In *Finnegans Wake* the male principal's desire to be a Shaun, to be prosperous and popular, necessitates the suppression of the opposite Shem and produces that opposite's constant tendency to ooze and trickle out. In "A Painful Case" a colorless bank clerk who fancies himself a Nietzchean *übermensch* must repudiate, precisely when she tries to get too close, the colorless housewife who more than anyone else resembles the self he is trying to suppress.

Finnegans Wake is full of terms for this "zeroic couplet" (*FW* 284.10), this coupling of hero-self and zero-self, self-definition and self-negation, but *Dubliners* has one of its own. That word is "counterparts," the title of a story that shows how the process works. "Counterpart" is one of those double-sided words, like "cleave," that can mean either one thing or the opposite thing. A counterpart is either something's double or its complement. The story begins with Farrington making a counterpart in the first sense—copying over a document—for a boss whose relationship to him (brain to brawn, master to servant, northern to southern Ireland) exemplifies the second. Throughout the story, the two senses sometimes alternate, sometimes converge. Farrington and his wife, in trading off domestic tyrannies according to whether Farrington is drunk or sober (*D* 97), are counterparts in both senses; in their arm-wrestling contest, Farrington and Weathers go from being one kind (two strong men, evenly matched) to the other kind (victor and vanquished); Mr. Alleyne and Farrington are, one, bully and bullied (second definition) and, two, both bullies (first definition), as when the latter in effect makes his son into the former's counterpart (first definition): two small creatures, one of whom he may not hit.

It is in this last relationship, between Farrington and his son, the pathetic Tom, that the double sense of the story's title is thrown into sharpest focus. Thrashing his son, Farrington is both a large man beating a small boy (one kind of counterpart) and a Farrington beating a Farrington (the other kind). Like Stephen's Shakespeare, whose "unremitting intellect is the hornmad Iago cease- lessly willing that the moor in him shall suffer" (*U* 9.1023–24), he establishes one self by subduing the other, the brutalized little boy we are, in retrospect, able to discern inside the brutish man. It is, after all, hardly a discovery of our time alone that child abuse is often a vicious circle, victims growing up into victimiz- ers: "I tell you," says Mr. Murdstone, preparing to whip David Copperfield, "I have been often flogged myself." Farrington's name, it has been observed, sug- gests "farrow," one of those newborns who according to Stephen Dedalus are eaten by the old sow Ireland, and with that as a clue it isn't hard to recognize, in the man Farrington, the boy Farrington, the swollen child of much of the story. The pleasures he takes with what he calls "the boys" are boyish—arm-wrestling and the like—and his taste in drink, for "hot punches," suggests a child's sweet tooth. His job sounds like elementary school at around the third form level—the copying of incomprehensible documents as in some infernal penmanship class, the fidgeting and daydreaming, the living for recess and day's end, the going- to-the-bathroom ploy, the mean master, the hyperacute sensitivity to certain sensations. Indeed it is remarkably like the world of *Portrait*, chapter 1, its pro- tagonist standing up to Mr. Alleyne as Stephen does to Father Dolan.

In fact that is the story, one of the oldest,[10] of the underling who with an un- expected comeback puts some officious bully in his place, of which Farrington is the hero, a story that as it happens is told several times in the pubs that night, and that has doubtless been told before, by other Dubliners, on other nights, with the names changed. That, probably, is why Farrington's comeback arrives automatically, in *his* distilling moment, "almost before he was aware of it" (*D* 91): given his cue, he adopts the readiest heroic role from those communally available, one in which he can take refuge and find an identity, becoming for a while not "the man" of the early story but the "Farrington" of its middle.

End "Counterparts" with a freeze-framing of Farrington's retort to Mr. Alleyne, and few would have trouble recognizing the kind of hero he is. (The same could apply to Chandler in "A Little Cloud," if only the last section were left out.) Nested in one Farrington story is another very different one, told in an idiom (either coarse or forceful, according to your druthers) that as usual reflects the sensibility (either brutish or brutalized) of the protagonist, and the former story prevails only because of where the story's maker chooses to draw the line, the particular configuration that the choice of frame throws into relief, in the process shifting the final vignette from one of Farrington's screaming victimizer to one of Farrington's weeping victim. As with the aftermaths of Stephen's defining distillations, the narrative admits new information that accumulates to form a new configuration, one including a helpless child, beyond the voice's range and incompatible with the heroic fiction it was telling. In the process Farrington's view of himself as a plucky underdog is overwhelmed.

As in this story, so throughout Joyce's work, counterparts in one sense tend to become counterparts in the other when the perspective shifts and, like Shem, the suppressed side seeps out, gathers, and distills. The picture in *Portrait*'s chapter 1 of Parnell as a hero dragged down by hypocrites is answered in the "Eumaeus" episode of *Ulysses,* where the cuckolded Bloom is a type of the cuckolded Captain O'Shea, humiliated by his wife's affair with a Parnell who in the context becomes counterpart to the odious Boylan. The other memorable trauma of that book's childhood chapter, the pandybat scene, is answered in "Nestor," where Stephen returns as a teacher, counterpart to Fathers Dolan and Arnall, before a classroom of spoiled and indolent boys who could drive many teachers to thoughts of the cane.[11]

As for *Ulysses:* it has its own scene of traumatic confrontation, the "Cyclops" set-to between Bloom and the citizen, and although in this case there is no sequel to supply a second look, the episode itself includes everything necessary to appreciate the extent to which the antagonists may be identical as well as opposite counterparts, and in the process to junk the reading given by almost everyone who has written on the subject. That reading is due mainly to the episode's crudely effective reverse psychology. So relentless is the narrative assault on Bloom that readers rally reflexively to his defense, nudged by irony as heavyhanded as anything Joyce ever wrote. (For a similar reading of Joyce's tactics, see Burns 2000, 122.) But if we pay attention to what is going on beyond the range of such manipulations, we come up with another story. It is the story of a recently humiliated man who comes into a bar and proceeds to make himself amazingly obnoxious, who at the most convivial hour of the day spouts off against drinking and treating, and in favor of flogging, hanging, and the British Empire, in the one place in Dublin where those sentiments are most likely to give offense, who then proceeds to in effect pick a fight with a broken-down ex-athlete obviously much older than he and in much worse health, by insinuating that the heart condition that will in fact soon kill him is his own fault, the result of the "violent exercise" that he has devoted his life to promoting (U 12.892–93), and then, with a kind of genius for saying the wrong thing, commending the one sport, lawn tennis, that epitomizes everything this man has campaigned against (U 12.945–46).[12]

Nor should Leopold Bloom be surprised about the consequences of this performance. He knows a good deal about the citizen (U 12.888, 13.1221–23) and his milieu. The resulting brawl is largely his own work, the result of some relentless egging-on by what a disinterested observer would likely see as a barroom troublemaker with a chip on his shoulder, acting from motives that the same observer, if aware of the events of the episode just past, might reasonably interpret as a classic case of return-of-the-repressed. The citizen's rage is largely Bloom's doing, is, in effect, *his* rage, brought to the surface and projected on the nearest candidate.

Three Joyce notes, I think, encourage this reading. One says that Polyphemus is Ulysses' "shadow" (Hayman 1978, 81), a hint confirmed in "Eumaeus," where Bloom recalls that the citizen had taken "umbrage" (from Latin *umbra*, shadow) against him (U 16.1081). The second reads, "Ulysses projects envy at each chapter" (Herring 1972, 192). The third, "Mark blind when he sees T & I [Tristram and Iseult] do it,"[13] recalls the tradition, probably most familiar from Chaucer's "Merchant's Tale," of the blindness of cuckolds, and invites us to consider that the citizen's Cyclopean blindness may also be a shadow, or projection, of the Bloom whose cuckolding became official just before the episode begins.[14]

Even the citizen's ugliest quality, his anti-Semitism, is to a degree generated out of, projected out of, Bloom. First, it arises as a specific response to Bloom's specific provocations; though spaciously xenophobic, the citizen shows no inclination to single Jews out until Bloom makes himself an irritant. And it is possible to take that anti-Semitism as a reflection, a "shadow," of Bloom's own. "The jew hates the jew in the jew" (Herring 1972, 82)—so Joyce's notes to the episode, with obvious pertinence to Bloom, who remarks of Reuben J. Dodd, "Now he's what they really call a dirty jew" (U 8.1159), who entertains apparently without qualm reports of Jewish ritual sacrifice of Christian children (U 6.1771–72; compare U 17.843–49), who goes out of his way to introduce, "with sudden eagerness," the implicitly anti-Semitic story of Dodd and his son (*U* 6.272–75). And who, in this episode—with his aggressive cosmopolitanism, his uncharacteristic, and uncharacteristically abrasive, volubility (he may do more talking in this chapter than in all others combined), his tactless refusal to treat or be treated, his conspicuous pulling of strings and splitting of legal hairs—*acts* like an anti-Semite's picture of a Jew, even down to the fat cigar.

In fact, it may be that in "Cyclops" Bloom is implicated in the preeminent anti-Semitic action of *Ulysses,* by using his (stereotypical) way with fine print to defraud a man of money owed him, all the while doing what the narrator says Jews are prone to do, swindling "his own kidney" (*U* 12.1090–91). As Hugh Kenner observes about the negotiations in which Bloom is engaged, "someone named Bridgeman lent money in good faith, and . . . what is proposed is to defraud him on a technicality."[15] To which we can add the strong suspicion that this Bridgeman is Jewish, that that is why the anti-Semitic Hynes calls him "old Shylock" (*U* 12.765). To be sure, there is room for doubt: "Bridgeman" could be either an English or a Jewish name, and "Shylock" denotes either generic Jew or generic moneylender. But if Bridgeman has earned the epithet solely by virtue of being a professional moneylender, then he is a notably incompetent one, given that his investment looks to be wiped out by just the kind of loophole it should be his business to know about.[16] Besides, as shown by the case of Reuben J. Dodd (a gentile moneylender, assumed to be Jewish and stigmatized accordingly), anyone in his line of work is a natural target for anti-Semitic animus, no matter what the facts of his origins. Whether a moneylender or not—not, I would bet—Bridgeman either is or is believed to be Jewish.

To this add the two other mentions of Shylock in *Ulysses* (*U* 9.741, 748), which both stress the character's Jewishness, and recall his story in *The Merchant of Venice,* and we may be prompted to look behind the foregrounded drama— that of citizens rallying around to provide for widow and orphans at the expense of some fat cat—to, once again, another story, Bridgeman's, with Shakespeare's play as guide. "Everyone," says Kenner, "would want the widow Dignam and her children to inherit what there may be" (1977, 389). Yes, but only because Mrs. Dignam is foregrounded as just that, "the widow Dignam," in a formulation automatically eliciting sympathy, while Bridgeman is kept in the shadows. What Kernan's "grizzled moustache" does for his picture of himself, what Shaun's host-receptive tongue does for his own self-presentation, the word "widow" does for Mrs. Dignam in the eyes of this community.

As with those others, "the widow Dignam" can become less accommodatingly poignant if we look behind the scenery, perhaps beginning with Bloom's rueful recollection that, rightfully hers or not, Mrs. Dignam (a pretty unpleasant sort, incidentally, in his memory) emphatically "wants the money" (*U* 13.1227). The reason she wants and needs the money is not that an act of God has smitten her family, but that after begetting more children than he could afford to support, her husband proceeded to first ruin and then kill himself with drink. The Dignams, that is, are casualties of those indulgences that Bloom thinks of as distinctively Christian (*U* 8.49, 8.31–37),[17] and although it would be hard that the children should suffer for their parents' folly, it is hard as well that the as far as we know blameless Bridgeman, who may have children of his own to support,[18] should be the one to pay for it.

So Bloom, himself famously careful not to make the same kind of mistake (*U* 8.985–88), is called on to out-sharp the backgrounded Bridgeman by Martin Cunningham, who in the process calls Bloom a "perverted Jew" (*U* 12.1365),[19] and whose reasoning may well be just this: send a dog to eat a dog. At the least, Hynes's "Shylock" remark, occurring as it does in the episode most concerned with names as identifiers of type and character, opens up this possibility, and with it the possibility that we readers have gotten everything totally, completely, one-hundred-percent and then some, wrong. If the "Cyclops" narrative manhandles us into reading the events one way, it allows us to read them otherwise—even, among its gallery of parodies, to behold ourselves caricatured as the gulls it has made of us. Judge Frederick Falkiner, we are informed, recently rebuked Dodd for trying to get his money back from one Gumley, whose plight ("How many children? Ten, did you say?" "Yes, your worship. And my wife has the typhoid" [*U* 12.1105–6]) is on a par with the widow-and-orphans tale of the Dignams. And like Dignam's, Gumley's turns out to be an old story, as Bloom recalls in "Eumaeus": that of the child of wealth and privilege who chose the familiar (Irish, Christian) path of dissipation, with familiar consequences (*U* 16.941–56). Whether or not his wife really has typhoid, Gumley's miseries are entirely self-inflicted. Given a second look, his story invites this question: why should Dodd be expected to pick up his bill, at the behest of a community and legal establishment that treat him with scorn—more than that, with a scorn fueled by anti-Semitism? After all, this same Frederick Falkiner had recently made a name for himself with an anti-Semitic tirade delivered from the bench.[20] Yet here Falkiner is, in "Cyclops," presented as the defender of widows and orphans, David against Goliath, the soul of, well, Christian charity. "Poor old Sir Frederick," says one of the "Cyclops" patrons, "you can cod him up to the two eyes . . . Tell him a tale of woe about arrears of rent and a sick wife and a squad of kids and, faith, he'll dissolve in tears on the bench" (*U* 12.1096–99). Frederick Falkiner, *c'est nous*.

It is, one might feel, a bit hard of Joyce. (And, in a way, cruel too: the next episode will implicate us in ridicule of a character, Gerty McDowell, whose pos-turings are then shown to be the result of her lameness—in effect, we are made to laugh at a cripple, and then reflect on our laughing.) In a book famous for its ambiguities, "Cyclops" has been one place at least where we can relax, where wrong is wrong, right is right, and we can check our quotation marks at the door when calling Joyce's "hero" a hero.

That alone should alert us. "Cyclops" is in fact full of marginalized evidence probably planted to reproach our aroused lust for melodrama, for David-and-Goliath stories and so on. The undersized Irish "pet lamb" who floors the British bruiser in the boxing match reported at *U* 12.960–87 is a David versus a Goliath if you like, but one who triumphs, it seems reasonably clear from the ac-count, through low blows that are allowed to continue because the Irish crowd is screaming for his opponent's blood; his victory may make the mob feel good, but the upshot is that two poor sods, counterparts whether they realize it or not, have beaten one another up in order to put more money in the pocket of the pro-moter, Blazes Boylan, who is incidentally elsewhere identified as an English col-laborator. So much, at least, for that analogue of the Bloom-vs.-citizen story.

Especially telling are the episode's premonitions of the Great War fresh in the memory of Joyce's first readers. There are to begin with the repeated allu-sions to the German origins of the British royal family (*U* 12.293, 1390–92, 1397, 1399, 1401), recalling to English readers one conspicuous irony of their late sac-rifice for king and country in the struggle against the Hun. There is the tactless mention of Roger Casement, man of the hour in 1904 but by the time of the episode's composition a patriot traitor, hanged knight, hero of the Empire, and ally of its enemy—by the standards of the Kiernan crowd either a martyr de-filed by English lies or the blackest of deviants, executed for trying to liberate one small country, Ireland, by an imperial power claiming to avenge the vio-lated sovereignty of another small country, Belgium: a figure, that is, whose memory is guaranteed to foul up any attempt to make a satisfying story of re-cent history. And speaking of Belgium, and the infamous German "rape" of that brave little land which so exercised British propagandists during the war, there is, planted in "Cyclops," by way of reference to Casement's exposé, this incon-venient memory: "—Well, says J.J., if they're any worse than those Belgians in the Congo Free State they must be bad . . . —Raping the women and girls and flogging the natives on the belly to squeeze all the red rubber they can out of them" (*U* 12.1542–47).

Joyce wrote this dialogue when the words "Belgians" and "Raping," juxta-posed, would automatically have crystallized in his readers' minds the phrase "rape of Belgium," and with it a story the opposite of the one here told. Like Farrington and the Irish "pet lamb" of the boxing ring, the Belgium of Joyce's memory was both victim and victimizer, depending on the configuration of the moment, the focal point chosen. The same is true for the Bloom who in facing a barroom full of bullies may be a bit of a hero, but who in dealing with one of them is a bit of a bully himself, and who in his dealings with Bridgeman may well be playing a Shylock's Shylock.

What seems to be Bloom's finest moment is actually his most compromised. In fact I would argue that it is partly because Bloom's business here is so dubious that the heroic rhetoric is so noisy and the narrative strategy so importunate: as in "Clay," the monocular narrative of this episode is the expressive extension of a character who powerfully wishes not to see what he is doing, and whose strategy of extreme self-deprecation, as enacted by the narrative's "I," is recognizably that of the Bloom who woos Martha Clifford by posing as a naughty boy who needs to be punished and who throughout "Circe" fantasizes dramas of self-degradation. "Noman" is the name Joyce's notes give to the "Cyclops" narrator who savages Bloom and others, and in the *Odyssey* "Noman" is of course another name for Odysseus himself. "The jew hates the jew in the jew": the citizen and his anti-Semitism give voice to the self Bloom has suppressed most vigorously, the kind of Jew (moneylender, caller-in of debts) he must deny in order to achieve apotheosis as Elijah, the other kind.

As with Farrington, then, there is implicitly in "Cyclops" a story pretty much the opposite of the one apparently being told, in which one kind of counterpart turns out to be the other kind too, against a background thick with examples of how the same thing can happen on other scales, including the grand narrative of history. Joyce peoples this world of his, garrulous yet lexically deficient because its detectable and determinable facts outnumber available verbal formulae (the neo-language of *Finnegans Wake* is one response to the deficiency),[21] with characters each of whom tries to make himself or herself into the narrative expression of a defining focal point on which relatively random data can converge to make satisfactory sense, and shows them repeatedly getting it more or less wrong. He inveigles us into doing the same, for what in retrospect seems the purpose of prompting us by a rough dialectic to getting things more right. (The history of Joyce criticism is full of such progressions-through-reversal: almost no one still considers Molly Bloom to be either an earth-mother [thesis] or slattern [antithesis]; the reassessment began with second looks at the list of her lovers given in "Ithaca.") In *Ulysses* in particular we are constantly required to contemplate characters who generate fictions out of an implicitly infinite plenum, catalogued in unprecedented complexity and detail, for which no one version presented in the book's pages, probably, completely suffices, though some come closer than others. Hence the proliferation of narrative styles, which increasingly in Joyce's work come to compete with, interrupt, and shout down one another, like talkers at a party each of whom wants to tell the So-he-says, So-then-I-say story of which he or she is the star, all of whom, whatever else the argument may be about, are arguing, most of all with themselves, about what is most real.

The cognitive dislocation sometimes resulting has led one astute critic to propose E. H. Gombrich's duck-rabbit figure as a model for the "oscillating perspectives" that Joyce induces (Riquelme 1983, 40–41). I find this analogy of limited use. You can like and dislike Stephen Dedalus by turns with each new reading of *Portrait,* but once *Ulysses* has shown you the aftermath of the earlier book's triumphant valedictory, you can never, I think, take its Stephen on his own terms to the extent that originally seemed possible. Every persistent reader has experienced such moments of radical reevaluation when some new datum simultaneously reverses and advances his or her reading, in a movement less circle—or oscillation—than helix. Joyce stage-manages such moments, both because he wants to keep us rereading him and because it is one way of bringing his reader to experience the world as he sees it, as something that, although it can never be grasped comprehensively, can be engaged with increasing degrees of success. Which is to say that *Ulysses* is not *Rashomon,* nor even *The Ring and the Book.* The operations its author induces are, as computer programmers say, recursive, non-reversible, toward readings incorporating and surpassing any found within its pages at first meeting. To conjure the implied reader on whom Joyce works we ought to envision rather a sequence of readers, each smarter than the one before. The single figure who comes closest is probably, again, polytropic Odysseus, dead-reckoning without compass or chart, learning his way as he goes along, who experienced some reversals and oscillations of his own but eventually, through much trial and error, made it home, wiser than when he'd left.

4

The Orphic "Sirens," the Orphic *Ulysses*

1

A FICTIONAL UNIVERSE whose characters are subject to reversals of perspective such as those just surveyed will likely tend toward instability in its presentation of other categories of reality as well. In general, the "nebuless" state preceding the distillations as they "idendifine" themselves will tend to shift and refract before our eyes. Latent from the first pages of *Ulysses*, these effects come aggressively into their own in the eleventh episode, "Sirens." Whatever may be going on with the verbal events on display, they are not following the same rules to which, despite some perturbations, we may have become accustomed over the first ten episodes. David Hayman made a memorable contribution to the conversation when he anthropomorphized the presiding spirit introduced at this point as "the arranger," a sometimes "perverse" "version of 'the artist-God as cosmic joker.' "[1] This is the guy—he is always or almost always male—who will henceforth be trying out, and showing off, the new-style-per-episode virtuosity that was to exasperate Ezra Pound and S. L. Goldberg, and whose "Sirens" voice brashly announces "Begin!" (*U* 11.63) the moment he steps forward to run the new show.

I think Hayman was right: the shift in "Sirens" constitutes a presence, even an identity, which it is possible to assay descriptively. For instance, it is possible to talk about what he believes in. What assumptions allow him to order the narrative material as he does? And not just the narrative: to a degree new in *Ulysses*, this character is in the business of rearranging the universe. "Sirens" introduces a kind of split-screen montage effect, of events in one venue intercut with events in another, and they are not merely juxtaposed. They are coordinated. Hints of such things have shown up before—notably in what Clive Hart (1974, 181–216) calls the "interpolations" (moments from one locale introduced without obvious transition into the action of another) of the preceding episode, sometimes with possible paranormal implications. There were similar effects in the composition of Stephen's villanelle, which strove to fuse a book's-worth of experience into one poem, which to that end entertained notions of telekinetic synchronicity, and which in so doing drew on a developmental hypothesis with cosmological applications.

All that, I think, is true of "Sirens" too, but at a new level of deliberateness and with a new range of repercussion. The arranger introduced in "Sirens" also believes in versions of telepathy and telekinesis, among other things. He has a theory of the universe that substantiates those beliefs, one that recognizably derives from the nebular hypothesis of *Portrait,* and this theory licenses not only the special effects of his own performance but much of what follows. And, with all that, he has a name: Orpheus.

According to Joyce's schema (Ellmann 1972, chart after 187), Orpheus is one of the mythical figures anagogically present in "Sirens." His Dublin reincarnation? Simon Dedalus. Simon is the one whose wife has died, who has visited her grave in "Hades," who calls, musically, for her to return to him, whose song transfixes everyone in the room (and whose son will later claim the power to raise the dead [*U* 14.1113–16]), and whose singing is "high in the effulgence symbolistic . . . etherial" (*U* 11.748)—that is, Orphic. He plays the piano, an instrument descended from Orpheus's lyre. As a "Dedalus" he is automatically an Orpheus type: two fabulous artificers, for that reason paired by Plato and others.[2]

Most of all, as the only widower present, Simon takes the male lead in the Orpheus and Eurydice story suffusing "Sirens." It is, essentially, the story of a man who cannot *wait* to *look* back, and who in consequence recondemns his wife to the land of shadows. The first conversation of "Sirens," between two *wait*resses *look*ing out a window, describes a man said to be "killed looking back" at a woman who then saunters "sadly from bright light" (*U* 11.77–81). From there until a point about three-quarters of the way through the episode (we will later consider why), two repeated words, "wait" and "look," along with derivatives and synonyms, dominate a narrative describing characters who spend most of their time doing one or both.

As for the Eurydice half of the story, that is supplied by the songs being sung and recalled, almost all of them, as Zack Bowen has shown (1967, 249–52), about the meetings and sunderings of lovers, about paradisiacal love found and lost. It is the right accompaniment for Bloom, whose marriage to Molly is threatened in this episode as Boylan approaches and reaches her, and who, as a result, succumbs, for a time, to the kind of self-pitying sentimentality such songs encourage.

For a time, but not for good: earlier in *Ulysses* Bloom had registered his disdain for exactly the kind of "symbolistic" (*U* 8.543) afflatus on display in Simon's song's flight into the "effulgence symbolistic," and that disdain returns in "Sirens," shortly after Simon's Orphic song is over. Like Odysseus—thrilling to the music, but by his own command tied to the mast—in the end Bloom steels himself against the siren song.

Which is to say that if Simon is Orpheus, Bloom is a kind of anti-Orpheus. Orpheus's followers had three prohibitions: against the eating of meat, against the eating of beans, and against the burial of bodies in wool. Of the three, Bloom has violated two—he eats meat while Simon sings, and has buried his child in a wool jacket (*U* 18.1448)—and his flatulent farewell violates at least the spirit of the third, meant to discourage gassiness. That farewell also amounts to a dismissal of the kind of "Dotty" music (*U* 11.1193) practiced in the Ormond: "Musemathematics. And you think you're listening to the etherial. But suppose you said it like: Martha, seven times nine minus x is thirty-five thousand. Fall quite flat" (*U* 11.836).

Yes it would—and so much for "Musemathematics," a phrase that nicely summed up the claim by the Orphics and their successors the Pythagoreans that their music was a sacred force attuning them to the mathematical laws of creation and thus to "the etherial." Bloom accompanies this hardheaded assessment of such claims with some cavalier treatment of Pythagoras's monochord, here a "slender catgut thong": "He drew and plucked. It buzzed, it twanged" (*U* 11.796). (The cords binding Odysseus to the mast are in there too.) Given his situation, such responses come naturally. Love songs, after all, are not something a new-minted cuckold will want to listen to for long. Bloom's final acts in "Sirens" are of rejection: he leaves the congregation, deliberately, before the climax of the latest musical rhapsody, and heads into the world of daylight and business, rudely mocking, with his own wind instrument, the whole musemathematical notion of music as some kind of transport to sublimity. Despite having been lured for a spell, he makes it clear with his departure that he is not one of the Orphic cult.

But the music-makers of the Ormond are, and so is the episode they inhabit. In particular, "Sirens" works from something with deep roots in Orphic doctrine—the power, earlier entertained in imagination by the Stephen of *Portrait*, to interact with distant objects by means of spells and incantations, musical or otherwise. The Orpheus of legend had set distant rocks and trees to dancing with his playing, and for hundreds of years his disciples were notorious for claiming similar powers (Gutherie 1966, 17–19). Although no theoretical explanation for such claims was given, a later age was to fill in the gap. The Neoplatonist vogue of the late eighteenth and early nineteenth centuries brought with it a renewed interest in Orpheus,[3] along with a new accounting for his telekinetic charms (Riffaterre 1970, 12). Creation was an organic interconnection of Swedenborgian correspondences, the motive power of which was music, and music was a matter of reverberating frequencies that, when they matched, produced the phenomenon known as "sympathetic vibration." There was now a plausible scientific rationale for such theories, supplied by the new experiments with electricity and magnetism, particularly as interpreted by the school of Franz Anton Mesmer, musical-medical-magical discoverer of "animal magnetism." (Thus, E.T.A. Hoffman, literary follower of this new Orpheus: "The musician has the same rapport with nature as the magnetist with the seer."[4]) Animal magnetism, as described by Mesmer, was a fluid, all-pervasive *"influence mutuelle"* through which *"toutes les impressions du mouvement"* could be communicated, even across great distances. It worked on humans by *"s'insinuant dans la substance des nerfs"* and often produced symptoms similar to those of passionate love. Like light, it could be augmented, reflected, and focused by glass.[5] As such, it was, as Maria M. Tatar writes, a logical extension of "the sympathetic nervous system of Romantic vitalists" derived from Galvani's discovery (the one cited in *Portrait* by Stephen) of animal electricity, an extension that "invested the word 'sympathy' with a new vitality" (Tatar 1978, 48, 22). Tatar cites, as one influential example, the new understanding of "sympathy" represented by the romantic physician Gotthilf Heinrich Schubert: "Schubert maintained that a bundle of nerves located in the solar plexus regulates the functions of the ganglionic system, just as the brain orchestrates the activities carried out by the cerebral nerves. The solar plexus, identified by Schubert as the organ of intuitive knowledge, figures as a link between the individual nervous system and an ethereal spirit or subtle fluid that organizes the universe into a living whole. That anatomical organ invests man with a sixth sense analogous to the faculty of instinct in animals and endows him with the ability to transcend spatial and temporal limitations."[6]

"Sirens" is full of curious occurrences recalling such theories. When Bloom attempts psychic communion with one of the barmaids, for instance, he urges himself, "Think in my stom" (*U* 11.1095)—that is, in Schubert's center of "sympathetic" influences. Along with such forays into telepathy goes the distinctively Orphic phenomenon of telekinesis. In Joyce's day the new name for it was "synchronicity,"[7] and a fascination with it was very much in the air. The *Journal for the Society of Psychical Research* frequently contained reports of such experiences; at the moment of his death in battle, so it was told, Wilfred Owen had appeared in a vision to his brother; newspapers reporting on the aftermath of the *Titanic*'s sinking told of distant relatives of doomed passengers becoming spontaneously hysterical just as the iceberg struck, in some cases in response to the sudden apparition of the image of the imperiled beloved.[8] Joyce knew of such stories from his childhood: one is recorded in *Portrait* (*P* 19). Later, according to an account given to Clive Hart by Stuart Gilbert, he took a lively interest in accounts of "psychic cross-correspondences" as reported by the Society for Psychical Research—that is, of cases where mediums, all strangers to one another and in different locales, transcribed different but consistent strands of one composite history known only to the defunct communicator and to the subject seeking contact.[9] There is redundant evidence of his lifelong fascination with what according to Margaret Anderson he considered "his curious telepathic experiences," especially his way of unconsciously divining and recording people's inmost secrets in his writing (Margaret Anderson 1990, 135). Such experiences have at least a familial resemblance to those of the young Stephen, whose mind "instantaneously" "met" Ibsen's "in a moment of "radiant simultaneity" (*SH* 40), or of the love-struck young Joyce given to similar talk about his communion with Nora.

With that background in mind, we may remark that *Ulysses* contains one generally recognized instance of synchronicity, and that it occurs in "Sirens": the stopping of Bloom's watch at 4:30, from something like sympathetic vibration, a kind of "magnetism" (*U* 11.987) responding to the coupling of Molly and Boylan. Actually, that is just the beginning of the business. There are in fact many such "magnetic" phenomena in this episode of musical and sexual convergences, cases of "coincidence" so remarkable that Bloom is twice struck by them (*U* 11.303, 713).

Consider just the first few pages. In them Bloom receives four pence change from the shopkeeper in the stationery store and, because he is preoccupied with thoughts of Molly and Boylan's appointment "at four," has to be reminded to take it: "And four," says the girl innocently (*U* 11.308). On the next page, Boylan asks whether a telegram has arrived and receives this answer: "Not yet. At four he" (*U* 11.354). When Miss Douce, taking a coin from Boylan of the "Bold hand" (*U* 4.244), strikes "boldly the cash register," the pub clock signaling the fatal hour chimes in (*U* 11.382–83). At the moment when this same Miss Douce concludes the performance with her garter, Simon Dedalus concludes his singing with the words, "Sweetheart, goodbye!" and Boylan announces, "I'm off" (*U* 11.426). The moment that Boylan begins jingling off to his tryst with Molly and Bloom lets out a "light sob" at the thought of the loss this meeting portends, Simon proclaims "God be with old times" (*U* 11.459), after which the conversa-

tion turns to the subject of Molly and her run-in with a(nother) priapic singer.
With Boylan jingling to her and Bloom fretting about what is going to happen,
Simon, unaware of Bloom's presence in the pub, offers the comment, "Mrs Mar-
ion Bloom has left off clothes of all descriptions" (U 11.496–97).

That is all in the first five hundred lines. It seems that in "Sirens" the influence of those two highly charged magnetic fields, music and sex, have con-
verged to heighten the potential for sympathetic influences, for the Orphic
phenomenon of synchronicity. And no wonder: animal magnetism, said Mesmer, "est augmentée et réfléchie par les glaces, comme la lumière" (Tatar 1978, 274);
the barmaids spend much of their time looking into the mirrors above the bar;
the Ormond setting itself is ideal for purposes of receiving and augmenting
such vibrations: "His spellbound eyes went after, after her gliding head as it
went down the bar by mirrors, gilded arch for ginger ale, hock and claret
glasses shimmering, a spiky shell, where it concerted, mirrored, bronze with
sunnier bronze" (U 11.420–23). That, jazzed up in the mid-Ulysses manner, is
also essentially a rendering of the same kind of mental/extra-mental operation
that the Stephen of Portrait envisioned when he compared his own mind's
working to a reflector or a cloud chamber, both of them implements for concentrating and augmenting scattered, far-flung influences. Miss Douce's bronze
hair, itself as we are constantly reminded a reflector of sunlight, is made yet
"sunnier" by the concerting action of the "gilded arch" of glass, just as that
"spiky shell," we will later learn (U 11.930, 934–36, 944–45) gathers, focuses, and
gives back the pulsings of the ear, which, come to think of it (U 11.930), is also a
shell, an acoustical reflector, yet another concavity designed to capture and con-
cert certain vibrations stirring in the air. This shell is the aural counterpart of the
spellbinding mirror-show that reflects and focuses it, an example of the "shell-
hearing" that Frederick W. H. Myers' Human Personality and Its Survival of Bodily
Death (a book Joyce read) called the "correlative" of the "crystal-gazing" practiced by clairvoyants.[10] And those vibrations, like the cloud chamber's cosmic
rays, like Stephen's accompanying intimations of psychic synchronicity, may
come by ways and from presences our daily experience knows not of, from
sources outside the range or beneath the thresholds of our five senses.

If "Sirens" is indeed Orphic in this way, then we may expect, paradoxically,
that the episode's anti-Orpheus, Leopold Bloom, would be the one most acutely
sensitive to its effects. Tied-to-the-mast Odysseus is after all the only one who
actually gets to hear the Sirens' music. And here let us note a strange thing
about Bloom in this episode—his uncannily acute sense of hearing. When Miss
Douce and her customer hold the shell to their ears, in an adjoining room no

less, we are told, amazingly, that Bloom can hear its roaring ocean-sound too, albeit (a concession to credibility) "more faintly" (*U* 11.934–36). Bloom can identify, correctly, the invisible pianist whose notes are reaching him from the other side of a closed door (*U* 11.537). He can pick up the "little sound" of "jing" coming from the street outside (*U* 11.457). He is, in short, an aural phenom, for the duration of this episode at least. No wonder that under its influence he feels that he might manage a bit of telepathy.

2

Whatever the success of his one deliberate try, in "Sirens" Bloom does, effortlessly, unconsciously, and unwillingly, experience a prolonged spell of telepathically-inflected synchronicity, of sensing, for the most part as a kind of subliminal hearing, from far away, the main phases of the main event of the day, an event that in accordance with Orphic dictates is both sexual and musical. (Much of the time he is also writing, like Joyce during his "telepathic experiences.") That event is Boylan's visit with Molly, to sing with her and have sex with her. It is conveyed to Bloom through a series of double entendres that correspond to the stages of Boylan's and Molly's convergence, beginning with Boylan's jingling off and the musically accompanied dalliance that follows. Stephen, we have seen, may already have anticipated such a connection in composing his villanelle, and Molly, in her way, seems later to have also sensed something similar: about her time in bed with Boylan, she will recall, "I suppose they could hear us away over the other side of the park" (*U* 18.1131–32). This is hyperbole, certainly, but the later episodes have a way of literalizing the hyperbolic: in the same monologue Molly calls men "pigs" (*U* 18.1356), about two hours after "Circe" 's magic turned a host of men into pigs. So it may pay to take such expressions seriously and to consider that, topographically speaking, anything happening at 7 Eccles Street audible from the far side of Phoenix Park would certainly be detectable to someone tuning in from the Ormond.

In tracing the main coordinates of the synchronic parallels that Bloom picks up, we can begin at 3:16, the time when, according to Hart's meticulous chronology of the preceding episode,[11] Molly is throwing a coin to a sailor (*U* 10.249–56). As this glimpse reveals and Molly later confirms (*U* 18.346), she has not yet begun preparing for Boylan, expected at 4:00. So we know what she will be doing during the next forty-four minutes: getting ready, *look*ing in the mirror, and *wait*ing.

Again using Hart's chronology, we find that the action of "Sirens" begins at

3:38,[12] by which point Molly must certainly have begun her preparations. "Sirens" opens with two women standing like Molly when last seen, at a window, gazing with interest at the men passing by ("Your *beau* is it?" asks the bootsboy), comparing notes on fashion and skin care as Miss Douce, worried that her skin may become unattractive when her sunburn starts to peel, turns "to see her skin askance in the barmirror." Molly, at about the same time: "I looked a bit washy of course when I looked close in the handglass powdering"; "I thought it was beginning to look coarse or old a bit the skin" (*U* 18.413, 464). Such thoughts lead her to remember the face lotion that she has asked her husband to get at the druggist's (*U* 18.459–61). Again there is a parallel development in the Ormond, where the conversation leads Miss Douce to recall the time she "asked that old fogey in Boyd's for something for my skin," which fogey is forthwith linked to Bloom (*U* 11.180).

From this point until the moment when Boylan greets Molly, the barmaids spend their time looking in the mirror, fretting, and—being waitresses—waiting. Their anxiety mounts after the clock strikes four, Boylan's scheduled time of arrival. At *U* 11.516 they "pined"; at *U* 11.640 Bloom, reminded of Bellini's *La Sonnambula*, thinks, "Too late. She longed to go," and Miss Douce, standing "in screening shadow" (compare Molly, "with blinds down" [*U* 18.146]), is being attentive to an "expectant" chord. The mood is of "desire" (*U* 11.706) and—the key, Orphic, word—of waiting: "Waiting she sang . . . full voice of perfume" (*U* 11.730). Compare Molly: "my hours dressing and perfuming and combing" (*U* 18.146–47). The mood of longing peaks when Simon sings "Come . . . To Me!"— but Boylan has not yet come, and the mood becomes one of nervousness and resentment. At *U* 11.781 we are reminded of the lines "false one we had better part . . . since love lives not"; at *U* 11.793 Bloom recalls the note of "lamentation" and envisions Molly abandoned by Boylan. In the remaining pages before the meeting, Bloom fiddles nervously with his thong as Miss Douce becomes "reproachful"; Martha is recalled writing "My patience are exhausted" and promising to punish Bloom; a shell is "forsaken." Just as Boylan turns into Eccles Street (Molly: "I was just beginning to yawn with nerves thinking he was trying to make a fool of me" [*U* 18.342]), Miss Douce feels compelled to protest that she is "not . . . lonely," "not alone" (*U* 11.956). As Boylan's car slows down before the Blooms' home, Cowley starts playing a melody from *Don Giovanni*, the opera that since "Calypso" has stood for the approaching adultery. Boylan raps at the door, and we have, "Come. He came, he came, he did not stay. To me," and then, in the interval between his knocking and Molly's answering, the episode's last concatenation of "waits": ". . . wife and family waiting, waiting . . . Deaf wait while they wait. But wait" (*U* 11.1004–5). Since the action began, the word in one form or another has been occurring at about three times the rate of its incidence hereafter.[13] Molly, after all, is finally through waiting.

From the moment of Boylan's arrival, the synchronicity becomes more detailed. There are, I think, two reasons for this. First, Molly and Boylan have sex, and sex, again, is supposed to be an especially powerful transmitter. Second, the listeners in the Ormond, especially Bloom, are at their most attentive: "Listen. Bloom listened. Richie Goulding listened. And by the door deaf Pat, bald Pat, tipped Pat, listened" (*U* 11.1028–30). The signal has been augmented from the transmitter at the same time that the volume has been turned up at the receiver.

The reasons those people in the Ormond are listening so closely is that they want to catch Ben Dollard's rendition of "The Croppy Boy," which begins at about the moment when Boylan is standing at Molly's door. And this performance happens to be a singularly appropriate accompaniment for what is about to occur, for a number of reasons. First, Dollard is a phallic symbol, thanks to the reputed size of his "organ" (*U* 11.536–37), a distinction that, according to the Blooms anyway, he shares with Boylan. Second, Boylan has earlier been identified with the song's hero, as "blazes boy" (*U* 11.290). Third, "The Croppy Boy" is a song about usurpation and betrayal.[14] Finally, as the following will demonstrate, its narrative parallels, or is made to parallel, the events at 7 Eccles Street.

I list what seem the most suggestive passages in the order of their occurrence in the text, with parallel commentary or corroboration from elsewhere. The "Sirens" passages, quoted in their order of occurrence in the left column, run from *Ulysses* 11.997 to 11.1242.

Bob Cowley's outstretched talons gripped the black deepsounding chords.	Having knocked, Boylan impatiently pulls the bell-pull as well.
Ruin them. Wreck their lives.	Molly is, because of Boylan, a "ruined" woman in the Victorian sense; Bloom's marriage is being threatened.
The voice of warning, solemn warning, told them the youth had entered a lonely hall.	The young Boylan enters Bloom's "bare hall" (*U* 452).
Bronze gazed far sideways. Mirror there. Is that best side of their face?	Molly takes a look in the mirror that hangs in the Blooms's hall before the door (*U* 11.689–90).

She looked fine. Her crocus dress she wore, lowcut, belongings on show. Clove her breath was always in theatre when she bent to ask a question . . . Hypnotized, listening.

Frank appreciation of the dressed-up, made-up Molly, her breath sweetened with "kissing comfits" (*U* 11.691, 17.301–2, 18.1140–41).

All gone. All fallen. Too late now.

Molly's resistance, that is. Which explains why it is too late now.

Big Ben his voice un-folded . . . . . . She listens. Who dares to speak of nineteen four?[15]
—*Bless me father,* Dollard the croppy cried. *Bless me and let me go.*

Flushed with success, the impatient Boylan dispenses with further preliminaries and urges immediate action.

Low sank the music, air and words. Then hastened. The false priest rustling soldier from his cassock. A yeoman captain. They know it all by heart. The thrill they itch for.

The undressing begins, with Boylan wasting no time: "pulling off his shoes and trousers there on the chair . . ." Just at this moment, Dollard is singing the words, "The robes were off, and in scarlet there / Sat a yeoman captain with fiery glare." "Fiery" recalls "blazes," and Molly later remembers Boylan undressing to reveal "that tremendous big red brute of a thing" (*U* 18.144).

With hoarse rude fury the yeoman cursed. Swelling in apoplectic bitch's bastard.

Compare Boylan's "hoarsely" guttural cry when coupling with Molly in "Circe" (*U* 15.3809–10).

Thrill now . . . For all things dying, want to, dying to, die . . .
    A liquid of womb of woman eyeball gazed under a fence of lashes . . . At each slow satiny heaving bosom's wave (her heaving embon) . . . Heartbeats her breath. . . . And all the tiny

A fairly graphic account of Molly's response. "Die" probably carries the Elizabethan double meaning.

tiny fernfoils trembled of maidenhair.
... Popped corks, splashes of beerfroth ...

... Fro, to: to, fro: over the polished knob ... her thumb and finger passed in pity ... a cool firm white enamel baton protruding through their sliding ring.
    With a cock with a carra.
    Tap. Tap. Tap.

Consummation. "Tap" has earlier (*U* 11.706–7) been equated with the Elizabethan "tup."

I hold this house. Amen. He gnashed in fury.

"*I*" hold this house is one of Bloom's significant blunders; the song says "We."[16] At this moment Boylan's usurpation in Bloom's house is complete.

Get out before the end. Thanks, that was heavenly.
... Walk, walk, walk. Like Cashel Boylo Connoro Coylo Tisdall Maurice Tisndtall Farrell. Waaaaaaaaalk.
    Well, I must be. Are you off? Yrfmstbyes. Blmstup. ... Ow. Soap feeling rather sticky behind. Must have sweated: music. That lotion, remember.[17]

Boylan is climaxing. "Get out before the end" confirms Molly's memory: "I made him pull out and do it on me" (*U* 18.155). As elsewhere the subject is "Boylo."[18]

At Geneva barrack that young man died. At Passage was his body laid. Dolor! O, he dolores!

Flopping down beside Molly, Boylan experiences post-orgasmic dumps.

By rose, by satiny bosom, by fondling hand, by slops, by empties, by popped corks.

The innuendo is obvious.

General chorus off for a swill to wash it down. Glad I avoided.

Molly washes off, perhaps reflecting, as she does later, that it is "so much the better" that Boylan did not "finish it in me," "in case any of it wasnt washed out properly" (*U* 18.155–57). Boylan is getting ready to leave.

—Ben machree, said Mr Dedalus, clapping Ben's fat back back shoulder blade.

Molly: "one thing I didn't like his slapping me going away so familiarly in the hall" (18.122–23).

Richie rift in the lute alone sat.

As usual "too quick" (*U* 18.316), Boylan has gotten ready to go out to check, probably by phone, on the wire he was earlier told would be in "at four." (He is hoping to learn the results of the Gold Cup horse race on which he wagered.) Molly is being left alone.

. . . And *the last rose of summer* was a lovely song . . .
    'Tis the last rose of summer Dollard left Bloom felt.

Left so abruptly, Molly, the Spanish "Rose of Castille," feels like the subject of Mina's melancholy song, which begins, "Tis the last rose of summer / Left blooming alone." Both Blooms feel alone.

. . . Wish I hadn't promised to meet. Freer in air. Music. Gets on your nerves. Beerpull. Her hand that rocks the cradle rules the.

Outside, Boylan walks along in the open air, feeling free and reflecting on how a woman can tie a man down and get on his nerves.

. . . Better give way only half way the way of a man with a maid.

Boylan, as above.

Under the sandwichbell lay on a bier of bread one last, one lonely, last sardine of summer. Bloom alone.

The abandoned Molly Bloom, lying in her bed and feeling lonely.

... a mermaid, hair all streaming (but he couldn't see) blew whiffs of a mermaid (blind couldn't), coolest whiff of all.

"Mermaid" is a cigarette brand; Molly consoles herself with the traditional cigarette. (Its butt will be in evidence at *U* 17.1306).

... Molly in her shift ... hair down. ... Sleep! All is lost now.

Molly recalls herself later "with my hair a bit loose from the tumbling" (*U* 18.593). Lying in bed, her dressing all undone, she falls asleep.[19]

3

The above observations converge, I think, on one general conclusion: that we have not begun to appreciate the extent to which Joyce's work was given over to what I have here been calling "Orphic" effects, of the kind first glimpsed in *Portrait*'s gropings toward a unified-field theory embracing macrocosm and microcosm, natural and supernatural, physical laws and psychical phenomena. The later episodes of *Ulysses* in particular reflect the author's openness to the ways in which the science and pseudoscience of his day seemed to have come together in a common quest to understand the mechanics of human sensation and communication, to explore the possibility of their extensions beyond established borders, and in general to find in the new theories of nature a new understanding of human nature. During the years when Joyce was setting his course—and, not incidentally, studying medicine for a time—the Mesmeric tradition was being not only revived (most influentially by Jean-Martin Charcot, mentor to Freud, celebrity in residence of Paris's Saltpêtrière hospital, and widely considered the world's greatest neurologist), but to all appearances substantiated by the findings of Hermann Helmholtz, William Wundt, and many others about the neuronal processes through which our bodies and brains transmute the universe's raw data into perceptions. William James summed up: "the brain is essentially a place of currents which run in organized paths" (James 1950, 1:70). So was the body a place of currents, as became clear the more its sensory receptors were studied in relation to the afferent and efferent neural conductors wiring them to the brain's central bundle of circuitry. And so, it seemed increasingly, was the universe: light came in beams that could be spectrally distributed, bent, their speed measured; sound was a successive reverberation of molecules and could be channeled in electrical pulses across wires or, later, through the air, which it turned out was already abuzz with previously undetected static. Members of the Society for Psychical Research (which, like the word *telepathy*, came into existence the year Joyce was born) never tired of saying that the new advances in communication just confirmed how in touch with the order of things were their own divinings, that "brain-waves" and spirit signals, like X-rays and radio waves, could cross distances and pass through walls.[20]

Electricity, including the electricity of the nervous system, was the central exhibit. One spiritualist journal was called *The British Spiritual Telegraph* (and an English translation of a French spiritualist tract was retitled *The Celestial Telegraph*);[21] phrases like "electro-psychology," "electro-biology," and "phreno-magnetism" were the order of the day; the effectiveness of mediums was monitored and measured with galvanometers; a representative theorist, in a formulation that may have contributed something to Stephen's understanding, in *Portrait*, of his own galvanic, mitotically expansive inner self, defined the soul as "the really vital part of the cell," as such a matter of (as summarized by Janet Oppenheim) "ionization and condensation, electric polarity, molecular dimensions, and electrons" (Oppenheim 1985, 338).

All of which was the kind of thing one might expect in an age whose histologists were writing books about the psychology of cells. No less a figure than Alfred Russel Wallace, the co-discoverer of evolution, was led by way of phrenology and mesmerism, scientifically accounted for, to "phrenomagnetism," thence to spiritualism (Oppenheim 1985, 305). In fact evolution figured heavily in the theorizing about psychic powers, most writers considering them an evolutionary advance, some on the contrary as a throwback to or vestige of what Myers called the "germ" of "undifferentiated continuous sensitivity" that preceded "our existing specialisation of sense" (Myers 1920, 1:224), still others as a morbid mutation, comparable to epilepsy, hysteria, or the genius that according to Cesare Lombroso was really a pathology of cerebral or neuronal hypertrophy. Even ghost-visitations, with such coinings as "ectoplasm" (from "protoplasm"), were reinterpreted in light of the "new fashions in science": " 'Literary' ghost stories were framed around drugs, psychiatry, mesmerism. Many, in short, tried to combine and compromise science and spiritualism, with occasionally peculiar results. At the end of the century one enthusiast published a pamphlet about 'Animal Electricity' in which he discusses the 'live thermometer or electric pile in man', and describes a spiritual conversation he had with the atoms of iron in some bearings" (Finucane 1984, 179). Thus, in updating the conception of sympathetic vibration advanced a century earlier, did contemporary science devise an explanation for what seems to be happening in "Sirens."

Such convergences, of traditional, "Orphic," doctrine and the new speculative science,[22] account, I think, for much of what is distinctive in Joyce's writing.
It is a convergence in evidence throughout his career, since before the *Portrait* in
which the hero's heart is spoken of in terms of its "ventricles" and artistic creation in terms of electrical phenomena observed in a laboratory frog. The
longest chapter of *Finnegans Wake* opens with a description of its central figure's
eyes, ears, brain, and nervous system in the language of electronic communication (*FW* 309.01–310.21) and later maps out his son's body as a branchwork of
phosphorescent conductions (*FW* 474.16–475.17), thus demonstrating Joyce's
familiarity with contemporary theories that phosphorous is the nervous
system's active agent.[23] In that book's many evocations of past or distant lives, it
often has recourse to a complex of Mesmeric, magical, electromagnetic, and
physiological correspondences, correspondences that can reach indefinitely
outward to mirror and participate in the universe's fundamental processes governing creation and destruction. Thus in one of her monologues Issy describes
herself as staring into a mirror while sending her dream by "telepath" "on my
hearz' waves" (*FW* 460.25)—Hertzian waves: wireless messages—to her faraway lover.[24] That Hertzian waves might go with the sympathetic signals that
quickened the heart was not just a verbal conceit: Sir Oliver Lodge, the eminent
physicist whose "experiments with Herzian waves led him to achieve the wireless transmission of signals before Marconi's far more famous . . . activity" (Oppenheim 1985, 397), had hoped to prove just that, as culmination of his lifelong
quest for a "modern physics" embracing both material and spiritualist realities.
Numerous passages in *Finnegans Wake* show that Joyce knew of such ideas, and
knew, as well, that the ether was where physical and metaphysical were said to
become one.[25] He also knew that those waves went out to the end of the universe, and if nothing else his rhyming of heart and Hertz makes clear that, as in
Portrait, he remained receptive to the idea that intense feeling is intensely electrical.[26] The inquisition of Shaun, which takes up most of book 3, is among other
things a seance in which the subject is induced to receive different
telepathic/telegraphic messages ("per Neuropaths" [*FW* 488.26]) over the Mesmeric ether: "pricking up ears to my phono on the ground and picking up airs
from th'other over th'ether" (*FW* 452.12–13).[27]

Looking forward to *Finnegans Wake* as it does, the new, modernized, science-
fictionish Orphism that emerges in "Sirens" extends as well, in different capacities, to the end of *Ulysses,* much of whose second half depends on effects
deriving from ideas most of us today would ordinarily dismiss as occult or
pseudoscientific mumbo-jumbo—telepathy, psychically-engineered correspondences, telekinesis, ghost-visitations, the apparition of etheric doubles,

and (of course) metempsychosis.[28] That does not mean that it thereby abandons its initial commitment to realism; it only means that Joyce's reality was different from ours. He believed, or at least entertained a belief in, all kinds of things that his readers (who, when they consider, say, Joycean metempsychosis, are likelier to feel comfortable with Plato and Nietzsche than with Bridie Murphy or The Amazing Kreskin) would most likely disparage. Alive today and writing a sequel to *Finnegans Wake,* he would likely find uses for the Bermuda Triangle, crop circles, that monkey face supposed to be on Mars, and Elvis sightings.

4

The following chapters will explore in detail some of the implications of such newly respectable "Orphic" effects, as they work themselves out from "Oxen of the Sun" through "Penelope." Before that, however, I would like to return briefly to "Cyclops," as well as to its successor, "Nausicaa," as they present themselves in light of these effects. Just what, after all, is going on in "Cyclops," if, as argued, Bloom there confronts a gigantified imago, a "shadow," of his hidden self? By what dispensation do fragments of his buried impulses emerge, swell, take on independent life, assume names, and start talking?

By the same dispensation, I suggest that, in this episode immediately following "Sirens" ' rendition of Boylan's offstage penetration of Molly, Bloom is confronted with a succession of grotesquely magnified replicas of that act, as on some huge X-rated screen—beginning with the first sentence, in which a "bloody sweep . . . near drove his gear into my eye" (U 12.2–3), and extending to the last one, in which the concluding "shot off a shovel," "at an angle of forty-five degrees" (U 13.1916–17), is as much ejaculatory as anything else.[29] In other words, the bigger question about "Cyclops" is: why are variants suddenly so prominent in this episode, including dramatized, come-to-life variants of the pornographic mental picture that since the events of "Sirens" has most haunted Bloom ("a cool firm white enamel baton protruding through their sliding ring" [U 11.1116–17]; "O, he did. Into her. She did. Done." [U 13.849])?

Perhaps the question answers itself. Writers of novels have long found doubles useful for purposes of psychological exposition, have long contrived to present their protagonists with props symbolic of their true inner states. Increasingly in *Ulysses,* such authorial manipulations come into existence as autogenous products of character dynamics, appearing more after the manner of, say, Macbeth's floating dagger than of Elizabeth Bennett's Pemberley. Increasingly, they emerge not as encounters arranged for them by the plotting author but as apparitions generated out of something about the way the inner and outer components of their lives are working together. Touched and animated by the Orphic arranger, people are redistributed, gigantified, and turned inside out.

A concession here: doubtless Barney Kiernan's is as real as anything in the book, and the citizen too, and probably a crossing sweeper really does stick his broom in the direction of someone's eye. Still, something else is going on here, something about the way these particular facts and features are chosen and presented, which belongs in the traditional domain of the uncanny. If "Sirens" is a hall of mirrors, psychically reflecting faraway events, "Cyclops" is the Brocken. Joyce's Linati schema lists Prometheus as one of the "Persons" anagogically present in "Cyclops," and Prometheus was the one who, according to tradition, made animate humans, in his own image, out of clay. (He also, of course, brought fire to mankind, as does Bloom, in Barney Kiernan's, when he lights his cigar.[30] In his meal of the previous episode he was replenishing his supply of liver.[31]) That was why *Frankenstein* was subtitled "The Modern Prometheus," and indeed there is a Frankenstein's-monster quality in the way the citizen rises up to beleaguer Bloom with a composition of his own worst humors, and in the way so many of the details appearing to Bloom inform against him. Even when Bloom is not yet present on the scene, the new narrator is acting out his new-forged fixation, on the apparition of long hard objects being poked into sensitive bodily apertures, when he introduces that picture of a broom handle going into an eye;[32] even though the citizen knows nothing of what has just happened in Bloom's bed, he speaks not just to but for him in lamenting "our ruined hearths" (read: hearts) and untended beds (*U* 13.1255–56), in furiously denouncing Boylan (*U* 13.949–50), and in finally erupting into impotent rage at the outsider's insult to his own home.[33]

Such Orphic phenomena—apparitions, doubles—not only continue into the next episode, "Nausicaa"; to a great extent they are its subject matter. It begins with a set of twins, long held to be telepathic adepts.[34] It is the episode in which Bloom notices his stopped watch and concludes that "back of everything is magnetism" (*U* 11.987). Gerty's half, the narrative of which in Joycean double entendre tells us that Gerty is dressed in "electric blue" and that she is "adamant" (that is, a magnet [*U* 11.587]), duplicates it, and the interaction of the two bears out the common, more-than-mundane vision of magnetism toward which they are independently groping.[35] They experience, in Gerty's version anyway, the love at first sight of preexistent sympathy ("she knew on the instant it was him" [*U* 11.431]); they share a mutual orgasm that lights up the sky.[36] In at least one instance their reciprocal electromagnetism seems to be of the most literal kind: the ball that Bloom throws toward Gerty's friends "rolled down the slope and stopped right under Gerty's skirt near the little pool by the rock" (p. 356) (to reiterate: "Gerty was adamant"; "under Gerty's skirt" is just where Bloom wants to go), and that pool (recall Mesmer on mirrors; recall the mirrors in the Ormond) is later imagined by Bloom to be a "dark mirror" (U 13.1260–61).

Night—a "good conductor," speculates Bloom (U 13.1013–16)—is supposed to be the best time for picking up such influences,[37] and it is accordingly as night approaches in "Nausicaa" that Bloom, reflecting that there's "Something in all those superstitions" (U 11.159), comes to contemplate the evidence of their presence: birds, insects, and bats homing in on subliminal signals (U 11.1117–20, 1127–32, 1143–47); intuitive attunements between women and the moon (U 11.782–85), the sea, children, animals, and one another (U 11.902–28); prophecies (U 11.1063–67) and prophetic dreams (U 11.1240–41). Supplementing the twin theme introduced by Jackie and Tommy Caffrey comes a host of doublings, in both halves of the episode, the halving itself being yet another variant of the theme: the two celebrants in the church; the two stars that signal evening (U 11.1077); the two girl friends; the "twofaced" non-friends (U 11.279–80); the baby crying "two great big lovely tears" until set right in "two twos" (U 11.399, 11.614); Gerty herself with her "Cupid's bow" (U 11.88) mouth of perfectly matched lips; her "Greekly perfect" (U 11.89) pairs of eyes, shoes, and stockings; her "splitting headaches" (U 11.327) and her household role of "second mother" (U 11.325); her friend who always wants to "dress the same" (U 11.419); her misremembering the marriage vow as "till death us two part" (U 11.216); her personal investment in the reduplications of photography, painting, and theatre; her election of Bloom as "the image of the photo" of a matinee idol (U 11.416)—the image of an image—who arrives as her soul mate, her other half. Inevitably, the thoughts of both Gerty and Bloom embrace notions of the telepathic synchronicity supposedly shared by such paired mates (Gerty: "she seemed to hear the panting of his heart" [U 11.699–700]; Bloom: "Still it was a kind of language between us" [U 11.944]). These notions are confirmed many times throughout the text. Gerty, for instance, senses correctly (U 11.667) that Bloom is in mourning for "an old flame" "from the days beyond recall" ("Days beyond recall" is a phrase from the song sung by Boylan and Molly this afternoon, at just about the time Bloom was indeed perhaps losing his old flame); Bloom senses, correctly, that Gerty is beginning to get her menstrual period; Gerty is aware that he is masturbating (U 13.700–707); that ball he threw, thinks Bloom, "rolled down to her as if it understood" (U 13.950–51).[38]

All of which supernormal doings at least adumbrate the theoretical basis for what I have been saying about Gerty for years:[39] that, like the citizen, she is a projection of Bloom's state at the time—in this case of his dialectically generated, masturbatorily incited longing to embrace a sensibility that is nurturing (therefore not-"Cyclops"), female (therefore, again, not-"Cyclops"), and genteel and pliant and true (not-Molly).[40] Besides those given above, there are, roundly, nine reasons supporting this reading, as follows: (1) Joyce's Linati schema gives the episode's "Sense (Meaning)" as "The Projected Mirage"— pretty much what, I would argue, Gerty is.[41] (2) According to Joyce, "Nothing happened between them [Bloom and Gerty] . . . It all took place in Bloom's imagination" (Power 1974, 32). Exactly. (3) Gerty and the "tumescent" style in which she flourishes disappear immediately after Bloom climaxes[42]—something which it seems safe to say almost never happens in real life, except in the case of prostitutes and—well, masturbator's fantasies. (4) That style itself recalls the namby-pamby parody of Bloom's own "love" speech in "Cyclops,"[43] with an admixture of the "costliest frillies" fetishism of *Sweets of Sin* (*U* 13.1492–1501; 10.608–17). Which is to say it has already been established as, under the right conditions, a Bloomian idiom. (5) To confirm which, the style twice returns as an outgrowth of Bloom's own voice, in Gerty's absence, as he sinks toward slumber (*U* 13.1166–81, 1292–1302). (6) The "Greekly perfect" Gerty is recognizably a type of the virginal nymph or goddess that Bloom idealizes in "Calypso," "Lestrygonians," and "Circe," doubtless in recoil from the overly carnal Molly.[44] (Both Gerty and the Nymph, for instance, disdain eating (*U* 13.228–29, 15.3393.) In "Ithaca" (*U* 17.2010–11) just such a nymph is promised as "tribute" to "Noman"—which, as Odysseus, Bloom became, at the end of the previous chapter. (He has no name in Gerty's half of the episode.) (7) Gerty's account of Bloom is by far the most flattering of the book. She thinks exactly the kinds of things a man like him in an emotional state such as his would want an attractive young woman to be thinking about him. (8) "O Lord, that little limping devil" (*U* 13.851–52): so Bloom, after his climax. He is thinking about, one, his now-limp penis, and, two, the limping Gerty. Earlier, when things were getting hot and then hotter between them, her face and form were "suffused" (*U* 13.723) with blood coloring her "crimsoning," glowing, rose-red flesh ("rosebloom," at the start [*U* 13.120])—and as "Sirens" (*U* 11.701–2), "Cyclops" (*U* 12.437–78), and "Penelope" (*U* 18.144–45) remind us, erectile tumescence is all a matter of congested blood.[45] Which is to say it is a matter of a "welfilled hose" *U* 13.793), to adopt Bloom's phrase for the kind of display that Gerty has just put on with her stockings. (Such double-entendres, applying suggestively to both Bloom and Gerty, are another variant on the doubling theme.)

(9) Pornography, as the volume in Bloom's pocket might remind us, is typically authored by a man, in the persona of a woman. Pornography is for masturbating to.

Again: such effects as I have here proposed to be at work in "Nausicaa" were quite within the boundaries of the speculative science of Joyce's day. As the "projected mirage," Gerty recalls the abovementioned Frederick W. H. Myers' theory of ghosts (and we meet one of those in *Ulysses* too [see chapter 19]), that they constitute a variation of "those hallucinatory figures or phantasms which living persons can sometimes project at a distance" (Myers 1920, 1:3) through the same kinds of occult forces that stop Bloom's watch. William James, no less, shared with the Bloom of "Nausicaa" a belief in woman's attunement to primal forces and what he called "peripheral visual attention" (James 1950, 1:437, 2:55, 369; compare Bloom: "Eyes all over them" [*U* 11.912]). He also took seriously accounts of synchronicity (James 1950, 2:118–19) and "hyperaesthesia of the senses," the faculty that allows Bloom to hear the barmaids' shell and Gerty to hear Bloom's heart; he even speculated about "the effects of magnets and metals" on such events (James 1950, 2:609–11). Many of James's contemporaries were at least as ready to credit such ideas and to explain them with references to the newly discovered electromagnetic currents vibrating through brain, body, and atmosphere, on the lines we have already noted. In fact, every one of the Orphic events of "Nausicaa," reported or imagined, can be traced back to its source in some sober theorist of the day. Even Bloom's hilarious idea that celibate priests attract women "like flies round treacle" (*U* 11.1037–38) because their bottled-up semen, working its way up and out, effloresces alluringly through their pores, was lifted intact from a book of pseudoscientific theory in Joyce's Trieste library.[46]

So: by the end of "Nausicaa," Joyce has pretty thoroughly established for his polytropic word-maker the "arranger" the right to call on a range of psychic resources in order to keep the show going. This figure continues as introduced in "Sirens": a virtuoso mystagogue, learned in the weird congruences of the old science with the new. If, besides naming him, we were to try to envision him as well, we could probably do no better than to picture a conductor (giving the word its Joycean double meaning), waving his baton before a Dublin, and outside that a universal, orchestra, working to weave the fields of magnetic correspondences into harmonies. Perhaps, in fact, he is so introduced. The beginning of "Sirens" consists of one and one-half pages of discontinuous snippets, later to be incorporated into the body of the episode. They have generally been taken as comprising this musical episode's overture. Overtures, however, are neither discontinuous nor dissonant. Instead, this cacophony seems to me to resemble, simply, the random plunks, toots, and sawings of an orchestra tuning up, waiting for the conductor to begin. With the last phrase of the introductory section, he does just that: "Begin!" (*U* 11.63). The "tap"s that repeat intermittently throughout the length of the episode thereafter may, I suggest, be the sound of his baton rapping against the music rest, calling his orchestra to attention for the next movement.

If so, they are the only salient signs of his personal presence. Like any good conductor—and like Orpheus—he is too absorbed in his music to intrude. And like any good conductor—and like Orpheus—he has his back to us.

5

The Erotic Gerty, the Pornographic Gerty

"NAUSICAA" 'S GERTY, I have suggested, emerges from Bloom's mind in reaction to his contemplation of Molly's rude physicality, recently made intolerable by the sexual transgression registered in the book's two preceding episodes.
Bloom thinks the non-carnal Gerty into being because he needs to think away
from the all-too-carnal Molly.

He especially needs to think away from the scene of the crime, Molly's orifices. Those orifices are in fact crucial coordinates of *Ulysses'* "epic of the human
body,"[1] what *Finnegans Wake* might have called its Bodyssey. Joyce delegated
them—Molly's "arse" and "cunt," along with her "breasts" and "womb"—as
indispensably among the four "cardinal points" around which her episode re-
volves,[2] in a Penelopiad beginning—the word "bottom" occurs twice on its first
page—with "arse." In the last pages before that last journey begins, Bloom will
to some extent relent from his earlier avoidance of such matters, to some extent
dialectically, when, settling into bed, he kisses Molly's bottom's "smellonous"
"furrow" (*U* 17.2242–43), that is—not to put too fine a point on it—on or in or
near her anus.

He does that to confirm that after all she is Penelope, not Calypso, wifely
woman, not goddess. This issue has been importunately with him since early
morning, when the art-print "Nymph," a nude but a nude with her "shame"
"shaded" away (*U* 15.3265), was encountered, framed, above his earthy wife,
with her lover's letter, her tea and toast for the hole on one end, her chamber
pot for the holes on the other.[3] The juxtaposition lingers in his mind thereafter
and lies behind his concern that the goddesses he checks out in "Lestrygonians" not have anuses. It becomes especially important, so much so that he runs
into the museum to see for sure, when he finds himself facing the man, Blazes
Boylan, who as he knows will soon be busy about Molly's orifices—will, as
Molly later recalls, be rooting around in one while his finger is exploring the
other, behind (*U* 18.586–87). In "Lestrygonians" the obscene apparition of that
act at its crudest, of, in Molly's words, Boylan's shoving his "tremendous big

red brute of a thing" into that "big hole in the middle of us" (*U* 18.144–51), helps explain Bloom's displacements into the physiology of food consumption, of "we stuffing food in one hole and out behind" (*U* 8.929). He concentrates on such ugly images as a screen for what for him is their uglier, indeed unbearable, correlate.[4] When he sums up the Burton's "sloppy eaters," the fellow "ramming a knifeful of cabbage down his gullet," for instance (*U* 8.382), as "Men, men, men" (*U* 8.653), he is thinking not about humanity in general but about male humanity, defined as the sex that rams things into holes. When, going to the opposite extreme in Davy Byrne's, he remembers his first day of sexual intercourse with Molly as a scene of mutual mastication only, of seedcake chewed and nipples licked, and draws the curtain before the real nitty-gritty starts (*U* 8.897–916), he is employing the two main techniques, of deflection and suspension, of kiss-kiss and fade-out, soon to be reinvented and patented in all countries by Hollywood.

Bloom's idea of acceptable thought-sex is defined by what it excludes—the nude woman without vagina or anus, the romantic revery that stops above the belt. Such thoughts are made erotic-not-pornographic by the suppression of the long-established touchstones of hard-core pornography, that being the depiction of the genitals in arousal, along with what the proprietresses of Rosalind Erskine's *Passion Flower Hotel* called *"La Penetration,"* and their vividness testifies to the internal pressure of the thing suppressed. Joyce was sufficiently Freud's contemporary to believe that sooner or later that pressure must find its release. So, in "Circe," when the pristinely unperforated goddess of "Lestrygonians" reappears, amalgamated with the similarly orificeless Nymph of the Bath, it is only a matter of time before her plaster cast breaks open from suppressed inner pressure, releasing a "stench" of body odors, "from the cracks" (*U* 15.3469–70).

This reappearance happens in a place of prostitutes, the literature of whom gives us, from the Greek, the word "pornography," that category of sexual imaging that Bloom has so far been avoiding. And, as long as we are being etymological, what does "prostitute" mean? It means, as *Finnegans Wake* will instruct us, correctly, a woman who "stands before a door" (*FW* 116.17). So, in "Circe," an episode obsessed with etymology, the first certified prostitute Bloom meets, identified as an "elderly bawd," will be introduced in "a doorway" (*U* 15.78–79). She will in turn introduce Bloom to the prostitute, Bridie Kelly, with whom he lost his virginity. Bridie will exit with a squeak and a flap of her "bat shawl" (*U* 15.365), which will remind Bloom of the bat in "Nausicaa" (*U* 13.1117), therefore of Gerty, who duly appears from the same doorway to display "her bloodied clout" (U 15.373–74)—the suppressed, therefore pornographic, secret of that earlier episode. She soon exits in turn, but not before the bawd has charged her with "Writing the gentleman false letters" (U 15.380). A woman in a doorway who writes letters to a man is, etymologically, a pornographer.

Which is to say that the U.S. courts might have been onto something after all when they singled out Gerty's episode as being especially, obnoxiously, pornographic.[5] What sets "Nausicaa" apart from the other transgressive stretches of *Ulysses* is not its sexual frankness—several passages are raunchier—but its cuteness, its college-humor-magazine dirty-jokester's fondness for smirky double meanings: the masturbating Bloom a "gentleman to his fingertips," another masturbator coming from the "Congested Districts Board," the fireworks orgasm, the "limping devil," the "welfilled hose." Such insinuating indecencies, forcing their way through the proprieties like those rude odors breaking through the nymph's plaster cast, are the inevitable correlate of a narrative voice as given as Gerty's is to deflecting all grossness by way of coyness and euphemism. If pornography begins with a sense of its own dirtiness, Gerty, and her "letters," belong in that pornographer's doorway.

She is there, of course, because Bloom, or his subconscious, has put her there. Her mental habits of deflection mirror his. Indeed, up to "Circe" they have been typical of Bloom's dealings with his female objects of desire. That is, again, especially true of the two orifices that make for the profane coordinates of Molly's episode, the arse and the cunt. The first of these was the word that Bloom once tried to get a prostitute to say, only to have it come back to him as "arks" (U 13.869)—no small transformation, for someone raised Jewish. The second was the word included in a letter to Molly during their courtship, the same word, as we will see in the next chapter, that Martha and her typewriter have transfigured and returned back to him as "world."

What these women did, Gerty does—displaces the obscene into the sublime, or faux-sublime. So, in her rendition, Bloom's ejaculation becomes a Roman candle, brightening, like Sweny's soap, the sky. It is of course a ridiculous idealization, and the question is, why? Why this prettification, this pulling of punches?

Not, certainly, because Joyce feels the need to resort to innuendo and double meanings. Bloom, on the other hand, does feel that way, in relation not to any audience, but to himself. As in "Lestrygonians," when he ricochets from the Burton to the genteel revery achievable in Davy Byrne's, or from the prospect of priapic Boylan to the museum's reassuringly impenetrable goddesses, the *cache-cache* rhetoric of Gerty's "Nausicaa" enacts Bloom's inhibitory recoil, in this case from the unfaceable phallic fact registered in the previous episode but one, "Sirens," set at the hour when the deed is done, and then in the next episode, "Cyclops." "Cyclops" is *the* all-male episode, the one where there is much talk of being firm or going soft, where Bloom, with unprecedented volubility, feels moved to lecture on the subject of hanging-induced erections, where Boylan is publicly named as Molly's lover and Bloom, his dispossession confirmed, collapses like a wet rag, where, as earlier remarked, the corresponding Homeric tale of red-hot stake shoved into eye is recast into a gigantified rendition of sexual penetration—that being the definitive tableau which Bloom wants most not to call to mind—projected and magnified, as on a huge pornographic movie screen.

Which leads back to my point of the preceding episode, that Gerty's person and voice are, largely and perhaps entirely, a matter of Bloom's projection. This letter-writing woman last seen standing in a doorway is his projected pornographer. She *is* that yielding female voice typically heard in works like *Sweets of Sin*. And speaking of *Sweets of Sin*, she may remind us as well that through that book, Bloom's imagination has recently been fired with visions of another "beautiful," "queenly" woman who has a thing about underwear. Again: I do not think it a coincidence that, in their encounter, Gerty heats up and turns red just as Bloom is reaching climax, or that, like many another masturbatory fantasy-figure, she is out of sight and out of mind within seconds after he has finished and the episode's style has detumesced. Above all, I do not think it a coincidence that she shows up when she does—that Bloom goes from being reduced to "twisting around all the opposite, as limp as a wet rag" (*U* 12.1497–98), to the telekinetic embrace of a woman with a limp, the two overlapping senses of that word—his and hers—later being joined in his phrase "that little limping devil" (*U* 13.851–52).

What happened to Bloom before encountering Gerty was that he was, in "Cyclops" terms, unmanned, which meant, in "Cyclops" terms, that he was docked, phallectomized, bobbed, bobbetized—what you will—with the result that his version of ecstasy, including sexual ecstasy, became a woman's version, or his version of that version. And now recall, again, Gerty's appearance in "Circe": She "shows coyly her bloodied clout" and tells Bloom, "You did that." What can she mean? A "clout" is a cloth used to patch up a break or wrap up a wound. In "Nausicaa" Gerty was getting her period, which would be one reason for that blood, and imagining herself being deflowered, which would be another. She is, then, talking about her vagina, bleeding. But she is also talking about her lame limb, here represented, with the surreal hyperbole typical of "Circe," as a still-fresh, still-bleeding amputation. It was her injury, even more than her sex, that was her episode's dirtiest secret, the last one to be yielded up to Bloom, the one thing she was "always trying to conceal" (*U* 13.651) even when revealing the rest—and did reveal, as a final treat, to the man who later reflects that he "wouldn't mind" sex with a lamed or otherwise defective woman, that "curiosity" might pique the experience (*U* 13.776–77). (In "Two Gallants," the secret dirtier than sex, to yield up which is to make a submission beyond sexual submission, turns out to be money. Here, it is deformity.) Likewise, in "Circe": Gerty is exposing her privates, and she is brandishing a stump, and the two things are the same thing. That bloodied clout signifies, simultaneously, a vagina and a wound from something lopped off. It is a *Grand Guignol* apparition of *phallus abscondicus*, of woman as genitally unmanned man, and as such it qualifies Gerty to be the voice of post-"Cyclops" Bloom. Pygmalion (Bloom: "O, I have been a perfect pig" [*U* 15.3397]) to her Galatea, he has made her in his own new-maimed image. Her concealment of her deformity services, mirrors, and enacts Bloom's of his, that brand of cuckoldry which in "Scylla and Charybdis" Stephen calls the wound of Shakespeare's undoing (*U* 9.459–60).

It also, I think, takes us to the heart of what is eating Bloom, which is not so much sex as the depiction, the envisioned witnessing, of sex. Not Molly and Boylan in bed, which winds up being memorialized, undramatically, by a scattering of crumbs, but the inflamed, gigantified, mythified, pornographied specter of it, that projected infantile trauma of wound and weapon, of violation and bloodbath, of amputation and invasion, which Freud was contemporaneously discovering in what he called the "primal scene," and to which *Finnegans Wake*, some of us think, keeps hearkening back, for instance when, with some help from Rabelais, Shem recalls his mother's "microchasm" as "the cluft that meataxe delt her" (*FW* 229.23–24).[6] Which ghastly stuff is not, probably, Joyce's version of what sex is or of how it is experienced, but rather of one way it comes across when witnessed or contemplated, when written about or thought about, when transformed into that kind of inner pornography that Lawrence called "sex in the head."

The catch, Joyce would say, is that sex always *is* in the head, more or less. Or, perhaps, almost always. Because say what you will about Blazes Boylan, he is no pornographer. Introduced with a "Bold hand" ([*U* 4.234]—the word missing there is "writing") on a letter that Molly tells us "wasnt much" (*U* 18.735), he is distinguished as a man of few words who "does it and doesnt talk" (*U* 18.592). The only remotely sexy word of his that Molly remembers is "titties" (*U* 18.536), which made her laugh but understandably does not seem to have done much to turn her on. With him, she says, "I wanted to shout out all sorts of things fuck or shit or anything at all" (*U* 18.588–89). Note: she wanted to, and she didn't. Boylan is not into talking dirty, or writing dirty, and although we never really get an *entrée* into his mind, it seems a good bet that his thoughts on the subject are strictly goal-oriented. So: if sex in the head is what you don't want, there's your man.

Well, it is not what Molly doesn't want, at least not for long. One thing she wants from Boylan next time is a longer letter (*U* 18.730), and she has given him some coaching on the tack it should take: "I gave my eyes that look with my hair a bit loose from the tumbling and my tongue between my lips up to him the savage brute" (*U* 18.592–94). The savage brute? Where did she get that? Again, say what you want about Boylan: he is no savage brute. A man walking around town in shiny tan shoes and a flower in his mouth is not a savage brute. Hugh Boylan is an overdressed jumped-up lady's man, one likely to find out next time or the next that that is not really all that Molly has, so to speak, in mind. In fact next week, having perused *Sweets of Sin*, she will probably want him to be Raoul, and may not be so amused if he uses that word "titties" on what she will have since learned to think of as her "heaving embonpoint."

She probably got that "brute" idea from Boylan's family connection (*U* 13.998–99) with horses (she also remembers him as a "Stallion" [*U* 18.152]), helped on by what thanks to Mary Power we know to be a suggestive illustration—whip, half-naked woman, brutal-looking man in a lion-tamer's suit—in *Ruby*, her most recent reading (Power 1981, 115–21). But, mainly, she wants something the opposite of what she has got, that being the middling, not-at-all-brutal Bloom. Who in turn conjures up, in the ethereal Gerty, someone about as far as possible from the all-too-earthy person he has got. "She must have been thinking of someone else all the time" (*U* 13.885) remarks Bloom about Gerty, after the fact. He is right, of course: Gerty was thinking of matinee idol Martin Harvey, of various and variously *louche* heroes of the day's pulp romances, of getting her own back at the boy on the bicycle. And Bloom, all the while he is in the throes of his semi-carnal vindication with his idealized not-Molly, is also in the sight of—under, as he later envisions it, the gaze of—that Howth which is his private metonym for his love for his wife. Who in turn, during that warm summer day up there when she said yes, was all the time thinking of another "he," on another hill, at the tip of Spain, the one with whom she never (quite) consummated, the one who wrote her the wonderful letters. Like Bloom and Bloom's Gerty, Bloom and Molly's Howth were all the while reciprocating gazes, as with the crossing eyebeams of a Donne poem—interchanging the erotic and the pornographic, the nice stuff on one side of the line and the nasty stuff on the other, in an ongoing oscillation that, for Joyce's characters, makes sex sexy.

6

Henry's Flower

FOR CENTURIES, one romantic couple, racy of the soil, dominated the imagination of Britain's balladeers. The man was Henry II, born Henry Plantagenet, his family name said to have derived from an ancestor's custom "of wearing a sprig of flowering broom (called *Genêt* in French) in his cap for a feather" (Dickens 1908, 77) The woman's first name was Rosamond, as in "fair Rosamond," a name ever since associated in English lore with romantic abandon.

Her last name was Clifford.

Henry's wife was Eleanor of Aquitaine. The legend goes that in order to keep her away from his fair Rosamond, Henry had constructed for the latter on his royal estate of Woodstock a house that "after some was named Labyrinthus, or Dedalus worke, which was wrought like unto a knot in a garden, called a maze" (Percy 1966, 2:155). (Apart from the maze, the estate's most remembered feature was its well—the "Rosimund's . . . wishing well" of *FW* 245.18.) The stratagem didn't work: like Ariadne before her, Eleanor followed down a thread, possibly trailed behind by Henry, confronted her rival, and gave her a choice between a dagger and a bowl of poison.

In his romantic other life, Leopold Bloom is Henry Flower, the name that like the Plantagenets with their sprig of (blooming, flowering) broom he wears in his hat and that, when it drops out, implicates him in a (labyrinthine, knotty) "Love entanglement" (*U* 15.742), with a woman named Clifford. Miss Clifford's first name is not Rosamond, but within half a page of receiving her letter Bloom associates her with "roses" three times (*U* 4.265, 277, 285), and that letter does make its slip of "world" for "word." (Later we will come to connect her given name of Martha with an opera whose signature song is "The Last Rose of Summer.") Although he never finds out the kind of yellow flower she sends with her letter, roses are the flower of June, and a yellow rose, in the "Language of flowers" (*U* 5.261),[1] can signify infidelity.[2]

Which is perhaps one reason it is unfortunate that Leopold/Henry, instead of discarding that flower along with the letter, should keep it, in, of all places, his "heart pocket" (*U* 5.261). His wife has a thing about men's pockets: "first Ill look at his shirt to see or Ill see if he has that French letter still in his pocketbook I suppose he thinks I don't know deceitful men all their 20 pockets arent enough for their lies" (*U* 1234–36). So she is likely to find that flower. (And she cares about such things, for instance about Boylan's carnation, signifying, in the language of flowers, boldness [*U* 18.125].) And she knows already that Bloom is corresponding with another woman, the "little bitch" to whom he was writing when she surprised him in the act (*U* 18.45–48). And she has already investigated the contents of his top drawer, the one with the "3 typewritten letters, addressee, Henry Flower, c/o. P.O. Westland Row, addresser, Martha Clifford, c/o. P.O. Dolphin's Barn: the transliterated name and address of the addresser of the 3 letters in reversed alphabetic boustrophedonic punctuated quadrilinear cryptogram (vowels suppressed): N.IGS./WI.UU.OX/W.OKS.MH/Y.IM" (*U* 17.1796–1801).

If Molly wants to track this Miss Clifford down, she will need to decipher that "reversed alphabetic boustrophedonic" script. That is, she will need first to reverse the alphabetic placement of the letters, replacing "Y" with "B," "X" with "C," and so on, then arrange them in four rows marked by the diagonals, then (the "boustrophedonic" part) read those lines, as the early Greeks among others read, like so:

"Boustrophedonic" tells us that this is the pattern made by an ox in plowing. Is it not, also, the basic pattern of a maze, of—"bous" can be "bull" as well as "ox"—a "Labyrinthus, or Dedalus worke"?

Bloom as Odysseus does not slaughter the suitors but dismisses them with a gesture of abnegation, and should Molly succeed in tracing back through the boustrephedonic maze and confronting her rival we can probably expect the scene to be similarly bloodless—no dagger or poison bowl, but this: "Id just go to her and ask her do you love him and look her square in the eyes she couldnt fool me" (*U* 18.193–94). Given her impatience with verbal perplexities, such a scene is probably not going to occur any time soon. But it is imaginable.

Perhaps, in fact, it has been imagined, by Bloom. The whole Molly-Martha business has, I think, the feel of stage-managed make-believe. Assuming Bloom to be a reasonably sane fellow, some of his behavior *in re* Martha Clifford does not compute. Why does he hold onto that incriminating flower, even bring it back with him into the marital bedroom? Why, knowing that Molly suspects something, does he leave those compromising letters in an unlocked top drawer, where she has been rummaging already? (Why not, if he can't bring himself to destroy them, just insert them between the pages of *Thoughts from Spinoza,* where they would be completely safe?) And why go to the trouble of encrypting, and thus preserving, Martha's address, when he knows it by heart? There is a juvenile secret-handshake-and-code-ring quality about all of this that has more to do with fantasy than with the serious management of a serious affair. After all, what more delicious for a humiliated husband than just such an adultery-detection scenario—wife tracking other woman to her lair, looking her square in the eyes, and demanding to know, because in the end and in spite of everything she does truly love him, whether the other does too?

It is the Woodstock scenario, as invented and patented in all countries by— well, to a great extent, by Eleanor of Aquitaine. There is considerable irony in the older Eleanor's having been memorialized in the role of the wronged wife at whose hand the fair sinner dies for love. It was the young Eleanor who, in Poitiers and then Paris, was chief patroness of the troubadours and their theme of courtly love, the woman who had most to do with promulgating the rules of love that were to govern the West's codes of romance into the age of the Leopold Bloom whose "Circe" incarnation of Henry Flower is a serenading troubadour, complete with guitar. As everyone knows, the first of these rules is that true love must be illicit, that romance is properly a triangular affair of deception and discovery. When Henry II set up his mistress in her maze, he was, like it or not, deferring to his wife's earlier determination of such matters, in effect playing her game, just as much as he was when he trailed that thread out to where she could find it.

Which brings us to the most obvious thing about Leopold-Henry's indiscretion with Martha, that it is entirely a function of his connection to Molly. She is the one running the show. To begin with, Martha's address of Dolphin's Barn, selected from out of forty-four candidates (*U* 8.326), is not just any old address. Here is its first mention in *Ulysses:* "He smiled, glancing askance at her mocking eyes. The same young eyes. The first night after the charades. Dolphin's Barn" (*U* 4.344–45). Seeing her still-young eyes, he is taken back here to the same memory that will return to Molly too, at the other end of their book—of "the night he kissed my heart at Dolphins barn I couldn't describe it" (*U* 18.330–31). Dolphin's Barn, where they played charades at the Doyles's, ranks with Howth among the consecrated sites in the history of the Blooms's courtship. (As for Howth, it was there that "flower" became his and Molly's special word [*U* 18.1756].) When at the end of "Cyclops" the "milkwhite dolphin" (*U* 13.1772) takes him off toward that neighborhood, Bloom is not, mainly, heading toward the other woman in his life (see Hart and Knuth 1976, 33). He is, mainly, heading to the place where he and the first love of his life had their first kiss.

The Martha connection is that way throughout—overdetermined, as the Freudians would say. In "Sirens," sympathetically vibrating with Simon-Lionel's yearning songbird's call of "When First I Saw That Form Endearing," Bloom is hearing the name "Martha" but thinking more of the young Molly whose endearing form he first saw at Dolphin's Barn. The connection between the two women in that musical episode might best be thought of as chordal (Bloom is doubling his catgut into a musical chord at the time), but if so it is a chord with no question at all about which is the "passion dominant" (*U* 11.736).[3] More generally, one might say that Martha "corresponds" to Bloom's image of the young Molly, that she completes what "Ithaca" calls a "clandestine correspondence" (*U* 17.2251)—again, with little question about which is the original, which the secondary correlative. Martha evidently senses this sad fact herself: why else would she want to know what perfume her Henry's wife wears, if not to wear it herself, in order to correspond? Even the distinguishing feature of her correspondence, its grammatical and linguistic inexactness (which, after all, ought properly to have disqualified her for the advertised position), repeats what Bloom thinks of as Molly's winning weakness for such things (*U* 16.1473–75).

And then there is that business of Martha's wanting to know that other "world," a word that occurs so often in Molly's episode (twenty times, more than in any other) as to count as part of her idiom. ("Other world" is in there too, at *U* 18.1211.) When Martha asks about that other world she is asking about a word included in Bloom's last letter to her, a word she either (1) does not recognize, because it is too esoteric, or (2) is pretending not to recognize, because it is too improper. Bloom's reflections make clear which. "Went too far last time," he worries (*U* 5.59). It is not the sort of thing he would think to himself if the word in question were something like "prestidigitation."

An improper word, then, deliberately inserted in order to test the waters and perhaps draw her out. And why not? The technique worked once before, as Molly shows when, right before recalling that first kiss from her future husband (*U* 18.330–31), she revisits the preliminaries leading up to it: "then he wrote me that letter with all those words in it how could he have the face to any woman after his company manners making it so awkward after when we met asking me have I offended you . . . and if I knew what it meant of course I had to say no for form sake don't understand you I said and wasnt it natural so it is of course it used to be written up with a picture of a womans on that wall in Gibraltar with that word I couldnt find anywhere only for children seeing it too young . . . he sent me the 8 big poppies because mine was the 8th then I wrote the night he kissed my heart at Dolphins barn" (*U* 18.318–30). Which identifies, I think, "that word," "written up with a picture of a womans," that Molly, living in the days of pre-*Ulysses* literature and dictionaries, "couldnt find anywhere." There it is, in plain sight: just take "couldnt," and subtract "old." This was the "word" that seems to have broken the ice, around the time "he kissed my heart," at Dolphin's Barn. In his correspondence with his latest Dolphin's Barn woman, Bloom is, I would bet, using the same word in the same way. That, by way of Martha's coyness and mistyping, Bloom's transgressive introduction of—not to be coy myself—"cunt" should thus be transformed into *Ulysses'* "other world" (the two words have already been yoked, in *U* 4.227–28) will not surprise readers of *Finnegans Wake* familiar with that book's handling of the sacred "Tunc" page of the Book of Kells, or with its variations on the "eternal geomater" 's triangle of page 293; nor, perhaps, will it seem outlandish to anyone who has seen a reproduction of Gustave Courbet's painting *L'origine du Monde*. What, indeed, is that word/world's "meaning"? A silly question, maybe, but it is the question Dolph and Kev keep asking themselves in *FW* 2.2 while returning or trying to return to their deltic origin.

Behind Martha, then, Molly. And also Nora. Because a real-life Martha, Marthe Fleischmann by name, was to appear in Joyce's life in late 1918, when the Martha Clifford theme had already been established in *Ulysses*, to play a brief but vivid role as extramarital temptress. In the "Ithaca" episode composed later, the encrypted name of this rival, as "N.IGS.," which, because "vowels" have been "suppressed," may be decoded as either "Martha" or "Marthe," occurs in the first line of that boustrephedonic labyrinth of this labyrinthine book that Joyce always hoped his wife would someday read. Realistically, the odds of Nora's having gotten that far into *Ulysses*, and of having then decoded the name of her nonce rival, were even slimmer than those of Molly's unpuzzling La Clifford's address. Still, it evidently mattered to Joyce that the evidence be there on the page.

It mattered enough that he offered a kind of reward for success. If, after all, Molly were to decipher the Martha code, might she not be struck and—being an emotionally shrewd woman—moved by that address? As for Nora . . .

As for Nora, it is time to introduce Mr. Richard Henninge of the University of Mainz, who in a December 7, 1996, submission to the j-joyce website points out something curious about that "boustrophedonic" code, that it breaks down in the last line. According to the established pattern, that last line, "Y.IM," ought to read right to left, giving not "B.RN" (thus "Barn") but "NR.B." Mr. Henninge astutely remarks that the name to which this seems to point is "Nora Barnacle." I think his conclusion, that "Martha Clifford is Nora Barnacle," goes too far, but not by much. "Martha Clifford was Nora Barnacle" would be closer to the mark—first in the familiar sense, pervasive throughout *Finnegans Wake*, that a young woman may for a middle-aged man reincarnate the wife he still loves, second in the sense that Rosamond Clifford can be said to have acted the role that her Henry's wife all but invented. Had Molly or Nora gone to the trouble of doing some decoding, either could have affirmed the lesson acted out for Molly's younger self during those Dolphin's Barn charades: "Think you're escaping and run into yourself. Longest way round is the shortest way home" (*U* 13.1110–11).

7

Approaching Reality in "Oxen of the Sun"

1

BEFORE CONSIDERING the next two episodes, a decent respect for the opinion of Joycean mankind requires situating this book's ongoing argument within the current critical consensus. Its position is one of I hope civil but in any case near-absolute disagreement. For a long time, that consensus has been that during its later episodes *Ulysses* disengages from its initial realism in favor of an aesthetic of textual play, in which style is by degrees dissociated from subject or occasion, that by the time of "Circe," this dissociation is confirmed beyond doubt, and that "Circe" thus fulfills an authorial bent at least latent from the start. I believe this position to be categorically wrong. In that belief, I have accordingly been seeking and pointing out what might be called the autogenetic principles behind the formal mutations of Joyce's texts, that is the extent to which stylistic effects continue to take their cues from characters' psychology and circumstance—Stephen's villanelle generated out of the eroticised "curve of an emotion," the inner dramas of Bloom's heart being projected into technique and even, Prometheus-like, into the generation of character.

It seems to me that the opposite camp has missed out on such developments through overlooking the variety of mimetic writing called imitative form—overlooking it, mainly, because unwilling to recognize or to play along with the extremes to which the author takes it with the newly-proclaimed "Orphic" powers that let him keep topping himself performatively while still telling the story of real people in real places. If various other novelists (J. D. Salinger, Kingsley Amis) can write oneirically about drunkenness or (Henry Miller, Anne Rice) heatedly about sexual passion without thereby becoming rebels against representationalism, it is not clear what there is about Joyce that should cause him to be singled out—aside, that is, that being Joyce, he does go at it with his own brand of obsessive thoroughness. All of which is perhaps a matter of talent and temperament, but not necessarily of ontology.

A frequent test case is "Aeolus." "Aeolus" is the episode with the oversized headlines, and the question of how to take those headlines pretty reliably divides those given to speaking of Joyce's realism from those given to speaking of his "realism." On the one hand, it could be argued that the newspaper office shown in this episode is an exceptionally loud and declamatory place, that in the conventions of typography such facts are indicated with what the trade once called "screamer caps" (a term Joyce knew: see *FW* 374.10), and that in using them Joyce is no more departing from mimetic principles than are those cartoonists who choose to have their characters shout in boldface. On the other hand, it could be argued that whatever mimetic origin they might once have had, the headlines are so obtrusive, so call attention to themselves, that the text's rhetorical properties are unavoidably foregrounded, at the expense of what up to then has been its presumed transparence.

Karen Lawrence, deservedly among the most influential members of the latter school, exemplifies the shift to this text-centered reading of "Aeolus" and much of what follows. She grants that the headlines may be seen as a "whimsical pun of form and content" (Lawrence 1981, 58), a "chain of mimicry" in which typography mocks the resident mockers of other's bombast (Lawrence 1981, 73), even that the episode's verbal playfulness may reflect the verbal playfulness of the characters (Lawrence 1980, 399). Still, she insists that the "flaunted artifice" of such a stratagem is the main point, and that its effect is to destroy "the illusion . . . of language as an instrument of representation" (Lawrence 1980, 392–93) in a way that forecasts the "games of language" to follow in the later episodes (Lawrence 1980, 398).

To a great extent, this reading has prevailed, both for "Aeolus" by itself and for what it is said to forecast about the subsequent course of *Ulysses*. Hugh Kenner introduced a version of the all-Cretans-are-liars conundrum into the discussion by suggesting that the sense of mechanical dissociation accomplished by the headlines might convey the "disembodied," "anonymous" quality of the words spoken in the newspaper office (Kenner 1980, 63), because by such a criterion too transparently realistic a rendering would have been false to the spirit of the subject. In any case, this line has not been pursued. Rather than examine ways in which the shifting styles and voices of the later episodes might be read as expressive extensions of the shifting ways in which the central characters process or fail to process reality, rather than exploring the possibility that for instance apparently disembodied styles might be grounded in dissociated sensibilities, most critics have joined with Lawrence in seeing the later episodes as progressively repudiating the realism of the "initial style."[1]

One complication confronting this approach is what Lawrence calls the "retrogressive" fact that the initial style supposedly superseded in "Aeolus" keeps returning, both in the succeeding "Lestrygonians" and in all or part of at least three other episodes set late in the book (Lawrence 1981, 12). More problematic still, even in most of the remaining episodes *Ulysses* may be plausibly read as persisting in the sort of punning of form and content that Lawrence allows in "Aeolus." However pronounced the artifice may become, up to "Oxen of the Sun," any given episode's technique remains arguably referable to some corresponding extravagance or aberration, some distinct concurrence of sensibility and circumstance, in the here-and-now discernible behind the text. This is clearly the case in the episode after "Lestrygonians," "Scylla and Charybdis," which renders a literary discussion in markedly literary idiom and turns dramaturgic when the discussion turns dramatic, and is at least arguably so in "Wandering Rocks," the next episode, which presents a fragmented environment in a series of fragments, the random juxtapositions of which may be said to echo the aimlessness of the lives depicted.

As for the next three: "Sirens" is an episode of music, rendered musically—what is more, as I have noted, an episode of preponderantly lachrymose music at the center of which is a musically inclined consciousness in the act of feeling sorry for itself.[2] "Cyclops" is an episode of bombast, rendered bombastically. "Nausicaa" returns to interior monologue, in two consubstantial voices. These episodes, certainly, do get generally denser and busier, their writing more writerly, but that too can at least in part be accounted for by mimetic standards, beginning with the observation that after all things do tend to pile up during the day as time passes (thus requiring more effort to get things in focus, plus the need for a final summing up and sorting out, culminating in "Ithaca") and that people do tend to open up, and sometimes let themselves go, in bars, and at evening, and at night. In addition, as I have attempted to show, those last three episodes do something else as well: drawing on the Orphic lore of the time, they introduce a narrative medium that is newly reactive—an increasingly good "conductor," like the gathering night—to the impulses and mental operations of their characters.

Undoubtedly Joyce's techniques in these passages are often ostentatiously performative; undoubtedly they can distract as well as dazzle. We may well feel at times that surface has lost touch with source. But suppose that feeling turns out to be misleading, that on examination the connection is found to have held after all? In that case we would be dealing with a book that instead of forcing us to abandon our traditional notions of novelistic representationalism would be challenging us to hold on to them, against mounting strain. What is needed for the former interpretation to prevail over the latter is at least one substantial case where the separation is decisive.

Hence the importance of episodes 14 and 15, "Oxen of the Sun" and "Circe," together often cited as the culmination of those anti-mimetic developments supposed to have begun in "Aeolus."[3] Here, at least, it is said, *Ulysses* finally breaks whatever tenuous links may remain between subject and technique. For its part, "Circe" adopts a "hallucinatory" technique without troubling to establish either of its principals as experiencing hallucinations, and its phantasms repeatedly take on lives of their own, losing any discernible contact with the minds from which they may or may not have originated, often in fact drawing on details unfamiliar to those minds. As for its predecessor, its repudiation of any mimetic program is in its way just as complete. "Oxen of the Sun" is the episode with a superstructure of schematic correspondences, in Joyce's account "a nineparted episode without divisions" reproducing in serial pastiches nothing less than a chronological history of English prose, from its Latin and Anglo-Saxon roots through dozens of distinct voices—Malory, Bunyan, Swift, Pater, and so forth—to the "frightful jumble" of modern slangs. All this is "also linked back at each part subtly with some foregoing episode of the day and, besides this, with the natural stages of development in the embryo and the periods of faunal evolution in general." And, oh yes: "Bloom is the spermatozoon, the hospital the womb, the nurse the ovum, Stephen the embryo" (*SL* 251–52).

Well, really now: how could any production so inwrought with effects of verbal surface possibly hope to keep up with the psychological or dramatic developments underneath them? Expecting Joyce to do both would be like expecting Bach to write program music. Besides, is it not obvious that a writer who turns so assiduously to such devices must have chosen to leave behind all naïve notions of the straightforward replication of reality?

"Circe" will be addressed in a later chapter, "Oxen of the Sun" in this one and several to follow. In regard to both, I would reply generally that, at least after *Stephen Hero,* Joyce never did believe that reality was easily, transparently reproducible, that indeed his appreciation of the difficulties involved grew on him as he matured, but that that does not mean that he stopped trying. (On the contrary: he liked a challenge.) Indeed one way of taking *Ulysses* is as an enactment of that realization along with the continuing effort to negotiate it: perplexities accumulate, veils multiply and thicken, greater and greater effort is required to see through surface to substance, but in the end the effort always proves not to have been in vain.

That is in part because the Orphic dispensation established in "Sirens" continues to license new varieties of expressive extension. I have compared "Sirens" to a hall of mirrors reflecting psychically outwards, "Cyclops" to a psychically generated Brocken spectre, "Nausicaa" to psychic ventriloquy; coming next, the active principle of "Oxen of the Sun" might be thought as one of the psychic devices of twentieth-century science fiction (*Forbidden Planet*'s Krellian id-projector, for instance) whose function is turning thoughts into images or actions. In "Oxen of the Sun" things get said or thought or done that change the psychic configuration of the moment in ways a standard novelist would render with a phrase such as "Her mood brightened" or "The situation became ominous," but rather than confine itself to third-person characterization the narrative responds by adopting a whole new projected voice, representing a whole new (usually nameable) personality, to render the change. Moods, thoughts, changes of mind—all are serially personified.

As in the previous episodes, "Oxen of the Sun" includes an instructive set-piece illustrating the psychic operation at work. It appears at lines 1078–1109, when Bloom goes into one of those trances in which mediums were supposed to hear the voices of the dead (and all the narrative voices here are dead), and, like the Stephen of the villanelle, implicates the action of the episode with the motions of the universe, including the stars and planets. This set-piece will be examined in detail in the next chapter. Here, let it be noted that its generation of a personal style from input both circumstantial and individual is, according to the verbal *jouissance* school, exactly what ought not to be possible at this point.

Right now, the more general question is whether or not "Oxen of the Sun" is, for all its twists and turns, consistently endogenous. My argument is in the affirmative. I believe that the episode's voices derive demonstrably from the events and conditions reported, as experienced by one particular consciousness or other, given focus and thus an identity through the processes explored in this book's first three chapters. In fact the process by which some cue sets off mental reverberations distilled in a vision that is in turn rendered in answerable style is itself a subject of the episode, as in "Newman" 's account of how a "chance word" will call forth "evil memories": "they will rise up to confront him in the most various circumstances, a vision or a dream, or while timbrel and harp soothe his senses or amid the cool silver tranquility of the evening or at the feast, at midnight, when he is now filled with wine. Not to insult over him will the vision come as over one that lies under her wrath, not for vengeance to cut him off from the living but shrouded in the piteous vesture of the past, silent, remote, reproachful" (*U* 14.1344–55). "Oxen of the Sun" contains a number of such occurrences, and in each case the result is a dramatic modification of narrative voice. For instance, the "chance word" quoted above, arousing "memories" from, in this case, Stephen's past, is "mother," the word that, spoken flippantly by Lenehan (*U* 14.1123), has reminded Stephen of the "recent loss" (*U* 14.1122–24) of his mother. So the "vision" evoked by that word for this youth now drunk ("filled with wine") is female ("her wrath"), "shrouded" (like a corpse), and "reproachful." That is why Stephen then initiates, after two intervening paragraphs of revery, the first centering on a childhood memory of his mother (*U* 14.1356–78), the second evoking a nativity scene (*U* 14.1379–90), the spree that follows—he wants to stave off the apparition that, still shrouded and reproachful, will win through in "Circe," where again it is preceded ("SIMON: Think of your mother's people!" [*U* 15.4137]) by that "word."

That is, events continue to generate style. Mimesis perdures.

The following will trace the episode's experiential determinants.[4]

Lines 1–166: As the vision of Stephen's mother summoned at the end of "Oxen" carries into "Circe," so its beginning paragraphs echo the end of its predecessor. On the last page of "Nausicaa" Bloom drifts off, with the sound of

Cuckoo
Cuckoo
Cuckoo,

tripled, in his ear; "Oxen" begins with the same trochaic beat (Senn 1984, 355)— "Deshil Holles Eamus"—then prolongs it for the next two paragraphs, then introduces a convoluted paragraph in the flaccid run-on syntax a version of which in *Finnegans Wake* is used to approximate hypnagogic reveries of the kind that Bloom has just fallen into (*FW* 572.21–576.09). That is, the opening of "Oxen" reflects Bloom's inner state—drifting along, with rhythmic interjections—as just witnessed. It also expresses those sentiments likely to be prompted by his contemplating a maternity hospital. "Humane doctors, most of them," he has earlier thought, musing on childbirth (*U* 8.400), and here continues to approve, heartily, of physicians (255–56, 901–2), especially obstetricians. These are the sentiments of lines 8–70—of "Sallust-Tacitus," for whom the greatest "splendour" is obstetric proficiency, of the "mediaeval chronicler," who seconds him, and of the "Anglo-Saxon" encomium on maternity hospitals.

As with the first page of *Portrait,* the order of the initial voices tracks a consciousness's evolving ability to discriminate the details of a new and initially obscure environment, the confusion gradually dissipating as particulars emerge against a murky background, so that by lines 69–74 we can recognize distinct individuals in a definite place. "Mandeville" in particular reflects "childe Leopold" 's (160) first impression of a room where something exceeding strange (Are those *sardines*? Is that *beer*? In a *hospital*?) is occurring. The meeting with Nurse Callan reflects the formality typical of Bloom on such occasions. Bloom begs pardon, and the style is courtly; the two exchange news of recent deaths, and the style turns grave and homiletic, generating "Everyman."

Lines 167–276: A "stray sound" influencing this sequence is the "cry" "on high" (170) of Mrs. Purefoy, in labor. It affects—probably prompts—the students' discussion about the perils of childbirth; it leads Bloom, shaken, to be "minded of" his son's birth and death, thus of his own sonlessness. In the resulting somber mood (rendered by "Malory") he turns his attention to his acquaintance's young son Stephen and the dangers facing him. (The cry also affects Stephen: "mother" occurs three times in his eleven-line speech.) "Malory" emerges for other reasons as well: because Bloom here meets some turbulent young men having a round-table discussion, disguising aggressive rivalry ("the other . . . pricked forward with their jibes wherewith they did malice him") in the idiom of mock-heroic chivalry, because the first figure to get Bloom's attention, Lenehan, is given to facetiously archaic versions of that idiom, as when "Malory" says that he "quaffed" his drink: "quaffed" is exactly the sort of word (see, for instance, *U* 8.273) Lenehan favors.

Again, the account of the scene follows Bloom's developing awareness: first Miss Callan at the entrance, then the cry, then a recognition of the person, Lenehan, with whom Bloom thinks that, because of their relatively close ages, he has most in common, then, as Bloom sits down, a taking-in of the whole company ("Now let us speak of that fellowship that was there . . .") and as, "becalmed," he listens, an account of the discussion; Stephen then becomes the center of attention mainly because his speech attracts Bloom's notice.

Lines 277–407: Stephen pours drinks and, amid the heightened vivacity, gives his longest speech since "Scylla and Charybdis." Reflecting his Shakespeare fixation, that episode was largely an Elizabethan production, and here, according to a like logic, the paragraphs dominated by Stephen's talk correspond to "Elizabethan prose chronicles." Their glasses refilled, the students loose their youthful spirits, like Elizabethans slipping free of the Middle Ages, in a riot of blasphemy, showy learning, and wit. Equally typical are the second thoughts that emerge as Stephen's native morbidity resurfaces and the "Elizabethan prose" chroniclers are succeeded (at 333) by late-Renaissance authors. "It is," said Stephen, speaking of this transition, "an age of exhausted whoredom groping for its god" (*U* 9.810). Just as, according to him, licentious Anne Hathaway turned to religion in later life (*U* 9.800–810), so Stephen's nostalgia for foregone certainties returns, rendered in scriptural reproaches of his apostasy and libertinage (the Puritans are emerging, and the King James Bible) followed by a voice ("Sir Thomas Browne") lamenting the times' benightedness.

Lines 408–73: Another "stray sound," a thunderclap, controls this sequence. Stephen, pathologically afraid of thunder, takes it as confirming his revived guilt, and the voice he hears is of a Puritan preacher, then "Bunyan," reproving his sins. (In *Finnegans Wake* a guilty humanity will hear similar voices in the thunder.) The noise "thunder[s] long rumblingling" (422) throughout this passage in spondaic blows demolishing the *"dedal"* "house" of "wisdom" built in Stephen's "Browne" phase, recalling him to brute realities like death. Thus do primordial facts hammer down intellectual constructs; thus did the round-heads deal with the arabesques of their adversaries.

Lines 474–798: The arrival of "Buck" Mulligan—self-named after Dublin's eighteenth-century bucks—and the spruce Bannon effects a seismic shift to Restoration and Augustan authors and their worldly age, for which Stephen's religious terrors are, as for "Pepys-Evelyn," "a mere fetch" (526–27), religion a matter of expediency exemplified by Mulligan's friend the turncoat Moore (496–97). Even before Mulligan's arrival, things have been getting more down-to-earth: Stephen relaxes; Bloom, testifying from his "experience" (569) with cattle, nudges the discourse further into the realm of fact (the Royal Society waits in the wings) and discerns that the Lenehan he greeted as a fellow knight (174) is "To tell the truth" a low leech. So the voice introduced at 529 is that of Defoe, English literature's premier realist, followed—as the disabused company launches a satire on Anglo-Irish history—by its premier deflater of illusions, Swift. "Swift" 's tale of betrayal and collusion reflects savagely (of course) on the worldliness of the "Pepys-Evelyn" Mulligan, introduced as a "gentleman's gentleman" (495)—which may suggest "supreme gentleman" but more commonly means "servant" (compare *U* 9.491)—first spotted in the center of Ascendancy Dublin, by the door (493–94) of a man known for his ridicule of the Irish cause and his association with Tim Healy, Parnell's Judas (*U* 7.791–808). When this "gay betrayer" (*U* 1.405) takes center stage we get "Addison-Steele," and Joyce despised Addison as an opportunist (Atherton 1974b, 326). Although Mulligan's wit is given its due, its relentless coyness suggests that Dublin's bucks might have gotten pretty tiresome pretty quickly. Coyness merges at line 738 into the facetiousness of Sterne's *A Sentimental Journey* when Mulligan yields to Alec Bannon, by Milly Bloom's account (*U* 4.407) one of those "swells" notable for such qualities in their pursuit of decorous dissipation. Also Sterneian, and typical of Bannon's class, is the paragraph's intermingling of French phrases: at episode's end Bannon will take his leave with the line *"Bonsoir la compagnie"* (1536).

Lines 799–1009: The raillery is terminated by a "larum in the antechamber"—the bell announcing the delivery. The ensuing fracas—ribald Costello, rebuked and repentant—recalls the youth of "The Deserted Village" who "came to scoff and stayed to pray" and similar exempla (Olivia in *The Vicar of Wakefield*, for instance) in the pious parables of "Goldsmith," the dominant author of 799–844. The event also brings out Bloom's officious "Ciceronian" side (Kenner 1956, 214), which, roused, generates "Burke," "Sheridan," "Junius," and "Gibbon," all of them writers concerned with public, parliamentary business. In joining, as an elder, the common censure of the "eccentric" Costello, Bloom plays the Burke (845–79) who defended traditional pieties against anarchy; the following paragraph, mainly "Sheridan" (880–904), is in the same vein.

"Junius," on the other hand (905–41), signals a self-corrective swerve of the kind seen before (*U* 5.311, *U* 13.1098) and much in evidence in "Circe." The cause of this self-recrimination, voiced by someone famous for exposing intimate secrets, is the bell announcing the Purefoy birth. It has this effect for two reasons. First, bell-sounds remind Bloom of Molly's ringing for him on the servants' house bells this morning (for this, see chapter 9), and thus of two other things, both dwelt on by "Junius," his indiscretion with a maid (921–25) and the humiliating facts of his domestic life (916–20, 929–41). Second, announcing a new birth, the sound reminds him that others older than himself are begetting children while he spills his seed (929–31), are having sons while his only son has died, due, he thinks, to its father's "stagnant . . . and inoperative" sperm (937–41; compare *U* 6.329). (Mulligan's recent commentary on "sterility" from "conjugal vexations" or "proclivities acquired" (668–72) may have facilitated the association.)

Reminded thus of Rudy, apparently born deformed,[5] Bloom recalls "Aristotle's *Masterpiece*" (976–77), an anthology of abortions and misbirths that he has recently scanned (*U* 10.585–90). Enter "Gibbon," encyclopedic historian with an eye for the lurid, rendering the student conversation about obstetric horrors, his focus on decline and fall mirroring Bloom's anxieties about the future of his line and his worry that things are getting out of hand. The concluding scriptural injunction against putting "asunder what God has joined," that is by marriage (1008–9), is probably influenced by Bloom's reviving anxieties about his recently traduced marriage.

Lines 1010–1173: Mulligan dominates lines 1010–38 by launching into a mock-Gothic account of how Haines had appeared at Moore's soirée and given everyone the creeps by ranting about his nightmare nemesis, the black panther (Kenner 1980, 115). (He has earlier adopted a similar tone to frighten Haines about Stephen [*U* 10.1071–75].)[6] Hence the "Walpole" voice, with the Irish Gothicist "Le Fanu" enunciated by Mulligan's interjection of stage-Irish patter inspired in turn by Haines's "portfolio full of Celtic literature" (Hyde's *Love Songs of Connacht* [*U* 9.513–14]).[7] Meanwhile Bloom, brooding on the "Junius"-rendered self-reproach (1005–7), goes into a trance induced by "staring" at the red triangle on the label of a bottle of Bass Ale (1182–83), which reminds him of the "redlabelled bottle" with which his father poisoned himself (*U* 6.359), a connection suggested when Mulligan renders Haines's bottle as "a phial marked *Poison*" (1013–14). Thus transfixed, Bloom, susceptible to "hypnotic suggestion" (*U* 17.852), enters a "mesmerised" (1176) revery compounded of the memories aroused by the red sign as they "blend" with the "voices" in the background (1078)—Mulligan's tale, Stephen and Lynch recalling their Clongowes days, the "noise of voices" reviewing the Gold Cup race, followed by Lynch's story of his time in the field with his lover—which, when he comes to, he remembers as "the moment before's observations about boyhood days and the turf" (1187–88). (For a detailed analysis of this sequence, which evokes the sensibility of Thomas De Quincey, English prose's acknowledged maestro of such mental phantasmagoria, see the next chapter.)

Lines 1174–1309: When Lenehan reaches for the bottle (1162–63) and Mulligan makes fun of Bloom's trance (1163–68), Bloom, startled, begins coming to (1174–81), generating a defensive paragraph (1174–97) aspiring to "Macaulay" 's dignity but resembling instead "Eumaeus" (Atherton 1974b, 334), whose prose registers Bloom's mind at its murkiest and most ponderous. As at the episode's beginning, when the "evolution" of early prose mirrors Bloom's coming-to, the transition from muddled "Macaulay" (1174–97) to "Macaulay" *tout court* in the next paragraph (1198–1222) follows Bloom's awakening "symptoms of animation" (1178) after his trance; the 1198–1222 synopsis springs from the same cause—Bloom's growing awareness, his taking-in of things—as the synopsis of 187–201.

The hostility toward Stephen then voiced by "Huxley" (1223–1309) arises as follows. His thoughts having been directed to the son born to the elderly Purefoy, then to his own sonlessness, then (1182–85) to his daughter, Bloom, poise regained, asks two questions—can one increase the chances of having a boy? (1129–31) and, why would such a baby die? (1273–77)—natural to someone just led by bitter thoughts about the son he has lost and warm memories of the healthy daughter he still has to hope that he might yet father another, healthy, boy. (There is also an aside about the "too long neglected spermatozoa" [1233–34]: earlier "Junius" has berated him for the "consort neglected" (936) in favor of masturbation.) Stephen's answer results from his own musings: brooding on his mother's death because of Lenehan's wisecrack (1123–25), he responds callously. Look, he says, any hangman god depraved enough to feed on my mother would think nothing of snacking on "staggering bob" (that is, a newborn baby; for instance, to Bloom, Rudy Bloom). The remark comes across as especially brutal because of Bloom's kindling hopes. His wounded reaction is to lump Stephen with what he has earlier called "Those literary etherial people" (*U* 8.543) and, in recoil against such "perverted transcendentalism," to urge his own ethos of "hardheaded facts." Hence "Huxley." Since "staggering bob" is also an arcane term familiar to Bloom from his days in the cattle business (*U* 8.724), he gets to demonstrate his practical knowledge by explaining it to the rest of the company: "For the enlightenment of those who are not so intimately acquainted with the minutiae of the municipal abattoir . . . it should perhaps be stated that staggering bob . . . signifies the cookable and eatable flesh of a calf newly dropped from its mother" (1293–99). This paragraph ends with a Bloom's-eye version of a "public controversy" between the two, in which version Bloom, being after all the one in control of the narrative at this point, wins.

Lines 1310–1439: Also Bloom-generated, the "Dickens" voice (1310–43) reasserts the domesticity that Stephen's remark had squelched, and which Bloom's (self-proclaimed) last word (1307–9) reestablishes. Though describing Mrs. Purefoy and child, the picture framed owes most to Bloom's memory of Molly and the newborn Milly ("the first *bloom* [my italics] of her new motherhood") revived in "De Quincey," as combined "in . . . imagination" with his revived hope for a male heir to appease the patriarchal demands of "Those who have passed on."

"Newman" next expresses Stephen's reaction to the memory of his mother, a memory awakened by Lenehan's "chance word," "mother." That hardheaded "Huxley," having been followed by soft-hearted "Dickens," should now be supplanted by three Oxonians—"Newman," "Pater," and "Ruskin"—known for their advocacy of spiritual and aesthetic values against Huxleyan scientism, indicates that Bloom has relented toward Stephen since their "controversy" to the point that there is a new convergence of Bloom sentiment with those Stephen qualities of university-educated aestheticism earlier spurned, an access of sympathy that has been stimulated by another "chance word," the "word of so natural a homeliness" last uttered by Stephen—"bob." "Staggering bob" assaulted Bloom's feelings; "bob" by itself, which could be heard echoing through "Dickens"—"darling little Bobsy . . . lord Bobs of Waterford"—is a different matter. It is the word that "disengages . . . in the observer's [Bloom's] memory" the moment when he first saw Molly, *bob*bing for cherries, nearby the child Stephen and his mother.[8] Envisioning, in the glow of this memory, the boy watched over by the mother he has lost, gazing at Stephen and detecting a "recession" of bitterness, so that as at the end of "Circe," when Stephen, unconscious, is in similar "recession," he recognizes the face "of his poor mother" (*U* 15.4949), Bloom, in both main senses, sympathizes, and a kind of fusion results: in styles combining both principals, "Newman," "Pater," and "Ruskin" recount first the evocative effect of a "chance word" (for Stephen, "mother," for Bloom, "bob") on both, then the memory common to both, of Molly bobbing within sight of Stephen's mother, summoned by those respective words, then, as both sit absorbed in memory, a mother-and-child tableau rendered as a nativity scene. The sequence of contemplative ("Newman") followed by two figures known for impressionistic criticism of static emblems suits both, brooding on private images.

Lines 1391–1591: As Atherton says (Atherton 1974b, 334), the "confusion" of these last pages is "suitably embodied" first in "Carlyle," then, as things become wilder, in the ensuing "frightful jumble." Also Carlylean is the celebration of high purpose, of the Purefoys' victory over "sterile cohabitation," which registers Bloom's resolution to try for another son.[9] This spirit, building through developments we have traced, prompts Bloom's remarkably forward remark to Miss Callan ("Madam, when comes the storkbird for thee?"), his participation in the binge (as celebration, as pledge of resolve, most of all as a sign of his newly-forged paternalistic solicitude for young Stephen), his decision to "Cleave to" his wife in spite of all: "To her, old patriarch!" (Words that echo, with a difference, the phrase "to her" in the suicide note of the patriarch Rudolph Bloom—*U* 17.1884.) "Ruskin" had ended with a description of "swollen masses turgidly distended," repressed impulses about to break out; the last paragraphs (1440–1591) are in the language of release, in words about as free as possible from linguistic structure and stricture. For the reading I have been pursuing, they also constitute the exception proving the rule: the first paragraphs not dominated by a distinct sensibility, they are accordingly the first not written in the style of a distinct author or school.

2

"Carlyle" 's exhortation on behalf of fatherhood amplifies an impulse that has been growing in Bloom because of forces acting on him in this time and place.

"Oxen of the Sun" is set in a maternity hospital on the street to which the Blooms moved after their son died, the flat taken after, traumatized by this death, they ceased "complete carnal intercourse" (U 17.2274–78).[10] One consequence was that Bloom started his "secret life" of aberrant sexual practices (Raleigh 1977, 154), that for instance the voyeurism and public masturbation of "Nausicaa" became habitual.[11] Meanwhile from their window the Blooms could see the hospital (U 18.703–5), could see the couples leaving, about once a day (77–78), with their newborns, implicitly reproaching them. Now Bloom returns to that scene after masturbating and drifting off while serenaded by a cuckoo clock, masturbation and cuckoldry both being results of, and reminders of, his enforced sterility. By the standard of those philoprogenitive values affirmed throughout, "Oxen of the Sun," because of the associations arising from what has recently occurred and where he now is, begins, for Bloom, at absolute low ebb. In an episode that links conception to sunlight,[12] much of Bloom's sojourn in the hospital, in this first nighttime episode, is the dark night of the soul by which spiritual pilgrims are traditionally tested. The voices that rebuke Bloom's sexual deviance and harp on his sonlessness express private demons aroused through associations connected with the episode's place and time.

On the other hand, a maternity hospital in which a healthy son is born is not a bad place to confront those demons. Especially heartening is the fact of the father's age. In contemplating another son Bloom has wondered if, at thirty-eight, he might be too old (U 11.1067). But Theodore Purefoy is in his fifties, a fact not lost on someone born to a father also in his fifties (Raleigh 1977, 15–16). So there's hope yet.

With these two alternatives—sterility and fertility, despair over the past and the reviving hope for the future, fatherhood rejected or reaffirmed—emerging from the circumstances in which Bloom finds himself and converging in his mind, "Oxen of the Sun" becomes a morality drama in which traditional virtues are assaulted by the voices of the desert and, finally, proved. Throughout, this middle-aged man cast among raucously irreverent youths, is, if only antithetically, drawn to paternal values. His, and the narrator's, final "Carlylean" resolve signals the triumph of those values.

That triumph does not come about easily. If the students tend to go overboard at times so do the patriarchal spokesmen. It is not accidentally that the loudest affirmation of fatherhood is given to the author of *Latter-day Pamphlets*, nor that Theodore Purefoy, exemplary paterfamilias, is an abject forelock-tugger, one who despite his supposedly devout Methodism attends a church of the establishment's religion (518), each of whose nine children (1329–34) is named after a member of the royal family or some establishment boss.[13] Purefoy illustrates how fatherhood can lock men into the system of subordinations that oppresses many of Joyce's characters, the link between paternity and paternalism. "Tyrannous" was Father Conmee's adjective for the urge to propagate (*U* 10.171), a sentiment echoed here (766–70), in an episode abounding with evidence as to why it deserves to be taken literally. To become a father is to take a place, probably low, in the hierarchy whose spokesmen preach, often obnoxiously, throughout this episode. Bloom knows this (for instance at *U* 15.3475–77), which is partly why the decision to proceed anyway should be so hard-won.

Nonetheless the decision is made, out of an impulse that the first word of that chant, "Deshil," forecasts. "Deshil" means "sunward," traveling or turning with the sun, hence in a blessed, lucky direction. (The opposite, widdershins, is bad luck. The introduction's triple "deshil" summons good luck for mother and child; such spells were once traditional for newborns.)[14] To inhabitants of the northern hemisphere, "deshil" has always signified circular movement from left to right, that is, clockwise—the direction in which we still deal cards, screw in light bulbs, and tell time, the direction that continues to be associated with the forward-looking. When Miss Callan, being of the Latin rite, crosses herself from left to right (83–84), she is signing herself *deshil*, for reasons that Sir James Frazer would have been happy to explain. Likewise when the students of "Oxen" pass the beer ("around the clock," as Edwardian slang had it), keep their eyes on the pub clock, discuss "axle drives" (1599), or open a sardine can in a clockwise circuit with a clockwise twist of the key, or when Bloom is mindful of the zodiac or the "whirligig of years" (1323), they are like it or not deferring, sunwise, to ancient pieties. So are Stephen and Lynch when they change course: "When Lynch sets off by the shortest route, turning left into Denzille Street, Stephen calls him back to make a slight detour through Denzille Lane . . . The route through the lane would enable Lynch and Stephen to separate themselves most readily from the others" (Hart and Knuth, 1976, 33). It also assures that all their corner-turnings will be to the right, and that in their boxing of the compass they will complete a *deshil* circuit.

Such intermittent revivals of tribal ways might seem to function like *The Waste Land*'s glimpses of ancient rituals—as reminders of how "inverecund habit shall have gradually traduced the honourable by ancestors transmitted customs" (25–26). But no one in *The Waste Land* does what Bloom does at the end of this episode: "Winding of his ticker" (1469–70). Resetting his watch by the pub clock, he is turning the stem *deshil*, after advancing the hands *deshil*, in hopes of setting it ticking *deshil*. That is, he follows the ritual injunction of the beginning as he has taken up the principle, fatherhood, for which it is made to stand—not incidentally recommencing the clockwise movement that in his mind anyway was interrupted at the moment his wife's adultery traduced that principle.[15] And although he isn't aware of the *deshil* angle (any more than he is aware of the *Odyssey*), "Oxen of the Sun," continuing the *Ulysses* engagement with occult affinities, persistently encourages us to reflect on the extent to which the heart might have occult correspondences with ancestral codes that a person of Bloom's generally bourgeois-progressive stamp would be surprised to know of. In particular, we are reminded of how in the collective system of equivalences that Bloom engages by thinking the thought "father," his wish to sire a son is simultaneously a wish to turn clockwise, sunwise, his guilt about masturbation a guilt about having turned aside, per-verted (the trope is "Bunyan" 's, among others: 451, 474), from the *deshil* path, toward death and darkness. The *deshil* injunction, after all, commands one to keep the ball rolling, away from encroaching night, toward the sunlight, to as Bloom mused earlier "steal a day's march" on the sun, so as to "never grow a day older technically" (*U* 4.84–86). Which is what, famously, Shakespeare's sonnets claim a man does by having a son and stealing a march on death's shade, what is implicitly claimed for fatherhood by talk of senior and junior, of handing on the torch and carrying on the name. The same claim is included in the venerable son-sun equivalence that runs throughout the episode (for example at 1074, 1095). In chapter 12 I will be arguing that "Oxen of the Sun" enacts, for Bloom, a cometary journey, from the sun outward, past the planets and out toward the Milky Way; let it here be observed that in that capacity he should at episode's end be making a sharp turn, back toward the sun (compare *U* 17.2013–23), and that this turn corresponds to his resolution to beget a son.[16]

Now, one thing remarkable about this episode's stress on fatherhood as continuity, as return to primal, solar source, is that it should occur in a book that, many believe, rests on the opposite idea. Stephen, whose own search for a spiritual father is generally taken to illustrate the truth of his words, has called paternity "a legal fiction," "founded . . . on the void" (*U* 9.842–44), on an "instant of blind rut" (*U* 9.860). Set against this passage, "Oxen of the Sun" admonishes that "blind" is a word to pause at. Faith, too, is proverbially blind, and the sun is blinding—as for instance at the end of "Cyclops" (*U* 13.1912–16). To turn or return to the sun, or son, or Son, following "Oxen" 's urgings, is to risk blindness, to behave blindly, to make a blind leap of faith, of pure-foy, across what Stephen in "Scylla and Charybdis" calls the "void" or "mystery" of paternity (*U* 9.842,

839). (So we are reminded that an ejaculation is etymologically an outflinging [1391].) And indeed the Bloom of "Oxen of the Sun" who, despite the fate of Rudy and despite many qualms, decides to try again, is willing such a leap.

Mirroring Bloom, "Oxen of the Sun" insists as stridently as it does on the *deshil* verities of continuity, reaffirmation of fundamentals, return to the sun-source, because those verities are both vital and problematic. They are problematic in two main ways, in the realities represented and in the manner of their representation: substance and the question of answerable style. In both areas, the primary value under attack is what a paterfamilias might call responsibility, the acknowledgment that acts have consequences and that writing is one such act, one that must tell or show the truth about its subject—the world—if it is any good.

From "Sallust-Tacitus" on, many of the episode's voices harp on the dire chain reactions certain to be set off by apostasy, and particularly by birth control, whose purpose is to break those lines of genetic continuity that are the episode's standard of cause and effect. Irreverence, contraception, masturbation—in short the specialties of the students and, in the last case, Bloom—are "irresponsible" in this sense.

And so, to turn to the second problematic area, would seem to be the episode's technique, which, again, has long been taken as either virtually divorced from or prior to, overbearingly imposed upon, any experiential component, for which the commonest critical metaphor is that of a "veil" or "screen." Against that background, it may appear that, either perversely or slavishly, I have been giving "Oxen of the Sun" the kind of "responsible" reading it demands, "demands" in the sense not of logical inevitability but of peremptory command. "Oxen of the Sun" "demands" because its continuity depends on— and it repeats often that continuity is all—recognition of a causal connectivity throughout, which has not been recognized, or at least not argued, until right now. In concentrating on the causal sequences that make "Defoe" or "Huxley" appear when they do, make Stephen recall his mother when he does, make Bloom decide to try for another son, I have been, like Theodore Purefoy, obeying the boss, going along with the patriarchal injunction, despite compelling reasons for disobedience.

Because clearly "Oxen of the Sun" begs for the opposite reading. Clearly any such sequence of acts, arranged chronologically and keyed—it says in the notes—to the stages of gestation and Lord only knows what else, is self-evidently too "writerly" to devote much attention to the imitative effects typical of the earlier episodes, to answering cause A (setting, event, sensibility) with

just-right effect B (mot juste, technique). Common sense and our common experience with parody and pastiche tell us that one condition of a writer's putting such energy into formal effects is a diminution of the energy devoted to
telling the story and registering facts, and that the result of such diminution
must be an uncoupling of material from style. Joyce's famous account of the
episode's schematic pyrotechnics ("How's that for high?") reinforces this impression, as did the dismay of early critics at what they considered the story
line's submergence.

My reading suggests, however, that rather than break the ligatures between
event and style Joyce has stretched them out and woven them together: not veil,
but web. The difference between an early episode and this one is not that one
registers events and the other entombs them in technique but that the experiential causes of the former are relatively immediate and apparent whereas those
of the latter are relatively remote and compound. They require searching out.
And such searching-out asks acceptance of, as it were faith in, the patriarchal
assurances that "the ends and ultimates of all things accord in some mean and
measure with their inceptions and originals" (387–89), that a search for the
deshil origins of apparently factitious effects will be rewarded. Reading "Oxen
of the Sun" is a matter of choosing whether to search for the father, of asking
whether everything might still be of a piece—effects derived from causes, fathers begetting sons, world begetting word.[17] That is to say, it is a matter of testing, and eventually proving—no other word, alas—phallogocentric validations
in an apparently decentered text. Pharmacologically, we are asked to choose between using contraceptives—separating derivative from source, replacing a
doctrine of bloodlines destiny with one of ludic randomness—or not. As mod-
erns (or postmoderns), we must choose between repudiating and affirming our
cultural origins in an episode where parody and burlesque, gestures of rebellion, in spite of themselves express an incessant impulse toward "retrogressive
metamorphosis" (390), where even the dissipated Punch Costello reverts to af-
firmations of how he "was bred up most particular" by father and mother (841),
where as we are reminded at lines 154–59 even the delirium-inducing beer of
the "guzzling den" is made from plants that seek the sun, fermented in the sun
(1436). In this first nighttime sequence, we can surrender to the "lutulent"
"tenebrosity" ("Forward, woozy wobblers! Night. Night." [14.1562]) in an
episode that from the first word looks to sunshine for its bearings, where even
at the end a bartender awaiting coins wants "shiners" (1499–1500). As a matter
of belief, we can agree or not with "Pepys-Evelyn" 's (523–28) skeptical dismissal of prophecies (perceived continuities with the distant future, evoked by

spells revived from the distant past) in an episode where such claims are mocked but where in fact the two prophecies cited, that Mrs. Purefoy's baby will be a boy (514–15) and that "after wind and water fire shall come" (523), both come true (945, 1569–70).[18] As spectators of Bloom's morality play, we are asked to choose between Purefoy and the medicals—asked to make this choice as Bloom, "Everyman," us, opts for the former.

Of course we can reject his lead—in today's critical climate are almost certain to. But it is worth remarking that the author has invited this reaction only to make it a participant in a drama working to reveal it as superficial. At a time when many, including many Joyce critics, have been advertising the hidden ruptures papered over by texts once thought constructed in conformance with a metaphysics of uniform connectiveness, "Oxen of the Sun" is set up to generate the opposite exegetical sequence. What appears to be all about sterilization, the interposition of a gap between source and derivative, turns out to be about successful fertilization: Mrs. Purefoy gives birth after long labor, rain soaks the earth after long drought, Bloom resolves on paternity after years of estrangement.

And, too, what appears to be exoskeletal, allegorical, metonymic turns out to be endogenous, symbolic, metaphoric: things register, connect, and reverberate, from the inside out, from origin to derivative, cause to effect. Apparently a ripe plum for the deconstructionists, this episode "demands" and demands not deconstruction but construction. Or, since the demand has been resisted, at least repays it. The resistance is understandable, as understandable as any resistance to any father. Unquestionably there is something onerous about so finished a system of dependencies, so many generations of authorial Anchiseses piling piggyback onto a narrative base so hard to see. In few works can the association between "father"—that "tyrannous" figure—and "author"/ity be made so much of.[19] My reading may well recall Theodore Purefoy, stooped as he is under layers of interlocking hierarchies.

Still, as I have tried to show, *eppur si muove*. One does *find* something when one looks more—to use a loaded, licensed (1409) word—deeply. To the other hierarchical oppositions can be added one more, "demanded" by the father-author: depth versus surface. "Every word is so deep, Leopold"—thus, once, Bloom *père* to his son, underscoring the message of a theatrical scene about an apostate Jew who left "the house of his father" (*U* 5.205–6). Like Bloom *fils*, the reader is urged to read deeply, unlike those whose "acumen is esteemed very little perceptive concerning" matters of study, who are so "unilluminated as not to perceive" the underlying reality—to join with the "wise" and "prudent" and eschew the "mean" and "lewd," "blind" and "deceived," "base minds" and "rash judgers" whose distinguishing feature is an excessive regard for surface, for "exterior splendour," "eyepleasing exterior." Throughout, patriarchal responsibility equates with readerly responsibility, the adherence to essential continuities with the capacity to look beneath the surface. The text's penalty for rejection of this injunction is benightedness, an inability to appreciate the occulted connections with which it is mined. Joyce has so set things up that those who obey the boss, who follow his narrator's commands, will see things that those led astray by surface effects, by that "veil" lamented or celebrated, will miss.

And if, as several critics have found, *Ulysses'* first predominantly expository "literary" episode, "Scylla and Charybdis," treats, largely according to the model of doctrinal dialectics, of how the book should be read,[20] then so does this, the second such episode.[21] The Stephen of "Scylla and Charybdis," battling the interpretive fashions of his own day and practicing a hybrid of psychoanalytic, phenomenological, and Old Historicism criticism, expounds *Hamlet* and the authorial life it is assumed to reveal as a "ghost story" of dead father speaking to consubstantial son. Not for him the dissipations of unmoored textuality represented, in different modes, by most of his Charybdian interlocutors—and if his theory is flawed,[22] it is still superior to any alternative shown us. I suggest that in reading through the later episode's chronicle of authors—all of them male,[23] all of them, in 1904, dead—we are maneuvered, or should be, into the position of Stephen's Hamlet, seeking consubstantial continuities stretching from the present moment back through the dimly recognizable ghosts ranged before us, back to an origin figured as the vital "outflinging" connections of fathering and authoring.

That this search for continuities is a difficult thing to do is in a way the point. Throughout *Ulysses,* the reader as well as the hero is being tested. Thus "Wandering Rocks" is full of "reader traps" (Hart 1974, 181–216), analogous to the shifting hazards threatening the mariner Odysseus; thus "Sirens" tempts to sentimentality and "Cyclops" to tunnel vision, to for instance overlooking the messy counter-melodramatic facts we have previously considered. "Oxen of the Sun" tests our resolve to pay attention, to struggle to discern the story being told, with its beginning and end, its real people and critical events. In the process it doubtless tries that Odyssean virtue, patience. But at least those who negotiate it have, in their voyage through the book, halfway doubled the Cape: after this and "Circe," the Ithaca of the substantial world will never thereafter be so remote. Joyce found the Homeric episode corresponding to "Oxen of the Sun" the most difficult to interpret (*L1* 137) (but did interpret it) and saw to it that his own version was similarly challenging—that what in Homer came closest to keeping Odysseus from Ithaca would in *Ulysses* give the most trouble to readers struggling to keep track of "from what region of remoteness the whatness of our whoness hath fetched his whenceness" (399–400).

Specifically, it tests those qualities that, through Joyce's eyes, we can see affirmed in the *Odyssey*, in which Odysseus's crew is lost at sea because, rebellious and impatient, it ignores the injunction of the sage prophet Tiresias, while the hero, steadfast to that word and his purpose, mindful of origin and destination, saves himself and his mission. Several critics have remarked that in "Scylla and Charybdis" Stephen clings as tenaciously as he does to the rock of "hard facts"—Shakespeare's life, the second-best bed, and so on—to avoid the whirlpool of indeterminacy prominently represented by the "formless spiritual essences" of the theosophist A.E. or the infinitely receding Wildean paradoxes of Mr. Best. True enough, I think—but in the *Odyssey* it is in fact during the story of the sun-god's cattle that Odysseus clings to a Scyllan crag above the Charybdis in which his ship has vanished, waits for mast and keel to resurface, and with them continues the course that will eventually bring him home to wife, to marriage bed rooted in the earth, to son, and to father.

8

Bloom as Thomas De Quincey

BLOOM'S "DE QUINCEY"-rendered revery in "Oxen of the Sun"—beginning with "The voices blend and fuse" and ending with "a ruby and triangled sign" blazing "upon the forehead of Taurus"—requires more attention than any other sequence in the episode. Fortunately, it is followed by "Landor," a voice especially helpful in retrospectively assembling the events that have generated it, including the crucial fact (noted at 1164–67, soon confirmed by "Macaulay" at 1174–197) that throughout Bloom has been in a trance induced by staring at the red triangle on a bottle of Bass Ale.

We will later explore the causes of this tendency of Bloom's—chronic, as it turns out—to drift off (see chapter 13). At such times he is not simply being oblivious; he is in an altered state as deep as any visited on Trilby or Peer Gynt, and, as always, the voice that emerges, in this case of a writer famous for such states, derives from that fact. When Dr. Mulligan diagnoses Bloom's condition as that of someone "far away," in a "vision" (1165, 1166),[1] he is telling the truth. "De Quincey's" description of how "voices blend and fuse" is not just a bit of rich writing; it is an accurate account of what is happening in Bloom's head, as he sinks deeper into his trance and the voices around him fade into the background, blending and fusing.

"Landor" also tells us in some detail whose voices those are and what they are saying. There are three main conversations, occurring at times simultaneously—blending and fusing—and at times sequentially, in a mix anticipating the overlapping dialogue of directors Howard Hawks and Robert Altman.[2] In the first conversation, Stephen, Lenehan, and Lynch are recalling their school days. The second, which has been underway from the outset and comes to the fore when the first topic lapses and Lynch and Lenehan become active participants (Lenehan may have been stereophonically participating in both) is a discussion of the Gold Cup race. "Macaulay" later sums up these two simultaneous conversations as "observations about boyhood days and the turf" (1188)—the turf observations coming mainly from Lenehan, who remembers having once seen the Gold Cup favorite Scepter as a filly (1140–42)—during which Bloom was "recollecting two or three private transactions of his own" (1189).[3] The third conversation is Lynch's reminiscence about the day's outing with his girlfriend. The blending of voices ends when Lenehan reaches for the Bass Ale and this sudden movement causes Bloom to begin coming out of his trance.

To illustrate cause and effect I include a chart (fig. 1) giving the "Landor" sequence (1110–73) in the left margin and the "De Quincey" sequence in the right, with lines drawn between labeled passages to indicate correspondences. In the paragraph preceding the sequence, Bloom's memories of high school days of a "score of years" before have been prompted by the background conversation, recounted by "Landor," of Stephen's school days from "years before," "together in Conmee's time" (1110, 1111). (The mention of Conmee also prompts Lynch to recall his afternoon of lovemaking, interrupted by Conmee's appearance [1142–61].) The memory of Bloom's father (1055–60) may have been induced by the Bass red label, reminiscent of the red label on Rudolph's poison bottle. The light suddenly flooding the world (1070) comes, I suggest, from a flash of lightning, whose thunder—please remember this—we will hear soon after.

Now to figure 1, beginning with two explanatory remarks. First, during the first half, some of the lines of correspondence crisscross, because the conversation is overlapping, because it is not until sixteen lines down ("Madden had lost five drachmas . . .") that "Landor" begins remarking the second track of the two-track auditory field that Bloom is absorbing, and because the locus where these influences coalesce, Bloom's entranced consciousness, possesses what De Quincey's contemporary Coleridge called the esemplastic power of combining and rearranging them creatively in answer to his own activated impulses. (In the second half, Lynch's soliloquy apparently quiets the rest, and the talk is sequential; with one exception, accordingly, all the correspondences follow in order.) Second, it should be stressed that in many cases "Landor" is not to be taken as origin or faithful transcription of the origin from which "De Quincey" is generated, but as an alternative source of evidence—and, because neither intoxicated nor entranced, probably a more reliable one—to that origin's exact configurations. To take, as an example, the correspondence labeled "R": it is not that the "De Quincey" phrase "currents of the cold interstellar wind" is a distortion of an original phrase recorded by "Landor" as "Corinth fruit"; it is rather that both are renditions of something else—something real—antecedent to them both, and that by juxtaposing both, we can (with the help of an etymo-

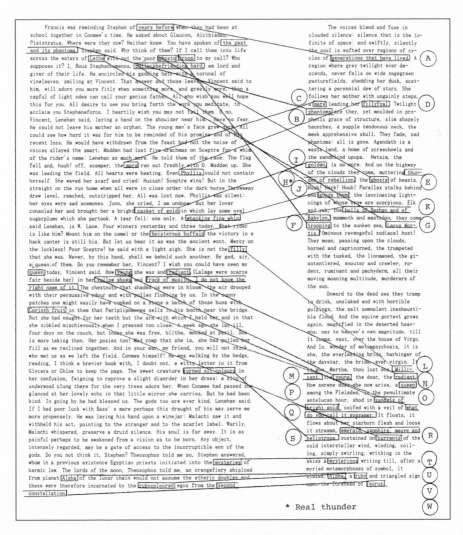

1. Parallel passages from "Oxen of the Sun." From the *Journal of Modern Literature,* courtesy of the author.

logical dictionary) triangulate to that something real: in this case the phrase "currant buns," which is nowhere on the page but which nonetheless accounts for two phrases that are. Were it not for the limitations of typography, figure 1 would properly be three-dimensional and semitransparent, the lines of correspondence usually going not to but through, toward a mix of shifting figures (it should properly be animated, too) coming progressively into focus.

To begin: "A," the "cycles of generation" being conjured up, like Lamb's preceding evocation of school days past, is prompted by Stephen and company's reminiscence about "years before." Likewise the phrase "the past and its phantoms" yields "B," the vision of "twilight phantoms." After this, things get more complicated. The account of the ongoing conversation about the Gold Cup has Lenehan using the words "mare" and Dixon remembering his "Phyllis," and so in "De Quincey" we get the picture of "a mare leading her fil-lyfoal"—"C" and "D." But of course for Bloom such an image, helped on by near-rhymes to "Marion" and "Milly," cannot help but recall Mrs. Marion and Milly Bloom (she who, Bloom will later remember, once "sustained her blond hair for him to ribbon it" [U 17.896], here distinguished by her "supple tendo-nous neck" [1084]), who therefore appear and will be present, mainly in dis-guise, throughout the rest of the De Quincey passage. They will be disguised, first, as horses—because of the background conversation about horses—and, second, as the constellated horses Pegasus and Equuleus ("Little Horse") that do indeed follow one another and are indeed right now climbing the sky. That they are climbing the sky is something the amateur astronomer Bloom would know from the moment about an hour ago when he dozed off, at the "grey twi-light" here preserved (1080), while looking out toward the eastern sea over whose horizon those constellations were just appearing, while thinking, as it happened, about "phantom" apparitions emerging in the dusk (U 13.1078)—that is, about "twilight phantoms."

While these visions are (nebularly) coalescing in Bloom's mind Stephen has been continuing to hold forth and now chimes in with some high-flown stuff, mainly facetious,[4] about how his poetic powers can summon herds of "ghosts" to "troop" like beasts from the land of the dead—and lo, what should appear in "De Quincey" but "ghosts of beasts" ("E") "trooping" ("F") to "the sunken sea, Lacus Mortis" ("G"). "H," "thunder of rebellion," I take to be the sound of, lit-erally, thunder, following the lightning flash mentioned earlier, and suggest that it as much as Lenehan's tactless remark about Mrs. Dedalus accounts for the sudden silence of Stephen, terrified of thunder.

The particular beasts numbered among the "zodiacal host" reflect Bloom's sky-watcher's knowledge of the zodiacal animals (lynx, ram, whale, bull, and others) that do in fact follow Pegasus. Pegasus was first glimpsed through the gathering clouds of late dusk, and accordingly Bloom now envisions it trotting along a "highway of the clouds." Dusk of course signaled the sun's disappear-ance, an occurrence here rendered as "Netaim, the golden, is no more" by virtue of the link established in "Calypso" (U 4.197–213) between a planter's company in Palestine (hence the sudden influx of biblical diction) named Agendath Netaim and sunniness in general; the "waste land" vision that succeeds in "De Quincey" traces to the "sandy tracts" (*U* 4.192) in which Bloom there envisioned the plantation being established; the "sunken sea, Lacus Mortis" in which the vision culminates, prompted by Stephen's reference to Lethe, river of the dead, is further informed by the succeeding moment in "Calypso" when a cloud covered the sun, darkening and chilling a prospect prominently featuring "a bent hag," and Agendath Netaim suddenly reemerged in Bloom's vision as a desolate desert (*U* 4.227).

At "I," Lynch's "casket of gold" is worked into the picture of that "golden" land, before its transformation into wasteland. At "J," Lenehan's "whacking fine whip" cues the herdsman "Parallax," goading the animals with his switch; the "lancinating lightnings" inflicted by that switch go, of course, with the thunder; the "Huuh!" sound of the cattle tells us that Bloom, his revery nudged to thoughts of death, is remembering the drover whose cattle momentarily halted the funeral party of "Hades": "—Huuuh! the drover's voice cried, his switch sounding on their flanks. Huuuh! out of that!" (*U* 6.390–91). That sounding switch, again, chimes with Lenehan's "whacking fine whip." The reverberating thunder—an earlier peal has been described as sounding "long rumblingly" (422)—conjures the rumbling stampede of the cattle, in their "thunder of rebellion." (Compare *CP* 44.) The drover's cattle were heading for their "killing day" (*U* 6.392); the "De Quincey" cattle are heading for the salt water of a dead lake whose main associative source is Bloom's idea of the Dead Sea. The "Hades" drover, incidentally, very likely corresponds to Orion, listed in Joyce's Linati schema as one of the mythical "Persons" of the episode (Ellmann 1972, 190) and present in the corresponding episode of the *Odyssey* as a herdsman driving beasts across the fields of asphodel: another constellation from Bloom's repertoire.

If the word "mare" made Bloom think of Marion, then it would automatically have made him think as well of Blazes Boylan and his morning letter of assignation blatantly addressed to "Mrs. Marion Bloom" (*U* 4.244).[5] And so, prominent in that thundering herd we encounter—"K"—"the bulls of Bashan and Babylon," a formulation that I suggest arises from a blending of Stephen's phrase "bullockbefriending bard" (1115) and Lenehan's "boisterous buffalo" (1138) with Bloom's own consciousness of his double-B nemesis. That alliterative link established, it does not take Sigmund Freud to recognize a good deal of displaced sexual anxiety about lengendarily endowed Boylan in the vision of what those boisterous bulls are doing to the "dead sea" that, we recall, "Calypso" identified with the "cunt of the world":

Elk and yak, the bulls of Bashan and of Babylon, mammoth and mastodon, they come trooping to the sunken sea, Lacus Mortis. Ominous revengeful zodiacal host! They moan, passing upon the clouds, horned and capricorned, the trumpeted with the tusked, the lionmaned, the giantantlered, snouter and crawler, rodent, ruminant and pachyderm, all their moving moaning multitude, murderers of the sun.

Onward to the dead sea they tramp to drink, unslaked and with horrible gulpings, the salt somnolent inexhaustible flood.

I particularly enjoy the presence of the pachyderm there. Those "horrible gulpings," by the way, probably originate in background sounds of drinking.

Following this scene, Lynch's sentimental account of his afternoon interlude with a young woman prompts a romantic vision of Milly whose outline owes something as well to the gold-sandaled Milly-type envisioned in "Calypso" (U 4.240–42). Lenehan's "filly" transmutes into "Millicent" ("L"), then Lynch's talk of a "queen" who is "young" and "radiant" in her "yellow shoes" becomes, clearly enough, Milly as a "young" "radiant," "queen among the Pleiades," in "sandals of bright gold" ("M," "N," "O," and "P"). (Mythically, incidentally, the Pleiades are a band of young virgins, clustered next to Orion in the sky; the two are linked in legend.) Phyllis's "flock of muslin, I do not know the right name of it" turns into "what do you call it gossamer" ("Q"). When the narrative has Lynch mentioning the "Corinth fruit" he enjoyed with his Phyllis, we may need to check the OED to confirm that "currant" is etymologically descended from "Corinth,"[6] and that Lynch is therefore really talking about currant buns, which we can then recognize sounding behind "currents of cold interstellar wind"— hence "R."[7] His description of this same Phyllis turning "all colours" yields the streams of "emerald, sapphire, mauve and heliotrope" radiating from that "what do you call it gossamer" ("S").

When Lenehan reaches for the bottle of Bass, Bloom, startled by the movement, begins to come to, which is why he (and thus we) can suddenly pick out the bottle's distinctive mark, then as now a bright red triangle. Starting to snap out of it, he becomes self-consciously aware that Stephen and Mulligan are making fun of his moonstruck state. The spoof of occult jargon, arising from their raillery about "incorruptible eons" and "karmic law"—especially from Stephen, who has recently discussed "planes of consciousness" (U 7.785–88) with the mystical A.E., here remembered as "Theosophos"—generates the occult note on which his revery concludes. Specifically, Stephen's word "mysteries" returns as Bloom's "mysterious"—"T"—and, for "U" and "V," his closing words about the "planet Alpha of the lunar chain" in "the rubycoloured egos from the second constellation" become Bloom's closing image: "it blazes, Alpha, a ruby and triangled sign upon the forehead of Taurus." Taurus—"W"— is the second constellation of the Zodiac; the red-orange Aldebaran is its alpha (brightest) star. Finally, although not confident enough of this to put it on the chart, I would bet that the cue for that talismanic word "blazes" is Stephen's word "orangefiery"—or rather the actual word behind it, which I would— again—bet was "blazing." (As we will see later, the pairing of the words "blaze" and "star" have a personal meaning for Bloom.)

About this sequence as a whole, two things seem to stand out. The first is the degree to which it is given shape by Bloom's informed musings about the sky's progress, acted out in a mind's eye capable of working as a private planetarium. This is especially striking near the end. Bloom's culminating—very De Quincean—vision of the radiant Millicent metamorphosing into a red triangle in the forehead of Taurus extends his imagined account of that night's story of the heavens into the next day's dawn, when the constellation rising above the horizon will indeed be Taurus, prominently including Aldebaran, its "alpha" or brightest star, fiery orange in color, close enough to the forehead to be imagined as "upon" it (see chapter 10). Also prominent in that morning sky will be the planet Venus—and sure enough De Quincey's radiant Millicent ("harbinger of the daystar [that is, sun] . . . the radiant . . . a queen . . . in the penultimate an- telucan hour . . .") is also Venus, both planet and goddess, her gold sandals the predawn glow in the east immediately beneath the planet, the gossamer veil its opalescent surface. It may even be that her metamorphosis into the "ruby" Aldebaran of Taurus is facilitated by the fact that at dawn on June 17, 1904, Venus was in a rare near-conjunction with Mars, the red planet.[8] (See fig. 11 in chapter 10.)

Second, it seems clear that to a great extent this visionary narrative forged by Bloom out of the available background material functions as wish- fulfillment. The essential story to emerge is that Molly and Milly appear in all their grace and beauty, are eclipsed by a nightmare stampede of the forces of darkness led by the boisterously buffalonian Blazes Boylan, then finally reap- pear, reborn as the goddess of love ascending into the house of Bloom's birth sign, Taurus, horned but happy.

Finally, a word about theory. This reading does not have one. Except in the trivial debater's-point sense that all discursive utterances assume assumptions, the above has been neither driven nor informed by any particular theoretical model. What happened was that I noticed some connections and set to tracking them down, to the point that eventually I was with some confidence able to construct the chart of figure 1. But I am aware of what, in the meantime, the more theoretically sophisticated readings of "Oxen of the Sun" have been saying, many of them impressively intelligent, and the conclusion I have come to is that if I am right then they are wrong, and vice versa. One, at most, or the other: not both.

The reading I have given here and in the previous chapter is flatly incompatible with a belief that in "Oxen of the Sun" Joyce completes his staged disengagement from the realist canons of the opening episodes, from any gesture of correspondence between word and world, and embraces a program of self-generating, self-reflexive textuality. Unless figure 1's chart of correspondences and the story of sensory and psychological effects it illustrates is an (alarmingly) elaborate hallucination, unless the echoes and influences it affects to trace are nothing but a combination of coincidences in the text and self-delusion in myself, the Joyce responsible for all of this has been paying at least as much attention as he was in "Telemachus" or "Calypso" to what is really going on behind the verbal events. He has got—and if we want to follow him, we have got to construct—a mental map of what is really happening, of a virtual source of psychological and physical facts, in which lightning flashes and someone speaks of currant buns, and bottles of Bass Ale bear their familiar red triangles, just as they do in what, once again, we might as well call the real world.

Talk of real worlds is not, to say the least, in critical favor. According to the received opinion, what I have just tried to show happening should not be happening. To which, once again: *Eppur si muove*. Working on figure 1 while mindful of what has come to be the accepted version of "Oxen of the Sun," indeed of *Ulysses* in general, I have taken to envisioning myself as someone sitting in a garden, reading through the fabled physicists' report said to demonstrate conclusively that bumblebees are aerodynamically incapable of flight, then looking up to observe a bumblebee buzz through the air. That, finally, is my answer to the chorus saying that what I see and have attempted to show going on in "Oxen of the Sun" cannot be, that everyone knows that it has been shown by all the best authorities to be incapable of working that way. In a word, Buzz.

9

Bloom's Bell

ABOUT THAT BELL that sounds in the middle of "Oxen of the Sun,"[1] and why it triggers the reaction it does in Bloom's mind: Bloom has already heard a similar bell-sound today, one that like some other *Ulysses* percepts has accreted its share of personal associations. "Ithaca" enlightens us about its origin. It is there that we learn that the Blooms's basement kitchen features a "row of five coiled spring housebells" (*U* 17.151). Their function is to call servants.[2] They go back to a palmier time when the building's former residents maintained a "downstairs" staff, answering to one room or other according to which bell was rung. Lately, their presence has been a reminder of a question never far from Bloom's mind: who at 7 Eccles Street is the master, who the servant?

On June 16, the answer is obvious. Two things in particular torment Bloom when he thinks of Boylan's affair with Molly: the idea that he has become a servant in his own home, and the sound of a (jaunty) jingle. Three times in "Circe" alone, the two appear juxtaposed in Bloom's imagination when thoughts of Molly and Boylan arise. In Molly's first "Circe" apparition, he, in sequence, hears Molly calling him, answers "At your service," hallucinates her as a houri with Raoul-Boylan, and hears the jingling sound of her "wristbangles angriling" (*U* 15.317). In the Bello Cohen sequence, he is taunted as a cuckold, turned into a maidservant, and auctioned off to the sound of a ringing bell (*U* 15.2972–3149). In the reenactment of the Molly-Boylan tryst, he wears "a flunkey's plum plush coat" and so forth, and the bedspring sounds from the next room remind Lydia Douce of the nursery rhyme about the woman with bells on her toes (*U* 15.3759–61). (She has been anticipated at *U* 15.2944.) And, of course, the reenactment of his domestic degradation is supervised by someone named "Bella" or "Bello." Clearly, there is in Bloom's mind a fixed associative link between bell-sound, Molly-Boylan, and servitude.

The obvious catalyst for all this is one moment in "Sirens": "Bloom heard a jing, a little sound. He's off . . . Jingling. He's gone. Jingle" (*U* 11.458). It might be proposed that all the "Circe" jingling results from Bloom's anticipa-

116

tion, at this moment, of the shaking of his bed's loose quoits. Yet when those quoits do put in an appearance, they go not "jing" but "Jigjag, Jigajiga" (*U* 15.1138), and for Joyce such nuances are not negligible. Moreover, there is nothing in the "Sirens" passage to explain the persistent connection with servitude, with livery or housework. Instead of looking forward from the "Sirens" jingle in order to understand its effect, we should perhaps, as usual, look backward, to an unrecorded event of the day: Molly's ringing for Bloom on the servant's housebell connected to the bedroom, just before his eyes lit on Boylan's letter.

Now, according to the plan of 7 Eccles Street in Clive Hart and Leo Knuth's *A Topographical Guide to James Joyce's Ulysses*, diagrams B and C, the Blooms's housebells should be located a few feet below and about fifteen feet to the left of where Bloom is standing as he enters the hall. Through the floorboards, the distance separating them from Bloom is about twenty feet; indirectly, sound would have to travel perhaps sixty feet to be heard by the unobstructed route from the kitchen, up the stairs, and down the length of the hall. Assuming that the door connecting hall and front room is open, there would also be an unobstructed route via the chimney connecting the kitchen fireplace and front room ingle.

My point is that a man standing in the entrance to Bloom's house would likely be able to hear a bell being rung in the kitchen, albeit as "a jing, a little sound." That granted, we may understand the following: "He walked on. Where is my hat, by the way? Must have put it back on the peg. Or hanging up on the floor. Funny, I don't remember that. Hallstand too full. Four umbrellas, her raincloak. Picking up the letters. Drago's shopbell ringing. Queer I was just thinking that moment. Brown brilliantined hair over his collar. Just had a wash and brushup" (*U* 4.485–89). After "Funny, I don't remember that," Bloom starts exercising his mnemotechnic, trying to locate the missing image of the hat by recalling his impressions in reverse order of occurrence; as initially recorded at *U* 4.240–46, the conclusion about the overloaded hallstand would naturally have come after he reckoned up the umbrellas and raincoat, which he must have noticed after rather than before picking up the letters, certainly the first things to catch his attention on entering. So far so good. Then an oddity: "Drago's shopbell ringing. Queer I was just thinking that moment." But he wasn't, according to the record; he was thinking poetically about the sunlight as a golden-haired girl, then staring at the mail. Where does Drago's come in? We are evidently facing one of those gaps of the kind first pointed out by Hugh Kenner.[3]

We can fill it in if we hypothesize that Molly rings one of those kitchen housebells, the one calling servants to the bedroom, just as Bloom enters, and that Bloom, hearing it, is reminded forcefully of his newly subordinate status— not unnaturally, since she is summoning him to wait on her. Then the sequence of associations from lines 240 to 246 goes like this: (1) yellow sunlight; (2) a girl with yellow hair; (3) Milly Bloom, a girl with *"blond hair"* (*U* 17.896), emphasis added);[4] (4) door opens, revealing letters on floor; (5) bell rings as Molly calls "Poldy!";[5] (6) bell-sound and image of hair act together to conjure up an affective memory of Drago's hairdresser, with its ringing shopbell; (7) where Bloom has recently seen Boylan's *brown hair;* (8) which formula, as Bloom is simultaneously spotting the letter, morphs into the *"bold hand"* of the man—Boylan, from the Drago's sighting—of whom he was certainly "just thinking" as soon as he saw that handwriting.

This hypothesis would explain two puzzles. First, it explains what seems to me the otherwise intractable passage at *U* 4.488–89 ("Drago's shopbell ringing. Queer I was just thinking that moment. Brown brilliantined hair over his collar"). Second, it offers a way of understanding why Molly should be calling "Poldy!" to Bloom just as he enters (*U* 4.246) even though she almost certainly would not have heard him come in. (In leaving he has set the door ajar deliberately to avoid making any noise.) If, on the other hand, we assume that she is virtually unconscious when he tells her he is going out ("Mn" is her reply), that on gradually waking she becomes impatient for her tea ("What a time you were!" are her words as he enters with it [*U* 4.302]), that she thereupon starts ringing and calling for him, thinking him downstairs, things makes sense.

Another reason for going with this hypothesis is that it has apparently been anticipated in the parallel episode, "Telemachus." Hart has argued that the *"Liliata rutilantium"* at *U* 1.736–38 of that episode arises in Stephen's mind from the otherwise unrecorded sound of a church bell, ringing nearby.[6] Because we know that the repetition of the phrase in "Ithaca" (*U* 17.1230–31) is triggered by the bells of St. George, the argument seems convincing. And the hypothesis would then lead back to a search for a similar origin to the phrase's first occurrence, at *U* 1.276–77—at just the moment when Bloom, miles away, would be opening the door and hearing the housebell, thus initiating yet another of the synchronicities between Stephen's first episode and Bloom's.

To weigh the probabilities of this earlier bell-ringing, it will help to determine the temporal correspondence between the two parallel sequences, in "Telemachus" and "Calypso," which follow from the clouding over of the sun. These seem to me the main stages:

"Telemachus" (*U* 1.248–80)

A cloud began to cover the sun Slowly, shadowing the bay in deeper green . . . For those words, Stephen . . .

Where now?
Her secrets: old feather fans, tasselled dancecards . . .
Phantasmal mirth . . .
Folded away in the memory of nature . . .
In a dream, silently, she had come to him, her wasted body within its loose graveclothes giving off an odour of wax and rosewood, her breath bent over him with mute secret words, a faint odour of wetted ashes.

Her glazing eyes, staring out of death, to shake and bend my soul. On me alone. The ghostcandle to light her agony. Ghostly light on the tortured face . . .

Liliata rutilantium te confessorum circumdent: iubilantium te virginum chorus *excipiat.*
Ghoul! Chewer of corpses!
No mother. Let me be and let me live.

—Kinch ahoy!

Buck Mulligan's voice sang from within the tower. It came nearer up the staircase, calling again. Stephen, still trembling at his soul's cry, heard warm running sunlight and in the air behind him friendly words.

"Calypso" (*U* 4.218–48)

A cloud began to cover the sun wholly slowly wholly . . . an old woman's . . .

Desolation.
Grey horror seared his flesh. Folding the page into his pocket he turned into Eccles Street, hurrying homeward . . . the gentle smoke of tea, fume of the pan, sizzling butter. Be near her ample bedwarmed flesh. Yes. Yes.

Quick warm sunlight came running from Berkeley Road, swiftly, in slim sandals, along the brightening footpath. Runs, she runs to meet me, a girl with gold hair on the wind.

Two letters and a card lay on the hallfloor. He stopped and gathered them. Mrs Marion Bloom. His quick heart slowed at once. Bold hand. Mrs Marion

—Poldy!

Entering the bedroom he half-closed his eyes and walked through warm yellow twilight towards her tousled head.

Stephen apparently notices the "warm running sunlight" some seconds after Bloom does because his moody brooding has rendered him oblivious: he has "heard" the sun in Mulligan's voice rather than experiencing it directly as Mulligan's call awakens him to it. If these passages are as carefully paralleled as they appear to be, and if there is indeed an unrecorded bell-ringing as Bloom opens his door, we should look for another bell a couple of seconds before Mulligan calls to Stephen and Molly calls to Bloom—at just the point where Stephen imagines, for the first time, the peal of *Liliata rutilantium.* Now consider the recurrence of the phrase in "Circe":

THE CHOIR

Liliata rutilantium te confessorum. . . . Iubilantium te virginum. . . .

(From the top of a tower Buck Mulligan, in particoloured jester's dress of puce and yellow and clown's cap with curling bell, stands gaping at her, a smoking buttered split scone in his hand.)

BUCK MULLIGAN

She's beastly dead. The pity of it! Mulligan meets the afflicted mother. *(He upturns his eyes.)* Mercurial Malachi. (*U* 15.4163–68)

And: after a brief exchange between Stephen and his mother, Mulligan then "*Shakes his curling capbell*" (*U* 15.4178).

Everything else composing Mulligan's apparition in "Circe" recalls "Telemachus" (although his bread, in a transaction to be considered later, is now fused with his scone in "Wandering Rocks" [*U* 10.1087–88])—except for that bell-ringing. Somehow it has gotten mixed up with what is otherwise a hallucinated reenactment of Stephen's feelings and associations when an incorrigible jester interrupted his memories of his mother with a call to breakfast. How? One plausible answer is that before calling to him Mulligan accompanied the call by ringing a dinner bell, the sound from which Stephen assimilated into his brooding about Mrs. Dedalus's funeral, as he had just assimilated the returned sunlight as "Ghostly light on the tortured face." (That would at least help explain, incidentally, why Stephen imagines Mulligan's reappearance in "Scylla and Charybdis" as accompanied by "Bells with bells with bells aquiring" [*U* 9.501–2].) It is exactly what happens, in reverse, in *Finnegans Wake*: "the scholiast has hungrily misheard a deadman's toller as a muffinbell" (*FW* 121.35–36). And just as Molly's ringing for and calling out to Bloom makes him feel like a servant in his own home, Stephen, on being rung for and called by Mulligan, feels himself "A server of a servant" (*U* 1.312).

So it seems, I would argue, that there are indeed two parallel bell-ringings in the two eight o'clock episodes, situated, respectively, between about 240 and 280 lines from the beginnings of, and between four and nine lines from the ends of, their respective episodes. The second of these is the one recalled to Bloom by the sound of the bell in "Oxen of the Sun," reminding him, in a way that is, as usual, registered in the narrative voice of the moment—in this case that of "Junius," summoning guilty memories of humiliations and derelictions at home, as well as a scandal involving a servant.

10

Dublin

Sun, Moon, Stars

ASTROLOGICALLY, we have seen, Molly and Milly ascend to the heavens as the constellations Pegasus and Equuleus. This symbolically celestial event occurs accompanied by Milly's birth constellation of Gemini, in Molly's astrological house of Virgo, under Bloom's astrological sign of Taurus, all moving toward the at least encouraging conjunction of Venus and Mars in that sign, at the hour when Molly should be acting on her resolution to give her husband "one more chance" (*U* 18.1498).

Obviously, Joyce was paying attention to the skies of Bloomsnight. Technology makes it possible for us to follow him. Using a selection of computer astronomy programs,[1] I have charted the Dublin skies for *Ulysses* and, while at it, *Finnegans Wake* as well.[2]

Ulysses begins at about 8 A.M. with the sun at an altitude of 36.46 degrees and an azimuth of 100.31—in other words about a third of the way up the sky toward the zenith and about ten degrees south of due east. It is a fact incorporated into the book's lighting effect from its first page, when Mulligan becomes "Chrysostomos," his teeth glistening "with gold points" (*U* 1.26), because, facing the tower's stairhead from the gunrest to its north, he is, at least approximately, facing into the sun.[3] As for Bloom at the same hour: since Eccles Street runs, approximately, west by northwest, the sunshine is falling almost on a line but more toward the south—the "bright side" (*U* 4.77), as the narrative has it (see fig. 2). In the rendering of these and later lighting effects we will recognize, I think, the Joyce who according to report would describe how a particular Dublin scene "looked at different times of the day, in different kinds of light" (Jackson and Costello 1997, 202). Thus Bloom's right turn onto Dorset Street Lower takes him along the sunny side of that street and, lit up by sun's rays, the links in Dlugacz's window are "shiny" (*U* 4.142). Because the bedroom window

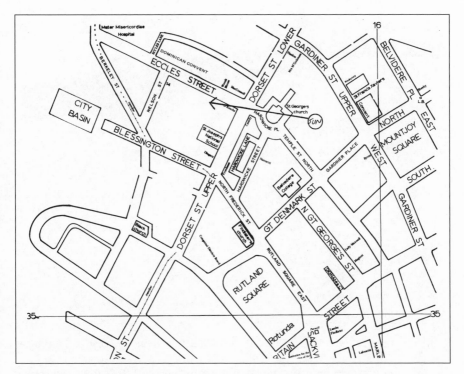

2. Morning sun on Eccles Street. From the *James Joyce Quarterly,* courtesy of the author.

of 7 Eccles Street faces east-northeast, Bloom can lift its blind (*U* 4.256) without letting in any glare.

At 10 A.M., the sun stands at an altitude of 52.20 degrees (high enough so that in "Nestor" it can stream through the leaves of a tree to throw checkerwork shadows "On [the] . . . shoulders" of Mr Deasy [*U* 2.448–49]) and has an azimuth of 132 degrees, almost exactly southeast. Standing in front of the Belfast and Oriental Tea Company, on the west side of Westland Row (running approximately north-south), Bloom is once again in the sun as he comments to himself on the warmth of the day, envisions a tropical land "in the sun," and imagines someone under a parasol floating in the Dead Sea, famously dehydrated by the sun (*U* 5.27–46). Likewise the fashionable lady whose stockings and veil "flash" "in the sun" is positioned in front of the Grosvenor Hotel, also on the sunny side of Westland Row (see fig. 3). After visiting Sweny's Bloom walks along Lincoln Place (and meets the dingy-seeming Lyons) on the south, in the shade. His spirits seem to lift ("He walked cheerfully . . .") as he comes on the gate of College Park, which at this hour is facing directly at the sun; it is here that he remarks

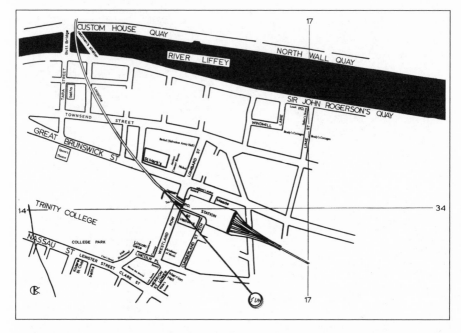

3. Morning sun in "Lotus Eaters." From the *James Joyce Quarterly*, courtesy of the author.

the "Heavenly weather" and muses pleasantly on cricket, Britain's summer game, with its sunshade-wearing spectators.

Near the end of "Proteus," at about 11:30 A.M., the sun, approaching apogee, has an altitude of 59.04 degrees (Stephen's shadow is here described as "ending" (*U* 3.408), and in fact it should be pretty stunted), and an azimuth of 169.69 degrees—"southing," as Stephen says. Turning his back to the sun to write his poem, he ponders what lies beyond the veil of daylight: "Darkly they are there behind this light, darkness shining in the brightness, delta of Cassiopeia, worlds" (*U* 3.409–10). Making poetry, he is thinking of Shakespeare, therefore of the nova that, as he will misleadingly relate in "Scylla and Charybdis," appeared near the delta (that is, fourth-brightest star) of the constellation Cassiopeia during Shakespeare's lifetime. Is he aware that behind the sky's blue, Cassiopeia is in fact roughly before him right now—with an azimuth of approximately 305, 135 degrees from the sun, it should be off to his left but well within his field of vision—at about the same altitude (around 52 degrees) as the sun? Stephen is no astronomer, but he has evidently noted, possibly last night, that at midnight in summer in the latitude of Dublin (and, virtually, Stratford), Cassiopeia, "eastward of the bear," is "lowlying on the horizon" (see fig. 4); noted too that it then lies to the northeast, where as he says Shakespeare would

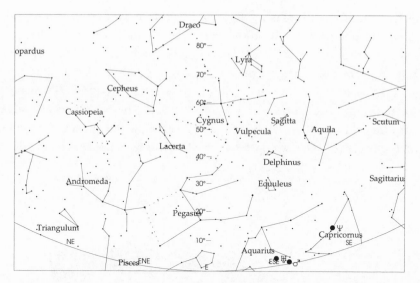

4. Mid-morning constellations. From the *James Joyce Quarterly*, courtesy of the author.

indeed have seen it as he was walking, through "the summer fields at midnight" along the eastward road from Shottery to Stratford (*U* 9.929–34). Knowing where it was approaching perigee, he should, in "Proteus," have a good idea of where it would be now, near apogee.

In the south-southeast, as "Hades" begins (azimuth 154.66 at 11:00 A.M.), the sun should be shining almost directly into the windows on the north side of Newbridge Avenue, where the cortege begins—hence the "lowered blinds of the avenue" (*U* 6.12). With Boylan standing in front of the Red Bank on the northeast side of D'Olier Street, his hat will have "flashed" as the sun strikes it at an angle of about twenty degrees to the storefront (*U* 6.199). Although the narrative does not specify just where Bloom is situated on his return out of the graveyard when the Glasnevin gates "glimmered in front" (*U* 6.995), according to the map of his walking route given by Jack McCarthy and Danis Rose he would at one point near the O'Connell Circle have been in position to see the sun directly over the cemetery's entranceway.[4]

Walking through Dublin when the sun is in the south-southwest (from 206.03 azimuth at 1 P.M. to 228.83 an hour later), Bloom in "Lestrygonians" is almost always on the sunny side: on the eastern sides of Westmoreland Street and Grafton Street as he heads south; to the north of Duke Street and Molesworth Street when he heads off to the east. (The exception is his stop at Davy Byrne's,

which he chooses on the rebound from his first choice, the Burton, to the north.)
It is as if his itinerary were illustrating the thought entertained in "Hades," that
the shady side of a street is liable to be spurned by pedestrians (*U* 6.316–18). The
sunlight's glare makes harsher the pitiless inventory of Mrs. Breen and illumi-
nates the "Gleaming" "Sunwarm" silks in the windows of Brown Thomas, on
the eastern side of Grafton Street (*U* 8.620–39, about a block from where, facing
south down the street and angling slightly to the right, Bloom blots out the sun
with his finger (*U* 8.565; see fig. 5). That when he meets Boylan coming down

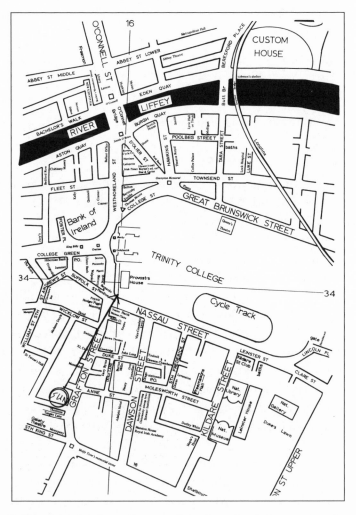

5. "Lestrygonians" sun. From the *James Joyce Quarterly,* courtesy of
the author.

Kildare Street he sees a "Straw hat in sunlight" and counts on there being "Light in his eyes" (*U* 8.1168, 1174) tells us that Boylan, besides walking south toward the sun, is on the far, eastern side.

Mrs. Breen and Bloom are nearly right when they say that there is a new moon (*U* 8.245, 584): it is three days old. At the moment of their meeting it has reached a height just short—by about two degrees—of apogee, which may have to do with the conspicuousness of the "two loonies" (*U* 8.478)—one of them incidentally based on a local character known as "Endymion"—that Bloom encounters. The latest full moon, seen last May 29 by Molly, Bloom, and Boylan in their east-southeast evening stroll along the Tolka, arose at 8:10 P.M. at an azimuth of 121.53—just about in front of them (see fig. 6).

The next time Stephen observes the sky, he is coming out of the National Library's reading room into the "shattering daylight" from a sun that, at a 2:30 P.M. azimuth of 242.26 and altitude of 46.34, should be, depending on his angle, approximately in front of him.[5] About his puzzling line "Wheelbarrow sun over arch of bridge" (*U* 9.1213), spoken at the moment he leaves the library, I hazard the guess that the sun has now begun its westering decline, a fact that in Stephen's Shakespearian mood may inspire his folkish picture of it as traversing its celestial arc like a wheelbarrow (its wheel the sun's disk) going over the hump of, for instance, the arched Ha'penny Bridge. Which bridge he might

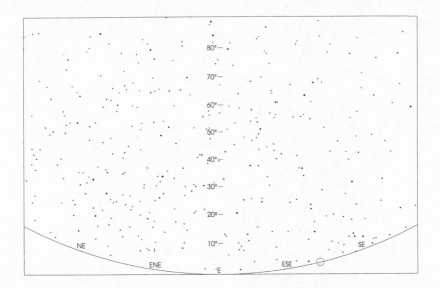

6. Full moon: May 29, 8:10 P.M. From the *James Joyce Quarterly,* courtesy of the author.

have noticed on his right while crossing the Liffey about an hour ago, with the sun hanging a few degrees off to the south, over Merchants' Arch, when first he would have glimpsed it as he came out of Sackville Street.

In "Wandering Rocks" the sun is at 44.9 degrees altitude and 245.05 degrees azimuth when Father Conmee begins his walk at 2:55 P.M.[6] The one-legged sailor he blesses before the Sisters of Charity Convent, on the eastern side of West Gardiner Street Upper, is accordingly "in the sun" (*U* 10.10): at this moment the sun's beams are only about eight degrees off meeting the street's eastern side at a right angle (see fig. 7). That eight-degree difference is enough to

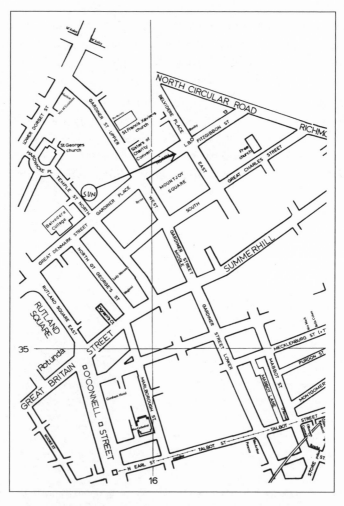

7. Sunlight, "Wandering Rocks." From the *James Joyce Quarterly*, courtesy of the author.

account for Mrs. David Sheehy's "beads of . . . mantilla inkshining in the sun" (U 10.31) as she stands on the northern edge (but south side of the street) of Mountjoy Square, a ninety-degree left turn off of Gardiner Street.

On the other hand, it takes some doing to explain, later, how the windscreen of a motorcar facing Tom Kernan might plausibly "flash" (U 10.759) into his eyes, given the route he is taking. Kernan at this moment is walking almost due east along James Street, which means that a car approaching him would have to be facing a due-west sun to reflect light into his eyes, whereas in fact the sun is almost twenty-five degrees off to the south. In correspondence with me, Clive Hart has kindly offered the suggestion that the car is not as I had supposed moving directly toward Kernan along the street but rather either parked at an angle (so that the flash occurs because of Kernan's movement rather than the vehicle's) or pulling out from an angled parking position.[7] To reflect a sun halfway down the sky, incidentally, the windscreen should be tilted slightly back from the perpendicular.

The other flashing glass of this episode is relatively easy to account for: Cashel . . . Farrell, standing at Wilde's house opposite the northern corner of Merrion Square, swivels his head from north-northeast (toward Merrion Hall)[8] to southwest (toward Duke's Lawn), catching the west-southwest sun in his eyeglass (U 10.1109–11). The observer who witnesses this, incidentally, would likely be standing on the corner diagonally opposite. The "glare" that makes Dilly Dedalus strain her eyes, on the other hand, does not come from any reflection. Her attention caught by the sound of the cavalcade approaching from the west along Dame Street, she looks up from her location in Fownes's Street (intersecting from the north) in its direction, into or almost into the west-southwest sun. Her vision is consequently dazzled: "In Fownes's street Dilly Dedalus, straining her sight upward from Chardenal's first French primer, saw sunshades spanned and wheelspokes spinning in the glare" (U 10.1226–29).

According to Hart's timetable, the action of "Sirens" begins at 3:38 P.M., when, in a "Wandering Rocks" interpolation, Misses Douce and Kennedy are first seen looking out, above the crossblind of the Ormond (U 10.962–63). By my calculations, the sun cannot be more than a few degrees from shining straight down the street in front of the Ormond. By 4:00 it should be out of the sight of anyone inside not pressing a nose to the window (at U 11.74–75 Miss Douce does just that); by 4:30 it should have withdrawn far enough to leave the bar in shadow (see fig. 8).[9] Which explains why when Miss Kennedy saunters from the window she is "gold no more" (U 11.82)—the light is streaming by the window more than into it—and why later Ben Dollard and Father Cowley, seen against bright doorway set off by dim surroundings, should become silhouettes

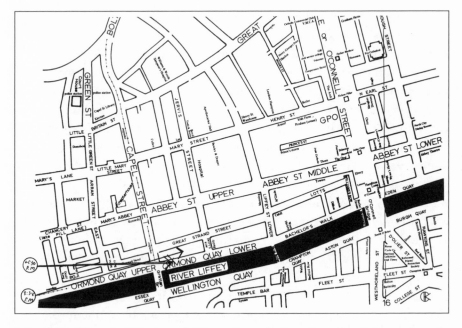

8. Sunlight, "Sirens"—3:38 P.M. and 4:30 P.M. From the *James Joyce Quarterly*, courtesy of the author.

(*U* 11.434). Added to all the other sources of the episode's gloom—including the fact that at about 4:00 Miss Douce lowers a dropblind (*U* 11.462)—we may perhaps add that things are getting darker at an accelerated rate, the normal dimming of this time of day accentuated by the sun's progression past the plane of the Ormond's front. It is getting darker for everyone, that is, except Boylan, who in contrast to the general atmosphere of "deepseashadow" (*U* 11.1137) is, perched on open-air jaunting-car, with "gay hat" and "skyblue clocks" (*U* 11.301, 978), at his flashiest, and whose approach and departure are very much in the sun. So, with a difference, is "the whore of the lane" encountered by Bloom at the episode's end; walking "glazily in the day" and looking "a fright in the day" (*U* 11.1252–53, 1259), she is heading west, facing into the sun.

Also facing into the sun is the citizen, at the end of "Cyclops," when he runs out of the pub and turns right (after Bloom, in the carriage) onto a street running about twenty degrees south of due west, so that the declining sun, only 21.28 degrees above the horizon, should be hitting his face at about a thirty-degree angle from its position at 280.88 degrees. (The testimony that he sends the biscuit tin "in a trajectory directed southwest by west" [*U* 13.1881] fits these directions.) As for Bloom, in his escape down Little Green Street his face—probably eight or nine feet above street level—might well be in a line with the sun, as seen from the angle of a sidewalk pedestrian on the eastern side of the street. I suspect that some such effect—Bloom standing, waving, the sun in aureole behind his shoulders and head—is behind the final vision of his ascent "in the glory of brightness, having raiment as of the sun" (*U* 13.1991–92).

"Nausicaa" begins at sunset—8:27 P.M.—and ends at about 9:00. It is the only period covered by *Ulysses* during which any of its characters can see the crescent moon, which has been following two hours behind the sun and will set shortly after 10:15, just about the time Stephen is intoning, "My moon and my sun thou has quenched for ever" (*U* 14.378).[10] Undoubtedly Gerty, gazing west toward Bloom and seeing the three-day-old moon hanging low in the sky behind him (see fig. 9), is affected; given the belief in the luck attendant on both new and waxing moons (Gifford and Seidman 1988, 163, 386), the juxtaposition may even have influenced her to reveal herself to this romantic stranger. Bloom seems to suspect something of the sort: "Must have the stage setting," he reflects about what has just occurred, "Moonlight silver effulgence" (*U* 13.855, 858). As suggested in that passage, as well as in his musings about menstruation or "the moon looking down" on a shipwreck (*U* 13.1164), he also seems conscious of its presence.

In terms of its effect on the narrative, the most important celestial event of *Ulysses* takes place during the unrecorded hour between "Nausicaa" and

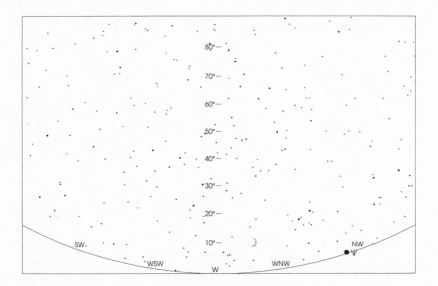

9. Moon in "Nausicaa." From the *James Joyce Quarterly,* courtesy of the author.

"Oxen of the Sun." Having nodded off at nine, Bloom will snooze, probably, for about half an hour before bestirring himself to catch the tram that will get him to Holles Street at about ten. Waking up, he will see before him—and recognize: as Lenehan says he knows them all, "the whole jingbang lot" (*U* 10.569)—the constellation Equuleus rising out of the sea, soon to be followed by Pegasus (see figs. 10 and 11). Perhaps because they chimed with his pre-sleep musings about Milly and Molly, he seems on waking to have forged an association between these paired constellations, little horse and big horse, on the one hand and his daughter and wife on the other. In any event, from whatever cause, his semi-hypnotic "De Quincey" evocation of Molly and Milly as mare and foal derives to a great extent from this earlier sighting on the beach.[11] Thus mother horse and "fillyfoal" emerge in the "dusk" as "Twilight phantoms," the one following the other,[12] then temporarily fade from sight (the clouds beginning to gather may have something to do with this) as they are followed by the "zodiacal host" trooping to drink from the "dead [that is, salt] sea"—the other beast-constellations rising over the horizon, arriving at the sea's edge—before following them up the sky "on the highway of the clouds." Chief among these constellations is Taurus, Bloom's birth sign,[13] which will be hanging just above the eastern horizon next morning during the "penultimate antelucan hour" before sunrise (at 3:35), with Venus, "harbinger of the daystar," or sun,[14] in its near vicinity,[15] only about ten degrees from the Pleiades (see fig. 12). Thus according

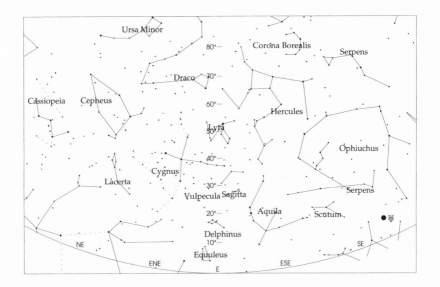

10. Equuleus rising. From the *James Joyce Quarterly,* courtesy of the author.

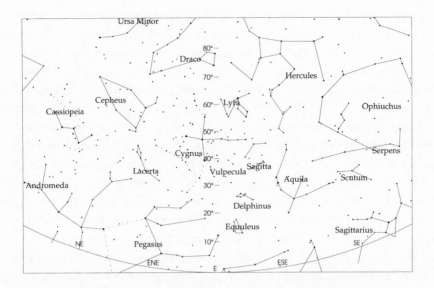

11. Pegasus rising. From the *James Joyce Quarterly,* courtesy of the author.

to "De Quincey" does Venus (as lambently radiant, mist-shrouded planet, as queen of love), "coifed in a veil of what do you call it gossamer," "arise," with some slight license, as "a queen among the Pleiades," "shod," as in "Calypso," "in sandals of bright gold"—the golden beams of the approaching sun, radiat-

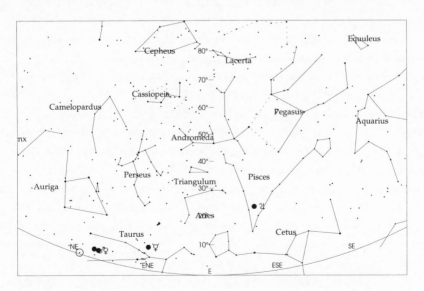

12. Dawn, June 17. From the *James Joyce Quarterly,* courtesy of the author.

ing up from the horizon. The conceit about the Pleiades enables the evocation of Taurus, on whose shoulder they are conventionally represented as perching, thus of "Alpha, a ruby and triangled sign upon the forehead of Taurus"—Aldebaran, the "alpha" star of the constellation, and at this hour of the whole sky, whose name means "fiery red." All of this takes place at least in the proximity of the zodiacal "house of Virgo" inscribed on the horizon.[16] With a certain minimal amount of pushing and shoving, Bloom's subconscious has taken his earlier night sighting, projected it forward with the aid of his knowledge of astronomy, and conjured from the resulting pageant a celestial fable in which a luminously matronly Molly appears, is momentarily obscured by the bestial Boylan ("the bulls of Bashan and of Babylon"), then, by means of the goddess of love, returns, as Virgo, to Bloom under his (highly ambivalent—we know what Shakespeare has to say about the horned foreheads of husbands) sign of Taurus.[17]

In "Ithaca," when Stephen and Bloom exit the rear of 7 Eccles Street, they are greeted by the brightest night sky either has likely seen in some time—moonless, shielded by house and fence from what astronomers call the "light pollution" of the city, its atmosphere washed clean by rain. Facing them as they exit, at about an angle of thirty degrees to their left, fifty-three degrees above the horizon, is Polaris, surrounded by the circumpolar constellations. The resplendent "heaventree of stars hung with humid [so there's still some moisture in the air] nightblue fruit" is Yggdrasill, Norse earth-tree said to transfix the heavens at the pole, with those constellations hanging from its branches like ornaments on a Christmas tree.

The scene in which Bloom and Stephen gaze at the heavens together requires little commentary. (I include a map of the sky they are seeing; see fig. 13). It may however be worth noting that the narrative's account of the meteorite's path, "from Vega in the Lyre above the zenith beyond the stargroup of the Tress of Berenice towards the zodiacal sign of Leo" (*U* 17.1211–13), is somewhat misleading: Coma Berenice, a dim constellation low in the sky, is almost certainly blocked from sight by the adjoining house and would probably be invisible in any case, and Leo is in fact below the horizon. (Hence, no doubt, the ambiguous "towards.")[18] As in the evocation of Pegasus, astronomical fact has been adjusted a little to accommodate myth. Having reached a point about halfway up the southeast sky, incidentally, Pegasus should now be hanging just about above the rear of the house and Molly's lighted window, as seen from the back of the garden.

Finally, two astronomical passages from *Finnegans Wake* that may help establish how that book is situated in time (I assume the Chapelizod-Dublin coordinates in space), and that I am especially happy to put forward because they

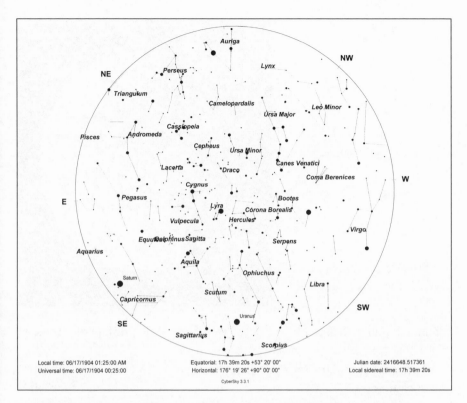

Local time: 06/17/1904 01:25:00 AM
Universal time: 06/17/1904 00:25:00

Equatorial: 17h 39m 20s +53° 20' 00"
Horizontal: 176° 19' 26" +90° 00' 00"

Julian date: 2416648.517361
Local sidereal time: 17h 39m 20s

CyberSky 3.3.1

13. Night sky, Bloomsnight. From the *James Joyce Quarterly*, courtesy of the author.

seem to support my long-standing belief (Gordon 1986, 37–43) that the book is set primarily on March 21, 1938, and on the morning of March 22. In *FW* iii.2, shortly after observing that the clock has just struck 2 A.M., Shaun sees himself tracking the "rugaby moon cumuliously godrolling himself westasleep amuckst the cloudscrums for to watch how carefully my nocturnal goose-mother would lay her new golden sheegg for me down under in the shy orient" (*FW* 449.34–50.2). The moon, that is, is a rugby ball rolling through the scrum of cumulus clouds.[19] Where does that idea come from? Neither Roland McHugh's *Annotations*, the *OED*, nor the Internet have anything on "rugby moon," and I have been unable to track it down in any of the usual sources on slang or folklore. I suggest that the coining is probably Joyce's own, to describe the moon when it most resembles the shape of a rugby ball (similar to the American football), alternately the egg of "golden sheegg," that is an oblate spheroid somewhere between the half-- and three-quarter phase. Which, as it happens, the moon was on the morning of March 22, 1938—61 percent toward the full and rising in the southeastern sky to an altitude of about seven degrees at the time

14. *Finnegans Wake* "rugaby"
moon. Courtesy of the author.

Shaun first notices it. (see figs. 14 and 15 for a large-scale printout of this moon and an inset picture of a rugby ball).

The second passage is the Muta-Juva dialogue of 609.24–610.34. For several pages leading up to this exchange there have been premonitions of the sun's imminent rising, which finally occurs at 610.03–4—"O horild haraflare! Who his dickhuns now rearrexes from underneath the memorialorum?"—at which point the sun is immediately hailed—"Fing Fing! King King!"—as the new lord

15. Rugby ball. Courtesy of the author.

of the day. And yet prior to this moment Muta and Juva have been talking about some other celestial monarch, "Old Head of Kettle puffing off the top of the mornin," a "thorly" figure who to Juva is "Dorminus master" and to Muta "Diminussed aster." I suggest that this figure is Jupiter, as planet and god, that the description of him as "twyly velleid" refers to the planet's barred, gaseous surface, and that his expression of "a leary on his rugular lips" gives us Jupiter's famous red spot (compare FW 582.32, where the father, to whom is later [FW 583.02] attributed a "juniper arx," has "Redspot his browband"), that as "Diminussed aster" he is a star fading in the dawn just as the pagan pantheon of which Jupiter was king faded before the Christian God, just as Lear—"leary"— was deposed, just as the night world over which he presided now gives way to day. That "he has help his crown [Lear again, parting his coronet in two] on the burkeley buy but has holf his crown on the Eurasian Generalissimo" (FW 610.11–13) bespeaks his intermediary position, at this moment, between the two worlds.

At 6:03 on the morning of March 22, 1938, as the sun was just beginning to show above the Irish Sea, Jupiter, the only planet in the sky (see fig. 16: the symbol in the lower right-hand corner is the astronomical sign for Jupiter), hung 7.33 degrees above the horizon, 38 degrees to the sun's south.[20]

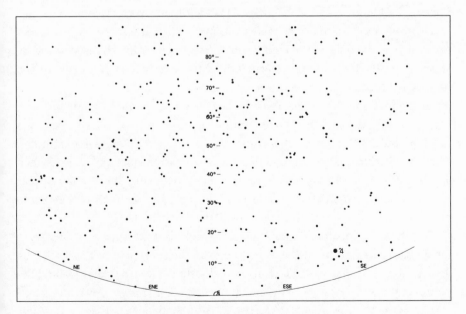

16. Dublin sky, 6:03 A.M., March 22, 1938. From the James Joyce Quarterly, courtesy of the author.

11

Bloom's Birth Star

THE "OXEN OF THE SUN" pageant summoned during Bloom's trance includes one other element both personal and astronomical. It includes Bloom's birth date, as established by the stars—one star in particular. That date was May 12, 1866. It can be arrived at as follows.

1. As we have just seen, at the climax of Bloom's vision a female figure traverses the sky from the house of Molly's astrological sign of Virgo to the constellation of Taurus and there, "after a myriad metamorphoses of symbol," "blazes" a scarlet *A*—"Alpha"—on its horned forehead (*U* 14.1104–9). We may, to begin with, take the hint that our resident cuckold is probably a Taurus, born between April 20 and May 20.[1]

2. "Eumaeus" narrows things further with Bloom's recollection of the Phoenix Park murders of May 6, 1882: "He vividly recollected when the occurrence alluded to took place as well as yesterday, roughly some score of years previously in the days of the land troubles, when it took the civilised world by storm, figuratively speaking, early in the eighties, eightyone to be correct, when he was just turned fifteen" (*U* 16.604–8). That helps, but "Eumaeus" is not the place for anything definitive. Twenty-three years ago is a pretty approximate "score," and in any case the "correct" number is twenty-two, since the year was not 1881 but 1882. Further, the syntax leaves it unclear whether Bloom had "just" had his birthday on the date, May 6, when the murders took place (which would put it around May 4 or 5) or at some time during the ensuing uproar (which would put it on May 7 or later). But the passage does confirm that Bloom was born in Taurus, probably some time in the first half of May.

3. "Ithaca," altogether a more reliable source, next informs us of "a star . . . which had appeared in and disappeared from the constellation of the Corona Septentrionalis [today called Corona Borealis, the Northern Crown], about the period of the birth of Leopold Bloom" (*U* 17.1123–26). This was, as Don Gifford (1988, 545) and John Henry Raleigh (1977, 15–16) both note, T. Corona Borealis, which did indeed flare from tenth magnitude to second magnitude in May of

1866. Now let me add two new pieces of information. First, among astronomers, T. Corona Borealis, which made quite an impression at the time, was and is popularly remembered as "the Blaze Star."[2] Second, the date of its appearance was May 12. Following the usual course of novae, it was at its brightest on that first night[3]—blazing into sight, so to speak—and faded away over the course of the week.

It could I suppose be a coincidence, but for reasons given below I don't think it is, that that star on the forehead of Bloom's birth-sign "blazes" there, thus making it a blaze star. More to the point at hand, the May 12 date perhaps gives us a *terminus ad quem* to the *terminus a quo* of May 4, though the borders may remain fuzzy. Bloom was born on one of the days extending from "just" the time of the fracas commencing with the first date to "about" the period of the nova commencing with the second date. The restricted range thus delimited may suggest that Joyce really did have a definite date in mind.

4. I think that "Ithaca" offers a further clue as to which one. It is there that we learn that on May 12, 1904, Bloom's weight was "certified by the graduated machine for periodical selfweighing in the premises of Francis Froedman, pharmaceutical chemist" (*U* 17.90–96). The word I would call attention to here is "periodical." It may be said to have two possible applications. In the language of the marketplace, it often means something like "intermittent," as in, " 'I was with Bob Doran, he's on one of his periodical bends' " (*U* 5.107), from which we are not really to conclude that Bob Doran goes on those bends according to a fixed schedule.[4] This usage is a colloquial derivative of the original, which is: recurring according to regular intervals longer than a day: usually, of a week, a fortnight, a month, or a year. The original *Saturday Evening Post* was called a "periodical" because it appeared every Saturday evening.

In the precisionist "Ithaca," usages of the latter sort are much likelier to apply. When "Ithaca" tells us that Bloom weighs himself on scales dedicated to "periodical" readings, the word probably does not mean "now and then." It probably means that the weighings are according to some regular established interval—that of, again, a week, a month, a fortnight, or a year. Which one? None of the first three, since the May 12 weighing was, the passage makes reasonably clear, the most recent. It might conceivably be quarterly or semiannually, but would we not then expect the date to correspond with the beginning of a quarter or half-year—to be April 1 or January 1? Why would anyone set up, for instance, a quarterly schedule keyed to the 12th of February, May, August, and November?

For the same reason, I suggest, that one would set up a routine of annual weighings each May 12, that there was something special about that day which made it an appropriate point to assess one's date-to-date progress. For example, if it were one's birthday. The list of Bloom's measurements given in "Ithaca" was compiled on the "chart" (*U* 17.1815) accompanying Eugen Sandow's *Physical Strength and How to Obtain It*, but for some reason skips the two first items listed on that chart, those of age and weight. Maybe that is because, lacking a scale, Bloom weighed himself away from home, on the day his age changed, in a separate self-assessing operation.

Or maybe not. In any case, if he does weigh himself at "periodical" intervals, they are probably annual intervals, and May 12 is not just a date in a cycle but the date in the cycle. People today traditionally reserve the resolution-making New Year's Day for such moments of truth. Birthdays would serve the purpose just as well. And May 12 is within the short period when Bloom's birthday should fall.

5. Finally, one other thing. If he was indeed born on the date of the Blaze Star, then Bloom, amateur astronomer, knows it, and, given the ways of his busy mind, it would not be surprising if he were to make something of it. I suggest that this knowledge, combined with Bloom's bent toward personalized myth-making, is behind the "Oxen of the Sun" account of how, "after a myriad meta-morphoses of symbol," that star, Bloom's star, "blazes, Alpha, a ruby and triangled sign upon the forehead of Taurus," his sign. I also suggest that for Bloom the meaning of a "blazes" mark fixed on the horned brow of that sign is all too clear: "Blazes" Boylan has branded our man with the insignia of cuck-oldry. As Molly will put it later, he is thereby "coronado" (*U* 18.1394)—crowned, with horns. Like Cain's red mark, the blaze sign broadcasts his shame.

In other words, Bloom, in his most prolonged brood on the most traumatic event of the day, has gone in for a spell of self-lacerating mythopoesis, confect-ing an interior drama out of astronomy, astrology, his cuckolding, and his birth date. But there is another story going on here too, made out of the same materi-als but amounting to the opposite of the first. In fact, the resemblance between the way the one imagined "Oxen" scenario yields to the other and the way sim-ilar glorious-to-ghastly morphings occur throughout Bloom's "Circe" halluci-nations (Lord Mayor Bloom to pariah Bloom, and so forth) is, it seems to me, one reason for taking the "Oxen" revery as strictly Bloom's own personal pro-duction. Another is the use it makes of the fact that he alone of the persons pres-ent would know his birth date.

In both cases, the key word is "alpha." Taking the second point first, let me quote again, one last time: "it blazes, Alpha, a ruby and triangled sign upon the forehead of Taurus." In astronomical terminology, as Bloom certainly knows, "alpha" is the brightest star (here, Aldebaran) in a constellation (here, Taurus). And, as it happens, the Blaze Star was an alpha too, for the duration, and only the duration, of the first night of its appearance, when it achieved a magnitude either equal to or greater than that of Alphecca, normally the alpha star of its constellation Corona Borealis.[5] That is, for one night, May 12, 1866, it could have been said of it that "it blazes, Alpha."

For the first point, we need only consider the meaning of the word itself, and attend to the resoundingly triumphalist tone of the passage in which it appears (U 14.1097–1109)—accompanying, as it does, the victorious homecoming being described. "Alpha," after all, means tops, first, best, number-one. It has also been, since "Nausicaa" (when the stars came out) Bloom's personal letter: "I" (U 13.1258) "AM. A." (U 13.1264) (Senn 1984, 355). Noting which, we may also reflect that to "blaze" is to be something splendid, and that Molly's coronado"—"crowned"—is, when non-ironic, a mark of elevation. As suggested in the previous chapter, the story being presented at this point of Bloom's astronomical allegory turns out to be not only of Boylan's ascendancy but, on second look, of the reverse, a story of Molly-as-Virgo (and Venus) crowning and rejoining her bright-blazoned Taurus while the usurper sinks back into darkness.

Where could Bloom have gotten the inspiration for this Uranian wish-fulfilling parable? I think he got it from his birth date. The Blaze Star that accompanied his birth certainly lent itself to personal allegorizing of the kind in which Bloom sometimes likes to indulge[6]—for instance in "Ithaca," in a passage that makes use of not one but two astronomical birth-blazings, one of them Bloom's and one of them Shakespeare's: "Whence, disappearing from the constellation of the Northern Crown he [Bloom] would somehow reappear reborn above delta in the constellation of Cassiopeia and after incalculable eons of peregrination return an estranged avenger, a wreaker of justice on malefactors, a dark crusader, a sleeper awakened, with financial resources (by supposition) surpassing those of Rothschild or the silver king" (U 17.2018–23). There's that ("coronado") crown again, this time unambiguously a mark of preeminence, in the form of the same Northern Crown in which T. Corona Borealis blazed into alphaic prominence on May 12, 1866. The story it is made to accommodate here is essentially that given in "Oxen of the Sun," a story of vindication over "malefactors" (for example, Boylan) confirmed by its reappearance as what Stephen, fudging outrageously, has earlier established as the birth nova of Shakespeare, who was also a Taurus and, according to Stephen, horned to boot.[7] (In "Scylla and Charybdis" Stephen had called the Shakespeare nova a "daystar"; in "Oxen of the Sun" Bloom's blazing alpha is also a "daystar" [*U* 9.928, 14.1100].)[8] And as in "Oxen of the Sun," the logic of the story dictates that it is the first blazing—alpha—appearance of the nova, and not the dwindling aftermath of the nights following May 12, that marks the critical juncture: having flared in one constellation, it will return to flare even more brightly (Bloom's nova having been one of "2nd magnitude," in comparison with Shakespeare's "1st magnitude" [*U* 17.1118–22] counterpart) in its metamorphically, metempsychotically, score-settling Ulyssean return. As the revived, returned alpha, Bloom will defeat that double-beta rival of his by, simply, outshining him. All of which is made possible by knowing, first, what "alpha" means in astronomical terms, and, second, that Shakespeare nova and Blaze Star were both, for a specific time, alphas.

I should add in conclusion that nothing else much seems to distinguish May 12 in any calendar of events, Joycean or public—no particularly pertinent battles or birthdays or saint's days or holy days.[9] May 12, 1866, was a Saturday, which would mean that, going by the old rhyme according to which Stephen "has far to go" (*U* 15.3687), Bloom "has to work for a living." Otherwise, it is just an ordinary run-of-the-mill day of the year. Like June 16.

12

Plotinus, Spencer Again, and the
Proliferant Continuances of "Oxen of the Sun"

WE HAVE REVIEWED how the changing voices of "Oxen of the Sun" reflect the internal changes of the principals, mainly Bloom; we have seen how intricate and far-ranging some of the resulting literarily rendered psychological composites can be. It remains to consider how both these influences, the centripetal and the centrifugal, play out according not just to the chronological sequence of events and the voices they generate, but also to the anagogical overlays that are probably this episode's best-known feature. As always, the starting point must be Joyce's tip to Frank Budgen that the episode's "progression" is "linked back" with, among other things, "the natural stages of development in the embryo and the periods of faunal evolution in general" (*L1* 140).

This last phrase can be taken as designating the phenomenon of growth on all levels, according to certain universal laws, as established by the Darwinian and post-Darwinian science of the day—and, again, by the derivative cosmology prominent in Joyce's youth. Chief among these is the "biogenetic law" that ontogeny recapitulates phylogeny.[1] It is this equation, after all, that best accounts for how an embryo's stages of development can parallel the history of "faunal evolution." It also licenses other evolutions, among them the "progression" of a language, a literature, a race, and a man.

In Joyce's day the biogenetic law was still cutting-edge science, useful for those, like Herbert Spencer, formulating universal principles of origins and unfoldings. But it was also, recognizably, an updating of the venerable doctrine, always attractive to Joyce's medieval mind, of correspondences, correspondences that it proposed to account for according to their developmental stages. As we have seen, Spencer saw these stages as microcosmically akin to the generation and dispersion of suns and the other astronomical hosts. Suns converge, incandesce, cool, and dissipate into increasingly far-flung and individuated epigones and epi-epigones; so with us: "we wail, batten, sport, clip, clasp, sunder, dwindle, die" (392–93). Joyce, I think, kept this school of thought firmly in mind, but also recognized its anticipation in another school also given to seeing life as a progression from the sun outward, into ever fainter and less integrated forms. Stanley Sultan has shown that throughout "Oxen of the Sun," the sun is a central presence, associated, from the first word, with conception (Sultan 1964, 248 ff.): hence the *deshil* theme covered in chapter 7. There is a long precedent for that connection, one that in the tradition Joyce inherited was most prominently represented by the neo-Platonists, in particular Plotinus: "When living things reproduce their kind, it is that the Reason-Principles within them stir them, the procreative act is the expression of a contemplation, a travail towards the creation of many forms, many objects of contemplation, so that the universe may be filled full with Reason-Principles and that contemplation may be, as nearly as possible, endless: to bring anything into being is to produce an Ideal-Form and that again is to enrich the universe with contemplation: So Love, too, is vision with the pursuit of Ideal-Form" (Plotinus 1956, 63). Procreation is a kind of contemplation because its proper goal is a return to the original unity that Plotinus and his followers symbolized as the sun. Both activities are prompted by the "Reason-Principles," which in turn derive from the One. In a Plotinian universe, where multiplicity equals nature's fall from the One, any act of union is a return, and sexual intercourse therefore enacts the soul's attempt at reintegration.

"Oxen of the Sun" is framed by this partly ancient, partly *au courant* conceit. It relates to the paradigmatic Plotinian journey from light and unity to darkness and disintegration the phenomenon of organic development in a variety of manifestations, each one as part of a journey from a sun-like realm of transcendent brightness and unity into darkness, through emanations progressively dimmer and more remote. In this it, once again, reflects the cast of mind of, mainly, Leopold Bloom, experiencing a time of spiritual testing in which failure equals sterility and salvation equals renewed marital relations resulting in conception. For Bloom the main story of "Oxen of the Sun" is of a progressive descent into self-absorbed surrender—his version of Stephen's "angenbite of inwit"—which is, perhaps, reversed near the end. On any number of levels (I have no idea how many) he follows an outward-bound Plotinian course up until the point where the prospect of "proliferant continuance," "Love," "procreation," the refilling of an emptying "universe," bids him to reverse course, or at least try. In the process he winds up first lamenting the disappearance of, and then affirming the return of, domestic and patriarchal values. Politically speaking, this is Bloom's most right-wing spell of the day, and as always its sentiments have their causes in the here and now, in a *mise-en-scène* that must seem to him—what with all the drinking and cursing and all-round bad behavior—like a slide into anarchy and dissipation.

There are other causes too: apart from the Holles Street associations noted earlier, Bloom is tired; he has recently masturbated and is feeling low and self-reproachful; he is an outraged husband newly goaded into appreciating the preciousness of home, hearth, and marriage vows; at such times he is prone, as "Ithaca" puts it, to "experience a sentiment of remorse" about having "in immature impatience . . . treated with disrespect" certain patriarchal "beliefs and practices" (*U* 17.1893–95). Like Odysseus he wants to return home, to the way things used to be—an impulse easily translated into the ideology of reaction.

The trajectory of this impulse is enacted through a number of journeys. Here are seven.

Linguistic. Joyce described the episode as "enclosed between the headpiece and tailpiece of opposite chaos" (*L3* 16). The chronicle of English prose styles evolves from one "chaos"—one kind of near-nonsense—to another. The first, paradoxically, is monistic—ridiculously long sentences, held together with overstretched syntax. By contrast the concluding pages are "modern"—a fragmented, slangy spray of dialects, over which any attempt at imposing hypotactic structure or any other kind of subordination has been abandoned. The newborn is the offspring of Theodore Purefoy, whose name combines Greek and Latin derivatives (to spell out Gift-of-God Pure-faith), and the Germanic "Wilhelmina"; the language whose growth parallels his evolves from the fusion of these two principles into the modern "strife of tongues" (952). His birth-cry is a babel.

Literary. Correspondingly, as Spencer would have affirmed, the growth of English prose is from homogeneity to heterogeneity, paralleling the evolution of literature from its ancient communal origins to modern ideas of "finding one's voice" and copyrighting it. The progression is most obvious if we contrast the early voices with those of the end: whereas the former tend to blend together in a general impression of medieval quaintness, the latter are much more distinguishable. To an extent this is owing to our greater familiarity with the recent past: For most of us, Joyce parodying Mandeville is a bit like some nightclub impressionist trying to amuse us with a take-off on Henry Clay or Dolly Madison. But it also reflects literature's embryo-like differentiation into specialists and eccentrics. Accordingly there is a good deal of generic or group authorship at the beginning ("Medieval prose," "Elizabethan prose," "Milton-Taylor-Hooker-Burton") but none toward the end. So too, toward the end, each paragraph is increasingly liable to be a distinct unit representing a new departure: each of the first six voices runs on for two paragraphs or more, while five of the last six last for only one paragraph.

Historical. Naturally enough, the episode's chronology of literary voices reflects historical changes in the human image.[2] The "Roman" is impossibly high-minded, marmoreal, res publica—hence that syntax, binding everything together as in a bundle of fasces; the "Medieval" section is wide-eyed and pious; the humanism of the Renaissance is, in a juvenile sort of way, assertive and boisterous; the Eighteenth Century is assured and personable, though occasionally refractory; the Nineteenth Century, once described by Joyce as "the full tide of rationalistic positivism and equal democratic rights for everybody" (*JJ* 648), is a gentleman's club of eccentrics, disintegrating into the anarchy of the modern age. The history of literature is a chart of civilization's journey from absolute unity into absolute chaos. Humanism and individualism are symptoms of disintegration, and eccentricity, as exhibited for instance by "Costello, the eccentric" (1208), corresponds to the malignant mutations of birth deformities, of a "wretch that seemed to him a crop-eared creature of a misshapen gibbosity born out of wedlock" (853–55).

Political. Viewed in this light, the episode's literary history is a middle term equating the progress of all civilizations with the stages of embryological growth. Its literary criticism is heavy with implied political commentary. The opening chant derives from the fertility rite conducted by the Arval Brethren (Gilbert 1958, 296), an elite Roman sect carrying forward the apostolic succession of Roman leadership, performing an incantation recorded in antique Latin and considered as among "the oldest documents of their mother-tongue."[3]

That is, the episode's opening words come from the most distant past of the civilization from which the European states have evolved. The fertility celebrated in them represents the renewal of connections with buried origins. The Anglicized "Sallustian-Tacitean" speaker who follows then acts as a spokesman for the importance of these connections over everything else:

> Universally that person's acumen is esteemed very little perceptive concerning whatsoever matters are being held as most profitable by mortals with sapience endowed to be studied who is ignorant of that which the most in doctrine erudite and certainly by reason of that in them high mind's ornament deserving of veneration constantly maintain when by general consent they affirm that other circumstances being equal by no exterior splendour is the prosperity of a nation more efficaciously asserted than by the measure of how far forward may have progressed the tribute of its solicitude for that proliferant continuance which of

evils the original if it be absent when fortunately present constitutes the certain
sign of omnipollent nature's incorrupted benefaction. (7–17)

However labyrinthine, the cast of thought here is simple. It may be translated
without much loss as "Anyone who knows anything agrees that a nation's first
priority should be the business of childbirth." Everything is measured against a
standard characterized by highness, brightness, ancientness, plenitude, and of
course unity. The association between the solar and the generative sources of
life established with the first line thus begins the long process of its discursive
elaboration. A political parallel is added. "Eccentric" deviation from the eternal
absolutes of national destiny will lead to decline and fall. "Universal" condem-
nation awaits anyone who denies what has been "constantly" maintained by
"general consent" of those most "deserving of veneration" because of their
"high mind's ornament," to wit that a nation's prosperity is directly propor-
tional to the extent of its progress in caring for "proliferant continuance"—
motherhood. The concluding description of maternity is thoroughly Plotinian,
with fertility the source of all good, the loss of which is comparable to the re-
moval of sun and God. The next sentence likewise emphasizes the need for continuity with this sun-bright, "omnipollent" "incorrupted" origin: it admonishes
us not to be so "unilluminated" as to sink into a national "downwardtending
lutulent" [that is, darkening] decline by consigning the "honourable by ancestors transmitted customs" to a "thither of profundity"; we are to tremble "lest
what had in the past been by the nation excellently commenced might be in the
future not with similar excellence accomplished" and reminded of God's original command at the beginning of history to be fruitful and multiply.

Delivered in public exhortation, with insistent references to national destiny
and the duties of "every most just citizen," this voice sets the tone for an episode
that typically inclines toward public addresses and documents. (Buck Mulligan's lechery is institutionalized as a "national fertilizing farm" [402], Mina
Purefoy's baby is certified "in the presence of the secretary of state for domestic
affairs" [41], and so on.) Speaking on behalf of genetic continuity, it begins by
celebrating not the great medical practitioners of the Irish but rather their great
medical families, who have "sedulously set down" (37) their findings for their
successors and are remembered for their establishment of public institutions,
hospitals. Throughout the public discourses to follow, communal values are repeatedly invoked at the expense of private impulse. Giving birth is an act of
civic high-mindedness, carried out by female citizens in the "high sunbright
wellbuilt fair home of mothers" while contemplating "images, divine and

human" selected for their inspiriting effects (66–67). In their own way, even the (traditionally) irreverent medical students are concerned with maintaining the standards of the aristocracy, of which they consider themselves members. They divide society into "high" and "low" orders, with themselves of course honored as "right witty scholars" (202) given to denigrating the "mean people" (212–13), "lay folk" (223), "the lewd" (311), and the "low" (836) who speak "the vile parlance of our lowerclass" (1298); when they hold a meeting it is as "the keenest in the land" "engaged on the loftiest and most vital" theme (1200–1201). When Mulligan facetiously repeats the "Medieval" recommendation that mothers be removed from "all very distracting spectacles," there lies behind his words an authentic "Sallustian-Tacitean" disgust with the "low" orders of life (1248); Stephen, with his "perverted transcendentalism" (1223–24), follows with a similarly supercilious catalogue of the "municipal abattoir" (1294). It is as if, according to them, the opening forebodings about a national decline into lutulence had come true. Stephen, as Jeremiah, charges the Irish with sliding into "tenebrosity," using language drawing on the identification between sun, Godhead, and life-source established on the opening page: thus the Irish have "sinned against the light," denying God "to the Roman and the Indian of dark speech," so that God's "moon" and "sun" have been "quenched for ever" (378). They have become uprooted from that past which the Arval Brethren and "Sallustian-Tacitean" orator considered vital for a nation's health. Like "Junius" Bloom they are "an exotic tree which, when rooted in its native orient throve and flourished and was abundant in balm but . . . [now] its roots have lost their quondam vigor" (940).

Plotinus describes procreation as a "vision with the pursuit of Ideal-Form" because he considers it as a return to the source. In "Oxen of the Sun," the political analogy is to those "re-affirmations" that high-minded orators are always urging. A nation whose "loftiest" citizens frustrate or, as here, celebrate the frustration of this act on one level will lose touch with their roots on another level, and the state will dwindle and fall.[4] Ireland's sin is a denial of the continuity that procreation symbolizes. Most specifically, its sin is a denial of memory: "Remember, Erin, thy generations and thy days of old . . ." "Return, return, Clan Milly: forget me not, O Milesian" (371–72). Catholicism's argument against birth control is thus mobilized to give the general rootlessness of these young Irishmen an ideological dimension. Personal and national vitality both depend on seeing backwards to origins (all "honourable by ancestors transmitted customs") and forward to ends (the province of "foresight," "anticipation," and "prudent" vision), "lest what had in the past been by the nation excellently commenced might be in the future not with similar excellence accomplished." This is what has been blocked off by use of the humble contraceptive commemorated in these pages.[5] Denying God in the act of frustrating conception, the students have become sunk in "hellprate and paganry" (411), even if they do have recrudescences of piety—for instance Costello's reaffirmation of love for the parents on whom he "looks back" (844). The central event of the episode, the renewed fatherhood of Mr. Gift-of-God Pure-faith, epitomizing the "Sallustian-Tacitean" values they flout, comes as reproach. It is announced as the birth of an "heir" (945), that is as the proper representative of family and civic continuity. As "Dickens" says, it is the "fruit of . . . lawful embraces" affirming the sovereignty of "One above, the Universal Husband," whose "good and faithful servant" Purefoy has been, as well as a community with past generations: "Those who have passed on, who have gone before, are happy too as they gaze down and smile upon the touching scene" (1314–22).[6]

The values associated with the Purefoy birth are thus translated into political agenda. When the medical students become irreverent about Mrs. Purefoy's accouchement, the voice of that old Roman bore returns in the diction of the Augustans to fret once again over the nation's decline, saying that he "want[s] patience" with those who "revile" the "ennobling profession" of medicine, that he fears for a future where "no right reverence is rendered to mother and maid" (833–34). This "right reverence" is, as always, for the memory of the past. As the episode develops and the characters more and more abandon "right reverence," the kinds of memory they experience undergo a change that is the clearest sign of the community's disintegration. The memory invoked on the first page is deep-rooted and communal, binding society together in a continuum reaching from unfathomable past to unfathomable future, by its nature based on a unity greater than any one time or individual. At the "Milton-Taylor-Hooker-Browne" passage this memory has been obscured by the "adiaphane" associated with the fall of man and the decline of the Irish nation, which has forgotten its origins.

By "Swift," the nation's history has become a witlings' plaything. By the time we get to the nineteenth century—that "full tide" of eccentric individualism—everyone is becoming lost in private memories: Stephen and Costello in the language of "Landor," Purefoy in "Dickens," Bloom in "Lamb," "de Quincey," and "Pater." Intones "Newman": "There are sins or (let us call them as the world calls them) evil memories which are hidden away by man in the darkest places of the heart but they abide there and wait . . ." (1345–46). This is what memory has become by the end—each individual's private signature of his own fallen state. The episode that begins with an appeal to memory therefore ends in a rush to forget, with the speaker of the closing pages ordering "absinthe"—famously the drink of oblivion—for "the lot" (1533).

The floodgates have really begun to open with the introduction of the Romantics—the name itself, from "Rome," ironically marks the distance declined—whose cult of private memory equals a repudiation of public legacies. Haines is described in the language of the pre-Romantic Walpole, with a "portfolio full of Celtic literature in one hand, in the other a phial marked *Poison*," confessing how he "tried to obliterate" his "crime" with "Distractions," among them "the Erse language."(1021–24). Like his laudanum, the novelty of Celtic offers distraction to the history-haunted Englishman, as imperial civilization, sick of its guilty past, repudiates the root and branch of its inheritance in turning, in "Romantic" gesture, to local dialects and literatures. (All this corresponds to the terminally "dissipated" stage in the nebular process.) In "Circe" the "End of the World" has a Scottish accent (*U* 15.2181), and likewise here the last few apocalyptic pages are characterized by an influx of Scottish ("Carlyle," Crotthers), American (Dowie), and other dialects from the extreme borders of Western civilization, along with various references to "injuns," "coons," "sheenies," "Rooshians," "Jappies," and so forth. It becomes, that is, provincial. Civilization has "evolved" from Rome to the provinces, from Latin into a multitude of dialects, from communal memory and veneration into a collection of private memories, from Roman classicism into provincial Romanticism, from one universal Catholicism into many Protestantisms, from unanimous "concordance" (389) into "tempers so divergent" that they can be united only in lewd "discursiveness" (954), from the noble "universality" of the first page into "Carlyle's" very different kind: "a universal grabbing at headgear, ashplants, bilbos, Panama hats and scabbards, Zermatt alpenstocks and whatnot. A dedale of lusty youths . . ." (1394–95). It has become a "dedale" in the sense used here and earlier in Costello's verse (405)—a hopelessly complicated maze, whose plan no one can understand.

The movement reflects the development of Western culture and its mirror, literature, in a geographical as well as a temporal sense. We begin in Rome, looking backward, and by the end have through the agency of Alexander J. Dowie—the idea of the Irish turning to an American for salvation is proof enough of national degeneration—nearly circumnavigated the globe, "from 'Frisco Beach to Vladivostok" (1585).

Biblical. Another one of the episode's temporal journeys is the traditional biblical history of mankind. The episode opens with the original *lux fiat*, introduces Man (Bloom), Woman (Nurse Callan), and a Tempter (Dixon and the revelers). When on the verge of getting carried away, the company is rebuked by an Old Testament prophet (367–80) and checked by a thunderclap (408) and, later, a flood. Midway through the episode its central event, the birth of a child named Purefoy, is announced, like the moment of consecration in the Mass, with the ringing of a bell (797); parallels to the nativity are drawn several times. Finally, the episode ends with a fire (1569–71) just as prophesied (the Old Testament prophet Malachi's prediction that "after wind and water fire shall come" has been mentioned by "Pepys-Evelyn" at line 523) while Alexander J. Dowie proclaims the end of the world.[7]

Astronomical. The episode's first word means "sunwards"; by the time we get to "Carlyle" near the end we are in the "starshiny *coelum*" (1408) and drinking from the Milky Way (1434–36); the concluding 150 lines are palpably a journey through outer darkness. The episode is on a course of first interplanetary and then interstellar space travel, moving from the sun outward, and the intervening heavenly bodies are more or less recognizable in both their astronomical and their mythical guises.[8] We begin in the vicinity ("Deshil") of the sun ("bright one, light one") and, in the company of the traveler Mercury (the "wayfaring" Bloom [71]),[9] start the journey into deepening lutulence.[10] Venus is Nurse Callan, introduced at line 80, an ever-luminous paragon of comely young womanhood (89–92, 120–21, 803–4, 829–30). For about the next 150 lines, the text draws heavily on the language of Genesis to present us with the earth— all of its four elements and their domains: ("seafloor," "good ground," "the air," "white flames"), its forests and mountains and caverns, its denizens (fish, "serpents," "buffalos and stags," "small creatures"), its terrestrial lands ("Chaldee," "Portugal," "the occident," the land of "Mahound," "Alba Longa," "Eblana") and extraterrestrial last things ("limbo," "purgefire," "heaven," the place of "swinking demons")—awaiting its inhabitants, who are reminded of the "earthly" (249) lesson (107–10 and throughout) that man, born of earth, must eventually return to it. "Circe" provides a hint to help spot the next planet: reading Stephen's palm, Zoe interprets his Mount of Mars: "Mars, that's courage" (*U* 15.2657). So, at line 274, Bloom thinks of his dead son as having been of "gentle courage," and turns his attention to Stephen, said to have—with unwonted violence—"murdered his goods with whores" (276); we will later hear of the students as a group having slaughtered innocents with a "stout shield of oxengut" called "Killchild" (467).[11] Stephen then asks everyone to "Mark him" (292), by way of initiating an exchange that soon becomes a "gasteful turmoil" (321)—if not exactly warlike, as obstreperous as anything in the episode. In lines 408–650 Jupiter—king of the gods, king of the planets—assumes influence under different guises. An echo of Anglo-Saxon ascribes the thunder outside to "Thor . . . the hammerhurler," "the god self" (411).[12] Stephen names him as the Blakean "Nobodaddy," "Bunyan" as the "god Bringforth" (436). The Swiftian parable that follows, recasting the ubiquitous oxen theme as a version of the Zeus-and-Europa story, describes the women of Ireland giving themselves to a godlike bull. Jupiter is, astrologically, jovial, and these lines are accordingly the most gregarious so far, culminating in Bannon's paean to God as the "Giver of good things" (752) and "Beneficent Disseminator of blessing" (766). Such language is also appropriate to the golden reign of Saturn, god of fertility and childbirth. (It may be a coincidence, but probably isn't, that one of the voices announcing Saturn's age of gold is "Goldsmith.")[13] At the conjunction of the influences of these two giant planets, at the height of the jovial Saturnalia in the hall, the Purefoy baby, happily enough, is born.[14] But Saturn has another aspect, preserved in our word *saturnine*; in the words of an astrology handbook, "Saturn represents cold, contraction, seriousness, stability, discipline, and practicality" (Goodavage 1968, 212). This influence takes over as the Purefoy birth is announced and we drift completely outside of Jupiter's orbit: "Goldsmith" denounces the "general vacant hilarity" (799), and "Burke," "Sheridan," "Junius," and "Gibbon" all follow in kind. The next planetary deity, Uranus, is traditionally represented by the image of a fatherly old man; his presence here registers in the many father-figures suddenly in prominence.[15] As husband of the Earth he is "the Universal Husband" (1319); as god of the heavens he is "Carlyle" 's "starshiny *coelum*" (1408). (Uranus's other name is "Caelus.") The last planet before outer space is Neptune, who as the sea-god Poseidon (or "pissedon," as he is called in the babble [1456]),[16] swamps Odysseus's crew in the flood recorded from line 1407 on. It should be noted that the nine stages of this journey—the sun plus the eight planets—match the nine stages of literary and embryological development outlined by Joyce, although Pluto was to foul all that up by being discovered eight years after the publication of *Ulysses*.[17]

The important thing about this Joycean *jeu* is that it literalizes Plotinus's metaphor for human life as a journey away from the sun. Even as we begin the outward voyage on the first page the narrator warns us against slipping into "lutulence" and a "thither of profundity"; by line 392 our "subsolar being" has become shrouded in darkness, especially when it tries to "backward see" into its origins; by 1073 "the bride of darkness" will never bear "the sunnygolden babe of day"; near the end we are in sight of the Milky Way ("See! It displodes for thee in abundance! Drink, man, an udderful! Mother's milk, Purefoy, the milk of human kin, milk too of those burgeoning stars overhead" (1432–35), with nothing else ahead of us but the darkness: "Forward, woozy wobblers! Night. Night" (1562). (Seeking money, someone is unhappy to see that "no shiners is acoming" [1500]; earlier there had been plenty of "glistering coins" on display [285–86].) The journey is almost entirely Bloom's. He is not (of course) really a spaceship but perhaps a comet, coasting the sun and traveling out to the verge of the cosmos past the planetary orbits. Thus he is introduced as a wanderer (72), a word that, as shown in "Ithaca," he has been taught to connect with comets:[18]

> Would the departed never nowhere nohow reappear?
> Ever he would wander, selfcompelled, to the extreme limit of his cometary orbit, beyond the fixed stars and variable suns and telescopic planets, astronomical waifs and strays, to the extreme boundary of space, passing from land to land, among peoples, amid events. (*U* 17.2012–16)

Biographical. Along with all the other -cosms, the episode charts the life of a microcosm, a single male human, from conception to death.[19] Like Blake's Mental Traveller, he assumes a series of allotropic identities. He is conceived with the seminal *lux fiat* of "Deshil Holles Eamus" (line 1) introducing the nineparted gestation theme (three sentences, each repeated three times) that will run throughout the episode. At line 60 he has become conspicuous enough to shift the narrative's attention away from the pregnant mother to the prenatal soul within her: "Before born babe bliss had." At line 71 the still unnamed figure is described as standing by the "housedoor." In the first lines of the next paragraph the gates are opened to him,[20] he leaps into the world in a gush of afterbirth (and a sudden flash of new light: lightning), is baptized with the sign of the cross, and sheltered in a hospital crib: "the watcher . . . to him her gate wide undid. Lo, levin leaping lightens in eyeblink Ireland's westward welkin! Full she dread that God the Wreaker all mankind would fordo with water for his evil sins. Christ's rood made she on breastbone and him drew that he would rathe infare under her thatch. That man her will wotting worthful went in Horne's house" (80–85). As an infant he is taught his first lesson, about death: "for as he came naked forth from his mother's womb so naked shall he wend him at the last to go as he came" (108–10). Nurse Callan, who blushed and beamed on him at his birth (91), assumes the motherly role of instructress and "nursingwoman" (112). In the "Mandeville" passage he shows the wonder and confusion of a child encountering the world for the first time: his bee-sting is a wound inflicted by a "horrible and dreadful dragon" who, curiously, seems to carry a spear (129–30), and a tin of sardines is "a vat of silver that was moved by craft to open in the which lay strange fishes withouten heads" (149–48). ("Malory" also calls him "childe Leopold" [160].) This is also the passage where he meets his first childhood friends, who by line 202 have grown into schoolmates: "For they were right witty scholars." The ensuing discussion is a catechism on the subjects of "birth and righteousness" (203) and "mother Church" (241), at the resolution of which Stephen administers a First Communion (277–83). Shortly after this, puberty arrives and things become bawdy and riotous. (Along with the matriarchal Nurse Quigley, Bloom, now transformed into father-figure as the focus shifts to Stephen, tries to restore order.) Stephen's adolescent sins of the flesh are recalled from the second chapter of *Portrait*. He is rallied for his "nefarious deeds" of lechery (338), and there is ceremonial deflowering. As in *Portrait*, lust leads to revulsion: Stephen sees himself as sunk in darkness (380–83) and is rebuked by God for having sold his soul to "Carnal Concupiscence" (484). The succeeding few pages are given over to the banter of the "covey of wags, likely brangling fellows" (505), then to the twenty-odd-year-old Mulligan; all are now a little older, the persiflage collegiate rather than adolescent. Things continue in this vein until the announcement of the Purefoy birth, at which point the narrative abruptly, like a young man awakening to responsibility at the arrival of his first child, grows up. "Goldsmith" and Dixon together rebuke Costello and reassert the "right reverence" due to motherhood (833), and "Burke" "reverts" the episode's attention to Bloom, praising him as a mature man who has passed "the middle span of our allotted years" (859). "Junius" likewise alludes to Bloom's adulthood, but censoriously, chastising him as a married man who should know better (905–41). The fatherly estate of our mental traveler is confirmed in the "Gibbon" passage. Fatherhood in Joyce's work is always associated with a *recherche* of one's younger self, and so the new father now begins recalling his own past, while contemplating his "sons," in the language of the Romantics: "Now he is himself paternal and these about him might be his sons" (1060–63). Although Bloom's vision of himself fathering a son turns out to be, according to "Lamb," an "illusion" (1074–75), his thoughts, in the "De Quincey" passage, turn to his daughter, Milly (1097–1109). And when in "Landor" we take up again with Stephen and the students, they also seem to have aged and fallen into reminiscence: "Francis was reminding Stephen of years before when they had been at school together in Conmee's time. He asked about Glaucon, Alcibiades, Pisistratus. Where were they now?" Stephen is also melancholy because of his own problematical fatherhood: "That answer and those leaves, Vincent said to him, will adorn you more fitly when something more, and greatly more, than a capful of light odes can call your genius father" (1117–19). In "Macaulay" and "Huxley," the principals wake from their reveries and, having come into the ripeness of years, are now dignitaries engaged in discussing the "loftiest and most vital" themes in "Socratic discussion" (1201–16). The rest is a gradual decline into the lean and slippered pantaloon. With "Dickens" the central figure is the aged Mr. Purefoy: "He is older now" (1322). "Newman" invites this figure to make a final confession, summoning up his "sins" (1344–45). "Pater" grants the patient one final vision of that "faroff time of the roses" invoked by "Dickens," as well as a glimpse of Heaven (Molly is remembered as "Our Lady of the Cherries" [1369]). "Ruskin" tells us that the vigil is a deathwatch (1397). "Carlyle" launches Purefoy into eternity, congratulating him on having nobly worked and propagated himself right up to the edge of extinction; he is the "old patriarch" who is finally ready to reap the fruits (1438–39). The final ten paragraphs are a slide into senility, delirium, and death, as the minutes are ticked off until "chuckingout time" (1453). When it comes we are regaled with lachrymose reminders of Dignam's funeral (1555–58) and, amidst impressions of fire, "abominable regions," blackness, and heaven, come face to face through the murk ("Christicle, who's this excrement yellow gospeller on the Merrion hall?" [1579–1580]) with the self-proclaimed Messiah, Alexander J. Christ Dowie. In the last line, "Just you try it on," the subject is measured for a shroud.[21] His has been a completely average life, lived within the confines of the Church (six of the seven sacraments are celebrated) and community (like Paddy Dignam, he dies drunk).

13

Approaching Reality in "Circe"

TO UNDERSTAND WHAT HAPPENS in the next episode, "Circe," we must first return to the subject of the condition that enables Bloom to experience the visions of "Oxen of the Sun," visions that as we have seen can take on hallucinatory intensity and astronomical range. That condition has a name, and the name is epilepsy.

About which, some background. Because its seizures could sometimes be precipitated by inducing trances, epilepsy in its various forms was long thought to be related to hysteria (including a hybrid condition named "hysteroepilepsy"), somnambulism, and catalepsy, all states—like Bloom's with the bottle of Bass—inducible by hypnosis.[1] As the legendary "sacred disease" of prophets and prodigies, it inspired mystical notions about the hallucinatory fugues that could accompany its seizures: by long-standing convention, its victims belonged in the ranks of those gifted with clairvoyance and second sight, with the Bloomian knack for hearing voices and seeing visions. Alternatively, such states, following Darwin, were diagnosed as cases of cerebral atavism, the lower centers of the brain (including, some thought, those same occult powers) taking over as the higher ones weakened. This latter version was all the more disturbing because it was believed to be highly hereditary.[2]

Against that background, the case for Bloom's epilepsy is as follows. In "Ithaca," the narrator reports that he had several times succumbed to "hypnotic suggestion"—"More than once, waking, he had been for an indefinite time incapable of moving or uttering sounds" (U 17.854)—and adds that Milly, "somnambulist" (U 17.929), having twice awakened with "a vacant mute expression," has inherited something of her father's predilection (U 17.852–64). This (usually reliable) testimony supports remarks in "Circe" about Bloom's "hereditary epilepsy" (1777),[3] hereditary "atavism," and "somnambulism" (944–51). In "Circe" as well we meet an apparition of Bloom's grandfather Virag as an epileptic (2598), witness Stephen and Bloom fusing into the epileptic Othello, "rigid" in the epileptic's symptomatic "facial paralysis" (3822), and see

156

Bloom "fall" before Bello Cohen—thus acting out "the falling sickness"—"With a piercing epileptic cry" (2851–52). So: an epileptic grandfather, a suicide father, a somnambulist daughter and congenitally unhealthy son, dead soon after birth, who in his one apparition "gazes, unseeing" ahead (4964)—taken together these would have been supererogatory evidence. In falling on all fours before Bello, Bloom is, so the alienists of the day would have said, being atavistic in one sense, and apparently in another as well—reverting to the ancestral affliction a genetic tincture of which has resulted in his susceptibility to trances.

With this diagnosis in mind, certain earlier episodes may make a new kind of sense. I have no doubt given enough attention already to the "De Quincey" segment of "Oxen of the Sun," but may here also note that the same episode contains one other Bloomian hallucination[4]—the sequence in which Stephen's "chance word" "call[s] up" what is twice named a "vision," alternately a "dream" and a "scene," which scene is rendered in vividly envisioned detail (the main voice comes from "Pater," famous word-painter) all of which we are to understand has been "evoked" and now "disengages . . . in the observer's [Bloom's] memory" (U 14.1344–79), that is, presents itself to him as a vision detached from the circumstances of his surroundings. (Which is pretty much what happened with "De Quincey" too.) A similar spell has come over Bloom in "Lestrygonians," this one calling up in comparable detail the scene with Molly on Howth, framed between the repeated phrase about two coupling flies as if to signal a minimal passage of clock-time,[5] which Bloom experiences while staring fixedly ahead (U 8.896–918). Another such spell may have been the remembered meeting with Molly, when "we stood staring at one another for about 10 minutes" (U 18.1183). (It is this moment that is summoned to mind in "Oxen" by Stephen's "chance word.") In fact Bloom's first unharried moment alone of the day, when he sits down to breakfast, results in what the narrator calls a "vacant" expression (U 4.421), the same word later used to describe the expression of the infant Milly as evidence that she may have inherited a family tendency to "hypnotic suggestion" and/or "somnambulism" (U 17.852–63).[6] That Bloom is aware of and sensitive about this genetic susceptibility—in "Ithaca" he is said to fear that like a somnambulist version of his father he might commit suicide in his sleep "by an aberration of the light of reason" (U 17.1776–77)—is apparent from his defensive reaction when Dr. Mulligan, remarking that transfixed gaze of his, describes him as "mesmerised" (U 14.1175).

It seems, then, that the trances of "Lestrygonians" and "Oxen of the Sun" are fairly common occurrences, for which Bloom has a natural susceptibility. Today the likely diagnosis would be what has been variously called "temporal lobe," "complex partial," or "twilight state" epilepsy,[7] in which the victim experiences elaborate hallucinations while outwardly appearing little more than dazed.[8] Unlike the subject of the more violent, better-known *grand mal* seizures, someone undergoing twilight state epilepsy is often sensitive, sometimes hypersensitive, to external influences (like the Bloom who is roused from one "Circe" trance by the sound of a button popping off his pants) but (also like the later Bloom, fuzzy about how he lost that button [*U* 16.35–37]) likely to forget all or most of the experience afterwards.

In "Circe" in particular,[9] Bloom does a lot of the prolonged gazing associated with such states, usually just before his hallucinatory spells begin. "He gazes ahead" (649) before meeting the watchmen who accuse his past. Before the Messiah sequence he "gazes in the tawny crystal" of Zoe's eyes so intently that Zoe makes the standard rebuke to rude starers, "You'll know me the next time" (1318–21). The Virag hallucination appears as Bloom "gazes at the veiled mauve light" (2406–7). The Bello Cohen sequence commences as Bloom, having just turned a "piercing eagle glance" (2722) on the door from which Bella emerges, is literally entranced by her rhythmically waving fan and "glitter[ing]" "falcon eyes" (2752–53); when finally the sudden "Bip!" of his button snaps him out of it, Bella, like Zoe before, remarks, "You'll know me the next time" (3481), which tells us that Bloom has been, once again, staring fixedly ahead. The Boylan apparition, which he experiences with dilated eyes (3815), begins as he is staring at his own hand in a fortune-telling game. The Shakespeare apparition arises when Bloom and Stephen both "*gaze in the mirror*" (3821).

And speaking of Stephen: in "Circe" he too has been rendered susceptible to such states, and for him, as well, the agent has a name: absinthe. Bloom gets it essentially right (along with the usual muddle) when he explains Stephen's "Circe" behavior with the words, "Taken a little more than is good for him. Absinthe. Greeneyed monster" (4486–87). (He means "green fairy": see *U* 3.217.) He was around when Stephen downed a glass of the stuff (*U* 14.1470), then ordered "Absinthe [for] the lot" (*U* 14.1533), rapidly swallowing both rounds in an undiluted, "green" state (*U* 14.1545).[10] What that can mean for someone in Stephen's condition going into "Circe" is forecast in the "Proteus" reminiscence of Kevin Egan drinking his "green," that is, straight, absinthe (*U* 3.5–6), rather than the heavily diluted mixture (usually at a five-to-one water-to-liquor ratio) favored by most drinkers.[11] Inevitably, Egan is a wreck. Small wonder one of the "Oxen of the Sun" drinkers, hearing Stephen's first order, cautions him to get something safer: "Caramba! Have an eggnog or a prairie oyster" (*U* 14.1470–71). Straight absinthe was understood to be extremely strong stuff—

strong enough to make one drinker sick (*U* 14.1565–68) and to make another, Lynch (who has had exactly half of Stephen's quantity), start hallucinating that an evangelist announced on a poster has come to life and is haranguing him (*U* 14.1579–81).

Absinthe was famous for inducing hallucinations of just the sort Lynch experiences. (See fig. 17 for an artist's rendering of such states, painted during absinthe's heyday).[12] In 1890 Marie Corelli was drawing on a voluminous medical

17. Artist's rendering of absinthe intoxication. Courtesy of the Musée de l'Absinthe, Auvers-sur-Oise, France.

literature when she wrote that just one glass "taken fasting is sufficient to cause temporary delirium."[13] (Stephen has eaten nothing since breakfast, and of course has already primed himself with lots of beer.)[14] Both Lynch's spell and Stephen's later phantasmagoria correspond to contemporary accounts, popular and professional, of absinthe visions: vivid, protean, often becoming nightmarish (the ranting evangelist, the dead mother), likely to lead to violence (the smashed lampshade) and to collapse.[15]

Which is to say that there are two sound reasons, physiological and physiological-psychological, for the fact that this next episode into which Bloom and Stephen enter should be full of hallucinations. Their appearance has been prepared in abundant and—it certainly seems—deliberate detail. All in all, for someone supposedly busily disengaging the signifier, the Joyce of "Circe" seems to have gone to a lot of trouble to establish a rationale for just the opposite. Both of the principals through whose eyes we have with some complications been experiencing most of *Ulysses* are steered into an episode of hallucinations only after each has been shown to be prone to experience them. Furthermore, since according to medical doctrine of the time absinthism could produce delusional states identical to those experienced by the epileptic,[16] both characters have been made liable to experience the same kinds of visions.[17] With his usual ingenuity, Joyce has supplied an elaborately mimetic, character-centered rationale not only for the hallucinations of "Circe" but for the fact that Stephen's and Joyce's hallucinations should be so similar in nature, to the point that at times they can fuse or mingle.[18] I do not think that such convergence of apparent cause and apparent effect can plausibly be either a coincidence or, like the fossils supposed by Philip Gosse to have been deposited by God in order to test humanity's faith in Holy Writ, a huge red herring.

On the contrary: it is in keeping with Joyce's stated views, before and during the writing of *Ulysses,* that such effects should always have their discernible causes. Those views were behind, for instance, his criticism of *La Tentation de Saint Antoine*: "We might believe in it if Flaubert had first shown us St Antoine in Alexandria looking at women and jewellers windows."[19] Fantastical literature was fine, that is, as long as its specters could be realistically accounted for. And so when Joyce wrote his own version (and several critics have remarked on "Circe" 's debt to that Flaubert fantasia), he made sure that this criticism could not be directed at him. The special effects of "Circe" are not free-floating visions but, again, "hallucinations," generated from perceptions discernibly deriving from three sets of real-world facts: (1) internal: a character's mental makeup; (2) external: circumstances and events; (3) intersection: between (1) and (2).[20]

An example:

(Bloom plodges forward again through the sump. Kisses chirp amid the rifts of fog. A piano sounds. He stands before a lighted house, listening. The kisses, winging from their bowers fly about him, twittering, warbling, cooing.)

THE KISSES

(warbling) Leo! *(twittering)* Icky licky micky sticky for Leo! *(cooing)* Coo coocoo! Yummyyum, Womwom! *(warbling)* Big comebig! Pirouette! Leopopold! *(twittering)* Leeolee! *(warbling)* O Leo!

(They rustle, flutter upon his garments, alight, bright giddy flecks, silvery sequins.

BLOOM

A man's touch. Sad music. Church music. Perhaps here.

(Zoe Higgins, a young whore in a sapphire slip, closed with three bronze buckles, a slim black velvet fillet round her throat, nods, trips down the steps and accosts him. . . . .
. . . .

. . . .

(Her hand slides into his left trouser pocket and brings out a hard black shrivelled potato. She regards it and Bloom with dumb moist lips.)

BLOOM

A talisman. Heirloom.

ZOE

For Zoe? For keeps? For being so nice, eh?

(She puts the potato greedily into a pocket then links his arm, cuddling him with supple warmth. He smiles uneasily. Slowly, note by note, oriental music is played. He gazes in the tawny crystal of her eyes, ringed with kohol. His smile softens.)

ZOE

You'll know me the next time.

BLOOM

(forlornly) I never loved a dear gazelle but it was sure to. . . .

(Gazelles are leaping, feeding on the mountains. Near are lakes. Round their shores file shadows black of cedargroves. Aroma rises, a strong hairgrowth of resin. It burns, the orient, a sky of sapphire, cleft by the bronze flight of eagles. Under it lies the womancity, nude, white, still, cool, in luxury. A fountain murmurs among damask roses. Mammoth roses murmur of scarlet winegrapes. A wine of shame, lust, blood exudes, strangely murmuring.)

ZOE

(murmuring singsong with the music, her odalisk lips lusciously smeared with salve of swinefat and rosewater) Schorach ani wenowach, benoith Hierushaloim.

BLOOM

(fascinated) I thought you were of good stock by your accent.

ZOE

And you know what thought did?

(She bites his ear gently with little goldstopped teeth, sending on him a cloying breath of stale garlic. The roses draw apart, disclose a sepulchre of the gold of kings and their mouldering bones. (1267–81, 1309–41)

1: Internal: a tired middle-aged man with an ear for music, the edge taken off any erotic interest by fatigue and a fairly recent masturbation, just emerging from a trance-like revery induced by the arrival of the night watchmen and the shameful memory they evoke of his sexual initiation, twenty years ago, with a prostitute (compare *U* 14.1063–77). Accordingly, the experiences and fantasies revived have been largely from the memories of his vexed relations with women, which began with that initiation. They continue the earlier evocation of Josie Powell Breen, the woman he left behind when he chose Molly, and to whom he once sent a "valentine of the dear gazelle" (435).

2: External: the entrance to a house of prostitution, its features just emerging through the fog, amid which beams of light from the *"lighted house"* are playing. As they will at the episode's end, the prostitutes are blowing *"ickylickysticky yumyum kisses"* to a potential customer, along with some come-hither baby-talk. There is piano music, later identified as Stephen's rendition of a composition by Benedetto Marcello (2087–89). Although as Bloom says it is a piece of "Church music" (1278), a vigorous march that to my hearing sounds suitable for a recessional,[21] it was in part based on an ancient Hebrew melody (2089–94), and evidently Stephen, aware of that fact, is emphasizing its oriental origins.[22] Introduced at line 1282 is a young prostitute dressed in *"sapphire slip"* with *"three bronze buckles."* She is made up with eye shadow of kohol, the common name for sulphuret of antimony, and rose lip balm, a forerunner of lipstick, compounded of dye, rosewater, and (*"swinefat"*) grease-based ointment, and her hair has a scent deriving from either perfume or the residue of a shampoo containing a resin fixative.[23]

3: Intersection: beguiled by the music, Bloom stops and attends. Lights flickering through shifting *"rifts of fog"* spangle patches on his clothes that—the first hallucination of this sequence—turn into bright perches for the birds conjured by the chirping, twittering sounds of the women accompanied by the treble tinkling of Stephen's piano (1268–76). (That "icky licky mickey sticky" kissing sound will, again, be heard again near episode's end, when another contingent of potential customers elicits *"ickylickysticky yumyum kisses"* from the whores at the window [4321].) Zoe enters the scene, engages Bloom in conversation, and arouses his senses: *"(His skin, alert, feels her fingertips approach.)"* As Stephen in the background plays what by now is being rendered as *"oriental music"* (1318), Bloom *"gazes"* into her kohol-ringed eyes and passes into a thoughtful trance. In a previous "Circe" hallucination he had been, in a revival of his "Lestrygonians" meeting ("Mrs Breen turned up her two large eyes" [*U* 8.228]), attracted to the "roguish eyes" of Mrs. Breen (387); this similar transaction opens a mental circuit to that earlier experience, and he takes up where he left off with the "dear gazelle" poem that he was there reciting,[24] a connection facilitated by what the episode's notes (but not the final version) specify as Zoe's "brown eyes, the eyes of a gazelles" [*sic*] (Herring 1977, 221). The gazelles then come to life in a phantasmagoric landscape whose *"mountains"* are Zoe's breasts and whose *"lakes"* are her eyes. The acrid scent of sulphur or resin (that hair stuff) or both conjures a premonition of a fire, burning in the *"orient"* because of the music, ascending into the deep blue sky deriving from Zoe's sapphire slip (the English literary tradition has routinely associated sapphire with the color of a paradisial sky), *"cleft by the bronze flight of eagles"* deriving from the slip's bronze buckles; the dream-logic seems to be that as the clasps take flight the slip they held together comes apart. Which of course gives us the naked body underneath, the *"womancity,"* in an odalisk vision whose heavy orientalism, again, owes much to the background music. The *"fountain"* murmuring *"among damask roses"* is the sound of Zoe's *"murmuring singsong,"* coming from the *"damask roses"* of her lips.

At about this point the hallucination begins to shift from the romantic to the horrific, largely because like Gulliver in Brobdingnag Bloom has gotten too close to sustain the illusion but also because of the powerful rose scent, which he has earlier disparaged as "Sweet and cheap, soon sour" (*U* 13.1009–10). That was shortly after masturbating to the vision of a young woman getting her menstrual period, whose scent, remembered, now brings back feelings of *"shame, lust, blood."* Just before the sweetness turns thoroughly sour Bloom, still *"fascinated,"* filters what is probably little more than Zoe's guttural tum-te-tum tum-te-tum hum (she may be humming along with the piano) through an orientalism tinged by the music and compounded by his own Jewishness, yielding the Hebrew *"Schorach ani wenowach, benoith Hierushaloim."* The anti-pastoral coming-to (registered with *"shame,"* then *"swinefat"*) is accelerated when Zoe bites Bloom's ear and her foul garlicky breath hits him with full force; opening, her mouthful of gold-filled teeth becomes a sepulchre of rotting flesh (rancid residue of her last meat meal, presumably supplied by the brothel cook, who later appears with a *"greasy bib"* [2923–24]) among gold and bones.[25] The spell now thoroughly broken, Bloom rejoins the world of the conscious, until the next time.

Now, it seems obvious to me that effects such as are displayed in this passage could be produced only through careful attention both to the details of the setting and to the subject's profile, in this case to Bloom's memories, condition, and susceptibilities. To understand the scene we must, I would say, take account of what the central figure is likely to be feeling and remembering at this time— here, why a memory of a woman's eyes revived in "Lestrygonians" and transmuted earlier in "Circe" should make Bloom think of gazelles, for instance.

Or, to cite another example, we must take account of how for Stephen an earlier sequence of encounters helps generate the hallucinated specter of his employer, Garrett Deasy, with "*A yoke of buckets* [which] *leopards all over him and his rearing nag a torrent of mutton broth with dancing coins of carrots, barley, onions, turnips, potatoes*" (3990–91). The "*dancing coins,*" a flickering effect from "the checkerwork of leaves," are from Stephen's last sight of Deasy (*U* 2.448–49), the horse-riding scenario from the connection established in their last meeting between Deasy and horses (*U* 2.286, 300, 333), the yoke because Deasy is famously henpecked, or to use Stephen's term, "shrewridden." The coins become carrots in mutton broth by way of the account Stephen has heard of "The night she [Deasy's wife] threw the soup in the waiter's face" (*U* 7.534), and "leaps" becomes "leopards" because Leopardstown is where Dubliners go for horse racing; the sloshing wetness of the whole picture may be expedited by the fact that it is raining outside.[26]

Recent theory, taking "Circe" as the site where all the components of the earlier episodes of *Ulysses* disengage and frolic, inclines to read such passages as instances of textual free-play. It seems to me that on the contrary they are as rigorously determined as anything in the book, as fixed as any other episode on the bedrock of real-world minutiae that Joyce liked to call the product of his grocery-assistant's mind, still governed by essentially the same elastic but resilient set of mimetic conventions that has applied throughout.

For one thing, during the hallucinations we pick up a fair amount of new information later confirmed as true. We learn that in the course of Bloom's disputed liaison with a maid he gave her a gift of garters and that she was accused of stealing oysters (876–81), facts later confirmed by Molly (*U* 18.56–68), as is the "Circe" datum that her name was Mary. We learn that his mother wore a cameo brooch (285)—confirmed in "Ithaca" (*U* 17.1794–95)—and that "Hegarty," as in "aunt Hegarty's armchair" (3173–74), was a family name—her family name, as it turns out (*U* 17.537). We learn that he received a "pamphlet," "incorrectly addressed," for an English invention promising to "afford a noiseless, inoffensive vent" (3274–76); we will see that pamphlet in "Ithaca," and learn the name (Wonderworker) and address ("Dear Madam"—*U* 17.1819–23). We learn that he possesses an obscene postcard depicting a "torero" and a "senorita" having intercourse (1067–69), as indeed it turns out he does (*U* 17.1809–11). We learn for the first time of a woman named Georgina Simpson and of a housewarming party she gave during which Bloom, though involved with Molly, flirted with his old flame Josie Powell (440–93); in "Penelope" Molly remembers it too (*U*. 18.171–74). We are informed that the time is 12:25 P.M. (2194), and all subsequent evidence is that this information has been at least approximately correct. During a hallucination scene with the Nymph, Bloom loses a button (3440–41), and in "Eumaeus" that button is still missing (*U* 16.35–37). At the height of his "Circe" delirium Stephen breaks into a whirling dance; in "Ithaca" Bloom still remembers his "velocity of rapid circular motion in a relaxing atmosphere" *U* 17.39–40); earlier he had summed up the sequence of events from "Oxen of the Sun" to "Eumaeus" as "meeting, discussion, dance, row, old salt" (*U* 16.1223). During his hallucinated trial scene Bloom claims a degree from the "University of life" (840), and later he refrains from using the phrase again for that reason.[27]

Bloom's vision of Zoe's woman-city and Stephen's of Deasy do not exemplify pieces of text coming together; they exemplify an individual's sensations, memories, and associations coming together, as always working on a dense field of particulars. That is why such scenes can sometimes reenact memories that have not been registered anywhere else in the text. Thus Virag, Bloom's grandfather, can occupy over three hundred lines despite the fact that he has never appeared before. Where does this Virag come from, if not from the memory of a man, Bloom, who has not thought of him today until now?[28] And to what does that memory refer, if not to a virtual source prior to and independent of a text that is not self-constituted but rather likewise derived, always imperfectly and incompletely, from that source? The effect, which also occurs in Joyce's earlier work, for instance when the Stephen of *Portrait* remembers details from his time at Clongowes that were not recorded in the earlier narrative corresponding to that time,[29] ought not to occur in an episode whose ground is the text it is in.

Objections to the kind of reading of "Circe" I have been giving usually begin with the observation that Joyce at least problematizes the psychological origins of its hallucinations by having Stephen and Bloom recirculate items of which they could not have had knowledge. There are, I think, two answers to this observation. The first is that, under scrutiny, there are not nearly as many such cases as is often supposed—indeed, as I will argue in the next chapter, there is none that qualifies without question. The most commonly cited example is the "Nebrakada! Femininum!" (319) of Bloom's hallucinated Molly, which repeats an earlier line read by Stephen *solus*. That expression, however, derives from a piece of public property that Bloom might well have encountered on his own, and that he would certainly be inclined to notice.[30] In fact the account of Stephen's encounter with the words may suggest as much: "Eighth and ninth book of Moses. Secret of all secrets. Seal of King David. Thumbed pages: read and read. Who has passed here before me?" (*U* 10.844–46). Bloom is a regular of these same bookstalls, and nothing would be likelier to attract his attention than a spell "to win a woman's love" (*U* 10.847) in a magical "book of Moses." Stephen is reading that book on Bedford Row (*U* 10.830), and according to "Ithaca" Bloom was browsing the Bedford Row stalls around the same time (*U* 17.204). As we will see later, most if indeed not all similar cases can be similarly accounted for.

The second answer is that such items are hardly unique to "Circe." They are scattered through the book, in line with what I have been calling its "Orphic" dispensations, psychic division. How does the Bloom of "Ithaca" know of the Mulligan coining "snotgreen" (*U* 17.1315–17), a word that so far as we can tell was never spoken in his presence? How does he know the titles of Stephen's grade-school essays (*U* 17.644)? How, in "Sirens," does he rethink, almost word for word, Stephen's "Scylla and Charybdis" formulation for Shakespeare's cuckolding? (See *U* 9.953, 11.907–8.) Whatever else it is, this last instance cannot be a matter of character-disintegrating textual *jouissance* or some such, because it comes directly out of Bloom's thoughts of the moment, which are about Shakespeare, cuckolding, and the latest step towards some compensatory adultery of his own, and which probably echo ("Do. But do.") the "How do? How do?" boomed out by Ben Dollard at the moment Boylan headed off for Molly (*U* 11.436). Yet at the same time, if only because allusions to Gerard's rosery and so forth are beyond Bloom's range, the words are indisputably Stephen's. So: how to explain?

By, I suggest, some version of the same forces and faculties behind Bloom's graphically detailed recapitulation of the distant Boylan-Molly tryst, behind the fireworks that go off when Bloom does too and the ball that rolls toward the object of his desires, behind the citizen who fishes up and gigantifies Bloom's worst impulses, behind the narrator of "Oxen of the Sun" who knows that the new Purefoy baby will be a boy and that rain will be followed by fire, and behind the other "Oxen" narrator who produces an extraordinarily intricate rendering of Bloom's entranced reveries in language coming from all over—coming from, for one, Stephen, who in turn, in *his* deepest brooding (*U*

14.371), all unconsciously incorporates Bloom's departed daughter Milly ("Return, return, clan Milly") into his lament for lost tribes.[31] Behind, that is, the book's Orphic impresario.

And, so, in "Circe," the few likely cases of apparently disengaged phrases or thoughts are all psychologically, not ontologically, problematic, requiring an altered understanding of the nature rather than the status of the book's substantiating reality. With notable consistency, those scenes in which Bloom or Stephen invoke details whose provenance cannot be firmly accounted for occur in sequences characterized by an orgiastic disintegration of inherited categories, especially those of personal identity, originating in moments of extreme psychological or perceptual disorientation—those moments, that is, carrying over from the state that in "Sirens" bestowed on Bloom his hyperaesthetic and telekinetic powers.

To the marginal extent that such sequences depart from the canons of realism, they may be said to do so in ways parapsychological rather than metatextual. Uncanny things happen on the page because uncanny things are happening in the minds of the characters. As such they are nothing especially new, either for *Ulysses* or the literature of the period, for which if anything they might be called clichés. They occur by virtue of the same telepathic dispensation that, on a larger scale, licenses the more-than-coincidental correspondences between Bloom and Stephen, even the metempsychotic correspondences between Bloom and Odysseus.

Critics made uneasy by such apparent strains in the book's verisimilitude (and several have been bothered by that psychically shared Shakespeare sentence) may too readily have assumed that Joyce's realism is theirs. Again: abundant evidence exists that Joyce believed in the existence of some things most of us consider nonsense. He held a vigil for his mother's ghost. He had horoscopes cast, even considered handing over the completion of *Finnegans Wake* to another writer, James Stephens, whose main qualification was that, having been born at nearly the same time and place, he was Joyce's astrological near-twin. He was "much attracted by" the new theory of serialism, of precognition in dreams made possible by multidimensional time fields, and reported having had a prophetic dream himself (Jolas 1998, 19). He lived, and published his books, by a calendar of lucky days. He wore certain colors, as well as various rings and ancestral talismans, according to an elaborate private ritual devised to attract certain influences and ward off others. Gerty McDowell, who chooses the colors of her underwear according to the calendar and the moon, is in that way anyway a portrait of the artist.

And he seems to have taken seriously the belief that in some circumstances thoughts might be migratory, permeable, even catalytic. He clearly believed that his daughter was psychically sensitive, at least to him. The letters he wrote to Nora in his youth show a more-than-sentimental belief in the power to evoke, very nearly literally, the lover's spirit through ritual or talisman or pilgrimage, in sleep or music or intense passion. With variable degrees of irony, such intimations found their way into his fiction. In *Dubliners*, "The Dead" is partway toward being what Joyce's brother called it, a ghost story (Stanislaus Joyce 1950, 20), and "Clay" features a fortune-telling that will probably come true. (So, arguably, does "An Encounter.")[32] In *Portrait* Stephen more than once embraces or swoons into mystical communion with the spirit of someone or something, and experiences a climactic vision, of a "hawklike man" winging through the sky, which is at least perhaps valid. He also, as we have seen, contemplates the kind of orgasm-induced telepathy that passes from Molly and Boylan to Bloom in "Sirens."

It may help to recall how conventional all of these beliefs once were. *Ulysses* was written when many of Joyce's contemporaries, literary and otherwise, were (1) intensely interested in how individual consciousness might be extended or rarified, often in frankly occult ways, and (2) not especially interested in the postmodernist project of dissolving consciousness for purposes of redistributing it into text. For many, it was understood that characters might pass beyond the borders of their minds—into the *anima mundi,* say, or the soul of the beloved—without ceasing to be themselves, that far from constituting the abandonment of individual autonomy such effects rather signaled the expansion or extension of especially powerful personalities.

It is by such conventions that Joyce's characters can sometimes exceed themselves, sometimes mysteriously, without necessarily being untrue to their established selves. The words and images that come to their minds, though sometimes implausible, are never uncharacteristic, never not what they would have thought or seen if they could. In this, "Circe" follows the same rules as the earlier episodes. In his exposition of "Circe," Hugh Kenner observes that the phrase *"Habemus carneficem"* in a Bloom hallucination is out of Bloom's range, and indeed it probably is[33]—as is the sentence "She calls her children home in their dark language," from a Bloom monologue of "Lotus Eaters." But it remains unclear why the "Circe" transgression should be destabilizing any difference between real and unreal whereas the "Lotus Eaters" equivalent is merely a case of the author's, in Kenner's words, "supplying a phrase that shall bridge the text's continuity across an instant Bloom did not verbalise, merely felt" (Kenner 1980, 120–23, 69). We are surely not to take "Proteus," for instance, as a direct transcription of Stephen's mind, but rather as a lyrical rendering of the reactions and movements of that mind—in Kenner's formulation not entirely what Stephen verbalized but the author's verbal equivalent or completion of what he felt.

Let it be conceded, certainly, that Joyce is more or less always pursuing other courses in addition to the mimetic, often with his patented tricks of verbal overlay—sticking his own name in here and there, for instance, or setting up his numerological correspondences, or, especially, scoring points: thus for instance in a "Circe" stage direction quoted above, the line "*She bites his ear gently with little goldstopped teeth*" has at its heart an impish send-up of the phrase "with little snow-white feet" from Yeats's "Down by the Sally Gardens," and probably constitutes an authorial commentary on what Joyce considered that poet's weakness for such phrases. Still, that commentary does not change the facts, the facts of real teeth with real gold fillings that will soon be transformed into a hallucination, thoroughly grounded, of bones and gold. What is distinctive in Joyce is not his authorial assistance in the character's selection of language but rather his concomitant attention to the ways in which such language is or might be generated by one particular mind in one particular time and place—process over product. After all, although not usually the man for literary parody, the Bloom of the "*little gold-stopped teeth*" line is temperamentally an anti-Yeatsian, has indeed earlier dismissed Yeats's colleague A.E. as one of "Those literary etherial people" (*U* 8.543).

As for Stephen: from the beginning, the distinctive feature of a line like "Stephen closed his eyes to hear his boots crush crackling wrack and shells" (*U* 3.10–11) is not the onomatopoeia of the last five words but the way the sentence becomes onomatopoeic at the moment Stephen closes his eyes to concentrate on such effects: we are tracking here not so much external reality *tout court* as attention to it, neither sound, sense, nor sense's virtual source but the interplay of all three. The distinctive feature of "Circe" is not its Flaubertian phantasms but the Joycean way in which they are generated out of discernible shifts in mood, venue, dramatis personae, and so on.[34]

Theory-driven commentators have been overlooking this component of Joyce's fiction. In following the critical shift from reality to textuality, from the street names and cellar flaps of Joyce's realism to the verbal mutations of his narrative, they have in effect traded one flatness for another, at the expense of the three-dimensional realm engendered by the interaction of the two. Joycean mimesis has been too quickly dismissed because too narrowly, too flatly, construed. As with the headlines of "Aeolus" and the typological conglomerations of "Oxen of the Sun," it has too readily been assumed that Joyce is giving up on mimesis at the moment when he may in fact be taking it to a new, unfamiliar extreme.

Joyce was indeed a cultural revolutionary, but of a particular kind—a *jusqu'aboutist* who liked to *épater* the establishment not by overturning conventions but by pushing them past conventional limits. He could (often did) explain every episode of *Ulysses*, emphatically including "Circe," in terms his contemporaries might deplore (because he was always going too far) but so far as is recorded did never not get, because the explanation was invariably in terms of (the common quest) rendering reality. That was, especially, what he said about "Circe": "In my Mabbot Street scene I approached reality closer in my opinion than anywhere else in the book except perhaps for moments in the last chapter" (Power 1974, 75). Maybe he was wrong about that: maybe, for reasons that critical theory can explain, he failed and was fated to fail. In any event, he was not trying to fail.

14

"Circe" Again

Thirty-Two Anomalies

INSTANCES such as the "Nebrakada! Feminum!" of "Circe" (319, 3463),[1] where either Stephen or Bloom appears aware of a datum to which he did not have personal access, loom large in the criticism of the school I am disputing: I think it fair to say that its case depends on them. Here is a list, as complete as I have been able to make, of all the passages that have been cited in advancing that case, plus some others that seem likely candidates, given in order of occurrence.

1. Bloom, attempting to ingratiate himself to the Watch: "You know that old joke, rose of Castile" (740; compare 1731).

Why included: This is Lenehan's joke, as told in "Aeolus" (*U* 7.588–91), when Bloom is not present to hear it.

However: Lenehan tells it again in "Oxen of the Sun" (*U* 14.1510–11), when Bloom is present to hear it.

2. Bloom, accosted by the Watch, makes Masonic gestures and says, "No, no, worshipful master, light of love. Mistaken identity" (760).

Why included: He means to use the Masonic phrase "Light, life and love" (*U* 8.963), but, flustered, comes out instead with the phrase "light of love" introduced in Stephen's Shakespeare symposium and repeated in this episode (112), in both instances when Bloom was not around. So we have a Freudian slip of the tongue, like "admirers" for "advisers," revealing an irruption not of the individual unconscious but of "textual memory" (Hampson 1994, 170–71).

However: The source of the "Light, life and love" version is Nosey Flynn (*U* 8.963), hardly an impeccable authority. Besides, "light of love" was a ubiquitous phrase. My Internet search through *Literature Online* turns up hundreds of hits, many of them—from Byron, Thomas Gray, both Brownings, Thomas Moore's melodies, Gilbert and Sullivan's libretti, Wesley's hymns, Tennyson, Longfellow, Lady Wilde, Denis Florence McCarthy, Wordsworth, and the age's most popular melodrama, Mrs Henry Wood's *East Lynne* (*U* 18.653)—likely included in Bloom's cultural background. Further, at the moment Bloom is, as he imagines, in the presence not just of the Watch but of a beseeching Martha Clifford, who has just addressed him as "Lionel, thou lost one." In "Sirens," for a Bloom brooding on Martha, that same line immediately prompted the response, "Alone. One love" (*U* 11.742). "Worshipful master, light of love" seems addressed more to Martha—whom he has after all been coaxing to assume the role of "master," punishing her naughty boy—than to the Watch. And "light of love" is a perfectly natural, if indiscreet, thing to call an inamorata begging, "Clear my name" (754)—that is, Henry, show that I am not your idle plaything by publicly declaring your devotion.

3. In the trial of Bloom, J. J. O'Molloy

> (*steps on to a low plinth and holds the lapel of his coat with solemnity. His face lengthens, grows pale and bearded, with sunken eyes, the blotches of phthisis and hectic cheekbones of John F. Taylor. He applies his handkerchief to his mouth and scrutinises the galloping tide of rosepink blood.*)
>
> J. J. O'MOLLOY
> (*almost voicelessly*) Excuse me. I am suffering from a severe chill, have recently come from a sickbed. A few wellchosen words. (*He assumes the avine head, foxy moustache and proboscidal eloquence of Seymour Bushe.*) When the angel's book comes to be opened if aught that the pensive bosom has inaugurated of soultransfigured and of soultransfiguring deserves to live I say accord the prisoner at the bar the sacred benefit of the doubt. (992–1004)

Why included: Much in O'Molloy's appearance and speech derives from some "Aeolus" recitations of the oratory of Seymour Bushe and John F. Taylor, which occur when Bloom is not present.

However: Calling from another building, Bloom is "at the telephone" (*U* 7.671) located in an adjoining room during these recitations. The door is open, and hearing between the rooms is good enough for MacHugh to pick up the sound of the telephone's whirring signal (*U* 7.656). Although Bloom's request to speak to the editor is rebuffed with an abrupt "Come across yourself," MacHugh never says goodbye, nor do we hear that "whirr" sound that accompanied the three previous occasions (384, 415, 656) when telephone contact was made, broken off, then made again.[2] Although Bloom, who shows up in person near the end of the episode, eventually gives up, we do not know just when; we can however determine that it was most likely some time after MacHugh left him waiting.[3] So it is possible that, while waiting for a response, he overhears the ensuing talk. What he heard would have been fragmentary and garbled, but then the "Circe" rendition *is* fragmentary and garbled. (The "Circe" bit about "the angel's book," for instance, is not in O'Molloy's original, but "Michelangelo" is.) What he heard would also have been very faint, but then the O'Molloy of "Circe" speaks, as he did not in "Aeolus," *"almost voicelessly."* And the visual features of the sequence are all plausibly Bloom's own: the *"hectic"* complexion from the ominous "hectic flush" that, he reflected in the "Aeolus" office, spelled "finis" for O'Molloy (*U* 7.293)—and that incidentally contradicts the "Aeolus" testimony that Taylor was not a dying man (*U* 7.818)—the phthistical (that is, tubercular) symptoms (pale skin, "galloping" blood) he would have witnessed during the last days of his old "companions" Philip Gilligan and Michael Hart (*U* 17.1252–54) who died of the disease (compare *U* 6.392), the physical features of Seymour Bushe, once one of his "exemplars" (*U* 17.792).

Besides, someone who chooses such a figure as Bushe for an exemplar might on his own be familiar with one of his most famous orations. As for John F. Taylor, his Moses speech made a big enough splash to be reported in the papers, reprinted in a pamphlet, and remembered in Yeats's *Autobiography*.

4. When Bloom's cuckoldry is announced in the papers, *"The very reverend Canon O'Hanlon in cloth of gold cope elevates and exposes a marble timepiece. Before him Father Conroy and the reverend John Hughes S.J. bend low,"* and the clock chimes "cuckoo" three times (1128–35).

Why included: Bloom heard the cuckoo in "Nausicaa," but it was Gerty's voice that supplied the names of the celebrants and the picture of the timepiece.

However: The cuckoo clock was actually too far away for anyone, including Gerty, to hear. The entire "Nausicaa" composite is imagined, by a mind that there as here is hard to pin down. In a conjunction noted earlier in chapter 4, all these details reappear, at the end of "Nausicaa," in a return of the voice of the absent Gerty apparently generated out of the subconscious of the dozing Bloom (*U* 13.1292–95). To me, the explanation is to be found in Joyce's Orphic effects, and in particular in what I have argued is Gerty's status as Bloom's "projected mirage." However the "Nausicaa" passage may be explained, these "Circe" lines are simply a Bloomian recollection of it.

5. Prompted by reminders of Boylan's tryst with Molly, the anonymous narrator of "Cyclops" shows up, as "THE NAMELESS ONE," to tell us, "Gob, he organised her" (1145).

Why included: His language here is taken from his favorite verbal tag in that episode, plus the sentence "That's the bucko that'll organise her, take my tip" (*U* 12.1001–2). Although Bloom was present, these words were not spoken aloud.

However: As David Hayman points out (Hayman 1974, 243–75), it is far from clear just what level of reality this voice occupies. He cannot be a regular first-person past-tense narrator, because such figures do not, for instance, urinate in synchronization with their recollected urinations, as this fellow does. He cannot, realistically, be telling us what is happening as it is happening. But then where, and what, is he? I have my own answer, expounded in chapters 3 through 5; here it suffices that, as with the Gerty-Bloom voice, "THE NAMELESS ONE" is equally problematical in both cases: the "Circe" lines by themselves represent no new modification of mimetic conventions.

6. When the mob turns on Bloom, a judge materializes to pass sentence: (*His Honour, sir Frederick Falkiner, recorder of Dublin, in judicial garb of grey stone rises from the bench, stonebearded. He bears in his arms an umbrella sceptre. From his forehead arise starkly the Mosaic ramshorns*) (1162–65).

Why included: "Stonebearded" is from an unvoiced thought of Stephen's (*U* 7.854), therefore unavailable to the Bloom who is experiencing this hallucination. It and *"Mosaic ramshorns"* both derive from O'Molloy's description of Michelangelo's statue of Moses, with its curious set of horns, delivered out of Bloom's presence. Bloom would probably not know about that statue on his own.

However: See number 3, above. Plus, in "Oxen of the Sun" (*U* 14.394–96), while Bloom is present, Stephen gives what is certainly a virtual and may be a literal repetition of the "Aeolus" speech containing the word "stonebearded." ("Ram's horn" is, incidentally, a Bloom locution [*U* 13.952], not to be found in the "Aeolus" original.) "Stonebearded" may be Stephen's word, but the mental image, of human features petrifying, is characteristically Bloomian as well (*U* 6.351–52, 8.486–90); so is the picture of a grief that would "Wear the heart out of a stone" (*U* 6.351–52).

7. The hangman of Bloom's fantasia is *"H. Rumbold, master barber"* (1177).

Why included: Rumbold comes straight out of a "Cyclops" parody, a purely textual excursion corresponding to almost nothing actually spoken or heard. Further, his name is an authorial dig at one of Joyce's enemies, in other words a bit of authorial japery.

However: The "Cyclops" parody in question derives from a letter from Rumbold that is being read aloud, signature included, as Bloom first enters Barney Kiernan's, and from the ensuing discussion, in which he joins (*U* 12.410–51). And many novelists before Joyce made in-jokes about real people without thereby throwing over claims to narratological consistency.

8. The "scorbutic" spirit of Paddy Dignam, metamorphosed from a beagle, looks for a lamp to "satisfy an animal need" and explains, "That buttermilk didn't agree with me" (1234–35).

Why included: The buttermilk remark comes from another "Cyclops" parody (*U* 12.356), which was neither spoken by nor generated out of any one individual present.

However: Wherever the "Cyclops" passage may have come from—a question that as in number 5 above, is problematic—its prescription of buttermilk for what is here described as Dignam's "ghouleaten" flesh is consistent with Bloom's earlier reflection that buttermilk is good "skinfood" (*U* 5.497), just what the scorbutic Dignam obviously needs. Dignam's lamp recalls the narrator's worry in "Cyclops" (when Bloom was present) that another dog "might take my leg for a lamppost" (*U* 12.702).

9. At the end of Dignam's hallucinated appearance before Bloom, *"Tom Rochford, robinredbreasted, in cap and breeches, jumps from his twocolumned machine,"* which then repeats its "Wandering Rocks" performance: *"Two discs on the columns wobble, eyes of nought"* (1259–66; compare *U* 10.373–74, 468–69).

Why included: "Wandering Rocks" is the only episode in which this machine appears, in a scene at which Bloom is not present.

However: Bloom has seen what he calls "that invention" of Rochford's (*U* 8.1035). The double-zeros that turn up here are different from the double-sixes of the "Wandering Rocks" scene. That the image of "eyes" repeats the earlier picture of discs "ogling" from their resting place may trace either to the "Wandering Rocks" language or to the fact that two discs, with 0's (or 6's) in the middle, sitting side by side, will just naturally remind someone of eyes (00—66: one set is, and the other contains, a pair of empty ellipses). It would help, in settling such questions, to have a picture or replica of Rochford's machine, but nobody has come up with one.

Let it be conceded that to some extent the rhythm and language of this passage, especially *"wobble,"* seem indebted to the stylist of the earlier scene—or rather, to the stylist more or less in evidence throughout the whole of the book, who like all such presences has his identifiable idiolect. (A point acknowledged, among other places, at U 11.519–20: "As said before he ate with relish the inner organs . . .") Lawrence is fond of "blood," "loins," and the Book of Revelations; in Dickens greatcoats are always "capacious" and a gentleman introduced in a "bottle-green" suit will be tagged with that phrase from then on; in *The Ordeal of Richard Feverel* a ponderous butler is forever "Heavy Benson." Likewise in *Ulysses:* from episode to episode Bloom is almost always "Mr. Bloom" and Stephen (himself never "Mr. Dedalus") almost always sports, not a cane or a walking-stick, but an "ashplant." One of the trademarks of the stylist given to these verbal habits is a fondness for words like "wobble." Which is to say that "wobbled" here may simply be a case of the *mot juste*, used twice.

10. As politician, Bloom playfully pokes Baby Boardman, who goes "Hajajaja" (1595–98).

Why included: Both "Baby Boardman" and "Hajajaja" are phrases from the Gerty half of "Nausicaa."

However: See number 4, above. As I have argued in chapter 4, Gerty's thoughts are a function of Bloom's. Besides, as the women of "Nausicaa" remark, Bloom was near enough to hear such things.

11. "MOTHER GROGAN" makes an appearance in the mob persecuting Bloom (1716).

Why included: Mother Grogan is a character invented by Mulligan in "Telemachus," when Bloom was not present.

However: Bloom gets a chance to hear about her from Mulligan's renditions in "Scylla and Charybdis" (U 9.1186) and "Oxen of the Sun" (U 14.732).

12. In a hallucination of childbirth, Bloom *"bears eight male yellow and white children"* named accordingly, one of them as *"Chrysostomos,"* Greek for "golden-mouthed" (1821–22, 1827).

Why included: "Chrysostomos" comes directly from Stephen's thoughts (U 1.26). Bloom obviously had no access to those thoughts, and could almost certainly not, on his own, know of the name, or of either of the two classical figures who bore it.

However: Actually, most of those eight names—names like *"Nasodoro," "Maindorée,"* and *"Panargyros"*—are multilingual hybrids of a kind unavailable to someone with Bloom's limited knowledge of languages. Which is to say that, as with Virag's vocabulary (see number 17, below), a personal impulse—here, the wish to have successful, money-making children—is being given expressive assistance through a dramatic medium capable of extending a character's verbal powers while still responding faithfully to the course of his or her thoughts and feelings. (That is, after all, what Shakespeare did.) And that medium, given the impressive scope of its erudition, need not necessarily have gotten "Chrystostomos" from Stephen, any more than it did "Panargyros."

13. The character "CRAB" wears a *"bushranger's kit"* (1872–73).
Why included: It appears as part of a Bloom fantasy but comes from Mulligan's skit, as presented to Stephen alone (*U* 9.1182).
However: Bloom was walking right behind them at the time (*U*.1197–1203).

14. Florry Talbot: "Well, it was in the papers about Antichrist. O, my foot's tickling." This conjunction (papers, foot) summons the appearance of *"Ragged barefoot newsboys, jogging a wagtail kite"* (2135–37).
Why included: The newsboys and the kite image come from a description of Bloom in "Lestrygonians," yet this is Stephen's scene.
However: Was Stephen's scene. Bloom has entered the room, and is about to be noticed (2142). He is therefore available to make his own contributions. And either Bloom or Stephen might have observed the "Aeolus" sight of a newsboy "zigzagging white on the breeze a mocking kite, a tail of white bowknots" in Bloom's wake (*U* 8.445–46)—in fact we know for sure that Bloom did observe it (*U* 13.1056–57).

15. Spotting Bloom, Stephen intones the apocalyptic line "A time, times and half a time," generating this:

(*Reuben J Antichrist, wandering jew, a clutching hand open on his spine, stumps forward. Across his loins is slung a pilgrim's wallet from which protrude promissory notes and dishonoured bills. Aloft over his shoulder he bears a long boatpole from the hook of which the sodden huddled mass of his only son, saved from Liffey waters, hangs from the slack of its breeches. A hobgoblin in the image of Punch Costello, hipshot, crookbacked, hydrocephalic, prognathic with receding forehead and Ally Sloper nose, tumbles in somersaults through the gathering darkness.*) (2143–53)

Why included: This is mainly based on a story told, in "Hades," to a group that did not include Stephen. The language echoes that scene's account of how Dodd, "stumping round the corner of Elvery's Elephant house, showed them a curved hand open on his spine" (*U* 6.252–53). The ensuing evocation of Punch Costello is triggered by Bloom's "Oxen" thoughts that, compared with his own dead Rudy, Costello is—like the junior Dodd—manifestly less worthy of survival. These thoughts were not shared with Stephen.

However: The Dodd story has been "going the rounds" (*U* 6.264), so Stephen might have heard it elsewhere. *"Open on his spine,"* like the "wobble" of number 9, certainly seems to derive from the language of the previous narrative, but the datum that it describes comes from public property familiar to everyone in Dublin, emphatically including members of the Dedalus family. ("We have all been there," says Martin Cunningham, speaking of the Dodd establishment [*U* 6.259].)[4] Likewise, the description of Costello is consistent not only with Bloom's perceptions but with those of everyone else in the "Oxen" drinking party, who upbraid Costello as an "abortion," an "ape," and so on (*U* 14.329–30). The reason that Stephen and Bloom both happen to think of Costello as freakishly big-headed, that Bloom calls him a "creature of a misshapen gibbosity" (*U* 14.854–55) (that is, sporting a head prominently round and oversized, like a gibbous moon), and that Stephen here envisions him as *"hydrocephalic"*—and probably, that he has been nicknamed "Punch," after the big-headed Punch puppet—is that that is what Costello really is.[5]

16.

(*A rocket rushes up the sky and bursts. A white star falls from it, proclaiming the consummation of all things and second coming of Elijah. Along an infinite invisible tightrope taut from zenith to nadir the End of the World, a twoheaded octopus in gillie's kilts, busby and tartan filibegs, whirls through the murk, head over heels, in the form of the Three Legs of Man.*)

THE END OF THE WORLD

(*with a Scotch accent*) Wha'll dance the keel row, the keel row, the keel row?

(2174–78)

Why included: the figure depicted here seems to emerge directly out of Stephen's Punch Costello vision, yet is made up mainly of Bloom's memories from "Lestrygonians," "Aeolus," and "Nausicaa." That its summoner bestows Scottish attributes on the *"twoheaded octopus"* of A.E.'s overheard dictation (*U* 8.520) shows that he understands, as Bloom did not, that one of those heads was supposed to be Edinburgh.

However: Whatever he understood, Bloom did hear A.E. say that one head "speaks with a Scotch accent" (*U* 8.521–22, 529–30)—more than enough to summon up visions of kilts and tartans. However close together in line-count Stephen's apocalyptic hobgoblin and Bloom's apocalyptic gilly, they are separated by a disruptive interlude (2165–73) during which Florry Talbot exclaims, "The end of the world!" and breaks wind, causing someone to open the window, which then lets in the sound of a gramophone, which is playing the hymn "The Holy City." These events are incorporated into Bloom's hallucination, which is not an outgrowth of Stephen's but rather a separate variation on the same last-days theme: any similarity between them arises from their common source.

17. Virag: "Insects of the day spend their brief existence in reiterated coition, lured by the smell of the inferiorly pulchritudinous female possessing extendified pudendal nerve in dorsal region" (2412–14).

Why included: This is one of many cases where Virag's erudition is beyond Bloom's reach. Stephen or Joyce or somebody else must be helping. Yet the entire Virag sequence is supposedly Bloom's solitary hallucination.

However: So what else is new? Bloom doesn't know Charles Lamb or Thomas de Quincey from Adam, yet in the previous episode has had his innermost memories written out in Lambian and De Quinceyan language, including words like "oleaginous" and "upupa." Since dramatic literature's dawn, the rule has been that an author can smooth out or jazz up any given character's dialogue so long as the result is a recognizable facsimile of what that character might have said. Joyce went easy on the convention during the early episodes, but by "Circe"—"Vision animated to bursting point" is its "Technic"—all such rhetorical resources are at full throttle: thus the Bloom who in "Calypso" did not know the word "hookah" (*U* 4.490) does, in "Circe," know the word "howdah" (315).

And this is indeed what Bloom might have said, given the vocabulary: in fact it comes directly out of his "Nausicaa" meditations on the role of pheromones in the mating rituals of animals (*U* 13.1026–38), including insects and those sailors who are, he thinks, forever "Smelling the tail end of ports" (*U* 13.1155). As for the vocabulary itself, both Virag's *"basilicogrammate"* word-hoard and his familiarity with vintage esoterica derive directly from the prior fact that Bloom specifically associates him with ancient learning. Virag is his grandfather, and in "Nausicaa" Bloom had remembered "the tephilim no what's this they call it poor papa's father had on his door to touch" (*U* 13.1157). He means, of course, a mezuzah, with its scroll of ancient texts from the Torah, which scroll shows up in "Circe" as the "roll of parchment" (2307) from which Virag, his "papa's father" repeatedly reads, and from which he has presumably derived much of that recondite learning of his. Just as De Quincey was the appropriate voice to render the deepest reaches of Bloom's hallucination in "Oxen of the Sun," so Virag is by Bloom's lights just the right figure to expound, and expand on, his own robust interest in scandalous erudition.

18. When Ben Dollard appears near the end of Virag's turn, "A VOICE" is heard saying, "Hold that fellow with the bad breeches," to which Dollard responds, "Hold him now" (2616–18).

Why included: Except for the substitution of "breeches" for "trousers," this recapitulates the "Wandering Rocks" exchange between Dollard and Simon Dedalus (*U* 10.905), at which Bloom was not present.

However: The whole passage is cued and conditioned by Bloom's memory of the time Dollard showed up to borrow a new costume from Molly because his tight pants were too revealing (*U* 11.554–60). Hence, perhaps, the change to "breeches," punned (at *U* 12.1342) with "breach," a word that throughout appears in such phrases as "breach of marriage" and "breach of the proprieties." (The magic word that brings him forth here, after all, is Virag's "Kok!") So what we have here is one of those peculiar cases where the thought—here, that Dollard has dubious, even actionable, "breeches"—originates in Bloom's memory, but some of the language is carried over from someone else.

19. The Nymph, turning on Bloom: "Sully my innocence! You are not fit to touch the garment of a pure woman. (*She clutches again in her robe*) Wait. Satan, you'll sing no more lovesongs" (3457–59).

Why included: The last line comes from a story told in "Sirens" by Bob Cowley (with "scoundrel" instead of "Satan" [*U* 11.928]), playing the piano while in a room adjoining Bloom's. How could Bloom possibly pick up his words?

However: See chapter 4. Bloom's sense of hearing throughout this scene is extraordinary. Besides, this is just the kind of story he would know on his own.

20. Bloom, countering the Nymph, shouts "Hoy! Nebrakada!" (3463)

Why included: This is the second instance of this word in "Circe," from a book that we saw Stephen but not Bloom reading. Yet it occurs as part of what is supposedly Bloom's fantasy.

However: Again, it is entirely possible that Bloom encountered the book on his own. In fact this reoccurrence reinforces the inference that the first instance

(319), delivered by Molly's apparition, derives from Bloom's memory. And, again: we should not be too quick to assume that Stephen or Bloom has not picked up some datum just because we never witness them in the act. *Ulysses* is full of instances where Bloom in particular must have registered something off-stage: the General Slocum disaster (*U* 8.1146–47: we never see him reading or hearing about that), the moment during the time frame of "Lotus-Eaters" when "the jarvies raised their hats" (*U* 6.173–74: we never see him seeing that), the news that Boylan was arriving at four ("Who said four?" "Sirens" asks us, taunting [*U* 11.351]), and many others.

21.

LYNCH
(*points*) The mirror up to nature. (*he laughs*) Hu hu hu hu hu!
(*Stephen and Bloom gaze in the mirror. The face of William Shakespeare, beardless, appears there, rigid in facial paralysis, crowned by the reflection of the reindeer antlered hatrack in the hall.*)
SHAKESPEARE
(*in dignified ventriloquy*) 'Tis the loud laugh bespeaks the vacant mind. (*to Bloom*) Thou thoughtest as how thou wastest invisible. Gaze. (*he crows with a black capon's laugh*) Iagogo! How my Oldfellow chokit his Thursdaymornun. Ia-gogogo! (3819–29)

Why included: Bloom and Stephen compositely, and it seems randomly, fig-ure in this apparition. The "Shakespearian" diction is mainly Bloom's version, but "black capon" is there because Stephen knows, as Bloom surely does not, about Robert Greene's "upstart crow" remark. (He has quoted from it at *U* 9.926–27.) As for "Iagogogo," that probably comes from the "Do. But do" line (*U* 9.653, 11.908) that, weirdly, has occurred separately to both. All in all, then, it is impossible to identify any single memory as the source. The confusion of voices is all the more striking because the sequence derives, literally, from one person's point of view—that of Stephen, when he looks at the mirror from an angle and sees Bloom's image with the hall hatrack poised behind, its "antlered" top (2032) hovering above the head.

However: Actually, the directions say that both Bloom and Stephen are si-multaneously gazing in the mirror, in other words that each is seeing the other's reflection. So the resulting composite should somehow incorporate both faces, not just Bloom's: indeed later, as the apparition fades away, melting into that of the Shakespeare look-alike Martin Cunningham, it will still be reflecting their double gaze (3863). How is that possible? Parallax. Hold your two index fingers, at the same level, a few inches apart, then focus on a third object closer to your face—say, the end of a pipe held in your mouth—located along the perpendicular reaching from the midpoint between them. Then draw your fingers together until the semitransparent outlines of both overlap to frame one central, hovering, opaque, bean-shaped figure. Notice that, so long as you keep your focus on the nearer third point, this figure is a fusion: a red dot inked in the middle of one fingertip and a green circle drawn around the edge of the other will give that bean a two-color bulls-eye. This, on a large scale, is the process at work. Stephen and Bloom each constitutes one point of view, each originating a line of sight extending to/through/from the mirror to the face of the other, but focused on the midpoint of the mirror itself, both of them coordinated in one common cerebralised sensorium. This was, after all, a routine experience in those millions of late-Victorian and Edwardian homes with stereoscopes in their parlors. Stephen, remembering one such implement, has earlier explained the principle at work: "Flat I see, then think distance, near, far, flat I see, east, back. Ah, see now! Falls back suddenly, frozen in stereoscope" (*U* 3.418–20). (He continues these thoughts into "Circe," at 3629–31.) "Frozen," incidentally, explains why the Shakespeare portrait has to be *"rigid in facial paralysis."* And the stereoscopic effect as Stephen explains it—tricking the eye by ("think distance") tricking the mind—should blend both visual and derivative formulations, what each thinks about Shakespeare as well as what each sees.

So the resulting picture is, first, beardless because both Stephen and Bloom are beardless (and also because the thirty-year-old Hamlet, as the midpoint between twenty-two-year-old Stephen and thirty-eight-year-old Bloom, is "beardless" [*U* 9.832]), and marked on both sides with the stigmata of betrayal: for the cuckolded Bloom, for the Stephen given to seeing himself as a stag at bay, for the horns-obsessed Shakespeare. "Reindeer" situates the horning in Hamlet's Denmark. The laugh is a *"black capon's"* because both Stephen and Bloom, like Hamlet, wear black, and because both, like Hamlet and Stephen's Shakespeare, feel unmanned. "The loud laugh bespeaks the vacant mind" is a sentiment to which both the Stephen wounded by Mulligan's mockery and the Bloom who at this moment suspects that Lynch is laughing at his marital travails might subscribe. Both, in different ways, have entertained fantasies of invisibility. As noted earlier, both have separately helped generate that strange "Iagogogo" line (its sensory source is probably Lynch's staccato laughter in the background),[6] and both, like operatic singers in one of those duets where the lyrics do not always match, contribute to the garbled last line—the Stephen who like Joyce blames some father-figure, some "old fellow" (*U* 9.614) for killing his mother as Othello killed Desdemona, the Bloom who, especially just now, has this day been, like Othello, goaded with images of sexual violation and betrayal.

All in all, then, it won't do to say that this Shakespeare portrait comes out of some textual free-for-all. As much as anywhere in the book, text here is at the service of a distinctive psychology—a composite psychology, true, but all the same one following rules determined by the contours of the remembered experiences of the characters whose composite it is. The facts of individual sensation, perception, association, and abstraction remain as they were. It is, to be sure, one of those cases in *Ulysses*—the two "Do. But Do"s constituted another—where it becomes necessary to posit something supernormal, something like telepathy, in the mind(s) responsible. But then after all the subject is Shakespeare, old myriadminded Will himself, the one who, everyone always says, contains multitudes. In "Scylla and Charybdis," Lyster had called him, in a partially recorded sentence, a mirror "in which everyone can find his own" reflection (*U* 9.582). That, as much as the mirror held up to nature recalled by Lynch, is the kind of mirror at work here.[7]

22. Patrick Dignam Jr. shows up in the Shakespeare hallucination with the porksteaks and unruly collar that accompanied him in "Wandering Rocks" (3844–55).

Why included: Neither Stephen nor Bloom was around to see him.

However: He was bringing those porksteaks home, where Bloom visited a few hours later.

23. Zoe Higgins starts up the pianola, and Professor Goodwin appears as impresario: *"Professor Goodwin, in a bowknotted periwig, in court dress, wearing a stained Inverness cape, bent in two from incredible age, totters across the room, his hands fluttering"* (4018–20).

Why included: Goodwin is a fixture of Bloom's private memory.

However: He is also a fixture of the public memory. See Cowley's recollection (*U* 11.466–68), which accords with Bloom's (and Molly's) judgment that Goodwin was ancient, far gone in drink, and losing his musical touch.

24.

(All wheel whirl waltz twirl Bloombella Kittylynch Florryzoe jujuby women. Stephen with hat ashplant frogsplits in middle highkicks with skykicking mouth shut hand clasp

part under thigh. With clang tinkle boomhammer tallyho hornblower blue green yellow flashes Toft's cumbersome turns with hobbyhorse riders from gilded snakes dangled, bowels fandango leaping spurn soil foot and fall again.) (4122–48)

Why included: "*Jujuby*" comes from a Bloom thought ("jujube") in "Lestrygonians" (*U* 8.04); Toft's whirligig comes from Kitty Ricketts' memory of the bazaar (2718–19); "*tallyho hornblower*" recycles a line from "Wandering Rocks" (*U* 10.1264) originating in that episode's anonymous narrator. Yet here they all are in one stage direction, thrown together. Clearly, no one consciousness is in control.

However: No, but perhaps a number of consciousnesses are, collectively. Do not the directions signify some such psychic synergy, what with "*Kittylynch*" and "*Bloombella*" all wheeling, whirling, waltzing in one Mixmastered round? This seems to me one of those (rare) places in the episode in which a disintegration of boundaries—including, here, the boundary of the body, or at least of the perception of the body—is accompanied by a partial disintegration of character, a genuine mingling of voices, including inner voices. It is not accidental that these passages cluster around the episode's end, when things are breaking down in all kinds of ways. Even so, a mingling of voices is as far as it gets. "*Tallyho cap*" may as a phrase belong to "Wandering Rocks," but the sight of that cap on the Trinity porter's head is, as Molly confirms, public property (*U* 1257–58). Likewise, everyone knows what a whirligig looks like and what a ride on one feels like. As for "*jujuby*": the only thing really proved by the prior occurrence in "Lestrygonians" is that Bloom knows the word and is partial to it.

25.

STEPHEN

Dance of death.

(Bang fresh barang bang of lacquey's bell, horse, nag, steer, piglings, Conmee on Christass, lame crutch and leg sailor in cockboat armfolded ropepulling hitching stamp hornpipe through and through. Baraabum! On nags hogs bellhorses Gadarene swine Corny in coffin steel shark stone onehandled Nelson two trickies Frauenzimmer plumstained from pram falling bawling. Gum he's a champion. Fuseblue peer from barrel rev. evensong Love on hackney jaunt Blazes blind coddoubled bicyclers Dilly with snowcake no fancy clothes. Then in last switchback lumbering up and down bump mashtub sort of viceroy and reine relish for tublumber bumpshire rose. Baraabum!) (4138–50)

Why included: Speaks for itself. The sequence is a jumble of tag-lines, about half of them from "Wandering Rocks," which is itself not attributable to any one center of consciousness, the rest from most of the other episodes of the book up to the present one. Obviously, this cannot be originating in the mind of any one character, nor even any psychically anastomosed set of characters.

However: Although the tags are variously derived, the center of consciousness coordinating them is unitary and identifiable. For the pirouetting Stephen Dedalus, spinning himself dizzy, the room seems to be whirling around: *"Stephen whirls giddily. Room whirls back"* (4151). The resulting illusion of blurred dancers circling rapidly around him at first reminds his morose medieval mind of a "Dance of death." (The association gets helped along by Simon's sarcastic injunction to "Think of your mother's people" [4137]: Stephen thinks of these people as inhabiting "Houses of decay" [*U* 3.105].) The introjection of the lacquey's bell, which in "Wandering Rocks" was made to double with the "lastlap bell" of a bicycle race (*U* 10.651–53), turns the whirling dance into a whirling race.[8] That race then follows its own delirious logic, recognizable once we imagine it as Stephen sees and processes it, as a sped-up succession of headlong figures going in a circle, like something witnessed from inside a zoetrope. So, logically, to help him keep up with the pack, the slow-moving Father Conmee is supplied with appropriate transport, as is his wealthier opposite the Reverend Love—a cab for the latter, an ass, reminiscent of Christ's, for the former, who in "Wandering Rocks" was seen frugally taking public transportation on a mission of mercy. Obviously the one-legged sailor is going to need special help, help which, because he is a sailor, should be nautical: hence a cockboat, hitched by a rope to an imaginary ship in front, which thus pulls him, at his ease and arms folded, along in its wake. Stephen's two arthritic *"Frauenzimmer"* get up to speed by the simple expedient of jumping, with baby, from atop the pillar where we left them; should the result prove fatal Corny Kelleher stands ready with his coffin, like the child's coffin being trundled along in "Hades." In their plummet they are joined by the prison guards hurled into the sky (and then back down to the ground), by a Fenian bomb (*U* 3.239–49), and by the Gadarene swine of the Bible, plunging into the ocean, cousins of the *Ulysses* cattle being driven down to the Irish Sea to be slaughtered (this is still a dance of death), and in the company of the whirligig horses whose spinning, just past, helped launch this spinning. Other riders fill out the rout. Dilly Dedalus, sadly, is the only one left standing, as she was by Stephen (*U* 10.875–80).

26. *"(From the top of a tower Buck Mulligan, in particoloured jester's dress of puce and yellow and clown's cap with curling bell, stands gaping at her, a smoking buttered split scone in his hand.)"* (4166–68)

Why included: Mulligan appears as part of Stephen's vision of his mother, with details mostly drawn from the moment in "Telemachus" when he wounded Stephen's feelings with his insensitive talk about her death. But *"smoking buttered split scone"* comes from his "Wandering Rocks" tea break with Haines, when Stephen was not present (*U* 10.1087–88).

However: Actually, as we will see in chapter 16, Stephen might have seen him eating that scone, too. And even if he didn't, this one detail is a close variant of the moment in "Telemachus" when Mulligan, in Stephen's presence, "impaled" a "thick slice of bread on his knife" and "filled his mouth with crust thickly buttered on both sides" (*U* 1.365–64, 446–47). The unflattering point being made about Mulligan by both those eating vignettes is the same point—and the same one being made by this "Circe" rendition, which clearly reflects Stephen's final verdict on him. It is, that is, no random collocation of verbal tags, but a focused fusion of recollections, one of which may or may not be beyond Stephen's ken, all of them selected in accordance with what Stephen is feeling and thinking at this moment, and possibly—as argued in chapter 9—conditioned, Pavlovianally, by the repetition of the sound of a ringing bell. And the item about Mulligan's bread being "buttered on both sides" can remind us that Joyce's leeway in such matters extends beyond this episode. Bloom has not witnessed either the "Telemachus" or "Wandering Rocks" scenes, but that will not stop him, in "Eumaeus," from warning Stephen that Mulligan "knows which side his bread is buttered on" (*U* 16.284).

27.

EDWARD THE SEVENTH
(levitates over heaps of slain, in the garb and with the halo of Joking Jesus, a white jujube in his phosphorescent face)
My methods are new and are causing surprise.
To make the blind see I throw dust in their eyes. (4475–79)

Why included: The description is from the Bloom of "Lestrygonians" (*U* 8.3–4): the words are from Mulligan's song, as recited in "Telemachus," with no Bloom present.

However: Actually, the words are from a verse of that song hitherto unrecorded in *Ulysses,* though doubtless Stephen, who has heard the whole rendition "Three times a day, after meals" (*U* 1.610) knows it by heart. So it is Stephen's memory, not textual reflexivity, that produces this apparent anomaly. And as with the Shakespeare apparition, it is only by postulating a mutual exchange of memories that this composite may be accounted for. Shakespeare inspired that treatment in part by virtue of being a universal cultural touchstone, someone of whom both Stephen and Bloom were and had been thinking in parallel, and much the same applies to the king: his are the likenesses and insignia that have been greeting both men from every coin, stamp, and uniform. Thus when he appears on the scene he shakes hands with both, the only apparition to do anything like that, and the only one besides Shakespeare to acknowledge both simultaneously. And the vision of him that emerges is truly, uncannily, a meeting of minds, beginning with the premise, shared by both, that he is an imperial bloodsucker. To this core conceit Bloom contributes (again) his jujubes, his phosphorescent crucifix (*U* 8.819–21), his pile of sucked-white slaves; Stephen as it were takes the hint, and with some help from Dante Alighieri (whose Satan chews, in the middle of *his* glowing face, the Jew Judas), turns Edward into Christ-as-Antichrist.

He does something else too, as eerie as any mind-reading. You are here, he had said to the soldiers at the beginning of this sequence, "By virtue of the fifth of George and seventh of Edward" (4370–71). But in 1904 George V was still six years away, and although it was a good bet that that would indeed be the name of the next monarch, asserting it as a fact would have been foolhardy of Joyce had he not actually been writing this book during his reign. "Fifth of George" is a prophecy, like all *Ulysses* prophecies destined to be borne out by events. As such it exemplifies the dispensation that allows Bloom and Stephen in tandem to form, in this passage, a prophetic political cartoon the gist of which is that the reign of Edward VII will lead to a Great War that will blight the reign of his successor: the king, rising up and boasting about those "methods" of his—personal diplomacy, *ententes*[9]—supposed by the blinded subjects into whose eyes he is throwing dust to be producing universal peace, in truth leading to the next decade's "heaps" of battlefield "slain." Levitating over his handiwork, he assumes the pose sometimes given in works of pictorial political hagiography to great foregone spirits who having ascended to heaven continue to look down, benignly, on their legacy below. Which means, in Edward's case, on those "heaps of slain."

Again, this is not achieved by textual bricolage. It is the product of two distinct minds working together, for the duration gifted with powers both psychic and prophetic.

28.

EDWARD THE SEVENTH

(dances slowly, solemnly, rattling his bucket, and sings with soft contentment)
On coronation day, on coronation day,
O, won't we have a merry time,
Drinking whisky, beer and wine! (4559–64)

Why included: Whatever the case with Mulligan's song, this one clearly derives from "Telemachus," and nowhere else. The bucket, on the other hand, earlier identified as *"a plasterer's bucket on which is printed* Défense d'uriner" (4456–57), just as clearly comes from Bloom's emergency evacuation into such a receptacle. Bloom probably does not know the song; Stephen certainly does not know of the bucket incident.

However: "Coronation Day" is "from nowhere else" but "Telemachus"? Why? It was a popular song in a major national festival of about two years ago. This is, after all, still the king, still a repository of public memory, here being viewed, like Shakespeare, in double focus. The composite picture is still of a merry monarch, coarse and gorged, blithely oblivious to the carnage wrought in his name: thus the dancing and singing here goes on while the Croppy Boy, being hanged by his soldiers, dances in a different way in the background. Which, pretty much interchangeably, is the kind of thing both Stephen and Bloom think of when they think of their sovereign.

29. During the pandemonium leading up to the fight, *"Laughing witches in red cutty sarks ride through the air on broomsticks. Quakerlyster plasters blisters"* (4678–80).

Why included: "Laughing witch" is exclusive Bloom property, but although he knows Lyster and has dealt with him today he has no way of knowing that during the library discussion Lyster was a peacemaker, soothing sore spots—evidently the idea behind his blister-plastering activity here.

However: Bloom surely shares the belief that Lyster is a Quaker and therefore a peacemaker,[10] and probably knows as well of Dr. Joseph Lister, also a Quaker, known for treating and curing wounds (with carbolic-soaked plasters), who was still around in Bloom's time and famous enough to have a mouthwash named after him.

30.

(Black candles rise from its gospel and epistle horns. From the high barbacans of the tower two shafts of light fall on the smokepalled altarstone. On the altarstone Mrs Mina Purefoy, goddess of unreason, lies, naked, fettered, a chalice resting on her swollen belly. Father Malachi O'Flynn in a lace petticoat and reversed chasuble, his two left feet back to the front, celebrates camp mass.) (4689–95)

Why included: The "barbacan" complex is Stephen's, from "Telemachus"; Mrs. Purefoy's sacramental parturition is a Bloom formulation, from "Lestrygonians." Never the twain have met. Likewise, the officiating priest combines Stephen's Malachi Mulligan and Bloom's Father O'Flynn.

However: First, O'Flynn comes from a popular song, widely known, and his connection of Malachi and O'Flynn may have a separate provenance: in "Cyclops" Malachi shows up, along with Saint Patrick, in O'Flynn's entourage (*U* 12.1727–28). More generally, as in the previous end-of-days sequence, the apocalypse here enacted naturally tends to compromise psychic boundaries. (Also physical ones: Stephen will wind up being punched in the nose.) In a way, Bloom has prepared us for such mingling of selves: trying to imagine the "last day idea," in "Hades" he had speculated on how, on judgment day, the graveyard dead would go about properly reassembling themselves from out of all the remains scattered around (*U* 6.677–82). As for Stephen, Lynch has it right when, watching him getting himself in trouble, he remarks, "He likes dialectic, the universal language" (4726). The structure of this hallucinatory finale reflects the temper of the young man whose dominant influence made "Scylla and Charybdis" into an episode the "Technic" of which was "dialectic." In both cases the word works in the two related senses of debate and thesis-antithesis. First, Stephen is getting, dialectically, into an argument, and, second, the oppositional scenario generated out of this face-off is reflected in the dialectical pairings running through the whole sheep-versus-goats scene: here, for instance, the gospel and epistle horns, the two light shafts, Malachi and O'Flynn; immediately before it such equal opposites as *"John O'Leary against Lear O'Johnny, Lord Edward Fitzgerald against Lord Gerald Fitzedward, The O'Donoghue of The Glens against The Glens of The O'Donoghue"* (4685–88). Which is one way of representing the home truth that people involved in a fight typically view everyone around them in for-or-against terms. And Stephen has from the beginning been prone to the idea that minor skirmishes may contain within them the seeds of major conflagrations: in "Nestor" the sound of a hockey goal conjured a vision of "Jousts, slush and uproar of battles, the frozen deathspew of the slain, a shout of spear-spikes baited with men's bloodied guts" (*U* 2.317–18), here recycled, as part of this street-scene apocalypse, as a "pentice of gutted spearpoints" (4611–12).

31. Continuing the *"camp mass,"* "THE REVEREND MR HAINES LOVE" *"raises high behind the celebrant's petticoat, revealing his grey bare hairy buttocks between which a carrot is stuck."*

Why included: The *"grey . . . buttocks"* are an intertextual irruption alerting those in the know to the fact that Malachi Mulligan is really Oliver Gogarty, bearing the same name as a character in a novel by George Moore whose posterior is there thus described (*JJ* 2:234). The imputation of homosexual anality comes from Mulligan's warning, when Bloom is not around, that Stephen should beware Bloom's buggerous attentions (*U* 9.614–15).

However: First, as with Rumbold, above, literary in-jokes do not a postmodern ethos make; if they did, just about everyone, including Shakespeare, Trollope, and T. S. Eliot, would belong to the club. Second, Mulligan repeats that warning of pederasty when Bloom is following just behind (*U* 9.1209–11), well within earshot. (What he says is, "Get thee a breechpad"; the carrot blocks his own breech.) Third, that carrot, placed as it is, illustrates Bloom's conventional conviction that vegetarianism and effeteness go together (*U* 8.533–44).

32.

(*Against the dark wall a figure appears slowly, a fairy boy of eleven, a changeling, kidnapped, dressed in an Eton suit with glass shoes and a little bronze helmet, holding a book in his hand. He reads from right to left inaudibly, smiling, kissing the page.*) (4965–70)

Why chosen: ?

However: Exactly. This, and the concluding stage direction that follows, bear no trace of Stephen's input,[11] even though he is still in the episode, still present. That is because, having been knocked unconscious, he is for the time being mentally blank and consequently has nothing to contribute to the generation of this apparition or to the memories that fill it out. This principle—that the hallucinations of "Circe" derive from the consciousness of those present (and awake) at the time—is the same that accounts for the fact that, once Stephen has bolted from the scene, every single one of the seventy-seven figures listed in the *"hue and cry"* following Bloom comes from Bloom's memory, with nary a Stephen character in the lot (4335–61). Which, I would suggest, tells us something about what is going on in those composite or severally inflected hallucinations that appeared when he was around, awake, and engaged.

It tells us that the hallucinations were essentially psychological, not textual, in origin. Admittedly, this thesis leaves some loose ends. But there are always loose ends in *Ulysses*. On the whole, what remains striking is how many such apparent anomalies melt away on inspection. Indeed, so consistently do apparently baffling questions about the origins of some phrase or image turn out on second look to find their answers somewhere in the preceding text that one suspects Joyce of doing it on purpose, of playing yet another puzzle-game with the reader. He is, after all, notorious for that. The first word of *Ulysses*, "Stately," poses a question—is this an adjective or an adverb?—that is not answered until the forty-fifth line of the seventh episode, where the word "statelily" shows us how the adverb option would have looked. Make a photocopy of the "Ithaca" list of Molly's lovers (*U* 17.2133–42), keep it at your side while reading through "Penelope," crossing off each name as Molly's narrative explains it away, and eventually it will probably dawn on you that you have been set up, that the "Ithaca" catalogue was misleading in a way the next episode systematically exposes. Going through the above "Circe" list, especially numbers 1, 3, 7, 9, 13, 16, and 20, such suspicions dawn anew. Rather than being challenged to abandon our archaically pre-postmodern fixation on character and character psychology, if anything we are being challenged to retain it, holding fast against cresting transformational forces that, like the Circean magic in Homer, are finally more bark than bite. Even changed into Circe's pigs, after all, Odysseus's men kept their minds, hence their identities, intact. Then they changed back.

The centrality of character and character psychology holds not only because almost all of the disputed cases turn out plausibly to have their origins in the memories of those experiencing them but because the few arguable exceptions continue to be consistent with the personalities and personal histories to which they are attributed. And about those exceptions from the list above, just three— numbers 9 ("wobble"), 15 ("open on his spine"), and 18 ("Hold that fellow with the bad breeches")—may stand up.[12] It should be remembered that they themselves constitute nothing new in *Ulysses*, nor do they occur in "Circe" with unusual frequency. As noted before, it is mainly a matter of allowing the narrator of *Ulysses*, "Circe" included, the same prerogative of establishing and recycling his own narrative idiom that we grant to every other teller of tales. In "Lestrygonians," even though absent the just-departed Bloom, the narrator still applies Bloom's phrase "snuffling it up" to Nosey Flynn while reporting on Flynn and his companions, none of whom had said or, as far we know, thought it (*U* 8.983). "Plodding toward their goal" (*U* 10.310–11), the sandwichmen of "Wandering Rocks" retrieve the word, "plodded," with which Bloom had earlier described them (*U* 8.155), plus Mr. Deasy's telling Stephen that history moves toward one great goal, but none of the parties is around to remember it. Also in "Wandering Rocks," the anonymous voice of the finale adopts Stephen's earlier conjecture, probably spurious, that the two old women he had seen in "Proteus" are cock-lepickers,[13] that in their bag "eleven cockles rolled" (*U* 10.1275–76; compare *U* 10.818–20), even though Stephen is not on the scene. The "ghostbright" glance from John Henry Parnell (*U* 10.1052) is probably informed by the absent Bloom's "Lestrygonians" picture of him as "poached eyes on ghost" (*U* 8.508). And so on.

Before "Circe," that is, there had already been established a rare but occasional tendency for memorable phrases to migrate, minus the mediation of their only begetters, to other occasions where they also seemed the right words for the job. As such, the practice is anything but new. It may be, certainly, that in the hands of so deliberate a writer this practice may come across as promoting some distinctively Joycean qualities—the verbal playfulness, the fuzzy borders, the self-referentiality, and, I would add, the book's Orphic dimension, that is, its ever-problematical openness to the possibilities of psychic transmigrations through some not-only-physical ether.

In any event it remains the case that such apparent transgressions, in "Circe" and out, continue to reflect the shifting conditions in which unchangingly coherent characters find themselves. That composite Bloom-Stephen Shakespeare shows up as *"Stephen and Bloom gaze in the mirror,"* just the thing to induce one of those trances to which both are especially, uniquely prone in this episode. Later, when Stephen gets dizzy, the action starts whirling around, blurring everything into everything else. And because from that point on Stephen continues at a newly increased level of disorientation up until the moment he is knocked out, that stretch of "Circe," about 20 percent of the total, is exceptionally disoriented too, which among other things means that as in earlier *Ulysses* moments of destabilizing psychic intensity (notably in "Nausicaa" and "Sirens"), identities, and the memories that constitute them, are liable to shift and intermingle to an exceptional degree. It is, to repeat, no coincidence that by far the most frequent and drastic cases of psychic breakdown and interchange occur during that 20 percent. Music, mooniness, and desire brought out Bloom's Orphic capacities earlier in *Ulysses;* now absinthe, dizziness, and fatigue, culminating in a final spell during which he is described as being "giddy," as moving "giddily," as speaking "ecstatically" (4210, 4151, 4654), do the same for Stephen. These destabilizations were, for Joyce, an ever-present potential, which like the mediums and mystics of his day he believed could best be brought out, preferably at night, through such alterations of inner equilibrium as the fasting, substance-abusing, dervishing Stephen has induced in himself.

Stephen, in other words, has worked himself up into a state, and the narrative reflects it, not only in its style and action but in what might be called its level of energy, its relative power to rearrange things, including psychic space. Indeed, throughout the examples cited above the principles governing mental and sometimes extra-mental phenomena seem to come from the same kind of elementary psychic/psychological physics that we have noted already, for instance in the villanelle episode of *Portrait*. The closer to the center of action people are, the greater the force of attraction they exert, the more energy they embody and radiate, the more they will impinge on or absorb the mental force-fields of others and with them the totality of the action. The "navvy" of the opening pages, drunker by far than anyone else around, is the one we see yank up a streetlamp and carry it away: no one else present could have generated such a scene, because no one else was far gone enough to think it possible, thus think it real, thus think it into existence.

In any case, the navvy's moment on stage is brief. For most of "Circe," things are less extreme, and cases of genuine psychic synergy are scarce. Then things change, because the principals change. It is as if in his spinning Stephen had stirred up a vortex—that pet symbol of the age—with the power to radiate ever outward and to suck in an ever wider range of just about anything, overwhelming former limits. Until, inevitably, he collapses, spent, and the psychic field is left entirely to Bloom and his own store of senses and impressions, his own powers of projection, operating at the normative level.

That is exactly the way things would not work if "Circe" were mainly a matter of text playing with text. It is instead mainly a dramatization, thus a highlighting, of the generation of those psychic constructs that, throughout *Ulysses*, Joyce mimetically registers in text. Nonce neologisms such as *"mudflake"* and *"snowcake,"* eponymic legacies like *"gladstone bag"* and *"bowieknife"* (and "Bloomite"), onomatopoeic coinings like *"angriling"* and *"smackfatclacking,"* though all in evidence before "Circe," occur throughout this episode with a new frequency and insistence, as a running reminder that all words have a generative history, beginning with a metaphoric moment of synaptic connection. The language of "Circe" foregrounds the issue of how it, and all words, and all the molecular composites constructed of words, were made.

There is accordingly much more of nineteenth-century historical philology (particularly Max Müller) behind this episode's presentation of that issue than there is of Saussure. The opening scenario establishes the action not only of the characters but of the required reader-viewer intent on understanding it, and it is essentially the action of an historically informed linguistic detective versed in the ways of etymological reconstruction. Thus, at the outset, in line 5:

"Rabaiotti's halted ice gondola." "Ice gondola"? Well, consider: *"Rabaiotti's"* is an Italian name. Italian immigrants were linked in the popular mind with the selling of ice cream ("Italian ice"). Gondolas come from Venice, which is in Italy. This gondola, oddly, moves ahead (*"forges on through the murk"*) not through some canal but along a street, as if on wheels. Ah: perhaps it *is* on wheels. Perhaps it is an Italian-owned ice cream wagon, outfitted as a gondola in order to reinforce the connection, hence an *"ice gondola."* Now, follow the hypothesis: if the gondola shape is real, like the wheels, then the *"swancomb"* is not real—there are no swans prowling the streets of Dublin after dark—but derives from the figural similarity, as seen at night and in silhouette, between the shape of a gondola's prow and the shape of a swan's neck. And *"the stunted men and women,"* sucking on sandwiches of wafers and snow? Well: what, in the vicinity of an ice cream wagon, might resemble snow and be edible? Ah. But *"stunted"*? Well: remember that the tourist wives spotted in "Wandering Rocks," next to their taller consorts, were seen as "stunted forms" (*U* 10.341–42). Thinking of shortness, remember that these forms are customers of an ice cream seller. Remember the silhouette effect. And note the last word of the sentence: *"Sucking, they scatter slowly, children."* In an earlier draft Joyce had written, *"They are children,"* but decided that he didn't want to make it too easy for us.

The unnamed fact of ice cream sandwiches (as usual, a perfect memory would help here—in this case of the "Rabaiotti's icecream car" glimpsed in "Wandering Rocks" [*U* 10.229]) is the Indo-European root behind the latter-day derivatives on show in this sequence,[14] allowing us to distinguish real (children, ice cream, wagon) from figurative (stunted adults, snow, swan) and to stipulate the principle of derivation by which the former has generated the latter. This principle is essentially metaphoric, with tenor (ice cream) jumping to vehicle (snow), because for Joyce as for his generation the production of signification is essentially metaphoric. That production, thus understood, is "Circe" 's central subject and activity. The episode's exponential increase in figurative language reflects an attention to process, and is therefore always taken up with the question of how some intelligence has worked on some given material to forge a phrase or image or scene or fantasia. Usually that intelligence can be given the name of either Stephen or Bloom, both of whom have previously shown themselves fully capable of such metaphoric leaps (as when Bloom, in "Sirens," compares an open semigrand piano to the open mouth of a crocodile [*U* 11.1054], a harp to the poop of a golden ship [*U* 11.1772]) and hyperbole as extravagant as any in the episode (as when Stephen in "Proteus" remembers a green dribble of absinthe as a green fang [*U* 3.226], the blue fire of a match as the "blue fuse"[*U*

3.239] of a terrorist's bomb).[15] (They are also capable of incipient hallucinatory flights: Bloom's of the land being inundated with porter [U 5.314–17], Stephen's of a "sowish" Salomé dancing in a dive [U 10.808–11].)

Named or not, the process continues the same. Shortly after the episode's beginning, as Stephen enters, an *"elderly bawd"* takes his chanting of Church Latin as a sign that he is one of those "all prick and no pence" "Trinity medicals," hisses dismissively through her protruding *"snaggletusks,"* and spits. The stage directions call her spit a *"jet of venom"* (96). Why? Because, hearing her hiss, whoever is producing these directions sees her protruding front teeth as fangs; then, putting sound and sight together, envisions her as a fanged serpent, whose spit is therefore venomous. It is exactly the kind of operation Stephen performed in "Proteus" in remembering the "fang" of absinthe, or that Bloom will soon perform when the "hissing" sound and glaring fire-red headlight of a sandstrewer turn it, in his eyes, into a serpenting "dragon" (185–86). That is, bawd and anonymous bawd-watcher are, after the model of Stephen and Bloom, alike framing metaphoric percepts ("All prick and no pence," snake) by applying certain distinct associations to what they experience. Müllerian philology in Joyce's day entertained the idea that language, including its very letters, memorialized the folk's forging of such mental connections, that for instance the letter S preserved someone's observation that the S-shaped animal made the S-sound. *Finnegans Wake* entertains the same idea (*FW* 19.12–13, and see chapter 17, below). So does "Circe." However high-flown, its hallucinatory sequences continue to arise from the same fundamental operation that has obtained throughout the book, that of someone experiencing something and thinking something else about it.

15

"Circe" Yet Again

An Operatic Finale

WHEN THE BLOOM of "Circe" meets Zoe Higgins as Stephen's piano-playing sounds from inside, the background music, as we have seen, helps establish the ambience. At other times, music can do much more. It can take over the hearer's interior and transform everything happening there, including the way the mind processes its environment. One such transformation scene occurs, appropriately, in Bella Cohen's music room.[1]

Let us, drawing mainly on the stage properties presented on entrance (2031–55),[2] set the scene. The flooring is of a multicolored oilcloth covered with footprints, probably tracked in recently by customers with shoes muddy from the rain.[3] From the narrator's description of these prints as occurring in *"a morris of shuffling feet without body phantoms"* (2045) we may surmise that they resemble the footprint-shaped cutouts laid down by dance instructors. (Sure enough, Professor Maginni, the dancing master, will later show up, on that oilcloth, to demonstrate the "Katty Lanner step" (4044). Although the prints seem *"all in a scrimmage higgledypiggledy"* [2045–46], it should be noted that morris dancers move in circles.) The walls are covered with green wallpaper representing a sylvan scene of yew trees and glades (2046–47). Opposite the door is a fireplace, complete with brass fire irons (2071), covered with a screen of peacock feathers (2047–48), above whose mantle is a gilt-edged mirror (2053).[4] Before it is spread a *"hearthrug of matted hair"* (2048–49). There is at least one window, which, as confirmed at line 2780, is open enough to let in the sound of a gramophone record (2145) coming from a nearby house (605–6) and will be opened wider in the course of the action, when (a) things heat up and (b) someone breaks wind. The weather outside has subsided into a drizzly mist but will soon return to the thunder and lightning that terrified Stephen in "Oxen of the Sun." Hanging from the ceiling is a chandelier (2041) of prismatically glinting cut glass (3988), outfitted with an erratic gas jet with a mauve tissue-paper lampshade (2040–41). To one side is the pride of the establishment, a brand-new (see 1991) Pianola (2072), so up-to-date that it boasts a Wonderlight, one of the Wurlitzer Company's latest and showiest accessories.[5] The Wonderlight is a rotating jeweled ball with a light bulb in the center; when in action, its swirling colors are reflected in mirrored glass petals that surround the center unit. Wurlitzer advertised it as being "ideal for dancing."[6] Although alas I have so far failed to get an adequate photograph or videotape, I can at least report having witnessed the operation of one.[7] The glass petals come in all colors. When a coin is dropped in the slot they send sparkles of rapidly circling rainbow lights across floor, ceiling, and walls. The effect is similar to that produced by a disco glitter-ball, but in color. (And the music is better.) All in all the Wonderlight does indeed seem "ideal for dancing."

Action: Stephen Dedalus is playing idly with the Pianola's keys. Vincent Lynch is sitting by the fireplace, fiddling with the poker. The young men are accompanied by two painted—as the saying goes—ladies, soon to be joined by a third, escorted by Leopold Bloom. The women are gaudily dressed, each with her own color scheme—blue for Kitty Ricketts, sapphire for Zoe Higgins, red for Florry Talbot. Bloom and Stephen, by contrast, wear black.

When Bloom and Zoe make their entrance and join the other two couples, the scene is set. Although smell, touch, and taste all come into play, most of what transpires will fall within the theatrical modalities of sight and sound. Outfitting the room with reflective surfaces and making all the light sources changeable and multicolored, Joyce has seen to it that those modalities are conducive to phantasmagoric effects. (A similar scene has already been established outdoors, where fog expressionistically blurs and refracts the streetlights, and lightning flashes, than which nothing is more efficacious for dramatic emphasis.) For this purpose, the temperamental gas jet turns out to be an especially versatile piece of stage machinery. Right at the start of the brothel scene, when Kitty Ricketts turns it *"full cock"* and the shaft in Lynch's hand immediately *"flashes"* into being as a brass poker instead of the *"wand"* it seemed in dimmer light (2049, 2071), the gas jet's fluctuations are at work transmuting the appearances of things.[8]

This gas jet's changeable influence continues the long-standing literary convention that gaslight, in its flarings and flickerings, is especially serviceable for setting almost any tone. Of Mr. Pickwick, for instance, Dickens had written that "like a gas-lamp," he "burst out" in "brilliancy" and then "flickered" into dimness (Dickens 1986, 23), and in many a novelistic interior since, both persons and the rooms they inhabit had been made to alternate between romantic glow and pitiless glare, fuzzy penumbra and hard-edged anatomy, by means of the same device.[9] Joyce, in his all-out way, extends this convention to its logical extreme. First, his gaslight, prone as it is to malfunction, is exceptionally inconstant. It can flare blindingly one minute and cast the room into darkness the next, change color from white to mauve to green. Second, these changes, working on the hallucinatorily susceptible Stephen and Bloom, alter not only their moods but their perception of reality, and with it the reality presented to us, the audience receiving impressions through their eyes and ears as mediated by their delirious or transfixed brains. So, to follow the transmutations of one sequence, from lines 2257 to 2293:

JOHN EGLINTON

(*produces a greencapped dark lantern and flashes it towards a corner: with carping accent*) Esthetics and cosmetics are for the boudoir. I am out for truth. Plain truth for a plain man. Tanderagee wants the facts and means to get them.

(*In the cone of the searchlight behind the coalscuttle, ollave, holyeyed, the bearded figure of Mananaun MacLir broods, chin on knees. He rises slowly. A cold seawind blows from his druid mouth. About his head writhe eels and elvers. He is encrusted with weeds and shells. His right hand holds a bicycle pump. His left hand grasps a huge crayfish by its two talons.*)

MANANAUN MACLIR

(*with a voice of waves*) Aum! Hek! Wal! Ak! Lub! Mor! Ma! White yoghin of the gods. Occult pimander of Hermes Trismegistos. (*with a voice of whistling seawind*) Punarjanam patsypunjaub! I won't have my leg pulled. It has been said by one: beware the left, the cult of Shakti. (*With a cry of stormbirds.*) Shakti, Shiva! Dark hidden Father! (*He smites with his bicycle pump the crayfish in his left hand. On its co-operative dial glow the twelve signs of the zodiac. He wails with the vehemence of the ocean.*) Aum! Baum! Pyjaum! I am the light of the homestead! I am the dreamery creamery butter. (*A skeleton judashand strangles the light. The green light wanes to mauve. The gasjet wails whistling.*)

THE GASJET

Pooah! Pfuiiiiiii!

(*Zoe runs to the chandelier and, crooking her leg, adjusts the mantle.*)

ZOE

Who has a fag as I'm here?

LYNCH

(*tossing a cigarette on to the table*) Here.

ZOE

(*her head perched aside in mock pride.*) Is that the way to hand the *pot* to a lady? (*She stretches up to light the cigarette over the flame, twirling it slowly, showing the*

*brown tufts of her armpits. Lynch with his poker lifts boldly a side of her slip. Bare from
her garters up her flesh appears under the sapphire a nixie's green. She puffs calmly at her
cigarette.)* Can you see the beautyspot of my behind?

Eglinton's shining lantern is "greencapped," from the greencapped lamps accompanying his earlier appearance in "Scylla and Charybdis" (*U* 9.29–30), because the gas jet has just flared to green, bathing the room in the (snot)
sea-greeny color that helps turn Eglinton's accomplice in that earlier episode,
the mystical, bicycle-riding A.E., into a seaweedy ocean god. In "Sirens" a light-
dimming dropping of a crossblind, casting Miss Douce into "cool dim seagreen
sliding depth of shadow" (*U* 11.464–65), had helped establish her, for Bloom
and reader, as a kind of mermaid; here the process is more drastic, a matter of
hallucination rather than mood, but follows the same associative logic. When
the gaslight then *"wanes to mauve,"* A.E.'s domain glooms into that of a *"darkhid-
den"* deity, just before a *"skeleton judashand"* dims it down far enough to summon Judas, Christianity's archetypal extinguisher of light. When Zoe Higgins
then adjusts the gas jet back to green her flesh assumes the color of *"a nixie's"*—
that is, sea-fairy's—*"green,"* as seen by an ensorcelled Bloom.

So much for the visual field. As for the audio: in this same scene the sound of
the defunctive gas jet as it *"wails whistling"* accounts for the Mananaun MacLir
soundtrack: accompanied by the cry of *"a cold seawind"* and the *"cry of stormbirds,"* MacLir *"wails with the vehemence of the ocean"* and a *"voice of whistling seawind."* I would bet as well that his spluttery monologue owes something to
sputtering gas. As here, much of the episode's stagecraft recalls that imaginative "theatre of the mind" invoked by the BBC radio dramas of the '20s, '30s,
and '40s, as reportedly heard, in Paris, by the purblind James Joyce.[10] A staple of
the sound effects accompanying such performances was the noise of silverfoil
being scrunched to produce various crackling or rustling noises (cowboys am-
bling through sagebrush, rain on woodland, and so forth), and so Zoe Higgins,
fiddling with the silverfoil in which her chocolate has been wrapped (2708),
produces the *"silversilent summer air"* (3378) through which Bloom is envisioned
falling, the *"crackling canebrake over beechmast and acorns"* (3421–22) through
which Virag treads, and, in a rare giveaway phrase, the yew tree's rustling *"silverfoil of leaves precipitating"* (3453). Those yew trees, to return to the modality of
the visible, obviously derive from the room's wallpaper.

So, to restate: by and large, the hallucinations of "Circe" are composites of
determinable auditory and visual stimuli as noticed, combined, and enacted in
the inner theatres of characters' consciousnesses, which consciousnesses fluctu-

ate between passively registering these stimuli at one end of the continuum and, at the other, incorporating and projecting them into a drama, in turn cued by something real.

My main exhibit is the drama prompted by the events preceding Stephen's hurried exit from Bella Cohen's establishment, especially as conditioned by the opera we know he knows (because everyone in Dublin does), Amicare Ponchielli's *La Gioconda*. The action begins at line 4001 as Zoe Higgins puts two pennies in the Pianola slot and starts up a rendition of "My Girl's a Yorkshire Girl," a robust waltz.

Frank Budgen records Joyce's reaction to a similar sight: " 'Look!' said Joyce. 'That's Bella Cohen's piano! What a fantastic effect! All the keys moving and nobody playing' " (Budgen 1967, 228). Here, the Pianola's keys summon the ghostly figure of the late music professor Goodwin, who appears and strikes *"vague"* (4047), *"handless sticks of arms on the keyboard"* (4021)—a fantastic effect combining a version of the Pianola's mechanical works with "nobody." The Wonderlight's colored array comes to life and sends a wheeling rainbow across the room's shiny surfaces. It is joined by the wheeling waltz patterns of Stephen and Lynch with their partners. As Professor Goodwin has materialized to accommodate the Pianola's handlessly moving keys, so dance professor Maginni now appears (4032) to choreograph the phantom dancers adumbrated by that—remember?—morris of footprints on the floor. The combination of automated music and the spinning of bright, many-colored lights reminds Kitty, she says (4109), of the merry-go-round she saw at today's bazaar. That is one bazaar summoned to memory; another is the earlier one at which Bloom witnessed the famous "Dance of the Hours" (*U* 3.525–26) from *La Gioconda*, in which the hours of the day are acted out by curvetting young women, each dressed in colors appropriate to her appointed time. Recalling it in "Calypso," Bloom had summed up: "Poetical idea: pink, then golden, then grey then black" (*U* 3.534–36). And so, when the Pianola is cranked up and its Wonderlight's array of *"gold, pink, and violet lights start forth"* (4016–17) and begins spinning around in a room of dancers, including three women dressed in bright, color-coded outfits and two men dressed in black, all whirling around in waltz-step, the associative link for anyone familiar with the operatic scene is a natural one. Which is why (starting at line 4054) the "Dance of the Hours" dancers join the spectacle, in what can probably best be conceived as an overlapping medley of the two tunes. Until, that is, the Pianola finishing its rendition, Stephen launches into a pirouetting *pas seul* in which everything blurs vertiginously together:

STEPHEN

Pas seul!

(*He wheels Kitty into Lynch's arms, snatches up his ashplant from the table and takes the floor. All wheel whirl waltz twirl Bloombella Kittylynch Florryzoe jujuby women. Stephen with hat ashplant frogsplits in middle highkicks with skykicking mouth shut hand clasp part under thigh. With clang tinkle boomhammer tallyho hornblower blue green yellow flashes Toft's cumbersome turns with hobbyhorse riders from gilded snakes dangled, bowels fandango leaping spurn soil foot and fall again.*) (4119–28)

To understand why that should happen when it does, we should check on the music being played in Stephen's head. Indeed the best advice I can give the reader is to find a recording of the opera and listen to the beginning of act 3, scene 2, where this music occurs. "The Dance of the Hours" comes in two movements, both of them widely familiar. The first, repopularized many years ago in Alan Sherman's joke song, still sometimes played, entitled "Camp Granada" ("Hello muddah, hello faddah," and so on),[11] is a slow-moving piece conducive to the kind of gradual procession assigned to the "Hours." The second movement is just the opposite—a deliriously fast-paced, whirling, fandango-ish revel. "Whirling" here should be taken literally: anyone who hears the piece will recognize it as an invitation to twirl rapidly around the dance floor; the more energetic will feel like jumping and kicking too.[12] If the first half of "The Dance of the Hours" could be a slow march, the second half could be an unusually vigorous cancan of the kind recently made familiar to Stephen, back from Paris (3886).

So: Stephen is dancing and high-kicking in his frenzied way because that is the music going on in his head, following in due order the operatic sequence that got established there by virtue of the associatively conditioned stimuli noted above. First *largo,* then *prestissimo,* just as in "Dance of the Hours." He is playing out the story of *La Gioconda,* act 3, and the stage directions of "Circe" are, for now, following suit. To understand what happens next, we can therefore do no better than to consult the opera's libretto. As we join the action of act 3, "The Dance of the Hours" is being performed at the palace of the nobleman Alvise, who thinks he has just had his wife, Laura, poisoned. (Actually she has taken one of those death-counterfeiting potions so useful for stories of this sort.) Also present are Laura's disguised lover, Enzo, and the La Gioconda of the title, a street musician in love with Enzo. Behind it all has been Barnaba, who because of his beastly lust for La Gioconda has both instigated Laura's supposed poisoning and, falsely accusing her of witchcraft, seized Gioconda's old blind mother, the pious La Cieca—the blind one—who throughout the opera is for-ever praying for the dead.

Immediately upon the conclusion of the "Dance of the Hours," Barnaba ap-pears before the horrified assemblage with La Cieca, whom he will later mur-der, accompanied by the sound of a death-bell (*"The slow tolling of a bell is heard, indicating that someone is dead or dying"* [Gorrio 1996, 36]), ringing for the sup-posedly dead Laura, whose body will be revealed at the scene's climax. Gio-conda cries out at the spectacle of her poor mother, and various parties sing duets about how terrible things are, in a dramatic plummet from gaiety to mis-ery. No wonder the chorus comments on how a fatal vampire—*"un vampiro fatal"*—has made all joy withdraw (Gorrio 1996, 37). In the ensuing debacle, La Cieca accuses Barnaba of murder (*"l'assassino sei tu!"*), the distracted Enzo begs to be put to death, La Gioconda sings weepily ("One by one, my tears are falling," and so on), and Barnaba gloats about all the misery he has caused. The scene ends when Laura's body is revealed and Enzo, *"Lunging at Alvise with a dagger in his hand,"* exclaims "Murderer!" (*"Carnefice!"*) and is stopped by guards as Barnaba spirits La Cieca away *"through a secret door."* The scene ends with the chorus going *"Orror, orror!"*, and who can blame them (Gorrio 1996, 38–39)?

Sure enough, in "Circe," as soon as Stephen rights himself from his dizzying spin, who should appear to him, accompanied by a ringing bell and incanta-tions from the burial service, and with the hollow eye sockets of the blind, but the spectre of his afflicted mother:

> (*Stephen's mother, emaciated, rises stark through the floor, in leper grey with a wreath of faded orangeblossoms and a torn bridal veil, her face worn and noseless, green with gravemould. Her hair is scant and lank. She fixes her bluecircled hollow eyesockets on Stephen and opens her toothless mouth uttering a silent word. A choir of virgins and con-fessors sing voicelessly.*)
>
> THE CHOIR
> *Liliata rutilantium te confessorum. . . .*
> *Iubilantium te virginum. . . . .*(4157–65)

Combining the dead Laura and the blind La Cieca, she works the same kind of condensation on Stephen. Like Enzo he will bring things to a head by lunging forward menacingly with his own weapon, his ashplant, but, with the Mulligan who accused him of killing his mother gloating in the background, finds himself instead cast as a Barnaba, charged with murder and ordered to beg forgiveness.

Again, much of the detail of this scene can be explained from knowledge of its setting. That the mother is green—first from grave-mould, later as a green crab—shows that the gaslight is again in its green phase. Thunder-fearing Stephen will testify in "Ithaca" that the crisis was precipitated by the atmospherics outside[13]—and if with that in mind we take another look at the text we may notice that there has been a sudden *"glareblarefare"* (4132) occurring just before the mother's appearance, followed by the sound of *"Baraabum"* (4133)—as in the flash of lightning, the rumble of thunder: the same sequence that broke Stephen's courage in "Oxen of the Sun." (The window, remember, is open.) The mother's *"scant and lank hair,"* I suggest, originates in the *"hearthrug of matted hair"* noted earlier, which, in the logic of delirium, might become draped over her head when she *"rises stark through the floor."* As for the ashes on her breath (4182), all this is happening in the vicinity of a fireplace.

Other hallucinatory consequences follow from that vicinity. Above the mantle of the hearth, we have noted, is a gilt-edged mirror. What happens in the ensuing sequence is that Stephen, with the *La Gioconda* narrative running in his head, finds the visible correlate of the drama's gruesome climax primarily in the image of his own face, reflected in that mirror. Looking at his mother, conjured as "La Cieca," he is looking at himself in that mirror. At the end of this episode Bloom will remark on how much he resembles his mother (4949). Here, in the reflection of that familial face, the mother's *"toothless"* grin gives back his own "toothless" state, real and contemplated, as established in the epithet applied to him by Mulligan in "Telemachus" (*U* 1.708) and adopted in "Proteus" (*U* 3.494–96). The opened mouth gives back the image of Stephen's open mouth, which has just shouted, "Ho!" (4156). Her La Cieca-like "bluecircled hollow eyesockets" reflect the outline of his spectacle rims. The *"emaciated"* face reflects what we are told are the *"drawn,"* indeed *"drawn grey and old,"* features of his skinny self. When he finds himself *"choking with fright, remorse and horror"* (4186) it is from the mother's mouth that a green rill of liquid drools (literally reflecting his own equivalent of Kevin Egan's "green fairy's fang"); when he is *"strangled with rage"* she is *"in the agony of her deathrattle"* (4223, 4238). She *"wrings her hands,"* and he is holding on to his ashplant *"with both hands"* (4232, 4243). The "fire of hell" (4282) with which she threatens him comes from his own overheated state; like his fellow dancer Zoe Higgins, exclaiming, "I'm melting!" and fanning herself (4206–7)—which produces the sensation of the mother "breathing upon him softly her breath of wetted ashes" (4182)—he has worked up a sweat during the recent exertions. As for the mirror itself, I think we can discern its gilt frame in the *"wreath of faded orangeblossoms"*—faded, presumably, to yellow—surrounding the mother's face. Delirious or not, he is therefore right, at some level seems to know what is going on, when he thinks to end this horror show by smashing not the apparition before him but the gaslight above, the gaslight that has been showing him his face in the mirror and making for this vision's lurid effects.

Those are some of the details. The essential pattern into which they are made to fit, the essential story being acted out, originates in that *Gioconda* narrative, lodged in Stephen's mind by the sounds and sights around him, in a process variably receptive and projective, through the membranes of a selfhood whose unstable permeability seems to me Joyce's most distinctive contribution to fiction. Intellectually committed to the most stringent brand of realism but emotionally given over to the most florid extravaganzas of, above all, music hall and opera, Joyce contrived to have it both ways when he hit on the solution of realistically rendering the inner lives of people who like him loved, and sometimes lived, this music and the stories it tells.

16

Haines's Hallucination

AT THE END OF "CIRCE," a semiconscious Stephen Dedalus answers "Who? Black panther. Vampire" (U 15.4930) when Bloom calls his name. Earlier in the day, a distracted Haines had shown up late for a party and ranted about being stalked by a "black panther" (U 14.1024–5).[1] This same Haines was the one who last night woke Stephen up with his nightmare screams about that same panther.

What, do you suppose, set those two off? Any number of things, perhaps, but one of them, probably, was, yet again, absinthe, known for inducing just such visions. In the 1899 "Absinthea Taetra," the habitué Ernest Dowson wrote, of an *absintheur* beset by "Memories and terrors," that "The past tore after him like a panther." Another jungle cat—this time a leopard—haunts the addict of Marie Corelli's 1890 anti-absinthe best-seller *Wormwood* (Corelli 1890 312). Did Joyce read this book, as he did two other Corelli novels (SL 55)? If we consult *Finnegans Wake* to check *Wormwood* against Atherton's Law, that Joyce always names his sources, it passes muster at FW 579.33–34 with "warmwooed." In *Finnegans Wake* we also find Butt, ii.3's version of the "absintheminded" Shem (FW 464.17), downing a toast of "absents wehrmuth" (FW 348.13) just before the appearance (FW 349.06) of a spectre who is among other things a pard or panther (FW 353.14), and who at the end of the nightmare of a later Shem-type called Jerry is dismissed with motherly assurances that there "are no phanthares in the room" (FW 565.18–19). That same Jerry has, shortly before the panther's expulsion, been given the epithet "greenafang" (FW 563.31), a clear echo of the "green fairy's fang" (U 3.226; compare U 3.238) that in *Ulysses*, as we have seen, marks Kevin Egan as far gone in absinthe.

So Stephen could be acting according to type when the last of his absinthean hallucinations is of a panther. In any case, he is definitely acting according to form. The whole black-panther-vampire sequence follows the kind of hyper-aesthetic perceptual logic that governs his other Circean visions, as outlined long before in the aesthetic theory of *Portrait*. There were, Stephen said in the course of outlining that theory, three stages of true apprehension of an object, which we can track here in the sequence of those three words. *Integritas* is achieved when Stephen separates Bloom's black form from the less-black background. He associates blackness with his own black clothes, Hamlet's black clothes, Hamlet's father's black clothes, and thence fatherhood; Bloom's suit therefore indicates that he is of Stephen's substance, and the "Hamlet" associations supply the framework. Second, Stephen sees Bloom as a distinct shape, assuming the *consonantia* that distinguishes some shapes from others: Bloom is a largish looming four-limbed mammal, still black against the background—thence panther. The memory of Haines's nightmare helps complete this connection, as Stephen's familiarity with the tradition, recently recalled (*U* 15.2599), that Jesus' real father was a Roman centurion named Panther or Panthera, helps establish the next one.[2] Coming to, Stephen discerns a human face, pale by contrast with the dark suit. (According to the stage directions Bloom's mouth is near his face (*U* 15.4927)—probably, because Bloom is trying to be heard, near his ear. Which is right above the jugular vein.) Night, pale face,[3] black suit, crouching down over "prostate form," open mouth prominent: anyone who remembers a *Dracula* movie will understand why Stephen, just back from Paris where among other things he attended a show featuring vampires debauching young women (*U* 15.3891–93),[4] should react with "Vampire." It is the third stage of this particular epiphany, Bloom's perceived (and, to be sure, bogus) *claritas,* this time probably reinforced by the synaptic click that occurred in "Aeolus" when Stephen, in the presence of the moderately mad Myles Crawford, whose mouth continued to twitch throughout (*U* 8.709), recalled his "Proteus" poem about a mouth-to-mouth kiss from a "pale vampire" (*U* 8.521–25). Why Crawford? Perhaps because he apparently wants to make Stephen over in his image (*U* 8.625) and thus—of course—to destroy his soul, and because that is what vampires, with their bloody kisses, do to non-vampires.

Thus, I suggest, does the black panther make its way into one absinthe-influenced consciousness. As for its other two apparitions, one in a nightmare and one while awake, experienced by Haines . . .

One unsolved puzzle about Haines's bizarre performance at the party involves his possessions, "A portfolio full of Celtic literature in one hand, in the other a phial marked *Poison,*" the latter being identified as "laudanum," from which he drinks, saying, "Dope is my only hope," to "obliterate" his English guilt. Of these two, the book at least is real: it is, we know from other testimony, a copy of Douglas Hyde's *Lovesongs of Connaught.* And the bottle? The signs are that it too is real. Haines's behavior certainly indicates that he has been taking something strong; that is why Mulligan thinks the story worth telling. Kenner has suggested, plausibly, that he might have been going native with a bottle of Irish whiskey (Kenner 1980, 115). In any event it should certainly be something alcoholic, if only because the laudanum specified by the "Walpole" voice is opium in a solution of alcohol. But there is a problem: anyone drunk enough to be seeing things would normally be in no condition to be making, let alone keeping, appointments in train stations. If by the time he shows up at Moore's Haines is far enough gone to be experiencing alcoholic delirium, the odds are that by the time Mulligan is waiting for him at Westland Row he will be dead to the world in some gutter or cell. Yet show up he does.

There is one drink, however, that is consistent with the account of Haines's actions: absinthe. It was, more or less, the fin-de-siècle equivalent of the laudanum of Walpole's time—alcohol raised to a new level of potency, a bestower of visions cultivated by aesthete and outcast. As such it was famously what one drank "to forget." As "Oxen of the Sun" shows, it was available in 1904 Dublin, was habitually called a "poison"—the drinkers in Burke's call it *"viridum toxicum,"* green poison; Corelli can scarcely get through a scene of *Wormwood* without using the word—and was known for inducing hallucinations in drinkers who, though dazed or delusional, were otherwise able to continue functioning: thus Lynch, after one dram, experiences an hallucination (of the ranting Dowie) but continues on to the station and is thereafter coherent enough. One reason absinthe was called "poison" was its reputation for eventually driving its users to insanity or suicide—the fate apparently feared by Haines in Mulligan's account (*U* 14.1021–25) and in fact awaiting Haines's real-life original, Trench, who killed himself between the time *Ulysses* was set and the time it was written. "There's nothing wrong with him except at night," says Stephen, in a rare relenting mood (*U* 1.177–78). An ambiguous phrase: does it refer to Haines asleep, with his noisy nightmares, or just after dark, when under some influence or other he predictably goes to the bad? Has he been making a habit of finishing the day by turning to the same poison he brandishes at Moore's?

In any case, let us consider the possibility that, like Stephen, Haines is seeing his black panther under the influence of absinthe, and furthermore that what he is seeing, under that influence, is a hallucinated rendition of something real. And one other parallel: that just as Stephen's hallucination arises from the sight of a man dressed in black, so does Haines's. Only his man in black is Stephen Dedalus.

To see how that might happen, it will help to review Haines's situation in Ireland. Here he is, this Oxonian, with his weak tea, his pale eyes, his mien arousing suspicions of effeminate proclivities,[5] his blueblood sports—tennis, shooting—duly cultivated. So what is he doing here? He is slumming. As he puts it in "Oxen of the Sun" (U 14.1024), he is "camping out" in the wilds of the "wild Irish" (U 1.731). And like other slummers on occasion, he has gotten more than he bargained on. Here he is, locked in a remote tower with this perfectly frightful Dedalus cad whose repertoire of social graces seems to consist of the glower and the sneer. "I blow him out about you," says Mulligan to Stephen, "and then you come along with your lousy leer and your gloomy jesuit jibes" (U 1.499–500). By the morning of the sixteenth, on which Stephen's first social act of the day is to ask when Haines is leaving, we may gauge how strained relations have become by the energy that Mulligan devotes to repairing them. Up until two-thirds of the way into "Telemachus," out of a cast of four (counting the milkwoman), the only conversation technically possible that has not occurred is the one between Stephen and Haines, who so far as they communicate at all do so through the mediation of Mulligan; when, encouraged by Mulligan, Haines finally addresses Stephen, it takes three overtures and a kick under the table to get a surly answer. For his part, the only time Stephen makes anything like a spontaneous gesture toward Haines it is to look back over his shoulder and inform him (U 1.540) that the tower's rent is paid "To the secretary of state for war" (translation: more bloody blood money to you bloody British), and although there is the slightest of thaws for a short spell, the upshot of Haines's feeble concession of historical guilt (spoken by a member of a culture given to understatement to a member of a culture given to overstatement, it could hardly come across as anything but feeble) is that Stephen pointedly announces his departure to Mulligan alone and pointedly refuses to answer Haines's farewell (U 1.720, 730). Pity, for all his venality, poor Mulligan, desperately trying to sustain some pretense of bonhomie between these two prigs, the insufferable one and the impossible one.

Thus, to Haines, Stephen: implacable Parnellite, snarling Anglophobe, nursing his seven-plus centuries' of grievances in a tower constructed during the violent rebellion against Haines's people by his people, a race whose fondness for random slaughter Haines knows all about from his reading of its literature. In this impression he may well have been encouraged by Mulligan, who despite his morning blandishments is incorrigibly given to egging on people's fears and animosities: in "Wandering Rocks" he tells Haines that Stephen's wits have been driven astray by visions of hell (U 10.1072), news hardly calculated to soothe any apprehensions. So Stephen is probably not the only one nervous about being "Out here in the dark with a man I don't know" (U 1.60–61), and we can perhaps understand why Haines's "Oxen of the Sun" appearance should be rendered in the "Walpole" idiom identified with bloody deeds in dark towers, especially considering that the actual tower in question reminds him of Elsinore (*U* 1.773), home of another young man in black who turns out to be a very bloody young man indeed.

For his part, Stephen assumes that it is mainly history that is haunting Haines. His phrase "the nightmare of history" twines two Haines vignettes, the panther nightmare and the line "It seems history is to blame" (*U* 1.649), Haines's weak excuse for the nightmare of Irish history at England's hands. Thus Stephen's comparison of Haines and the English to Lady Macbeth (*U* 1.481–82), washing her hands, and to a "penitent thief" (*U* 9.101). (For their parts, A.E. and Eglinton, in Mulligan's version, think Haines suffers from "The vendetta of Mananaun"—ancient Irish god—and the "*Lex talionis*" [U 14.1029–30].) And with that attitude toward what Haines at least ought to be losing sleep over, and his studiously offensive way of making such opinions known to the people they concern, Stephen would not be the one to blame if Haines went to bed on the night of the fifteenth untroubled by intimations of native retribution, personified in an erratic young man who by his analysis—he can say this blandly enough in the light of day—has an idée fixe (*U* 10.1068). A hungry panther has an idée fixe, too.

A panther is also famously adept at stalking its prey. The most puzzling part of Haines's appearance in "Oxen of the Sun" is his testimony that someone or something, markedly Irish and soon to be identified as the black panther, has been following him around town all day, has been "after me the like of a soulth or a bullawurrus" (*U* 14.1020–21). Well, obviously, no one has been stalking him. Who would bother? And yet if we retrace their steps it becomes apparent how Haines might come to feel that Stephen was doing just that. At twelve-thirty Haines and Mulligan begin their wait at the Ship, 5 Lower Abbey Street. About a half-hour later, Stephen, having sent along an insulting telegram and stood them up, arrives with his newspaper friends at Mooney's, 1 Lower Abbey Street. Then Haines heads for the National Library where, shortly after, who should appear but Stephen. Declining the offer to join in (*U* 9.93–95), Haines heads off to Gill's and after that to the D.B.C. to have tea with Mulligan, at the window, from which they view the viceregal cavalcade outside (*U* 10.1046, 1223–25), starting at 3:22.[6] The timing of Stephen's itinerary at this point is less exact, but as Hart points out he should be heading to the Moira, just around the corner from the D.B.C., by a route taking him across the street on which Mulligan and Haines are looking out (Hart and Knuth 1976, 28). There is no direct evidence that either Haines or Stephen has actually seen the other during any of these convergences.[7] But in every case it would have been easily possible—at the library it would have been hard to avoid—and combined they certainly make for a strange sequence of coincidences. Or so, assuming he noticed them, it must appear to Haines: here, that is to say, is this fellow who having with the utmost bally rudeness neglected to honor an appointment then keeps popping up wherever one goes—not *saying* anything, mind you, just showing up in one's shadow.

So it may well be a certain amount of desperate calculation that leads Haines to the one place in Dublin where Stephen is certain not to be, to make an appointment on the last train. The reasoning is clear: one, it's too far to walk, so Stephen will not show up later; two, if he arrives earlier, he will, Mulligan having extracted the key this morning, find himself locked out, on a wet night, with no one home to let him in, and go away. The only hitch is the possibility that he might be on the same train . . . but no, if he drinks up his wages according to form there's every reason to expect that by 11:10 he should be out of commission. All in all, Haines can trust that for this night anyway he has seen the last of his tormenter, that tonight anyway he should sleep safely.

Then occurs something eminently calculated to give him the most thorough pip. After all, consider his case. It is a dark and stormy night. Back at the lonely tower to which he will soon return is a sportsman's gun (*U* 1.263–64) that he brought along in all innocence, never thinking . . . A good job that that baleful, brooding aborigine, dressed like Hamlet, like an anarchist, like a black panther, the one who has so unaccountably seemed to know and dog his whereabouts, is out of the picture. Haines makes his way to the station. Mulligan arrives on schedule. The train is due any moment. All is well. And then . . . Good God, out of the shadows . . . surely not! . . . a black form . . .

It is at this point that a disputed something happens at the station. Kenner proposes that Stephen and Mulligan get in a fight (Kenner 1980, 116). Over what? Stephen is there to take the northbound train to Nighttown (*U* 14.1572–73). Mulligan and Haines are heading south to Sandycove. Haines might find it hard to believe, but their convergence is yet another coincidence: Stephen really did just happen to hit on the weird idea of taking a one-stop train ride to Nighttown, with no regard to what the other two were doing. Why, therefore, should he pick a fight on discovering, assuming he does discover it, that they are going in the opposite direction? Without giving them a thought, he has already set on a course of action ruling out any return to the tower. For his part, although Mulligan may well experience some unpleasant feelings when Stephen comes into view, none of them should be of the sort to make him advance with his fists extended. He has, or so he likely thinks, been caught in the act of betraying an old friend who was buying him drinks not fifteen minutes before. The natural reaction, surely, is to skulk. Especially since, including as it does Lynch and Bloom, Stephen's party outnumbers his by three to two. Nor should one expect fisticuffs from Haines, who by this point is to be pardoned if he has been utterly spooked. Everything, in short, counsels evasive action.

Which is pretty much how Bloom, the soberest party present, remembers "the very unpleasant scene at Westland Row terminus when it was perfectly evident that the other two, Mulligan, that is, and that English tourist friend of his, who eventually euchred their third companion, were patently trying as if the whole bally station belonged to them to give Stephen the slip" (U 16.263–67). Bloom's account, the only one available and no doubt fairly trustworthy, is nonetheless influenced by his newfound paternal interest in Stephen, perhaps reinforced by the memory of Simon Dedalus's saying that Mulligan is out to "ruin my son" (U 6.49, 70). (An estimate that Bloom, acting out of parental esprit de corps, in effect hands on to Stephen at U 16.279–86.) Yet even he remarks that Stephen "didn't notice as much as I [Bloom] did" (U 16.283–84)—a strange thing to say if what he noticed was a fistfight to which Stephen was a party— and on reflection wonders whether Stephen had "let himself be bamboozled" or rather had "allowed matters to more or less" transpire without interference (U 16.303–6).[8] So it seems that Stephen did not notice, or anyway did not care about, the hurried efforts of Mulligan and Haines to get out of his way.

In fact there is probably a touch of farce in the Westland Row scramble, of surprise entrances and frantic exits according to a scenario fully perceived by none of the parties. Stephen and Lynch are for all intents oblivious to the two men standing on the opposite side of the tracks when they come up into the station. Mulligan, thinking incorrectly that he has been found out, runs down the nearest stairwell or behind the nearest pillar, probably with Haines hot after him. Bloom, seeing this, knowing that Stephen is staying with the two of them to the south, not having heard that he is heading to Nighttown to the north, concludes, half correctly, that Stephen is being "euchred" by his mates, who are giving him the slip.

And Haines? Alas for the stiff upper lip. We may understand Bloom's impression that he and Mulligan seemed to have felt that the whole station belonged to them if we imagine Haines's reaction, beholding his dark stalker turn up yet again: "You! Again! My God! You! What are *you* doing here?"

It used to be a custom to predict what was likely to happen after *Ulysses* ends. I have two predictions. The first is that Bloom, following the example of Bantam Lyons, will shave off his moustache. The second is that Haines is going to have a nightmare that will make last night's seem like nothing.

17

"Ithaca" as the Letter C

APRÈS LE DELUGE, LOI. After the culminating turbulence of "Circe," a protracted spell of sifting and sorting out, equilibrium reestablished and new ideas of order put in place. The last three episodes of *Ulysses*, set apart and collectively entitled "Nostos," or "homecoming," constitute a stage-by-stage enactment of this process. As always, this action is character-centered: you would want things settled down, too, if you had just had the kind of night Bloom and Stephen have had.

The phase of this sequence that most clearly counterpoints its dialectical predecessor is the middle episode "Ithaca," and one critical component of the difference is in what Stephen would call the modality of the visible. Visually, "Circe" was a kinetic sequence of vividly surreal animation. Visually, "Ithaca" is a book of diagrams, mainly Euclidian, progressing from one to another, as with the turning of pages. These diagrams tend to fall into set patterns, composed out of geometry's limited store of elemental shapes. In fact, they consistently tend to break down into just one of those shapes, that of the arc. This is so both in the mind's eye, what the narrative tells us to envision, and in the reading eye, what we see when we look at the page. For the first: from the "arc" subtended by the walkers at its beginning (*U* 17.8–10) to the "flexed" postures adopted by the sleepers at its end (*U* 17.2313, 2315), from macrocosmic Northern Crown (*U* 17.2018–19) to microcosmic "protruding part of the great toenail" (*U* 17.1489), the figurative landscape of "Ithaca" is a field of arcs and composites of arcs. For the second: reinforcing this predominance is a proliferation of arc-shaped marks on the page: the parentheses (approximately one every three and one-half lines; only "Circe," with its parenthetical stage directions, has more), the record number of question marks (sickle-shaped, bent arc above dot), and, most of all, the letter C. C appears more frequently than in any other episode of *Ulysses*, at a rate of incidence way off the curve.[1]

So far as I can determine, nothing about subject or format accounts for that rate of incidence. A sequence of questions and answers, "Ithaca" has lots of

"Where"s "When"s, "What"s, and so forth, and we might therefore expect a disproportionate number of Ws and Hs, but not of Cs. Nor does it appear in either "Stephen" or "Bloom," the two names occurring most frequently. Remembering Wallace Stevens' poem written on the premise that C is the most protean of letters, we might speculate on its being emphasized in an episode so concerned with metamorphosis, but then what about "Proteus"? Or we might hypothesize that for some reason Joyce found the letter prosodically suitable for this episode, but in that case we would also expect K to show up with extraordinary frequency, and it does not.

So: why? Why this shape, insinuated in so many ways? *Finnegans Wake* readers may be reminded of its ubiquitous rainbow, its arcs and arks. But there is another arc-shaped icon closer to the story of *Ulysses*, and to "Ithaca" in particular. Hugh Kenner identifies it: "when the unremarkable drooping trajectory of Bloom's urination in 'Ithaca' reminds the implacable catechist how when a schoolboy he 'had been capable of attaining the point of greatest altitude against the whole concurrent strength of the institution' . . . it would be a pity not to let that heroic arc remind us of Odysseus' power manifested in his great bow" (Kenner 1980, 320). Whatever else they may do, this and the other arcs of "Ithaca" should recall the bow with which Odysseus, home in Ithaca, turned the tide and set the Odyssey toward its resolution.[2] And like that bow, they are emblems of homecoming, straight-shooting, hitting the target, satisfactory completion. The "star" that, in one of the episode's arcing transits (*U* 17.1211–13), is "precipitated" across the sky from Vega in (harp-shaped, bow-shaped) Lyra is one variant of the theme; another occurs shortly thereafter when Bloom, with the "bow" of his key, sends the "centrifugal" Stephen off into the night air, to fall to earth he and we know not where, another when he buries his face in the furrow at the intersection of Molly's "female hemispheres" (*U* 17.2329–43), a final one when he composes his "flexed" limbs in the bed above which hovers a target composed of "concentric circles" (*U* 17.2301; compare *U* 17.897–900),[3] and the narrative asks and answers its final question:

"Where?

."

Bulls-eye.

To begin with, then, this most abstract of *Ulysses* episodes advances its effects through the most concrete of means. It works to induce in the reader a visual sense, in fact sensation, corresponding to its main parable, of the returning voyager who draws his bow, finds the target, hits the target, and, as arrow and archer reach their goals, comes to rest. Visibly (besides those Cs, and so forth), it is a series of discrete typographical blocks, typically following a short-long pattern, which correspond to the text's rhetorical closures. The distinctive formal unit is this: a short question elicits an exhaustive answer ending with a period and followed with a border of blank space. Ask the narrator about water, and, by God, he tells you about it: it may take 473 words, but by the end the book's main symbol for flux has been reviewed, catalogued, put within borders, reduced to, as the saying goes, manageable proportions, and filed away.

The water question-and-answer is one of the longer arrow-flights of the episode, powered by release of the mental tension, of expectation, that any nonrhetorical question generates. It follows the archer's exercise reiteratively performed in "Ithaca"—tension, release, and a tension-annulling completion—bringing to a close the fundamental neural operation, which as it happens had long been called the "reflex arc,"[4] the action-reaction unit that at the time of *Ulysses* was the main experimental subject of Sir Charles Sherrington, the age's best-known British neurologist, and becoming the basis of behaviorism, the new science behind Bloom's "modern art of advertisement" (*U* 17.581).[5] It is the operation that according to the narrator governs neurally-determined actions, from storytelling ("by which potential narration was realised and kinetic temperament relieved" [*U* 17.637–38]) to sexual intercourse (transit between "the selfprolonging tension of the thing proposed to be done and the selfabbreviating relaxation of the thing done" [*U* 17.2214–15]). Time after time, an unstable state is posited, followed by its resolution, through a discharge of directed energy, into what is variously called "rest," "equilibrium," "equanimity," "apathy," "seeking its own level," "quiescence," "satisfaction," "crystallized state," "successful completion," "repletion," "logical conclusion," and so on. It is the main story behind the episode's action, the Homeric fable it enacts, its technique, and its style.

Most of all, it is the story of the mental operation that on all those levels "Ithaca" works to induce in the reader. In this, it constitutes a refinement of the preceding episode, "Eumaeus," which repeatedly enacts the process of seeking the target, some goal or terminus, and missing. "Ithaca" is a sequence of targets set up and hit—ping! *chunk*; "Eumaeus" shoots wild and wanders around. As in "Ithaca," this feature is manifested in various details of the narrative. We hear of firearms going off accidentally (*U* 16.83–84), of people falling off cliffs (*U* 16.561–62), of "reading in fits and starts" (*U* 16.600–601), of various wrecks and capsizings, of a staggering sailor trying to relieve himself who manages to miss the urinal (*U* 16.939–40), of all kinds of mistakings, misfirings, and missed connections, of people missing one another's point or not seeing eye to eye or failing to see the connection or being out of their depth. As in "Ithaca" as well, there is an equivalent in the way the episode is written:

> it being a case for the two parties themselves unless *it ensued* that the legitimate husband happened *to be a party to it* owing to some anonymous letter *from the usual boy Jones,* who happened *to come across them at the crucial moment in a loving position locked in one another's arms, drawing attention to their illicit proceedings and leading up to a domestic rumpus* and the *erring* fair one begging forgiveness of her lord and master *upon her knees* and promising *to sever the connection* and *not receive his visits* any more if only the aggrieved husband would *overlook the matter* and let bygones be bygones *with tears in her eyes* though possibly *with her tongue in her fair cheek at* the same time as quite possibly there were several others. (*U* 16.1832–42)

I have italicized words and phrases having to do with physical positioning or movement to or from a point. Such terms are extraordinarily dense. An episode in which people are forever bumbling and lurching around, "Eumaeus" takes place in an English that is itself in similarly fuddled transit, in which the language becomes a business of situation and re-situation, direction and (much) mis-direction.

This is, as usual, a case of imitative form: the principals are tired, their brains fagged out, and the prose reflects it by repeatedly reenacting the process of unfocused or misfired movement. Simply by imagining the opposite of this episode's mental operations, one might hypothesize what a lucid mind, as demonstrated in "Ithaca," would do: it would complete those journeys snappily and smartly, hit the nail on the head, score bulls-eye after bulls-eye.

This conceit, of thought as target-shooting, is a common enough one,[6] which in Joyce's day had been given new authority by anatomical studies on the brain the broad conclusion of which was that thought was movement, from point to point, down a bundle of wires and across a spark-gap named, by Sherrington, the "synapse." The brain was a concentration of nerve cells, bunched into "ganglions," a word that by 1930 had become so familiar that even P. G. Wodehouse's addled Bertie Wooster uses it familiarly (1930, 151), and those nerves were relays of distinctively hairy neurons, each transmitting stimuli along one of many branching dendrites. Human thought, when examined with that in mind, seemed also to be a matter of rapid relay from ganglion to ganglion, sometimes in a straight line but often every which way. "In terms of the brain-process," wrote William James, "all these mental facts resolve themselves into a single peculiarity: that of indeterminateness of connection between the different tracts, and tendency of action to focalize itself, so to speak, in small localities which vary infinitely at different times, and from which irradiation may proceed in countless shifting ways" (1950, 2:366). (A variant of the nebular psychologisms remarked earlier.) The consciousness, he wrote, "Like a bird's life ... seems to be made of an alternation of flights and perchings" (1950, 1:243), perchings that are the "halting-places" along the mind's incessant journey (1950, 1:269).

That was the medical background when former medical student Joyce wrote "Eumaeus," an episode to which he assigned the organ of "nerves," from the Latin for "bowstring."[7] Writing about the episode earlier, I once remarked that the authorial style moved from formula to formula "like a drunk lurching from one lamppost to another" (Gordon 1981, 115). I might have added that this was true as well of the action, which is mainly a matter of people moving from one coordinate to another, to "focalize" "in small localities," against a murky background, or of the way the characters' minds move from one focal point—coin, coffee cup, newspaper, knife, tattoo—to another, like a bird hopping from perch to perch, or like a thought shooting from node to node, there, eventually, to distill, like Stephen's nebular droplets of association, around their particulate centers of concentration.

In "Eumaeus" those relays, and the nodes punctuating them, are fatigued, the result being all those misfirings. And just what, clinically, did it mean to be suffering from mental fatigue? The answer had been given when Angelo Mosso, modern founder of the field, had exercised a dog to the point of exhaustion, injected some of its blood into another, rested, dog, and observed that the latter suddenly became tired. From then on, fatigue, both physical and mental, was understood as the chemical result of what happened when too many metabolic by-products had piled up in the system. In particular, mental fatigue meant that the brain was encountering interference when it tried to make the essential connections. This interference resulted from an accumulation of what were sometimes called the "fatigue toxins" or carbonic "waste products" left over from the chemical processes of neural excitation. To be fatigued as "Eumaeus" and its principals are fatigued was by Joyce's day understood to be, especially at the polar points, clogged and cumbered with detritus slowing down and blocking the thinking process.[8]

In their last excursion of the episode, Stephen and Bloom find themselves "stepping over a strand of mire" left by a colleague of the horse who immediately before has deposited his "three smoking globes of turds" before them (*U* 16.1876–82). It is hard to see how Joyce could be more explicit here. "Eumaeus" is horseshit. Its style results from a mental apparatus overcharged with waste products. It begins in "the distinctly fetid atmosphere of the livery stables" (*U* 16.22), moves to a hut heavy with coal and coffee fumes and with the collective funk of its long-unwashed company, and ends as we have seen. It is an episode of dregs, pollutants, waste, sedimentation, and so on, the episode in which the sailor urinates and Bloom wants to, in which newsmen are "mudslinging" members of the "gutterpress" (*U* 16.1482), prostitutes "reeking with disease" (*U* 16.729), the coffee a clotted deposit, the food gone stale or bad—gone, as the saying goes, to waste—and absolutely everything that anyone says is "pure buncombe" (*U* 16.1286). An episode, that is, of horseshit—and at its conclusion the much-needed sweeper, with his proleptically emblematic sickle-shaped scythe on his car, arrives to sweep it away, as if to clear the field for the clean lines and curves of "Ithaca," for its battery of sickle-shaped question marks.

What distinguishes the "nerves" of "Eumaeus," then, and especially the central bundle of nerves called the brain, is that they are exceptionally crudded up with waste. Why? Because "Eumaeus" follows "Circe," that "hallucinatory" episode in which Stephen and Bloom, and the technique reflecting their internal states, are at their most cerebrally stimulated.[9] In particular, the hallucinations to which both are subject in "Circe" result from a heightened nervous suscepti-bility, which, as I have attempted to show, in effect means a greatly increased predisposition for the matchings of metaphor, as enacted through the forging of neural connections. (The environment gets into the act, too, with intermittent electric storms, discharges across the synapses between sky and ground. Periods of pathological cerebral excitation—those induced by epilepsy or absinthe, for instance—were commonly compared to electrical storms in the medical literature of the period; our term "brain storm" preserves the connection still.)[10] Thus: huddled in a wet, dark alley, Bloom hears the approach of a night patrol, and instantly his mind activates the associative connection to the wet, dark alley in which he encountered the *"raincaped watch"* of twenty years ago (*U* 15.675; compare *U* 14.1066–67). Thus: bleary-eyed, Stephen hears someone use the word "pandybat" and instantly resurrects Father Dolan, from the sixteen-year-old compartment lodged in his memory, pandying him for breaking his glasses (*U* 15.3663–72).

And, as we have seen, the stage directions follow suit:

Bloom, raising a policeman's whitegloved hand, blunders stifflegged out of the track. (*U* 15.190–91)

From a bulge of window curtains a gramophone rears a battered brazen trunk. (U 15.606–7)

ZOE: (*Spouts walrus smoke through her nostrils.*) (*U* 15.2560–61)

In the first example, Bloom raises his hand, palm flat, in a gesture like that of a policeman halting traffic—and to whoever is seeing this, that is what he becomes. In the second, the same observer glimpses, poking through window curtains, the flaring trumpet of a Victrola, and sees an elephant's trunk, therefore an elephant raising it. In the third, jets of white smoke shot from the nostrils instantly become walrus tusks. That is the essential psychological operation behind the hallucinatory fugues we have traced. Like Bloom and Stephen, whoever is recording these transformations—or Bloom's oriental "womancity," or Stephen's operatic evocation of his mother—is being synecdochally hyperactive: all three enact a powerful impulse to turn any perceptual fragment into a recognizable whole by completing it with associations from private or collective memory. In the terms of this book's first chapter, they are working overtime to resolve the nebular mass of potential alternatives, the "different tracts" with their "indeterminacies of connection," into one focused, distilled composite. It is, most simply, the impulse to completion—to linking whatever offers to whatever memories and images are available in the mind's repertoire, thus crystallizing sensation and memory into perception. The result is the episode's "hallucinatory" technique.

We know, if only from *Portrait*, what the aftermath will be like. Bloom foresaw it: "Drugs age you after mental excitement. Lethargy then. Why? Reaction. A lifetime in a night" (*U* 8.474–75). From De Quincey to accounts of fin de siècle absintheurs to *Naked Lunch* to recent public-service anti-cocaine advertisements showing the ganglia of an overtaxed brain being clogged with synaptic precipitate, the convention is that after a night of neural excess comes the dawn when one's nerves are shot, when one is blitzed, dazed, blank, flat. After a spell of gestaltic frenzy the cerebral orgiast cannot connect the dots, like the overburdened narrator of *The Waste Land* "can connect nothing with nothing." Of the eight occurrences of "connection" in *Ulysses*, four are in "Eumaeus": Bloom reacts to one of sailor Murphy's stories by wondering "what possible connection" (*U* 16.386) it could have to something else, assures himself that there could be "no possible connection" (*U* 16.1272) between one letter in the newspaper and another, considers an adulterous wife's promise to "sever the connection" (*U* 16.1539), and advises Stephen to "sever his connection" with Mulligan (*U*

16.1868–69). That is the lot of connections in this episode, as the nothing-if-not-cerebral Stephen, described throughout "Eumaeus" as needing all his might to concentrate on anything at all (for example, *U* 16.108, 186, 386), illustrates neatly when his associative meanderings about Baird the stonecutter—"Stephen thought to think of Ibsen, associated with Baird's the stonecutter's in his mind somehow in Talbot place" (*U* 16.52–54)—invite comparison with his steel-trap certainty in *Portrait* that "as he went by Baird's stonecutting works in Talbot place the spirit of Ibsen would blow through him like a keen wind" (*P* 176).

After a mental binge, then, a spell of frazzle and wool-gathering. "Eumaeus" is something of a rest cure for, in the language of the time, the brain's higher functions. It is also—framed as it is with accumulations of horseshit and full of waste products—a purgative, like the "horse piss and rotted straw" the Stephen of *Portrait* self-administers as an antidote to a spell of "maddening" mental "vapours" (*P* 86). The waste dump of "Eumaeus," like the reeking pig-keeper's hut in which Odysseus sleeps before claiming his kingdom, constitutes an administration of concentrated unpleasantness of the kind traditionally considered therapeutic to those, like kings and ecstatics, prone to getting above themselves. (For instance Edmund Spenser's Redcrosse Knight, who, having gone to extremes in the House of Pride, must spend three months sleeping in his own accumulating excrement.) Without their stay there, Bloom and Stephen could not have gone on to the arcs of "Ithaca" that begin showing themselves—the "swingchains" (*U* 16.1771) outdoors, the scythe on the sweeper's car—as, breathing fresh air at last, they exit from the shelter.

Those arcs, again, are of Homeric as well as Euclidian provenance. And they signal something else as well,[11] as spelled out earlier: "Beauty: it curves: curves are beauty" (*U* 8.920). Thus Bloom in "Lestrygonians," getting back on an even keel after a sequence prefiguring the one we have been following: a near-hallucinatory flight of what *Finnegans Wake* calls "reminiscensitive" fancy (*FW* 230.26–27) ("Hidden under wild ferns on Howth . . . Kissed, she kissed me" [*U* 8.897–916]), followed by a return to reality at its most dispiriting ("Me. And me now" [*U* 7.917]). As with the hallucinations of "Circe," this visionary voyage is cued by a specific stimulus, a taste of Burgundy, which makes Bloom think of grapes ripening in Burgundy, which make him think of the sunny South, which makes him think of Molly's southern origins, which make him think of Molly on that hot, hot-blooded day. The literary inspiration here, presumably unconscious, is surely the call in "Ode to a Nightingale" for a beaker full of the warm South, tasting of Provencal song and sunburnt mirth, which call imaginatively transports the poet to a sunlit South where youth and beauty never fade. In the courtship (Howth-era) days Bloom made Molly a present of a book of poems, and the one line she remembers is from Keats, about beauty (*U* 16.1177–78). It is the line Bloom recalls as well in "Circe" when contemplating the Nymph's ideal beauty, in language coming from the "Lestrygonians" revery: "Your classic curves, beautiful immortal, I was glad to look on you, to praise you, a thing of beauty, almost to pray" (*U* 15.1367–68).

In fact "curves" is a word seldom far from Bloom's mind when he is feeling Keatsian, that is, in the escapist mood easily associated with the sentimental- ized poet too noble of soul to live. (And whose epitaph for himself was that his name was written in water; compare Bloom at the end of "Nausicaa," giving up on his self-identifying message in the sand: "Useless. Washed away" [*U* 13.1259].) Curves are at once ideally abstract and ideally sensuous, Euclidian and womanly, which is to say they are the right sign both at the beginning of "Ithaca," as Bloom disengages from the post-passional turbidities of "Eu- maeus," and at its end, to convey him to what he more than once, speaking of Molly, has called her "opulent curves," and what Joyce, speaking of her episode, called its "amplitudinously curvilinear" form (*JJ* 501). Joyce's testi- mony ("It turns like the huge earth ball slowly surely and evenly round and round spinning" [*JJ* 501]) indicates the figural connection between the two episodes. "Ithaca," rising out of the muck, retrieves and isolates the curve, as C. "Penelope," giving it flesh, completes it, turns C to O (and then, doubling it, to infinity's doubled O, ∞).[12] Missile's arc yields to planetary ellipse.

That is, one kind of reality principle, the reassertion of the physicality of page and type,[13] of black arcs on white space, precedes and mediates another, Molly's. Moving us from the murk of "Eumaeus," *Ulysses* takes us down to earth by way of taking us down to the page. Thus does the resident maker of marks join in the episode's project of radical simplification, as exemplified in Stephen's and Bloom's detection of "increasing simplification traceable" to the history of the alphabet (*U* 17.770–73), or in Bloom's final desideratum of the perfect advertisement, "condensed in triliteral monoideal symbols" (*U* 17.581–82), or in the final dot. At least in this component of its technique, *Ulysses* at this point is recognizably an artifact of a time when many writers were at work trying to reach new, unorthodox registers in both writer and audience. What would later be called concrete poetry had been revived by Apollinaire, and variants on it were in evidence in the pages of such publications as *Blast* and *transitions*; Gertrude Stein, prize pupil of William James and, at Johns Hop- kins, specialist in the physiognomy of fatigue, was extending her researches into the realm of literary effects, of what kinds of cues produced the optimum pattern of stimulus and relaxation in readers; others, including Robert Graves and William Carlos Williams, were pursuing similar, if less programmatic, inquiries; there was of course great interest, both clinical and popular, in the mechanisms of association. The writings of Bergson, Whitehead, Claude Bernard, the Symbolistes, and in their different ways both of the brothers James had revived an interest in what, early in the nineteenth century, the French philosopher Maine de Biran had named the *"sens intime"* of one's *"coenesthese,"* which he defined as "one's immediate awareness of the presence of the body in perception" and "the simultaneity of a composite of impressions inhering in different parts of the organism." [14]

Joyce, I think, missed little of all this. In his later writing he intends to engage every faculty he has a chance to reach, including visual, visceral, and associative faculties supposedly dismissed from the contract of writer with reader. His ideal readers are an attentively impressionable lot, more so than almost anyone really is, which is why he works to educate them in how to read. He teaches us to revive those distracting habits that our grade-school reading masters were at pains to purge: to see the letters on the page and the patterns they fall into (the two eyes in the middle of "look," the felicitous x in the English "connexion," the serried ranks and rhomboids of stanzas), to hear the sounds they correspond to and notice how they affect us associatively, what images or memories they provoke. In "Ithaca" especially, such an exercise suits his purpose of making his reader feel brought down to earth in tandem with his hero's being brought home. In general he appeals to us to widen our range of receptivity, to be ready to recognize any pattern we pick up, to be prepared to bring together whatever visualizes the scythe at the end of "Eumaeus" with whatever notices all the scythe-shaped question marks of "Ithaca." And along with that, we are to tune into our own kinesthetic interior, to hear ourselves hearing and feel what we are feeling, bumping along the rutted tracks of "Eumaeus," internalizing the long rhythmic sweeps of the "Ithaca" catalogues as, time after time, each comes to rest on its terminal target. The sequence from at least "Circe" to "Ithaca," of cerebral excess, cerebral relapse, followed by a period of lucid, dispassionate reorientation, is, or should be, the reader's too.

The reader of "Ithaca" who sees the inked arcs on the page, envisions them when the narrator describes them, feels a liminal mental organ tensing and releasing in time with archer's exercise of question and answer, picks up with inner ear the corresponding rhythmical pattern of voluminous passage/terse passage, consolidates these responses in some inner chamber where sensorium communicates with cerebrum, and attends to that consolidation, will have become a Joycean reader. Many critics have observed that from the outset Joyce fought with the words he worked with, the words Stephen calls "heaps of dead language," that in effect his work constantly seeks communication outside the conventional media of speaking and writing. It is an impulse we can find at work in "Penelope," whose style is at the least a powerful gesture toward canceling syntax, and whose heroine's memory and imagination focus on certain luminous nonverbal moments—the love interlude on Gibraltar where because of language problems "everything was whatyoucallit" (*U* 18.820), a fantasy tryst with a Stephen "not knowing me from Adam . . . without a Gods notion where he is" (*U* 18.1485–86), the final embrace of a "he" who is alternately or simultaneously two men and more.

I suggest that "Ithaca" prepares for "Penelope" by working to activate responses beyond what, conventionally, reading is. It puts in its superabundance of C's in the hope that in some capacity they will register, and thus reinforce, certain effects approximated by other means. Such a purpose would after all be, in its quirky Joycean way, in keeping with the ancient effort of writers to use marks on paper to move us and show us things—as Conrad puts in the preface to *The Nigger of the Narcissus*, "to make you hear, to make you feel, before all to make you see."

Maybe that's one other meaning of "Ithaca" 's C. See.

18

Passport to Eternity

THE WHITE-SPACE BREAKS between "Ithaca" 's question-and-answer units are gaps as well as borders, signatures—again, visible signatures—of how much its homecoming certainties depend on the blanking-out of incommensurable data. The reason all its questions can be answered is that certain questions are not asked. In particular, it is difficult to imagine "Ithaca" taking on Stephen's query posed in "Proteus" and again in "Circe": "Tell me the word, mother, if you know now. The word known to all men" (*U* 15.4192–93). With all its know-it-all ways, "Ithaca" doesn't touch that kind of thing. Yet if *Ulysses* has an ultimate question, this is it. Or at least it is the question that matters most to Stephen—and, in a different key, to Bloom, who also wonders throughout about the meaning of "that other world," that is, originally, "word."

In its own way, as we shall see, it will instead be the next and last episode, "Penelope"—"Bloom's passport to eternity," to which "Ithaca" is the "countersign" (*L1* 160)—that does take up the question to answer it, even enact it. That is probably just as well, because in "Ithaca" it would come across as something like this:

What is the word known to all men?
Love.

Well, of course. Didn't we all know that, in some sappy little corner of our souls?

Bloom certainly did. He demonstrates as much in "Cyclops," testifying about how "everybody knows" that love is what really matters (*U* 12.1432–35). So does Stephen, at least according to the Gabler edition's version of "Scylla and Charybdis" (*U* 9.429–30). And Gabler or no Gabler, he knew it before *Ulysses:* "26 April: Mother is putting my new secondhand clothes in order. She prays now, she says, that I may learn in my own life and away from home and friends what the heart is and what it feels. Amen" (*P* 252). Even back then, the sentiment was anything but remarkable. Since the troubadours, it has not been possible to grow up without knowing that love is what the heart feels or ought to feel. Indeed it has barely been possible for those whose heart is not thus preoccupied to be unconcerned about the fact. Ask Gabriel Conroy: "He had never felt like that himself towards any woman but he knew that such a feeling must be love" (D 223). The Stephen of both *Portrait*'s chapter 5 and *Ulysses* is of this company. He knows the word for what he is missing, that word linked with the memory of his mother at least since Cranly admonished him (P 241–42) with an expression he remembers (U 2.143), that a mother's love is the "only true thing in life."

So Stephen in "Circe" is asking for knowledge that he already has. What kind of request is that? To answer, recall how it begins: "Tell me." Where have we heard that before? In *Ulysses,* we have heard it one other place, in Stephen's first words of the day, spoken by a Greekly-named man who twenty-eight lines later will be called a bard: "Tell me, Mulligan" (U 1.47). And where have we heard that before? In many works, usually with titles like *Ulysses,* with one variation—"Tell me, Muse."[1] Stephen's address to his mother is of the nature of an invocation, which is to say a request to be given information with which the speaker simultaneously reveals his familiarity: Tell me, Muse, about Troy, how so and so did such and such and then . . .

That peculiarity of the convention may illuminate a peculiarity of *Portrait,* that its invocation ("Old father, old artificer, stand me now and ever in good stead" [P 253]) occurs at its end. Stephen's muse, old artificer Daedalus, has not been revealed until well into the book, and not addressed until its last line, when (because now we know the story) we are finally ready to begin with the first line, which is not "Once upon a time"—though these words are spoken by another "old father"—but the epigraph *"Et Ignotas animum dimittit in artes."* Thus does the old artificer set about his *artes,* telling us the story we have just heard, which could not be told now had it not been told before.

Stephen's invocation to his mother is of this odd kind, beseeching something already known, an appeal that, like the "Old father" address, becomes possible only when the response has been learned. In "Circe," the oddity is redoubled because Stephen not only knows the word ahead of time but has taught it:

THE MOTHER

(*a green rill of bile trickling from a side of her mouth*) You sang that song to me.
Love's bitter mystery.

STEPHEN
(*eagerly*) Tell me the word, mother, if you know now. The word known to all men. (*U* 15.4188–93)

So Stephen cannot not know the answer; it was his, embedded in "love's bitter mystery," to begin with. Then what does he want? Why do people, bards included, make such appeals? *Because* the answer is known. This is, after all, a son addressing his mother. The idea is to confirm shared truths, to secure the beachhead of the established familiar. On the first page of *Portrait*, moocow story and wild rose song ("his song") are fixtures of Stephen's world as reassuring as parents. Now, in "Circe," at the end of his tether, as much in need of reassurance as he was those twenty years ago, Stephen takes his cue from the song he sang to his mother—a song, about love, known to both—on her deathbed, a song that constituted, lovingly and bitterly, a reversed reenactment of childbed tableau of mother singing to son. His request to her traces back to the lost verities of lullaby and bedtime story.

One could I think argue that to Joyce all literature owes something to such wishes. In *Finnegans Wake* the washerwomen, who know all stories already, try to stave off the night by telling them again: "Tell me of John or Shaun? Who were Shem and Shaun the living sons or daughters of? Night now! Tell me, tell me, tell me, elm!" (*FW* 216.01–3). As Daedalus is not invoked until *Portrait*'s end, so too in *Finnegans Wake* the muse—this time Mnemosyne, mother of muses—is invoked on last rather than first page ("Bussoftlhee, mememormee!" [*FW* 628.14]), and the opening, in speaking of what has not yet ("passencore" [*FW* 3.04–5]) reoccurred but is going to, reassures that we are about to hear ofttold tales. As for *Ulysses*, title and Homeric superstructure by themselves amount to reassurances that the fundamental things apply as time goes by, that the book's bewildering panorama is really an old story we already know.

All such reassurances are of course questionable. Night does fall; *Finnegans Wake*'s stories keep going off the rails; readers will argue forever about how adequate a key the *Odyssey* is to Bloom's Dublin. And for Stephen, anyway, love's adequacy, the extent to which love really is *the* answer to *the* question, is similarly open to challenge, if only because of its manifest debasement in the adult world. It is not accidentally that he should feel compelled to ask his question when in a whorehouse. He asks it not because he wants to know the answer but because he needs to hear it.

In this he is not much like the Telemachus, setting out in search of news, to whom he is supposed to correspond. He is more like Odysseus, who in visiting the underworld asks two shades, Tiresias and his mother, to reassure him about his love, Penelope, in the "other world." And here it helps to recall something persuasively argued by John Paul Riquelme: that the fifteenth episode of *Ulysses* corresponds to two classical episodes rather than one, to both the visit to Circe's den and the visit to Hades.[2] Hence, for instance, Stephen's muddle about "Circe's or what am I saying Ceres' altar" (*U* 15.2091–92): Ceres/Demeter, as a mythologically inclined contemporary of Frazer would likely have known, was supposed to have once been a goddess of the underworld, a role taken over by her daughter Persephone. So: Circe = Ceres and, therefore, "Circe" = "Hades."

Which means that in considering the two principal encounters of "Circe," it is permissible to seek correspondences in Odysseus's two main encounters in Hades, with Tiresias and his mother, Anticleia. (As we will see later, one encounter in the other Hades, "Hades," is with his father.) Once that is allowed, the connections become obvious. As Riquelme says, Tiresias is Bella/Bello Cohen, sex-changer and prophet, whose report on the doings at Bloom's home (*U* 15.3136–37) corresponds to Tiresias's on Ithaca (compare *Odyssey* 11.116–21). The second encounter, of Stephen with his mother, just as clearly corresponds to that of Odysseus with Anticleia. In Homer's account, son-Odysseus is as cavalier to his mother as Stephen is supposed to have been to his, holding her off with his sword until he can first get the inside word from Tiresias.[3] And how did she die? When he lets her tell him, Anticleia minces no words. It was your long absence, Odysseus, she tells him, my loneliness for my wandering son (not, as you may want to suppose, illness) that did me in (11.229–36). "Perplexed," Odysseus bites his lip, and no wonder. After all, had he not insisted on sticking out the war, or never left at all, his mother would not be here. For all her tenderness, Anticleia makes clear that it was no "illness" that did her in, it was *him*. (To which Stephen, slipping into denial mode: "Cancer did it, not I" [*U* 15.4187].) And both mothers are remarkably eloquent about the fates of their sons. Anticleia rubs it in that "All mortals," for example, you, are coming to her state (11.220–22); Mrs. Dedalus keens to her son, "All must go through it, Stephen. . . . You too. Time will come" (*U* 15.4182–84).

Despite these lugubrious pieties, Odysseus manages, and Stephen attempts, to gain one reassuring word about the other world to which they will be returning. For Odysseus it is the news that Penelope remains faithful. Is there a sense in which Stephen's question to his mother corresponds to Odysseus's, seeking a similar answer? To see how that might be, it will help to look at another author's treatment of the scene:

Ulysses: Alas, alas! and mother, she? she lives—
But stays she true to me?

Anticleia: Child, I have come
But lately to this place, and when I died
Still was she true to thee, and knew not time.

Ulysses: At last, at last the word that lighteth hell!
One word! and thou alone, mother, couldst speak it!

(Phillips 1902, 90)

"At last the word," spoken by mother to son, the "One word." This scene is from Stephen Phillips's *Ulysses,* a play now forgotten but highly thought of in 1902, when with the help of Beerbohm Tree's stagecraft wizardry it became one of the talked-of shows of the season.[4] Joyce probably never saw it performed, but he did read it,[5]—and, I suggest, went on to pick up from its climactic "Hades" scene some ideas later incorporated in his own handling of the climactic "Circe" episode.[6] Aside from the coincidence that both questioners seek the one "word" from their mothers, there are similarities in the treatments of the events following. Phillips's Ulysses, urged on by his mother, *"rushes to the foot of the descent, and stumbles upward,"* fighting off the throng of ghosts surging around him: "I gasp and fight toward thee! . . . / Think me not dead! / . . . The light, the light! The air, the blessed air!" Stephen—overheated, faint—suddenly becomes aware of himself as being in hell (his mother uses the word twice) and makes a break for it, against the resistance of the whores. For both, it is a matter of escape from a hot, suffocating place into the open air—for Phillips's Ulysses to continue on to Penelope, for Stephen to resume his ludicrously Wagnerian quest, brandishing the Siegfried sword that at the end of *Portrait* he left his mother in order to "forge."

And Phillips's script also throws into relief a critical difference between Stephen's encounter and the Homeric original: in Homer, the mother answers the question; in "Circe," despite prompting, she does not. Anticleia supplies Odysseus his reason to return to the living and continue his voyage; Mrs. Dedalus tries to drag her son back down into the Ireland of religious fanaticism, marinating animosities, and death. Odysseus sets out with his mother's blessing; Stephen runs away to escape his mother's curse.

That is, both Odysseus and Stephen ask for the same thing, a reason to go on, but receive opposite responses. One reason for the difference is that unlike Homer's (or Phillips's) Odysseus Stephen is talking not to a genuine apparition but to a "hallucination," something largely a projection of his own impulses and associations—indeed literally, as we have seen, the reflection of his own face. Seeking an affirmation of the word he knows in the abstract, he is also talking to—asking his question of—himself, which is to say he is asking the young man who was to a great extent also talking of himself when in "Scylla and Charybdis" he recast Shakespeare, the sweet myriadminded Will of the library's literary set, as an embittered outcast, compulsively recalling the moment when love left him: "Belief in himself has been untimely killed . . . The tusk of the boar has wounded him there where love lies ableeding" (U 9.455–60). These words, typical of Stephen's Shakespearean portrait/self-portrait, occur some twenty-five lines below the restored "Love" passage of the Gabler edition, which is also, like the Circean exchange, a query to which the answer is known, seeking affirmation not information: "Do you know what you are talking about? Love, yes. Word known to all men" (U 9.429–30). "Do you know what you are talking about"—like "What the hell are you driving at? I know. Shut up. Blast you. I have reasons" (U 9.846–47)—is Stephen's question to himself testing, again, not the answer, but the possibility of arriving at it along his present course. As in "Circe," Stephen knows what he wants to hear but not how to get to it.

It is I think possible to triangulate from passages like the above toward what Stephen is driving at, the Aquinian *amicitia inter multos* (U 9.771) that he wishes to plot as developing from Shakespeare's "undoing," much as Christian agape unfolds from the Fall. But in any case the fact remains that none of his library interlocutors is going to come away with the faintest idea that "love" was what he was "talking about." For reasons both internal (slights and betrayals, real and imagined) and external (Eglinton's baiting, Mulligan's hectoring), Stephen never earns the answer to his question. The Shakespeare he is left with is the hornmad paralytic reflected—again, as self-portrait—from his and Bloom's face in Bella Cohen's mirror (U 15.3820–29). And he himself is "a most finished artist" (U 15.2508), going to the dogs in the appointed way, winding up by episode's end in a red-light district (Stephen on Shakespeare: "Assumed dongiovannism will not save him" [U 9.458–59]), eventually lying in the gutter.

Among the reasons that belief in himself has been thus untimely killed, there is one whose genealogy he spells out to Bloom: "The collapse which Bloom ascribed to gastric inanition and certain chemical compounds of varying degrees of adulteration and alcoholic strength, accelerated by mental exertion and the velocity of rapid circular motion in a relaxing atmosphere, Stephen attributed to the reapparition of a matutinal cloud (perceived by both from two different points of observation, Sandycove and Dublin) at first no bigger than a woman's hand" (*U* 17.36–42). Ever the exponent of "phenomenon," Bloom traces the collapse to Stephen's booze-and-absinthe binge on an empty stomach and to the dizzying pirouettes he performed during the *Gioconda* fantasia. That is part of the truth, certainly, but Stephen was the one it happened to, and his version is the one to go with. It will help if, noting that phrase about the cloud no bigger than a woman's hand, we remember what "A Little Cloud" did with its biblical original. Once again, here, we have a storm grown out of a wisp. The thunderstorm that scared Stephen with the threat of divine reproach in "Oxen of the Sun" (*U* 14.414–15) has returned at the end of "Circe"—that is why Bloom cloaks himself (*U* 15.4324) and the crowd, escaping the "pelter" (*U* 15.4333), huddles under a scaffold (*U* 15.4365)—bringing with it yet another peal of thunder, which becomes the source of Mrs. Dedalus's "deathrattle" (*U* 15.4238). Why Stephen, always afraid of thunder, should on this occasion hear in it his mother's deathrattle becomes clear when we remember the cloud's "matutinal" original (or harbinger) in "Telemachus," when it was "no bigger than a woman's hand." The associational link was forged when Mulligan, trying to make up for his remark about Stephen's mother, adverted to the sea, then exited while singing Yeats's "Who Goes with Fergus": "And no more turn aside and brood / Upon love's bitter mystery / For Fergus rules the brazen cars" (*U* 1.239–41). As Sonja Basic has pointed out,[7] the first words of the meditation that follows, "Woodshadows floated silently by through the morning peace from the stairhead seaward where he gazed" (*U* 1.243–44), rather than describing the vista—there are no trees in the vicinity, therefore no "woodshadows"—arise from Stephen's knowledge of the song's next line, "And rules the shadows of the wood." With that line, the seascape Stephen contemplates becomes mingled in his mind with this song, the song he sang his dying mother. So when that little cloud, later remembered as "no bigger than a woman's hand," covers the sun and darkens the scene, the bay becomes a "bowl of bitter waters" (*U* 1.249), from the bowl of green vomit earlier remembered (a memory itself provoked by Mulligan's lines about "Our mighty mother" [*U* 1.85, 78]) from the death scene (*U* 1.106–10), and brings with it the remorse from Stephen's failure at that scene to honor the request of "Her glazing eyes, staring out of death" (*U* 1.273).

And so, in a sequence anticipated in *Portrait* and "A Little Cloud," that cloud is established as a synecdoche for Stephen's anxieties about mother, church, and death, and so the thunder from the cloudburst of "Oxen of the Sun" arouses his guilty fears (*U* 14.408–54), and so in "Circe" another peal of thunder, conceived of as coming from that same cloud, recalls the mother, with her glazing death-eyes (*U* 15.4160–61) and her curse.

Such psycho-symbolic metamorphoses are, as we have been seeing, all over

the place in the later chapters of *Ulysses*, a major concern of which is the generation of symbols over time: a figure in a raincoat becoming the mystery man
McIntosh, the "jing" of a jaunting car (*U* 11.457) becoming a leitmotif for adulterous bed-banging, a misheard "throw it away" (*U* 5.534) becoming a
prophecy. (And, by extension, the fabled travelings of some wily Greek becoming the *Odyssey*.) Stephen's repudiated request for reassurance, for an affirmation that love outlasts the grave, results from one such generation, tracing back
to the first pages of the book. So, perhaps, does another, more heartening answer. As a result of the nightmarish encounter with his mother's apparition
Stephen runs into the street, gets mixed up in a row, and winds up flattened,
muttering again those lines from "Who Goes with Fergus." Why that poem,
here? Because, as usual, of a convergence of associations: the revived memory
of his mother and of the death scene where that song was sung, the echo of that
catalytic phrase "wood shadows" in Corny Kelleher's "He's covered *with shavings* anyhow" (*U* 15.4891, my italics), and in *"woodshavings"* (*U* 15.4937) amidst
mention of "Cabra"—site of the Dedalus home—and "Burying the Dead," spoken by the man who may well have arranged his mother's funeral. And, especially, this detail: *"Stephen, prone, breathes to the stars"* (*U* 15.4887).

The last line of the Yeats poem, which Stephen never reached in
"Telemachus," is "And all disheveled wandering stars." The anthropomor-
phism latent in that "disheveled"—not to mention the poem's earlier line, "And
the white breast of the dim sea"—will become explicit in "Ithaca," when the
two men watch a meteorite connect their two nonce-signs, Lyre and Leo, with
the (disheveled) "Tress of Berenice." That is the last thing we see Stephen see,
and considering his Dantesque pose it seems pertinent that each of the three
books of *The Divine Comedy* ends with a vision of the stars, that the entrance to
the garden where these constellations are beheld is accompanied with a psalm
(*U* 17.1030) famous for the use Dante was supposed to have made of it, even
that the name "Berenice" does not sound all that different from "Beatrice."

It is at the end of the hellish "Circe," when, as the "Eumaeus" narrator remarks, "it [has] cleared up after the recent visitation of Jupiter Pluvius" (*U*
16.40–41), that Stephen first sees those stars, and prompted by them and other
cues recalls and rounds off the poem with which he began the day. With that, at
the end of one sequence of misprisions, another begins: Bloom, picking up on
his "Fergus now" and "white breast" (*U* 15.4932, 4943), thinks that Stephen is
dreaming of a girlfriend surnamed Ferguson,[8] and, as always most right when
most wrong, humanely concludes, "Best thing could happen him" (*U*
15.4949–51). In the next episode Stephen says that he left his father's house "To

seek misfortune" (*U* 16.253); Bloom hears it as something like "Miss Fortune," and imagines that she, whether Miss Fortune or "Miss Ferguson," was "very possibly the particular lodestar who brought him down to Irishtown" (*U* 16.1559–61). So through a myriad metamorphoses of symbol the poem recalled at the outset, prompted by Mulligan, has come, in "Circe," to fork—first toward Mrs. Dedalus's underworld, second toward the stars, especially the "lodestar" associated with "some girl."

And there is reason to think that this latter path might extend further, to one Nora Barnacle, that it points to the answer, love, which Stephen sought and did not receive from his mother. In *Finnegans Wake* Bloom's misfortune/Miss Fortune confusion is behind a pun relating ALP in Professor Jones's reference to his rival's ally "the fiery goodmother Miss Fortune" (*FW* 149.22–23)—"fiery" because her red-brown auburn hair is often represented as afire, as "auburnt" (*FW* 139.23). Indeed the book insists on how fortunate (*FW* 175.29, 327.26) or, simply, lucky (*FW* 28.23, 148.32, 200.08, 232.36, 249.05, 299.20, 315.15, 326.35, 358.24, 438.35, 531.24, 556.10, 587.17, 606.24) was the "lover-lucky" (*FW* 55.28) swain to be chosen, by his lucky woman, who more than once recalls Nora, as when we are told that but for the "tiddywink of a windfall . . . there would not be a holey spier on the town *nor a* vestal flouting in the dock . . . *nor a* yew *nor an* eye to play cash cash in Novo Nilbud . . . *nor a'*toole o'tall o'toll" (*FW* 23.34–24.02, my italics). Nora—the purblind Joyce's seeing-eye "spier," the vessel's vestal of their elopement—is the man's "windfall" here.

A windfall (an unexpected fall of fruit, for instance apples), like Miss/Fortune, can be taken as signifying opposite kinds of luck: at *FW* 589.25–27 the woman is involved in the calamity that "misflooded his fortunes," and throughout she is at least partly responsible for the apple-fall of original sin. But then we know what the book has to say on that subject: "O fortunous casualitas!" (*FW* 175.29). If *Finnegans Wake* asserts anything without qualification, it is that both mankind's and the author's fall into the calamities of life—heartache, begetting, bringing forth, the new heartaches of parenthood—is good, is lucky, that wretched though he may be it is the crushed and pickled Gripes, not the pristine Mookse, who has "luck enoupes" (*FW* 158.17–18), and that the condition of *felix culpa* is sexual, especially married, love.

Which is to say that the Stephen of Bloomsday, who for all his hauteur badly wants some woman to fall for him ("How to win a woman's love. For me this" [*U* 10.847; compare 3.434–36, 9.261]), looking for love as well as "Love," is indeed seeking Miss Fortune. *Ulysses*, everyone agrees, commemorates the day when the author, at Stephen's age, found her. Is it not odd that nothing of the kind happens to Stephen?

Maybe not to Stephen, but I think that by tracing one last sequence of associative mutations we can see that something like that does happen. Of the parallels between Stephen and Bloom, perhaps the most striking is that they should have had such similar dreams last night. Stephen's is of encountering, at the entrance to a "Street of harlots," a dark man resembling Haroun al-Raschid who beckons him into an interior covered with a red carpet, holds up a cream-fruit (later melon) to him, and speaks cryptically comforting words. He also dreams of a visit from his mother's corpse and of flying, his "foes beneath" him (U 15.3930, 3935). Bloom has dreamed of seeing Molly in red slippers and (later, according to the "Pepys-Evelyn" of "Oxen of the Sun") Turkish trousers—a harem outfit, in short. These dreams derive from the same source, the *Arabian Nights's Entertainment*, that communal quarry of the bedtime stories and Christmas pantomimes that shaped the fantasies of the young men of "The Sisters" and "Araby." In "Araby," simply the title name, posted around town, had been enough to induce a dream of Persia. Just what in the Dublin of June 15 might have called up similarly eastern images into the dreams of Stephen and Bloom is less certain; perhaps as in "Araby" the placards for the Mirus Bazaar (perhaps, indeed, just the word "Bazaar," with its Arabic origin and associations) spotted here and there, acted as catalyst, and perhaps Bloom, lying next to a woman given to smoking "Muratti's turkish cigarettes," to wearing "outsided ladies' drawers" "redolent of . . . jessamine" (U 17.2094) and reading *Ruby, Pride of the Ring*, was reminded before drifting off of Aladdin's Slave of the Ring,[9] as, next night, the circle of light above his bed reminds him of the roc's egg of the Sinbad saga.[10] It may be, considering his habit of inducing sleep by "the automatic relation to himself of a narrative concerning himself" (U 17.1755–56), that he usually drifts off with stories of Sinbad in his head. Anyway, the congruence of Bloom's and Stephen's dreams, though certainly owing something to *Ulysses'* intermittent field of telepathic possibilities, owes something as well to the fact that both have grown up in the same community, with its limited inventory of imaginative furniture; for them, as for the characters of *Dubliners*, fantasy lies in the East, and more than any other source the stories of the *Arabian Nights* define its contours.

And the story acted out when Stephen's and Bloom's oriental dreams are put together is of the triumph of, the finding or re-finding of, love. Stephen, having met his Haroun al-Raschid in the street of harlots, having, in his way, like Aladdin, flown (U 15.3935–36, 4128), giddy from whirling dervish-like to the accompaniment of a Pianola whose revolving "Wonderlight" probably gets its name from an Englishing of German *Wunderlampe,* Aladdin's lamp, and having confronted his mother's "ghoul" (an Arabic word, prominent in the *Nights* [*U* 15.4200; compare *U* 1.278]), escapes this dream-scene and makes his way, in Bloom's company, to another. In "Ithaca," Stephen will "obey his [Bloom's] sign" and enter his hallway leading to the door behind which lies Molly, she of "plump mellow yellow smellow melons" (*U* 17.2241–42) in which Bloom will later press his own face, she whose photograph, showing her "fleshy charms," Bloom has earlier presented to him while harboring regrets that it does not display the melonous "opulent curves" of the real thing (*U* 16.1428, 1448).

That Stephen does not stay around to inspect this caliph's gift—he has identified Bloom with the figure of his dream since *U* 9.1203–08—may have to do with his subconscious recollections of what happens to Aladdin in the stories. (In one, the Haroun who purchases Aladdin a wife winds up sentencing him to death; in the commonest pantomime version the false uncle who lures him into an underground cavern with promise of splendid fruit leaves him to die.) In any case, we have seen enough by the time he leaves to have a pretty clear notion of where his dream, if only as wish-fulfillment, was heading. Zoe, who interpreted his dream's melon as meaning "Go abroad and love a foreign lady," and Lynch, who added, "Across the world for a wife" (*U* 15.3924–26), got it right. So did Florry when she added, "Dreams goes by contraries" (*U* 15.3928), given that Stephen is not, to all appearances, the man for melons, any more than young James Joyce seemed the man for Nora Barnacle. That the melon should be a "creamfruit" evokes both Aladdin's beloved wife Zabadiah ("A popular name, dim. of Zubdah, cream, fresh butter, 'creamkin' ")[11] and Molly, who in *Ulysses* is repeatedly associated with cream, who has sent her daughter a birthday present of a box of creams, who lathered herself with cosmetic cream for Boylan, and who in her monologue wonders indignantly if Bloom would "like my nice cream" (*U* 18.1506). As well she might; Bloom has served "the viscous cream ordinarily reserved for the breakfast of his wife Marion (Molly)" (*U* 17.364–65) to Stephen, who should be hearing yet another strange bell go off when his "attention [is] directed" to this mark of hospitality. Here, one can imagine Bloom saying jocoseriously, just for you, my wife's cream.

We may speculate whether behind Stephen's bland composure the wheels are turning feverishly: just what the *hell,* he could be wondering, is going on here? What has gone on is that he has received in a prophetic dream confirmed in his waking hours a full-blown symbolic introduction to the creamily, amplitudinously melonous, melodious Molly Bloom, of the Turkish cigarettes and

234 / JOYCE AND REALITY

Moorish lineage—and, behind her, to Nora, from the city whose Spanish, therefore Moorish, connections Joyce liked to stress. He has found out, or been given
the means to find out, that his dream was prophetic. As, come to that, was
Bloom's. When Stephen, his revery fulfilled, leaves the scene to Bloom, it is like
one relay runner handing the baton to another. Like Stephen's, Bloom's dream
derived primarily from the Aladdin stories of the *Arabian Nights*—in particular,
from the scene in which Haroun al-Raschid purchases at auction the slave Jes-
samyn[12]—and like Stephen's it comes true. In "Oxen of the Sun," as we have
noted, the "Pepys-Evelyn" narrator reports of Bloom's dream that it "is thought
by those in ken to be for a change" (*U* 14.509–10), and though one might incline
to dismiss the prognostications of someone who is himself skeptical of such
things, we have already observed that both of the other prophecies he reports—
along with all the others in the book—come true (*U* 14.945).

And so does his prediction about Bloom's dream, as follows. In a variant of
the Aladdin story the hero demands of the genie the one thing that will make
his palace complete: "the egg of a roc to be suspended from the center of this
dome" (Foster 1886, 548). Staring up from bed at the lamp's round reflection on
the ceiling, composing himself for sleep by calling to mind the bedtime stories
of his childhood, Bloom is reminded of that story, therefore of the roc, therefore
of Sinbad, whose best-known adventure occurs with a roc, and drifts off muttering about Sinbad and that egg. The half-awake Molly, coming to as he drops
off, hears him, in the process commencing the last of the book's luminous misprisions. Hugh Kenner (1977, 392) was the first to suggest in print that Molly's
notion of Bloom's asking for breakfast in bed traces to a mistaking of Bloom's
last muttered word, "egg," as recorded in the beginning of her monologue: "Yes
because he never did a thing like that before as ask to get his breakfast in bed
with a couple of eggs since the City Arms hotel when he used to be pretending
to be laid up" (*U* 18.01–3). Thus does "egg" cue the memory of the City Arms incident, which in turn supplies the framework for much of what follows—
Bloom, in bed, being served breakfast by Molly. Kenner's point about the
conjunction is confirmed if, taking the hint that the last words of "Ithaca" are a
more or less accurate transcription of Bloom's murmurings, we note that Bloom
says "bed" shortly after "egg" (*U* 17.2329), that the sounds of "Darkinbad the
Brightdayler" (*U* 17.2329–30) might suggest someone in bed as the day dawns
bright, and that Molly's later elaborations on Bloom's supposed demand plausibly derive from his last words, as heard by a groggy listener: the "tea and
Findon haddy" (*U* 18.930–31) from, respectively, "Tinbad the Tailor" (Irish
"tea" is pronounced "tay" and comes in tins) and "Finbad the Failer."[13]

Though ambivalent, Molly, her husband's rigmarole having wakened her for good on the verge of a high-summer dawn, decides to humor him. She will saunter out and fetch his breakfast, including eggs ("No good eggs with this drouth," Bloom remarked twenty hours ago [U 443–44], but the drought is over now) and possibly, adopting the *Arabian Nights* idiom, some "splendid fruits" (U 18.1500). And something else: imagining Stephen in Milly's room, she muses, "Id have to get a nice pair of red slippers like those Turks with the fez used to sell" (U 18.1494–95). Voilà.

How much of that will happen is anyone's guess, though it is worth noting that something very like this projected scene is reported to have transpired between the married couple of *Finnegans Wake*,[14] a book that begins where *Ulysses* left off, on Howth, and that ends with that couple heading there, on their trip back to the book's first page, via the last. (The opening "fall" [FW 3.16] is, in part, from the top of that destination, as imagined by Bloom at U 15.3377–81.) But at the end of *Ulysses* there is at least the prospect that Bloom will wake up next morning to find that his dream of the previous night has come true, and that a reader of *Ulysses* observing the scene would be struck by the way events also complete Stephen's dream: this exotic dark-eyed woman, playing the houri in her red Turkish slippers, bringing cream and fruit into the habitation of the beckoning dark-eyed stranger he met in the street of harlots. And it seems fair to expect this same hypothetical reader to take notice of the fact that these two men are to some extent youthful and mature versions of the author, an author who said, and wrote *Ulysses* from the conviction, that what changed him from a boy to a man was that woman's love. I have considered, in the preceding chapter, some of the ways in which in its final movement *Ulysses* seems to be settling down, its midcourse turbidities sedimenting into stable patterns (arc, circle), destinations (bulls-eye), and tales (homecoming), and it accords with such a development that the mysterious dreams of the two male principals should be resolved, or at least made resolvable, that the resolution should come into focus around the person of the one female principal, and that in so doing it should implicate the one personal event that started the writing of the book. Also, that this one event should be an act of love.

That the whole sequence should be conditioned by, indeed engendered by, the language of pantomime fantasy and facilitated by one mistake after another is nothing unique in Joyce's work. The ALP of *Finnegans Wake* is an accomplished pantomime *artiste* who like her daughter repeatedly tells her husband "all sorts of makeup things" (FW 625.05), fooling him and letting herself be fooled, to keep his spirits up and his love alive. In fact Joyce's connection with

Nora, we are told, began with a misprision; she thought from his outfit that he was a sailor and found that intriguing. Maybe that mistake has something to do with the fact that *Ulysses,* dedicated to that meeting and its sequel, calls on the story of one of literature's two most famous sailors, Odysseus, and why "Ithaca" ends with a meditation on the other one, Sinbad. In *Finnegans Wake* the male half of that Howth-wending couple remembers first greeting the auburn-haired woman as "goldilocks" (*FW* 615.20–26), a name from the pantomime stage, and, as the dawning sun turns the Liffey's waters to gold (*FW* 619.19), she goes along, like Molly seconding Bloom at that time on Howth when he called her a flower of the mountain (*U* 18.1576–78)—affirming that yes, "I am leafy, your goolden, so you called me" (*FW* 619.29–30).

19

The Mysterious Man in the Macintosh

A Prize *Titbits* Story by Mr. James Joyce

THE MAN IN THE MACINTOSH is the forgotten figure of the Joyce world. Once, the riddle of his identity cast a spell potent enough to draw out a dozen or so candidates, like claimants for a disputed inheritance.[1] Those were the days when almost everyone was reasonably sure that *Ulysses* conundrums could be expected to have *Ulysses* resolutions. Today, fewer are inclined to make that assumption, and an influential cohort, as avid for indeterminacies as was an earlier generation for epiphanies, rejects it out of theory-driven fiat. Coupled with recent genetic controversies over which if any *Ulysses* is definitive and a natural disinclination to enumerate old themes, this dispensation has brought most around to the line first taken by Robert M. Adams, that M'Intosh should be taken as an "unfulfilled curiosity," destined to remain so.[2]

Writing, as I am, a book, this one, arguing that that dispensation is wrong-headed, I take this opportunity to remark on how, in re M'Intosh, it can come with its own built-in traps. In particular, there is the characteristic overwillingness to collapse *is* into *ought*. I have elsewhere presented the thesis of this chapter in various forums—papers, e-mail, publications, conversations—and overwhelmingly the gist of those objecting to it has been not that the evidence doesn't add up but even that if it does it shouldn't, because everyone knows now that Joyce is a lot more indeterminate than those formalist modernist fifties-types were able to realize, and so that's the way to go. There is in effect a kind of canonicity being lent to the feeling that what has not yet been satisfactorily resolved cannot and, really you know, *ought* not to be resolved, that Joyce must have *meant* for it not to be resolved. Ponce de León sought the Fountain of Youth in Florida; Florida has by now been pretty thoroughly canvassed and no Fountain of Youth discovered; therefore Ponce de León was seeking that which was not. *Ulysses* has by now surely been explored in enough detail that the absence of some fabled presence from the charts constitutes prima facie evidence of authorial intention to keep it unmapped, to mystify and withhold. Hence Phillip Herring, who in the process of rejecting the argument being advanced in this chapter has written, in the name, ironically, of "uncertainty": "the M'Intosh mystery was clearly *intended* to mystify Bloom and thus the reader."[3]

Well. For me, for one, Joyce's intentions are seldom what one can confidently call "clear," and *Ulysses* remains in any number of areas a dark and indeterminate narrative, full of things that I still don't get, don't know for sure if I ever will get, but for that very reason cannot feel certain that I never will get. Even if Joyce were well known to be fond of frustrating his readers in such matters, any such assertion as Herring's would amount to a doubly dubious compounding of the intentional fallacy (we can't figure it out because Joyce didn't mean for us to) with tautology (and the reason we know he didn't mean for us to is that we can't figure it out). In any event, and whichever way the Zeitgeist may blow, the easily verifiable fact remains that Joyce does not as a rule go in for such tricks, that most of his puzzles, at least up through *Ulysses,* have by now received quite satisfactory solutions. Let it be noted as well that of the two puzzles Joyce particularly liked to put to his friends—Who is M'Intosh? and What is the title of "Work in Progress"? (*JJ* 516, 708)[4]—the latter at least had a definite answer, which answer was *Finnegans Wake.*

So we should not be too quick to assume that the M'Intosh question did not also have such a definite answer, just because we have not all agreed on what it was. Accordingly, I propose to approach the M'Intosh question from what seem to me a few commonsense premises, the first of which is that it might, after all, be solvable.

The second premise is that M'Intosh's identity is indeed a puzzle, the most naggingly reiterated one in *Ulysses,* unpuzzling which is therefore part of the proper business of reading the book. A puzzle, that is—or, call it, rather, a mystery, set up to tease the reader into thought as deliberately as any Agatha Christie. *Ulysses* makes a point of embracing a range of different genres, and M'Intosh is its main mystery story. Bloom hints as much while contemplating yet another figure whose name he does not know: "Ask yourself who is he now. *The Mystery Man on the Beach,* prize tidbit story by Mr. Leopold Bloom. Payment at the rate of one guinea per column. And that fellow today at the graveside in the brown macintosh" (*U* 13.1061–62). His idea is that that graveside "fellow" could make for another mystery story, entitled, perhaps, *The Mystery Man in the Cemetery,* which a reader of such things might hope to crack.

How? In the usual way: by gathering and examining the evidence made available by the author—if there is one point on which mystery readers agree, it is that any solution exceeding these limitations constitutes cheating—then listing the plausible suspects, then narrowing them down, process-of-elimination-wise, to the final candidate. That is how you "Ask yourself who is he now."

Let us, then, testing the hypothesis that M'Intosh is a definite detectable somebody whose identity corresponds to some character in the fictional world of James Joyce, consider the available testimony about him. Most of it seems pretty flimsy. We are told that M'Intosh wears a dusty brown raincoat, that he looks "lanky," that at different times he drinks Bovril and eats dry (that is, unbuttered) bread, that he is spotted at three different locations, once in a cemetery and twice in downtown Dublin, and that before that someone saw (and apparently heard) him in the vicinity of the Richmond Asylum. So far, this is discouraging: anyone might eat this or that, wear this or that, be here or there. There are, however, two pieces of testimony to more substantial attributes. In "Cyclops" we hear that he "loves a lady who is dead" (U 12.1498), and in "Oxen of the Sun" we hear that this lady was his wife: he is a "Man all tattered and torn that married a maiden all forlorn. Slung her hook she did" (U 14.1451–52)—that is, she ran off and/or died.[5]

Neither of these statements carries as much authority as one would like. The first appears in the middle of a parody, where it consorts with similar statements, some of them probably true and some of them probably not; the second, taken from the chaotic last ten paragraphs of "Oxen of the Sun," is an overheard something coming from a drunken someone. On the other hand, critical scrutiny of those ten paragraphs has shown them to be a remarkably accurate account of facts and events,[6] and the passage in question does corroborate the earlier testimony from "Cyclops." Although not that much to go on by themselves, taken together and matched with the fact that M'Intosh does first appear in a cemetery, apparently as a mourner, they add up to a coherent composite that amounts to the best evidence we have to go on as to who M'Intosh is.

Who, then, fits the profile? How many bereaved widowers—that is, men who (1) have lost their wives and (2) regret the fact—does the fictional work of James Joyce, up to and including Ulysses, contain? Nobody in Exiles or A Portrait of the Artist as a Young Man. Nobody in Dubliners either: the candidate proposed independently by John Henry Raleigh and John O. Lyons, Mr. Duffy, is not married to Mrs. Sinico, and the book's only certifiable widowers, Mr. Sinico himself and Mr. Hill of "Eveline," are not loving sorts. In fact none of the solutions proposed so far fulfills the criteria.[7]

That leaves Ulysses, in which there are two, and only two, eligible candidates. The first is Simon Dedalus, a widower who does, certainly, miss his wife, but who, both in Bloom's original sighting and in the *Evening Telegraph* report of the "Hades" funeral (*U* 16.1259–61), is obviously distinct from the M'Intosh also present in both.

Subtract Simon, then, and one man is left standing. He seems an unlikely choice, but let us steel ourselves with the words of Messr. Dupin: when you have eliminated the impossible, then what remains must be true. So. Here is the man who, by process of elimination, must be M'Intosh, if anyone is: "Tomorrow will be a week that I received. . . . it is no use Leopold to be. . . . with your dear mother . . . that is not more to stand . . . to her . . . all for me is out . . . be kind to Athos, Leopold. . . . my dear son . . . always . . . of me . . . *das Herz . . . Gott . . . dein*"(*U* 17.1883–86). This is Bloom's recollection of the suicide note of his father, Rudolph Bloom, who killed himself eighteen years before Bloomsday, out of grief over the death of his wife and from a desire to be "with" her, to go "to her"[8] To me, the choice is clear: either M'Intosh is a definite character, discernible in the work of James Joyce, or he isn't. And if he is, then he is the ghost of Bloom's dead father, Rudolph.

So there is my suspect, the one to whom what facts we have point. I can foresee three immediate objections. First, James Joyce was a writer with a fanatical devotion to realism, and such writers do not do ghost stories. Second, even granting that M'Intosh might be a ghost, he can hardly be the ghost of Rudolph Bloom, who has been buried for years in a city, Ennis, many miles from the scene of his appearance. Third, even granting that M'Intosh is not only a ghost but a ghost capable of traversing the width of the country, why should he? Why on earth, after all, should the late Rudolph Bloom be hanging around in Glasnevin Cemetery on Bloomsday?

The answer to the last objection is that as a matter of fact he has an excellent reason for being there, of exactly the kind that ghosts are known to find most compelling: having killed himself in order to be, in his words, "with" his dead wife, he is now, against his express wishes, buried miles away from her. Ellen Bloom is interred in Glasnevin, a Catholic cemetery where the suicide Rudolph was presumably not welcome.[9] "Mine over there towards Finglas, the plot I bought," thinks Bloom, in "Hades," about his future Glasnevin grave site, and then, "Mamma poor mamma, and little Rudy" (*U* 6.862–63). That is, Bloom's mother, Rudolph's wife, is buried near Bloom's plot and Rudy's grave,[10] in the cemetery being visited by M'Intosh, who from Bloom's perspective is "over there" (*U* 6.805), as her grave is "over there" (*U* 6.862).

Which motive, I think, pretty much answers the second objection: Rudolph may be buried in faraway Ennis, but his spirit has come to Dublin for the most compelling of traditional ghostly reasons. Also traditional have been the terms of his entry into the company of the unquiet dead, suicides being, along with murderers and murder victims (like Hamlet's father, about whom more later) one of the categories of the departed most likely to return as ghosts.[11] Which is why, as Bloom recalls in "Hades" (U 6.346–48), suicides were once buried, like vampires, with a stake through the heart: to prevent any untoward returns from the dead. As Professor MacHugh put it earlier, "The ghost walks" (U. 8.237). That is, after all, what unquiet ghosts proverbially do, and there is traditionally no limit to the range of their travels. ("Walking Mackintosh," our mystery man is called at one point in "Oxen of the Sun," and, a little earlier, "Dusty Rhodes" [U 14.1552, 1546].) Like (in Gabriel's imagination) Galway's Michael Furey in "The Dead," and like Bloom himself during one "Circe" hallucination (U 15.3137–71), he has traveled here to haunt at the place of his beloved.

As for the first objection, that a writer like Joyce would never have included a ghost among his cast of characters, I return to the theme of what I have earlier called his "Orphic" propensities. To repeat: James Joyce was a realist, but his reality was different from ours. He believed in things, or in the possibility of things, that most of us consider beyond the pale, and the evidence is that one of them was ghosts. Richard Ellmann records that as a young man Joyce and his sister Margaret "got up at midnight to see their mother's ghost."[12] His brother Stanislaus, dealing with approximately the same period, confirms Joyce's involvement in spiritualist circles (1958, 131–33, 176); Stanislaus assumes that these interests must have lapsed, but Stuart Gilbert later found the Joyce of the Ulysses years not only "conversant . . . with spiritualist literature" but willing to grant such doctrines a "validity no higher and no lower than that of many of the fashionable and fluctuating 'truths' of science and psychology" (Gilbert 1958, vii-viii), and we have already considered how the hypothesis of occult phenomena scientifically explained may have licensed some of the wilder flights of Ulysses' later episodes. Peter Costello has discovered that Frederick W. H. Myers' Human Personality and Its Survival of Bodily Death, whose purportedly scientific theories about ghost-hauntings, table-rappings,[13] telepathic apprehensions of far-distant relatives at the moment of death, and so on we have earlier cited, was consulted by Joyce shortly after the vigil for his mother's ghost (1993, 212). Myers' book, where Joyce could have learned of the Morton Prince-Sally Beauchamp case that was to figure importantly in Finnegans Wake (Glasheen 1954), draws on various contemporary scientific developments, along with the writings of Freud, Josef Breuer, and Pierre Janet, to advance a theory of ghosts as the result of a "manifestation of persistent personal energy" (Myers 1920, 2:4) some-

242 / JOYCE AND REALITY

what like radioactivity, and through two thick volumes gives example after example of such manifestations being identified by the clothes they wear.[14]

So M'Intosh could conceivably be a ghost, because ghosts are conceivable. Once allow the possibility, and a number of otherwise incongruous details fall into place. It becomes simply of course that he should suddenly materialize out of nowhere ("Where the deuce did he pop out of?" [U 6.826]) and disappear in the same way ("Where has he disappeared to? . . . Become invisible. Good Lord, what became of him?" [U 6.899–900]). We can now perhaps understand why he is described as passing "unscathed" across the viceroy's path (U 10.1772). His drink of Bovril, mentioned in "Oxen of the Sun," becomes newly apt: Bovril is beef tea, a meat extract recommended as fortifying to the infirm; we hear of it in an episode paralleling the *Odyssey* account of the killing and eating of sacred herds; its imbiber is introduced in an episode paralleling the Homeric episode in which famished ghosts drink from the "black blood" of sacrificed cattle; in the next episode Bloom, viewing the carcasses of cattle, emphatically links such a diet with ghosts: "Hot fresh blood they prescribe for decline. Blood always needed. Insidious. Lick it up, smoking hot, thick sugary. Famished ghosts" (U 8.729–30). In short, it would be hard to imagine a more appropriate beverage for anyone returning from the dead.[15] Or, for that matter, wishing to: in the first chapter of *Portrait*, Brother Michael brings Stephen a cup of beef tea just as Stephen is awakening from his dream of being dead and buried (P 24); in the second section of "Grace" Mrs. Kernan brings the convalescent Mr. Kernan a cup of beef tea (D 156) to help him recover from what according to Joyce's Dantean scheme for the story would be his fall into the lavatory's land of the dead.[16]

Nor should the fact that M'Intosh drinks a real drink, or apparently performs other earthly functions, disqualify him. Among his spectral contemporaries were many who ate, drank, and smoked, who took carriages, taxis, and boats, made telephone calls, and so on.[17] (There was also one—well known early in the century—supposed to have worn a macintosh;[18] perhaps inspired by his example, at least one fictional ghost—in "The Hollow Man" by Thomas Burke, written after *Ulysses*—does the same [Cox and Gilbert 1986, 411–20]. Indeed the age's ghost-sightings and similar reports of occult apparitions typically feature some distinctive garment, often from the past life.)

And the "Oxen of the Sun" passage that tells us about M'Intosh's Bovril contains other hints that M'Intosh may be not only a ghost, but the ghost of Bloom's father. It is worth quoting in full:

Golly, whatten tunket's yon guy in the mackintosh? Dusty Rhodes. Peep at his wearables. By mighty! What's he got? Jubilee mutton. Bovril, by James. Wants it

real bad. D'ye ken bare socks? Seedy cuss in the Richmond? Rawthere! Thought
he had a deposit of lead in his penis. Trumpery insanity. Bartle the Bread we calls
him. That, sir, was once a prosperous cit. Man all tattered and torn that married a
maiden all forlorn. Slung her hook, she did. Here see lost love. Walking Mackintosh of lonely canyon. (*U* 14.1546–53)

Here we learn what would seem to be another substantial fact about M'Intosh
besides those that originally permitted us to single out Rudolph—that although
now "seedy," he was once a "prosperous cit" who has since come down in the
world. In addition to being a sorrowing widower, he is what the novels of the
time would call a ruined man. And so, as it happens, was Rudolph, able to accumulate enough capital to become owner of the quite respectable Queen's
Hotel until, as Molly recalls, he "ruin[ed] himself altogether . . . in Ennis" (*U*
18.982). Bloom's memory seems to support hers: "I am ruined," he says in
"Circe," while reenacting his father's suicide (*U* 15.1966–67). Molly is also the
one who recalls that Rudolph "felt lost" when his wife died" (*U* 16.1062), which
may remind us of "Here see lost love." And there is perhaps one other hint here
of biographical testimony: the woman he married is called a "maiden," a word
denoting virginity and connoting youth, therefore right for Rudolph's wife,
who was somewhere between ten and forty-four years his junior.[19]

Aside from this incidental information, the "Oxen of the Sun" passage contains several verbal clues of the kind familiar to readers of Joyce. M'Intosh is, as
we have seen, called "Dusty Rhodes," a name that occurs twice in "Circe," once
in the Bloom genealogy (*U* 15.1864–65), once as the near-homonym "dusty
brogues," which Bloom is described as wearing at the moment when, in one of
his hallucinations, he turns into his father Rudolph (*U* 15.1959–68). As a stock
name for a tramp, Dusty Rhodes would, after all, be the right moniker for
someone who, like Rudolph Bloom, has been financially ruined, someone who,
like Rudolph Bloom, had been a traveling salesman (a frequenter of dusty
roads, ready to "go a piece of the road with every one" [*U* 12.1584–85]),[20] someone who, like Rudolph Bloom, is dead (dust to dust)—and also someone who,
like Rudolph Bloom on the Homeric level, corresponds to Odysseus's father,
Laertes, once prosperous but now ruined, presumed dead by his son but in fact
eventually found to be (though wishing for death because of the death of his
wife,[21] though driven to cover himself with "dust and ashes" when he believes
that Odysseus has died as well), still alive, albeit (compare "tattered and torn")
looking like a beggar, "patched and unseemly," all skin and bones.[22]

As long as Laertes is the subject, this is perhaps the place to answer one of
Herring's main objections, that according to my reading Bloom sights the ghost

244 / JOYCE AND REALITY

of his own father but, incredibly, fails to recognize him (Herring 1987, 113). Well, yes: just as, in the scene cited, Laertes fails to recognize his son Odysseus, after a comparable passage of time, in fact demands that Odysseus give proof by showing his scar. (Which scar, back in *Ulysses,* corresponds to Bloom's bee-sting, which sting is loudly discussed, in Burke's, in M'Intosh's presence.) For his part, the only reason Odysseus knows Laertes when he sees him is that the latter has already been pointed out and described, with particular stress on how much he has changed—he too was once a prosperous cit, now withdrawn to the country to pine away in grief (in Samuel Butler's translation, familiar to Joyce, "he never comes to town now, and lives by himself in the country" [Homer 1968, 6]; Ennis is definitely the country, by Dublin standards). Nor, *pace,* again, Herring, does Bloom necessarily get a good look at this strange apparition who pops up and then disappears so suddenly: he glimpses him once, in a crowd from which he himself is standing "far back" (*U* 6.1344), as a strange figure presumably with his head bowed and possibly seen from behind. (At *U* 11.1249–50 he seems to remember him as having been "Muffled up.") Likewise for the second sighting in Burke's: a crowded pub, packed tight in a common effort to make the last call, where there is some dodging and hiding by people not wanting to be seen.

Besides, it is in general a predictable feature of Joyce's work that people see what they expect to see, that for instance people like Bloom who do not believe in ghosts (see, for instance, *U* 6.677) do not recognize them. In "Hades" we hear a story of two Irishmen who fail to recognize Jesus Christ—surely a familiar figure—because they expect to see Mulcahy from Coombe. On the other hand, in "Cyclops" Alf Bergan, ignorant of Paddy Dignam's death and burial, meets or thinks he meets Dignam walking the street. And if that is true in general is it doubly so for fathers and sons: is it really necessary to point out, considering that it has an entire episode devoted to the theme, that for *Ulysses* the recognitions between fathers and sons are problematical?

Speaking of fatherhood, consider as well those "Oxen" words "Seedy cuss in the Richmond," which may fit Rudolph in three different ways. "Seedy," in this verbally acrobatic episode on the theme of fatherhood, is an irresistible pun (inevitably repeated in *Finnegans Wake,* which gives us "seedy ejaculations" (*FW* 183.23), for a down-at-heels patriarch, particularly a Jewish one. (Rudolph smoked a "Jacob's pipe" [*U* 14.1451–52] and implicitly compared himself to Abraham [*U* 5.200–206]; both Jacob and Abraham were promised that their "seed" would flourish.) "Cuss" is slang for "curse" or, here, "one who is cursed," which, as a suicide, Rudolph Bloom, according to the Church, is: that is probably why he is buried away from his wife. "The greatest disgrace to have in the family," says Mr. Power when the subject of suicide comes up, to which the diplomatic Martin Cunningham, thinking of Bloom's father, replies, "Temporary insanity, of course" (U 6.639). Which phrase supplies one other link between Rudolph (intermittently thought to have been or gone crazy)[23] and "Seedy cuss in the Richmond," since what is being referred to is the Richmond Lunatic Asylum, the institution where someone has apparently spotted M'Intosh earlier in the day (and which is [1] near the terminal for trains from Ennis and [2] right next to Dublin's main workhouse for the poor). That same someone refers to him as a case of "trumpery insanity," which as Joyce's notebook entry—

trumpery insanity
temporary insanity[24]—

confirms, quite definitely repeats Cunningham's "Hades" diagnosis of "Temporary insanity," intended as an excuse for the suicide of . . . Rudolph Bloom.

Other clues may lurk elsewhere. "Where the deuce did he pop out of?" asks Bloom in "Hades"(U 6.826), and "Pop," in Joyce's notebooks, is the most frequent term for "father."[25] As for the phrase "pop out of," the hint that M'Intosh is popping up (and, in his later "invisible" exit, down) like a theatrical apparition from beneath the stage seems confirmed in "Circe":

(*A man in a brown macintosh springs up through a trapdoor. He points an elongated finger at Bloom.*)

THE MAN IN THE MACINTOSH
Don't you believe a word he says. That man is Leopold M'Intosh, the notorious fireraiser. His real name is Higgins.

BLOOM
Shoot him! Dog of a Christian! So much for M'Intosh! (*A cannonshot. The man in the macintosh disappears. Bloom with his sceptre strikes down poppies.*) (U 15.1558–66)

Given Joyce's use of "pop," it is at least a neat coincidence that the flowers Bloom strikes down while ordering M'Intosh's execution should be "poppies." Why M'Intosh, or anyone else, should call the temperate Bloom a fireraiser is less clear, but it may be pertinent that during Rudolph's last years the young Leopold was going through a phase of what he remembers as "ultra ideas" (U

16.1581–1602), above all the "immature" abjuration of Jewish doctrines and customs, for which he now feels "remorse" because of the pain this may have caused the father (*U* 17.1893–1901), who in his story about attending *Leah, or the Forsaken* was clearly trying to shame him back into the fold. As for M'Intosh's assertion that Bloom's "real" name is Higgins: well, given that Higgins was Bloom's mother's maiden name, and that she seems to have been a native-born Christian, such a statement, spoken by a Jewish father, might be one way of saying that Leopold is no true Bloom.[26]

Robert Crosman, noting the scene from "Circe," proposes that M'Intosh "reminds us of Satan," materializing dramatically in some production of *Faust* (1968, 130). I would suggest instead another stage apparition, equally famous: the old fellow in the cellarage who appears to his son Hamlet.[27] That Joyce's central character should be mysteriously visited by the ghost of his own father simply completes a central theme of the book, the return of the father after long absence (the *Odyssey*) or death (*Hamlet*). Stephen envisions himself as the Hamlet figure going forth to encounter his "old father," but Bloom, who also wears black and who at thirty-eight is just as close to Hamlet's age of thirty as the twenty-two-year-old Stephen, is the one whose father has died.

There are other parallels. Like Hamlet's father, Rudolph Bloom was killed by poison and, because he is buried away from the wife he died to join, has reason to protest her abandonment. Hamlet's father is "doomed for a certain term to walk the night"; M'Intosh is a walker ("Walking M'Intosh") and, as a "cuss," cursed, or doomed. And there is also one significant divergence, captured in Bloom's misremembrance of the *Hamlet* lines: "Hamlet, I am thy father's spirit / Doomed for a certain time [not "term"] to walk the earth [not "night"]" (*U* 8.67–68). Perhaps not too much is to be made of the change from "term" to "time," but "earth" substituted for "night" is a substantial alteration, and one that, again, fits, first because M'Intosh initially appears during the day, not night, second because as "Dusty Rhodes" (or Laertes) he is, obviously, earthy.

Hamlet Senior is one of the ghostly fathers called up from the array of shadow texts that underlie *Ulysses*; another is, again, Laertes, who fills the role admirably except for the stubborn fact that, though dusty and decrepit, he is not actually dead. That is a problem, all right, but one to which Joyce is equal. Because "Hades" turns out to have not one main classical analogue but two, and the second dictates that Leopold Bloom should indeed be encountering the ghost of his father. The Linati schema hints as much by including Laertes among the presences in "Hades"—and it is worth noting that once the other names listed have been paired up with their Dublin counterparts there are very few at all prominent figures other than M'Intosh left with whom Laertes might correspond.[28] Now, Laertes is not in the underworld chapter of the *Odyssey*. Neither are Prometheus, Eriphyle, Cerberus, Hades, or Proserpina, all names on Joyce's list for the episode. Where the last four named of these figures do appear, and where Roman analogues of the other two, Anchises (for Laertes) and Tityos (for Prometheus), can also be found,[29] is the underworld episode of the *Aeneid*.

The *Aeneid* rivals Homer as a source of the episode's classical echoes and allusions.[30] In addition to supplying much of the cast of characters, it is behind Bloom's unconscious reincarnation of Charon in a canal bargeman,[31] his vision of mortuary statuary as a crowd of dead souls beckoning with outstretched hands,[32] his fancy that a somnolent bird might be dead,[33] and his parting sight of the cemetery exit: "The gates glimmered in front" (*U* 6.995).[34]

I am of course pointing all this out because it is in the underworld journey of the *Aeneid* that the hero encounters the ghost of his father. (The Homeric version, in which the encounter is with the mother, occurs later, in "Circe," where Mrs. Dedalus rises from the dead, keening about the "fires of hell," and Stephen, like Odysseus in Hades, fends her off with his sword—the ashplant he dubs "Nothung," after Siegfried's sword, for the purpose.)[35] For Joyce, in fact, that theme, of "the descent into the underworld of Aeneas searching for his father," was, according to testimony remembered by Thomas MacGreevy, paramount in *Ulysses* (Dawson 1988, 309).

A minor complication in the *Aeneid* parallel is that according to that same schema, Laertes—the listing is "Laertes, etc."—also turns up in "Penelope" (Ellmann 1972, chart), where once again (the other two "Persons" are "Ulysses" and "Penelope"; we know who they are) he is the mystery entry. Still, the connection between Penelope and Laertes is after all clear enough. It was his shroud that she was endlessly weaving and reweaving. Does anything in "Penelope" correspond? This does: "I suppose I oughtnt to have buried him in that little woolly jacket I knitted" (*U* 18.1448). The "jacket" here is the burial garment—a shroud, in effect—that Molly knitted for "him"—her son Rudy, soon dead. Or, to give him his full name, Rudolph Bloom. So the Laertes of "Penelope" is Rudolph Bloom, named after the Rudolph Bloom whom I have just nominated as the "Laertes" of "Hades."

One last lingering complication in this identification is that "etc." in Joyce's "Laertes, etc." Who or what could that be? I don't know, but venture the observation that in a cemetery the one group most liable to be summed up in a term for unspecified "others" is the dead, that in "Hades" these dead are often simply "they," lying around in their unnamed numbers, that in the *Odyssey* as in the *Aeneid* the ghosts of the dead appear as anonymous throngs. In any event, Laertes, father of Odysseus, apparently leads the list in "Hades"—a role, which in the *Evening Telegraph* report of the funeral read in "Eumaeus," is taken by, it gratifies me to report, "M'Intosh and several others" (*U* 14.1261)—or, as one might say, "M'Intosh, etc."

And finally: I have become ever more convinced that the man in the macintosh is Rudolph Bloom from a general sense that his identity is a "mystery" in precisely the tradition of the genre designated by that word. *Ulysses* was written during the golden age of the English mystery story. One point that has struck me during an unsystematic survey of the field is how many of these stories are variants of Poe's "The Purloined Letter." In such works as G. K. Chesterton's "The Invisible Man," Thomas Burke's "The Hands of Mr. Ottermole,"[36] Lord Dunsany's "The Two Bottles of Relish," and countless butler-did-it tales, the mystery concerns a crucial clue that rather than being hidden or encrypted is presented frontally as a routine part of the furniture, in order to be taken for granted and thus overlooked. "You see," says Holmes to Watson, "but you do not observe." Might this not, I have asked myself, be the story of M'Intosh as well? With that in mind, I conclude with a bit of Holmes-and-Watson deduction in the hope that some will find in it a solution to this particular mystery.

Q: Well then, what is the single most obvious thing about the man in the macintosh?

A: That he wears a macintosh.

Q. And what obvious thing might that tell us about him?

A: Not much. That he owns one, I suppose.

Q: Yes, of course, but why does he wear it? Why is the man in the macintosh the man in the macintosh?

A: Why is . . .

Q: Hint: Why did the fireman wear red suspenders?

A: Yes, yes, I know that one. So along that line a man in a macintosh, that is, a raincoat, wears a raincoat to . . .

Q: Keep off the rain. Quite. He wears it to keep off the rain. Now, let us try this one again: Why is the man in the macintosh the man in the macintosh?

A: ?

Q: *The* man in the macintosh. Why, in one of the world's wettest climates, should a man with a raincoat be any more distinctive than a man with, say, pants? Why is no one else in *Ulysses* equipped with a raincoat, and almost no one with even an umbrella?[37] There is raingear of some sort in most of the stories of *Dubliners.* Yet when the rain arrives in *Ulysses,* it catches everyone, even the prudent Bloom, in whose hall are four umbrellas and a waterproof (*U* 4.67, 407) all left behind this morning, without "brollies or gumboots" (*U* 14.483–98, 696–701, 1442; 15.4323–25). Also without macintoshes. Why?

A: That one I know too. There's a drought on. It hasn't rained for so long, and the morning of Bloomsday is so sunny, that nobody expects rain.

Q: Almost nobody. One person is prepared for the downpour that ends the drought: M'Intosh. What do you make of that?

A: Well, he's obviously peculiar. And wearing a macintosh on a sunny day, during a drought, when there's no sign of rain, is a peculiar thing to do.

Q: It also turns out to be a smart thing to do, doesn't it? Our friend M'Intosh gets the last laugh when the rain comes and he's the only one in the vicinity who's ready for it, doesn't he? So again: what do you make of that? How comes it that the one person in Dublin prepared for rain turns out to be right, and everyone else wrong? *How does he know?*

A: Eh? How does he *know?*

Q: Is there any *Ulysses* character who *knows* when it's going to rain?

A: Who knows? . . .

Q: Oh dear, dear. The answer is that there is one, and only one, who knows ahead of time when it will rain, who is, so to speak, a barometer to atmospheric changes.

A: Hm? Barometer? Hm. Ah.

Q: Ah.

A: You mean . . .

Q: Precisely. In "Circe," when Bloom, bending down, feels a twinge of sciatica, he fears it may be hereditary.[38] And then, at *U* 15.2783–84, he adds, about his father, Rudolph Bloom . . .

A: Bless me, Holmes, you've done it again. Allow me. He adds, "Poor dear papa, a widower, was a regular barometer from it."

20

Seeing Things in *Finnegans Wake*

ITEM, from a 1934 text reviewing recommended treatments for glaucoma: "The use of the trephine had been attempted many times during this period, but it was not until 1909 that Robert Elliot originated the most successful method in his scleo-corneal-trephine operation. The procedure here is to cut a triangular flap in the conjunctival layer of the sclera into the anterior chamber. The wound is then closed and a permanent draining scar, or fistula, is obtained. This is the operation most extensively used at the present time and has rightfully placed its originator among the greatest ophthalmic surgeons of all time."[1]

In an earlier book, *"Finnegans Wake": A Plot Summary*, I suggested that the doubled circle and triangle design on page 293 of *Finnegans Wake* arose from the befuddled double vision of the protagonist (see fig. 18 here and hereafter for the following; for the triangular flap of the quotation, see fig. 19)[2]. I would like to further propose here that the diagram also outlines the treatment for that condition. It represents an act of incision and trephination, as experienced from the point of view of the patient, whose out-of-focus "doubleviewed seeds" (296.1)[3] come to concentrate, naturally enough, on the locus of the operation. In the process of this forced concentration, they are being trained to focus in tandem, to cease seeing double.

When, like Joyce, a patient has one eye sounder than the other, the danger is that the good one will do all the work and the weak eye correspondingly will become what the literature calls "lazy," falling into disuse and losing what health it had, so that the subject becomes "exophoric," that is inclined to view with diverging rather than parallel axes of sight and to see double in consequence. (This symptom is especially common among those, like tailors and writers, who do minute work at close range.) Hence those "doubleviewed seeds," and the doubled figures of the diagram. The point of the operation is to help the patient both to see and to see straight.

As rendered in *Finnegans Wake*, this operation proceeds according to the following sequence, keyed to the numbered points in the text reprinted below.

The "mud, son" with which the procedure begins (286.31) is the medicine scopolamine, regularly given to Joyce before his operations. It is a sweet-tasting mixture that he compared to cough syrup and that, according to the footnote to "mud, son" [medicine] tastes like chocolate mixed with sugar (286 n.4). As "Scoppialimina," it has shown up in an earlier passage alluding to Joyce's eye ailments (183.1) and, in the sequence under discussion, as [1] "EBONISER" (304 R2), there by way of "ebona," Shakespeare's term in *Hamlet* for henbane, the poison that killed Hamlet's father and the principal ingredient of scopolamine. Scopolamine is a hypnotic that dilates the pupils and induces a "twilight sleep" state that liberates the patient's free-association (hence its reputation as a truth serum). The trance is often preceded by a period of high mental excitation. As Joyce described it,

> Twould make staid Tutankamen
> Laugh and leap like a salmon
> And his mummy hop Scotch on the green.
>
> *(JJ 573)*

granyou and *Vae Vinctis*, if that is what lamoor that of gentle breast rathe is intaken seems circling toward out yondest (it's life that's all chokered by that batch of grim rushers) heaven help his hindmost and, mark mo, if the so greatly displaced diorems in the Saint Lubbock's Day number of that most improving of roundshows, *Spice* and *Westend Woman* (utterly exhausted before publication, indiapepper edition shortly), are for our indices, it agins to pear like it, par my fay, and there is no use for your pastripreaching for to cheesse it either or praying fresh fleshblood claspers of young catholick throats on Huggin Green[1] to take warning by the prispast, why?, by cows ·.· man, in shirt, is how he is *più la gonna è mobile* and .·. they wonet do ut; and, an you could peep inside the cerebralised saucepan of this eer illwinded goodfornobody, you would see in his house of thoughtsam (was you, that is, decontaminated enough to look discarnate) what a jetsam litterage of convolvuli of times lost or strayed, of lands derelict and of tongues laggin too, longa yamsayore, not only that but, search lighting, beached, bashed and beaushelled *à la Mer* pharahead into faturity, your own convolvulis pickninnig capman would real to jazztfancy the novo takin place of what stale words whilom were woven with and fitted fairly featly for, so; and equally so, the crame of the whole faustian fustian, whether your launer's lightsome or your soulard's schwearmood, it is that, whenas the swiftshut scareyss of our pupilteachertaut duplex will hark back to lark to you symibellically that, though a day be as dense as a decade, no mouth has the might to set a mearbound to the march of a landsmaul,[2] in half a sylb, helf a solb, holf a salb onward[3] the beast of boredom, common sense, lurking gyrographically down inside his loose Eating S.S. collar is gogoing of whisth to you sternly how — Plutonic loveliaks twinnt Platonic yearlings — you must, how, in undivided reawlity draw the line  somewhawre)

[1] Where Buickly of the Glass and Bellows pumped the Rudge engineral.
[2] Matter of Brettaine and brut fierce.
[3] Bussmullah, cried Lord Wolsley, how me Aunty Mag'll row!

292

(2) *(5)*

Uteralterance or the Interplay of Bones in the Womb.

The Vortex. Spring of Sprung Verse. The Vertex.

 Coss? Cossist? Your parn! You, you make what name? (and in truth, as a poor soul is between shift and shift ere the death he has lived through becomes the life he is to die into, he or he had albut — he was rickets as to reasons but the balance of his minds was stables — lost himself or himself some somnione sciupiones, soswhitchoverswetch had he or he gazet, murphy come, murphy go, murphy plant, murphy grow, a maryamyriameliamurphies, in the lazily eye of his lapis.

WHY MY AS LIKEWISE WHIS HIS.

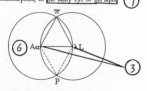

Vieus Von DVbLIn, 'twas one of dozedeams a darkies ding in dewood) the Turnpike under the Great Ulm (with Mearingstone in Fore ground).[1] Given now ann linch you take enn all. Allow me! And, heaving alljawbreakical expressions out of old Sare Isaac's[2] universal of specious aristmystic unsaid, A is for Anna like L is for liv. Aha hahah, Ante Ann you're apt to ape aunty annalive! Dawn gives rise. Lo, lo, lives love! Eve takes fall. La, la, laugh leaves alass! Aiaiaiai, Antiann, we're last to the lost, Loulou! Tis perfect. Now (lens

[1] Draumcondra's Dreamcountry where the betterlies blow.
[2] O, Laughing Sally, are we going to be toadhauntered by that old Pantifox Sir Somebody Something, Burtt, for the rest of our secret stripture?

293

18. Pages 292–305, *Finnegans Wake*, annotated. Viking Penguin, courtesy of the author.

Sarga, or the path of outgoing.

Docetism and Didicism, Maya-Thaya. Tamas-Rajas-Sattvas.

your dappled yeye here, mine's presbyoperian, shill and wall) we see the copyngink strayed-line AL (in Fig., the forest) from being con-tinued, stops ait Lambday¹: Modder ilond there too. Allow me anchore! I bring down noth and carry awe. Now, then, take this in! (9) One of the most murmurable loose carollaries ever Ellis threw his cookingclass. With Olaf as centrum and Olaf's lambtail for his spokes-man circumscript a cyclone. Allow ter! Hoop! As round as the calf of an egg! O, dear me! O, dear me now! Another grand dis-cobely! After Makefearsome's Ocean. You've actuary entducked one! Quok! Why, you haven't a passer! Fantastic! Early clever, surely doomed, to Swift's, alas, the galehus! Match of a matchness, like your Bigdud dadder in the boudeville song, *Gorotsky Gollovar's Troubles,* raucking his Bigdud turvku in the smukking precincts of lydias,² with Mary Owens and Dolly Monks seesidling to edge his cropulence and Blake-Roche, Kingston and Dockrell auriscenting him from afurz, our papacocopotl,³ Abraham Bradley King? (ting ting! ting ting!) By his magmasine fall. Lumps, lavas and all.⁴ *Bene!* But, thunder and turf, it's not alover yet! One recalls Byzantium. The mystery repeats itself todate as our callback (10) mother Gaudyanna, that was daughter to a tanner,⁵ used to sing, as I think, now and then consinuously over her possetpot in her quer

¹ Ex jup pep off Carpenger Strate. The kids' and dolls' home. Makeacake-ache.
² A vagrant need is a flagrant weed.
³ Grand for blowing off steam when you walk up in the morning.
⁴ At the foot of Bagnabun Banbasday was lost on one.
⁵ We're all found of our anmal matter.

294

The Vegetable Cell and its Pri-vate Properties.

homolocous humminbass hesterdie and ist-herdie forivor.¹ Vanissas Vanistatums! And for a night of thoughtsendyures and a day. As Great Shapesphere puns it. In effect, I re-mumble, from the yules gone by, purr lil mur-rerof myhind, so she used indeed. When she give me the Sundaclouths she hung up for Tate and Comyng and snuffed out the ghost in the candle at his old game of haunt the sleeper. Faithful departed. When I'm dream-ing back like that I begins to see we're only (11) all telescopes. Or the comeallyoum saunds. Like when I dromed I was in Dairy and was wuckened up with thump in thudderdown. Rest in peace! But to return.² What a wonder-ful memory you have too! Twonderful morrowy! Straorbinaire! *Bene!* I bring town eau and curry nothung up my sleeve. Now, springing quickenly from the mudland Loosh from Luccan with Allhim as her Elder tetra-turn a somersault. All's fair on all fours, as my instructor unstrict me. Watch! And you'll have the whole inkle. Allow, allow! Gyre O, gyre O, gyrotundo! Hop lala! As umpty herum as you seat! O, dear me, that was very nesse! Very nace indeed! And makes us a

The haves and the havenots: a distinction.

daintical pair of accomplasses! You, allus for the kunst and me for omething with a handel to it. *Beve!* Now, as will pressantly be felt, there's few tricklesome poinds where our twain of doubling bicirculars, mating approxe-metely in their suite poi and, poi, dunloop (12) into eath the ocher! Lucihere.! I fee where you

¹ Sewing up the beillybursts in their buckskin shiorts for big Kapitayn Killykook and the Jukes of Kelleiney.
² Say where! A timbrelfill of twinkletinkle.

295

Zweispaltung as Fundemaintalish of Wiederher-stellung.

mea. The doubleviewed seeds. Nun, lemmas quatsch, vide pervoys akstiom, and I think as I'm suqeez in the limon, stickme punctum, but for semenal rations I'd likelong, by Araxes, to mack a capital Pee for Pride down there on the batom¹ where Hoddum and Heave, our monsterbilker, balked his bawd of parodies. And let you go, Airmienious, and mick your modest·mock Pie out of Humbles up your end. Where your apexojesus will be a point of order. With a geing groan grunt and a croak click cluck.² And my faceage kink and kurkle trying to make keek peep.³ Are you right there, Michael, are you right? Do you think you can hold on by sitting tight? Well, of course, it's awful angelous. Still I don't feel it's so dangelous. Ay, I'm right here, Nickel, and I'll write. Singing the top line why it suits me mikey fine. But, yaghags hogwarts and arrahquinonthiance, it's the muddest thick that was ever heard dump since Eggsmather got smothered in the plap of the pfan. Now, to compleat anglers, beloved bironthiarn and hushtokan hishtakatsch, join alfa pea and pull loose by dotties and, to be more sparematically logoical, eelpie and paleale by trunkles. Alow me align while I encloud especious! The Nike done it. Like pah,⁴ I peh. Innate little bondery. And as plane as a poke stiff.⁵ Now, *aqua in buccat.* I'll make you to see figuratleavely the whome of your eternal

¹ Parsee ffrench for the upholdsterer would be delighterer.
² I'll pass our if the screw spliss his strut.
³ Thargam then goeligum? If you sink I can, swimford. Suksumkale!
⁴ Hasitatense?
⁵ The impudence of that in girl's things!

296

Destiny, In-fluence of Design upon.

geomater. And if you flung her headdress on her from under her highlows you'd wheeze whyse Salmonson set his seel on a hexen-gown.¹ Hissss!, Arrah, go on! Fin for fun! You've spat your shower like a son of Sibernia but let's have at it! Subtend to me now! Pisk! Outer serpumstances beiug ekewilled, we care-fully, if she pleats, lift by her seam hem and jabote at the spidsiest of her trickkikant (like thousands done before since fillies calpered. Ocone! Ocone!) the maidsapron of our A.L.P., fearfully! till its nether nadir is vortically where (13) (allow me aright to two cute winkles) its naval's

Prometheus or the Promise of Provision.

napex will have to beandbe You must proach near mear for at is dark. Lob. And light (16) your mech. Jeldy! And this is what you'll say.³ (15) Waaaaaa. Tch! Sluice! Pla! And their, redneck, (for addn't we to gayatsee with Puhl the Pun-kah's bell?) mygh and thy, the living spit of dead waters,² fastness firm of Hurdlebury Fenn, discinct and isoplural in its (your sow to the duble) sixuous parts, flument, fluvey and fluteous, midden wedge of the stream's your muddy old triagonal delta, fiho miho, plain for you now, appia lippia pluvaville, (hop the hula, girls!) the no niggard spot of her safety vulve first of all usquiluteral threeingles, (and (14) why wouldn't she sit cressloggedlike the lass that lured a tailor?) the constant of fluxion, Mahamewetma, pride of the province⁴ and when that tidled boare rutches up from the (17) Afrantic, allaph quaran's his bett und bier!⁵

¹ The chape of Doña Speranza of the Nacion.
² Ugol egal ogle. Mi vidim Mi.
³ It is, it is Sangannon's peach.
⁴ And all meinkind.
⁵ Whangpoos the paddle and whiss whee whoo.

297

Ambages and Their Rôle.

Paa lickam laa lickam, apl lpa! This it is an her. You see her it. Which it whom you see it is her. And if you could goaneggbetter we'd soon see some raffant scrumala riffa. Quicks herit fossyending. Quef! So post that to your pape and smarket! And you can haul up that languil pennant, mate. I've read your tunc's dimissage. For, let it be taken that her littlenist is of no magnetude or again let it be granted that Doll the laziest can be dissimulant with all respects from Doll the fiercst thence must any whatyoulike in the power of empthood be either

Ecclasiastical and Celestial Hierarchies. The Ascending. The Descending.

greater T H a N or less T H a N the unitate we have in one or hence shall the vectorious ready-eyes of evertwo circumflicksrent searchers never film in the elipsities of their gyribouts those fickers which are returnally reprodictive of themselves.[1] Which is unpassible. Quarrellary. The logos of somewome to that base anything, when most characteristically mantissa minus, comes to nullum in the endth:[2] orso, here is nowet badder than the sin of Aha with his cosin Lil, verswaysed on coverswised, and all that's consecants and cotangincies till Perperp stops repippinghim since her redtangles are all abscissan for limitsing this tendency of

The peripatetic periphery. It's Allothesis.

our Frivulteeny Sexuagesima[3] to expense herselfs as sphere as possible, paradismic perimutter, in all directions on the bend of the unbridalled, the infinisissimalls of her facets becoming manier and manier as the caliculom of her umdescribables (one has thoughts of that eternal Rome) shrinks from schurtiness

[1] I enjoy as good as anyone.
[2] Neither a soul to be saved nor a body to be kicked.
[3] The boast of the town.

298

---

to scherts.[1] Scholium, there are trist sigheds to everysing but ichs on the freed brings euchs to the feared. Qued? Mother of us all! O, dear me, look at that now! I don't know is it your spictre or my omination but I'm glad you dimentioned it! My Lourde! My Lourde! If that aint just the beatenest lay I ever see! And a superbposition! Quoint a quincidence! O.K.

Canine Venus sublimated to Aulidic Aphrodite.

Omnius Kollidimus. As Ollover Krumwall sayed when he slepped ueber his grannyamother. Kangaroose feathers. Who in the name of thunder'd ever belevin you were that bolt? But you're holy mooxed and gaping up the wrong palce[2] as if you was seeheeing the gheist that stays forenenst, you blessed simpletop domefool! Where's your belested loiternan's lamp? You must lap wandret down the bluishing refluction below. Her trunk's not her brainbox. Hear where the bolgylines, Yseen here the puncture So he done it. Luck! See her good.

Exclusivism: the Ors, Sors and Fors, which?

Well, well, well, well! O dee, O dee, that's very lovely! We like Simperspreach Hammeltones to fellow Selvertunes O'Haggans.[3] When he rolls over his ars and shows the hise of his heels. Vely lovely entilely! Like a yangsheepslang with the tsifengtse. So analytical plausible! And be the powers of Moll Kelly, neighbour topsowyer, will be a lozenge to me all my lauffe.[4] More better twofeller we been speak copperads. Ever thought about Guinness's? And the regrettable Parson Rome's advice?

[1] Hen's bens, are we soddy we missiled her?
[2] I call that a scumhead.
[3] Pure chingchong idiotism with any way words all in one soluble. Gee each now tea eye smells fish. That's U.
[4] The Doodles family, Hoodle doodle, fam.?

299

Primanouriture and Ultimogeniture.

Want to join the police.[1] You know, you were always one of the bright ones, since a foot made you an unmentionable, fakes! You know, you're the divver's own smart gossoon, aequal to yourself and wanigel to anglyother, so you are, hoax! You know, you'll be dampned, so you will, one of these invernal days but you will be, carrotty![2]

Wherapool, gayet that when he stop look time he stop long ground who here hurry he would have ever the lothst word, with a sweet me ah err eye ear marie to reat from the jacob's[3] and a shypull for toothsake of his armjaws at the slidepage of de Vere Foster, would and ccould candykissing P. Kevin to fress up the rinnerung and to ate by hart (*leo* I read, such a spanish, *escribibis*, all your mycoscoups) wont to nibbleh ravenostonnoriously ihs mum to me in bewonderment of his chipper chuthor for, while that Other by the halp of his creactive mind offered to deleberate the mass from the booty of fight our Same with the holp of the bounty of food sought to delubberate the mess from his corructive mund, with his muffetee cuffes ownconsciously grafficking with his sinister cyclopes after trigamies and spirals' wobbles pursuiting their rovinghamilton selves and godolphing in fairlove to see around the waste of noland's browne jesus[4]

No Sturm. No Drang.

(thur him no quartos!) till that on him poorin sweat the juggaleer's veins (quench his quill!) in his napier scrag stud out bursthright tam-

SICK US A SOCK WITH SOME SEDIMENT IN IT FOR THE SAKE OF OUR DARNING WIVES.

[1] Picking on Nickagain, Pikey Mikey!
[2] Early morning, sir Dav Stephens, said the First Gentleman in youreups.
[3] Bag bag blockcheap, have you any will?
[4] What a lubberly whide elephant for the men-in-the-straits!

300

Illustration.

quam taughtropes. (Spry him! call a bloodlekar! Where's Dr Brassenaarse?) Es war itwas in his priesterrite. O He Must Suffer! From this misbelieving feacemaker to his noncredible fancyflame.[1] Ask for bosthoon, late for Mass, pray for blaablaablack sheep. (Sure you could wright anny pippap passage, Eye bet, as foyne as that moultylousy Erewhig, yerself, mick! Nock the muddy nickers![2] Christ's Church varses Bellial!) Dear and he went on to scripple

Ascription of the Active.

gentlemine born, milady bread, he would pen for her, he would pine for her,[3] how he would patpun fun for all[4] with his frolicky frowner so and his glumsome grinner otherso. And how are you, waggy?[5] My animal his sorrafool! And trieste, ah trieste ate I my liver! *Se non è vero son trovatore.* O jerry! He was soso, harriot all! He was sadfellow, steifel! He was mistermysterion. Like a purate out of pensionee with a gouvernament job. All moanday, tearsday, wailsday, thumpsday, frightday, shatterday till the fear of the Law. Look at this twitches! He was quisquis, floored on his plankraft of shittim wood. Look at him! Sink deep or touch not the Cartesian spring! Want more

Proscription of the Passive.

ashes, griper? How diesmal he was lying low on his rawside laying siege to goblin castle. And, bezouts that, how hyenesmeal he was laying him long on his laughside lying sack to croakpartridge. (Be thou wars Rolaf's intes-

[1] And she had to seek a pond's apeace to salve her suiterkins. Sued!
[2] Excuse theyre christianbrothers irish?
[3] When she tripped against the briery bush he profused her allover with curtsey flowers.
[4] A nastilow disigrable game.
[5] Dear old Erosmas. Very glad you are going to Penmark. Write to the corner. Grunny Grant.

301

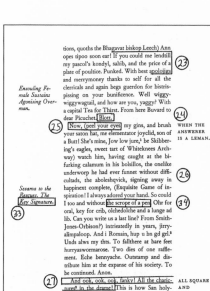

Ensouling Female Sustains Agonising Overman.

tions, quoths the Bhagavat biskop Leech) Ann opes tipoo soon ear! If you could me lendtill my pascol's kondyl, sahib, and the price of a ㉓ plate of poultice. Punked. With best apoloijgs and merrymoney thanks to self for all the clericals and again begs guerdon for bistrispissing on your bunificence. Well wiggywiggywagtail, and how are you, yaggy? With a capital Tea for Thirst. From here Buvard to ㉔ dear Picuchet. Blott.

㉕ Now, (peel your eyes) my gins, and brush your saton hat, me elementator joyclid, son of a Butt! She's mine, Jow low jure,² be Skibbering's eagles, sweet tart of Whiteknees Archway) watch him, having caught at the bifurking calamum in his bolsillos, the onelike ㉖ underworp he had ever funnet without difficultads, the aboleshqvick, signing away in happinext complete, (Exquisite Game of inspiration! I always adored your hand. So could I too and without the scrope of a pen, Ohr for ㉞ oral, key for crib, olchedolche and a lunge ad lib. Can you write us a last line? From Smith-Jones-Orbison?) intrieatedly in years, jirryalimpaloop. And i Romain, hup u bn gd grl.¹ Unds alws my thts. To fallthere at bare feet hurryaswormarose. Two dies of one raffement. Eche bennyache. Outstamp and distribute him at the expense of his society. To be continued. Anon.

㉗ And ook, ook, ook, fanky! All the charictures² in the drame! This is how San holy-

Sesama to the Rescues. The Key Signature.

㉓

WHEN THE ANSWERER IS A LEMAN.

ALL SQUARE AND

¹ I loved to see the Macbeths Jerseys knaeking spots of the Plumpduffs Pants.
² Lifp year fends you all and moe, fouvenirs foft as fummer fnow, fweet willings and forget-uf-knots.
³ Gag his rubes yourself.

302

polypools. And this, pardonsky! is the way Romeopullupalleaps.¹ Pose the pen, man, way me does. Way ole missa vellatooth fust show me how. Fourth power to her illpogue! Bould strokes for your life! Tip! This is Steal, this is Barke, this is Starn, this is Swhipt, this is Wiles, this is Pshaw, this is Doubbllinnbbayyates.² This is brave Danny weeping his spache for the popers. This is cool Connolly wiping his hearth with brave Danny. And this, regard! how Chawleses Skewered parparaparnelligoes between brave Danny boy and the Connolly. Upanishadem! Top. Spoken hath L'arty Magory. Eregobragh. Prouf!³

And here Missers the boour worumbeld... But, (that Jacoby feeling again for forebitten fruit and, my Georgeous, Kevvy too he just loves his puppadums, I judge!) after all his autocratic writings of paraboles of famellicurbs and meddlied muddlingisms, thee faroots hof cullchaw end ate citrawn woodint wun able rep of the triperforator awlrite blast through his pergaman hit him where he lived and do for ㉘ the blessted selfchuruls, what I think, smarter like it done for a manny another unpious of the hairydary quare quandary firstings till at length, you one bladdy bragger, by mercystroke he measured his earth anyway? could not but recken in his adder's badder cadder way our frankson who, to be plain, he fight him all time twofeller longa kill dead finish bloody face blong you, was misocain. Wince

Force Centres of the Fire Serpentine: heart, throat, navel, spleen, sacral, fontanella, intertemporal eye.

Conception of the Compromise and Finding of a Formula.

Ideal Present Alone Produces Real Future.

ACCORDING TO COCKER.

TROTHBLOWERS.

FIG AND THISTLE PLOT A PIG AND WHISTLE.

¹ He, angel that I thought him, and he not aebel to speel eelyotripes., Mr Tellibly Divilcult!
² When the dander rattles how the peacocks prance!
³ The Brownes de Browne - Browne of Castlehacknolan.

303

㉙ wan's won! Rip!¹ And his countinghands rose.
Formalisa. Loves deathhow simple! ㉚ Slutningsbane³. Thanks eversore much, Pointcarried! I can't ㉛ say if it's the weight you strike me to the quick or that red mass I was looking at but at ㉜ the present momentum, potential as I am, I'm seeing rayingbogeys rings round me. Honours to you and may you be commended for our exhibitiveness! I'd love to take you for a bugaboo ride and play funfer all if you'd only sit and be the ballasted bottle in the porker barrel. You will deserve a rolypoly as long as from here to tomorrow. And to hell with them driftbombs and bottom trailers! If my maily was bag enough I'd send you a toxis. By Saxon Chromaticus, you done that lovely for me! Didn't he now, Nubilina? Tiny Mite, she studiert whas? With her listeningin coiffure, her dream of Endsland's daylast and the glorifires of being presainted maid to majesty.³ And less the pity for she isn't the lollypops she easily might be if she had for a sample Virginia's air of achievement. That might keep her from throwing delph.⁴ As I was saying, while retorting thanks, you make me a reborn of the cards. We're offals boys ambows.⁵ For I've flicked up all the crambs as they crumbed from your table um, singing glory allaloserem, cog it out, here goes a sum. So

Service superseding self.

Catastrophe and Anabasis.

The rotary processus and its reestablishment of reciprocities.

WITH EBONISER.
IN PIX.
EUCHRE
RISK, MERCI
BUCKUP, AND
MIND WHO
YOU'RE
PUCKING,
FLEBBY.

¹ A byebye bingbang boys! See you Nutcracker Sunday!
² Chinchin Childaman! Chapchopchap!
³ Wipe your glosses with what you know.
⁴ If I'd more in the cups that peeves thee you could cracksmith your rows tureens.
⁵ Alls Sings and Alls Howls.

304

① read we in must book. It tells. He prophets most who bilks the best.

㉟ And that salubrated sickenagiaour of yaours have teaspilled all my hazeydency. Forge away, Sunny Sim! Sheepshopp. Bleating Goad, it is the least of things, Eyeinstye! Imagine it, my deep dartry dullard! It is hours giving, not more. I'm only out for celebriding over the guilt of the gap in your hiscitendency. You are a hundred thousand times welcome, old worttsampler, hellbeit you're just about as culpable as my woolfell merger would be. In effect I could engage in an energument over you till you were republicly royally toobally prussic blue in the shirt after.¹ Trionfante di bestia! And if you're not your bloater's kipper may I never curse again on that pint I took of Jamesons. Old Keane now, you're rod, hook and sinker, old jubalee Keane! Biddy's hair, Biddy's hair, mine lubber. Where is that Quin but he sknows it knot but what you that are my popular endphthisis were born with a solver arm up your sleep. Thou in shanty! Thou in scanty shanty!! Thou in slanty scanty shanty!!! Bide in your hush! Bide in your hush, do! The law does not aloud you to shout. I plant my penstock in your postern, chinarpot. Ave! And let it be to all remembrance. Vale. Ovocation of maiding waters.² For auld lang salvy steyne. I defend you to champ my scullion's praises. To book alone belongs the lobe. Foremaster's meed³ will mark tomorrow when we are making pilscrummage to whaboggeryin with

The Twofold Truth and the Conjunctive Appetites of Oppositional Orexes.

Trishagion.

COME SI
COMPITA
CUNCTITI-
TITILATIO?
CONKERY
CUNK,
THIGH-
THIGHT-
THIGHT-
TICKELLY-
THIGH, LIG-
GERILAG,
TITTERITOT,
LEG IN A TEE,
LUG IN A
LAW, TWO
THREE ON A
THRICKY
TILL OHIO
OHIO
IOIOMISS.

¹ From three shellings. A bluedye sacrifice.
² Not Kilty. But the manajar was. He! He! Ho! Ho! Ho!
³ Giglamps, Soapy Geyser, The Smell and Gory M Gusty.

305

This initial drug state is rendered, I think, by the passage of semicoherent fantasy-reminiscence (289.18–92.320), during which, "as we gang along to gigglehouse" (289.18), the subject fuses memory and desire with visions of himself as

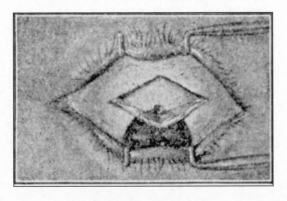

19. Operation for glaucoma.
Perera 1949, 251.

young saint (Patrick), lover (Tristram), and, probably, Swift, bound for the giggle-house. The tale of comings and goings, culminating in references [2] to a "circling" subject whose story ends in a dynamic diorama's whirling "roundshow," probably conveys that the subject's head, unsurprisingly, is spinning. The initial surgical punctures are signaled by the triangularly arranged dots of the doubled circle and triangle design [3]. Thus penetrated, the subject pretty quickly loses his euphoria, like the Joyce who described himself thus after one such operation:

> The clinic was a patched one,
> Its outside old as rust,
> And every stick beneath that roof
> Lay four feet thick in dust.
>
> *(JJ 571)*

The subject has started coming down to earth at 293.1 [4], as the knife-wielding doctor has begun to "draw the line somewhawre" [5], making the incision from point A to point L [6], "in the lazily eye of his lapis" [7]. Lapis lazuli is blue, and Joyce had blue eyes, one of them, in the sense noted above, "lazy." The patient is then directed to "lens your dappled yeye here, mine's presby-operian" [8]—a word that may be roughly translated as old-eyed-one—and, gruesomely enough, to [9] "take this in." (The "dappled yeye" related to the fact that glaucoma patients typically see spots before their eyes: Earlier, at 251.26–27, the "specks" of Shem's vision make him a maculate "Smachiavelluti," sooty and spotted, like Joyce with his left eye covered by a patch [251.26].) In the next few pages the subject's drug-induced twilight musing, his "callback" [10] revery of mother and childhood, mingles with the doctor's procedure. On page 295, preliminary progress toward proper focal vision is adumbrated when Shem goes from the observation [11] that "we're only all telescopes"—telescopes being monocular, not binocular—to perceiving "two tricklesome points where our twain of doubling bicirculars, mating aproxemately in their suit poi and poi, dunloop into eath the ocher" [12]. Recalling Stephen and Bloom's double-focused summoning of Shakespeare in "Circe,"[4] this is a thumbnail version of the previous century's discoveries in the mechanics of depth perception, discoveries that had produced binoculars, stereoscopes, and *Ulyssean* parallax.

From lines 296.23 to 298.6 the triangular flap—variously called the "trikkikant," "maidsapron," "pennant," and "triagonal delta"—is folded back, so that apex of upper triangle meets "nether nadir" of lower triangle [13] and a "safety vulve" [14] is opened up to drain the viscous waters that have come gushing and spraying out [15] as light breaks in [16]. (The footnote reports an eagle-eyed ogler, now seeing ["Mi vidim mi"] himself.) The "tidled boare" of [17] is a tidal bore, spewing pressurized liquid through a constricted aperture. (Glaucoma results from excessive pressure of the eyeball's fluid; the purpose of the operation is to relieve that pressure.) Pages 298–99 render the patient's new vision as he looks around and tries to get his bearings: "see" occurs six times on these two pages, along with admonitions about where and how he should be looking.

Next, [18] gives directions on how a seer now equipped with two functioning eyes, the "vectorious readyeyes of evertwo circumflicksrent searclhers," can bring them into focus on one figure. The observation [19] about how "Doll the laziest can be dissimulant with all respect from Doll the fiercst," makes contextual sense if we keep in mind that (1) "doll" is the etymological origin of "pupil," as in the "pupils" of the eyes; (2) one of the eyes of this optically asymmetrical subject is, again, "lazy"; and (3) the other one is what's left of that piercing, flashing stare, marking him as the "fiercest freaky" in her experience, which ALP remembers so vividly from her husband's courtship of her (626.11–16). (A friend of Nora Barnacle's from the days when Joyce was courting her remembered him, with his steady stare, as "the man with the X-ray eyes";[5] some of his early photographs show what she meant.)

I think we can take the "greater than or less than" and so on [20] business as a graphic rendering of a pupil expanding and contracting in an effort to reach parity with the other "searclher." At [21] we are told that the final trephinic "puncture" has been made, amid a lot of mirror-image wordplay—p's reversing q's and so on—which probably means that we're looking through the puncture into the back of the eye, where of course images are reversed. Much of the rest of the chapter up to the essay-writing that begins at line 306.8 concerns the efforts of the two eyes/brothers, last one and first one, lazy one and fierce one, to reach some parallel accommodation of their respective visions, now clearing, to come to a focus and [for example, 22A, 22B] cohere perceptions from the swarming reality appearing before them. (It is in this section that Shaun says that the new sight will be a "lozenge" to him [299.28], which shows that he is finally seeing the lozenge drawn on line 293, from π to A α to P to λ L; the footnote to his remark even gives some geometrical illustrations, unseeable before.) Next the subject, coming to as he is, awakens to the pain of his eye condition; at 302.2–4 [23] he begs for a "poultice," which is supplied ("Blott") at [24]; in the next line, addressed as "my gins . . . joyclid" (that is, Jim Joyce], he is urged to "peel [his] eyes" [25]—it's always a good idea in *Finnegans Wake* to take such expressions literally—for improved vision. Around [26], it seems to me, surgeon's trephine mutates into writer's pen (compare Stephen in *Ulysses:* "He fears the lancet of my art as I fear that of his. The cold steel pen" [*U* 1.1513]),[6] as the patient, urged to "ook, ook, ook" at "All the charicatures in the drame" [27] sets out as Promethean author to render his newfound vision in writing. And of course it makes sense that he should immediately start getting graphic, drawing caricatures, as soon as his sight, however temporarily, has been restored to him. I have trouble distinguishing Shem-type from Shaun-type, patient from surgeon, writer from reader, in the dialogue of these last pages—it may be one of the passages where the two have been "singulfied," and in fact there are a number of phrases such as "A bluedye sacrifice" (305 n. 1) (blue-eyed Shaun, bloody-eyed Shem) incorporating both—but someone is either reliving the illuminating ordeal of the operation or reenacting it by performing it on his opposite, giving a smarting "blast through his pergamen" with an awl-like trephine, "the triperforator awlrite" [28]. This trephine, again, is the surgical implement, a refinement of the trepan used in skull borings, long employed in such eye operations. (Its inventor took its name from *"a tribus finibus,"* "from the three ends thereof.")[7] That the victim/patient, on receiving a "Rip!" [29] from his "Pointcarried" opposite [30] should see not only a "red mass" [31] but "rayingbogeys rings" [32] before his eyes suggests that for the nonce anyway he is a Shaunian figure whose surgical gift of clear sight to Shem has been repaid with what from the first page the book (3.13–14) has identified with the infliction of artist's rainbow-vision, from the spectral refraction of light that was Joyce's first sure sign that he had glaucoma.

Considering the invitation, beginning at line 292.12, to "peep inside" the subject's "cerebralized saucepan," and the many ways in which the whole passage reenacts the *Wake*'s ubiquitous Acteon/Peeping Tom etc. story of young-

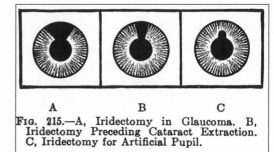

20. Result of glaucoma operation.
Perera 1949, 248.

Fɪɢ. 215.—A, Iridectomy in Glaucoma. B, Iridectomy Preceding Cataract Extraction. C, Iridectomy for Artificial Pupil.

sters peeking in at forbidden sights, it may be relevant that in an eye success-fully operated on according to the procedure given above a section of pupil is extended to the edge of the iris, forming a shape that quite strikingly resembles a keyhole (see fig. 20 [from Perera 1949, 280]).[8] Thus the final flourish of the sur-geon-author's implement at [33] 302 L2 is "The Key Signature," a version of "the prick of the spindle to me that gave me the keys to dreamland," perhaps pro-ducing "the keys to" (the two keys?) of the end (628.15). And if the key-shaped incision, the signature with the "scrope of a pen" that [34] equates to the "key signature," really did dispel the glaucomal miasma, has really "teaspilled all my hazeydency" (305.4), it makes sense for Shaun [35] to give that signature credit for dispelling his vague uncertainties. In any case, the conceit of the eyes as a pair of keyholes functions as a modern surgical equivalent of the trepan-ning of The House by the Churchyard—a way of opening up the head and looking inside. A medical fact established by Joyce's time was that the optic nerve grew directly from the brain. So the opening injunction to peek inside this subject's brainpan has been answered, through the anatomically most direct route.

Further—one last time—in so doing, the operation has not only dispelled ("teaspilled") all his hesitancy; it has distilled ("teaspilled") all his (nebular) hazy density into another of those epiphanic precipitates, condensing around the incisive puncture-points, experienced by Stephen Dedalus when memories "condensed within his brain" around the incisive penetrations of sword's blade and ray's trajectory. That is probably why Shem acknowledges this moment of invasively enforced concentration with the debater's tag "Pointcarried"—point carried, of course, but also Henri Poincaré, who at about the time Joyce was be-ginning Portrait was concluding an illustrious scientific career in becoming the latest (and last) major champion of Laplace's nebular hypothesis, which in spite of all intervening discoveries he considered still the best explanation around.[9] The endorsement was, to be sure, not unqualified: adjustments had to be made, especially in accounting for Jupiter and Saturn, which were accordingly the main concerns of his revisions. Which is perhaps why, in the passage cited above, Shem's moment of sclerotic incision, ocular illumination, binocular equilibrium, and mental resolution also incorporates planetary processes, specifically involving Jupiter's "red mass" and Saturn's "rayingbogeys rings."

This book is finished; a study of *Finnegans Wake* along these cosmological lines would require another one, probably as long, and prequel would morph into sequel. But in concluding I would like to note that, at least at times, *Finnegans Wake*, like *Portrait* before it, appears to instantiate a universal protocol of creation and destruction that applies equally to the formation of thoughts and the formation of stars. Everybody knows that Joyce wanted *Finnegans Wake* to be a book of everything, and that to that end applied a definite set of, roughly speaking, cosmological theories. It appears to me that *Finnegans Wake* was the culmination, not the beginning, of an ambition present from the outset, and that the house rules brought to bear—what Stephen Dedalus calls God's "court etiquette" (*U* 16.760)—may not have changed that much in the interim.

Notes

References

Index

Notes

Introduction

1. Notes and sketch are in the Frank Budgen file in the Richard Ellmann collection of the McFarland Library, Univ. of Tulsa, Tulsa, Oklahoma. The letter with the questions, dated April 5, 1933, and dictated by Joyce to his daughter, is in the collection of the Zurich, Switzerland, James Joyce Center.

2. On the one hand, the name "Saussure" has been found, written once, in one of Joyce's notebooks. On the other hand, there are thousands of other notes testifying to Joyce's career-long near-obsession with linguistic origins, including a special fascination with the genealogy of names. As a boy he read Skeat straight (and, somewhat later, seems to have kept up with the *Oxford English Dictionary* as its volumes came off the presses (see Deane, Ferrer, and Lernout 2001, vi.B.10.6–7); while writing *Ulysses* (see Downing 1998, 37–68), he was studying and incorporating the etymological researches of Richard Chevenix Trench among others; a recently published *Finnegans Wake* notebook shows him deep into Otto Jespersen's *Growth and Structure of the English Language,* accurately described by the editors as a "wholly practical and empirical" survey of "the essential stages in the evolution of English" (Deane, Ferrer, and Lernout 2001, vi.b.10.7).

1. *A Portrait of the Artist:* A Domino Theory

1. A promoted white pawn would be on the eighth rank, thus under attack from the opponent's rook if, through castling, the intervening black king were to be moved out of the way, subject to mate if the seventh rank were also covered. All of which is in its way logical but technically illegal: a pawn can be promoted to anything but a king, because no side can have more than one, as Stephen should have realized before he started playing games with Mulligan.

2. At 31 occurrences in 6,639 words, "like" appears once in every 214 words of this section. The second highest frequency occurs in 1.4, where Stephen returns to a newly mysterious ("smugging") and threatening (Father Dolan) scene at Clongowes, after the disorienting Christmas dinner at home.

3. See Darwin 1888, 1:53; and Oppenheim 1991, 186, 269.

4. Kimberly J. Devlin remarks *"Portrait's* implicitly porous boundary between self and otherness," as contrasted with *Stephen Hero.* Devlin 2002, 15.

5. For Lombroso, see *L2* 156–57, in which Joyce reports having passed along a magazine because "it contained an article either on Lombroso or of Gorki," and Stephen's remark in *Stephen Hero* that "Italy has added a science to civilisation by putting out the lantern of justice and considering the criminal in production and in action" *(SH* 186). As Sidney Feshbach has remarked to me, this is al-

most certainly an allusion to Lombroso. For Upward, see *L1* 156. For Berman—who for a while was one of Joyce's doctors—see *L1* 201, *L3* 409, and *L3* 410, including footnote. For Weininger, see *JJ* 463.

6. See Ball 1893, 526–30. Ball begins by calling the theory a "conjecture," but winds up effectively endorsing it.

7. See Jeans 1946, "Cosmogony," *Encyclopedia Britannica*, 6:489.

8. Thus Henri Poincaré (1952, 261–62), whose updating of the nebular hypothesis will be taken up later, could, in a book first published in 1914, refer to the Milky Way as looking like a "flattened disk."

9. For the neo-Platonist element in particular, see chapter 12.

10. James Joyce, "A Portrait of the Artist," *P* 258. Spencer also sees consciousness as "rhythmical," a matter of "rapid oscillations" building into "intervals of increasing and decreasing intensity" (1916, 240).

11. "Darkly" will occur in the next section. Mr. Dedalus's "glass," literally a monocle, may also recall the glass partition through which fathers in the maternity hospital traditionally peer at their newborn children; a similar connotation is probably present in the "glass" of "Ecce Puer." In yet another sense of the word, of course, Stephen's father is all too prone to looking at life through a (raised) glass.

12. Compare Joyce in "Aesthetics" (*CW* 147).

13. According to Christy L. Burns, Stephen here "learns through binary oppositions" and "relative comparative measures" (2000, 32).

14. For the revised version, see the 1982 *JJ* 297.

15. Conveying Stephen's life in his own terms, the fluidic imagery of such passages may owe something to his early indoctrination on the subject of masturbation. To begin with, priestly concern about a future inclination toward masturbation is probably what gets him pandied. Stephen comes close to intuiting this when he thinks that the punishment has been part of a general crackdown brought about by the "smugging" of Corrigan and others (*P* 54). The word "smugging" can convey a wide range of schoolboy sex, including mutual masturbation, which Christopher Hitchens remembers as the commonest of such activities (2000, 26). The pandying, after all, makes little sense in its own terms. If Father Dolan really believes that Stephen deliberately broke his glasses in order to avoid work and then lied about it, he surely ought to give him at least as many smacks as he delivers to the hapless Fleming, who may have written a bad lesson but at least tried. Instead, Fleming gets twice six and Stephen gets—well, twice one. As a warning for the future, however, the punishment has a certain logic, against a vice supposed to drive one blind, given to someone weak of sight, especially when administered to his hands. Later, adolescent masturbation drives Stephen to loathe himself. It figures in Father Arnall's sermon (*P* 124) and seems to be what really worries the old priest in the confessional. And, as we will see later, an unrecorded act of masturbation concludes the villanelle. Stephen's own thoughts on the subject are typically in the "precious bodily fluids" vein: he is surprised that the "wave of vitality" he feels leaving his body with his first ejaculation has not "maimed" him (*P* 103) and continues to think of the act in terms of vitality leeching vital juices out of his "marrow" (*P* 140), as he imagines that E. C.'s first menstruation must have left her in a state of "frail pallor" (*P* 222–23).

16. In English the *locus classicus* is in *Paradise Lost*: "Part hidden veins digged up (nor hath this earth / Entrails unlike) of mineral and stone" (*Paradise Lost*, 6:516–17). *Finnegans Wake* features a warning against a "netherworld" of enemies undermining from "earthveins, toadcavites, chessganglions" (*FW* 571.35–36).

17. Again, this conceit, and much of the rest of the chapter's imagery, seems to owe most to *Paradise Lost*, whose famous ending lines will be echoed in Stephen's conclusion that "life lay all before him" (*P* 146). For a parallel to the wind-and-volcano effects just described, see *Paradise Lost* 1:230–38.

18. On pages 127–28, going from "Now of all these" to "pain of loss." This is the paragraph in which we hear of hell as the "greatest torment" and "pain" and "worst damnation" and so on as defined by the "greatest" doctor of the church," of its "infinitely painful" loss of the "infinitely good" God, the "centre of her [the soul's] existence." The word "God" appears eleven times, a record; there are also four of the book's seventeen occurrences of "greatest," making for more "-est" superlatives than in any other paragraph. Calculation of the exact word-count center will depend on whether or not one includes title, author's name, epigraph, and "Dublin 1904—Trieste 1914"; excluding all of these, I come up with the two words "from God," in the last sentence: "This, then, to be separated for ever from its greatest good, from God, and to feel the anguish of that separation knowing full well that it is unchangeable, this is the greatest torment which the created soul is capable of bearing, *poena damni,* the pain of loss."

19. The parallel is pointed out in Magalener and Kain 1956, 115–17.

20. See entries under *pseudogamy* in the *OED,* which elsewhere records several instances of "anastamosis" between veins and other internal vessels.

21. In light of the following, see McBride 1996, especially pages 169–71. Observing that by itself "the syllable *cloud* introduces over forty words" in *Finnegans Wake,* McBride cites Issy in particular as a case of the "clouded consciousness," alternately "twilight state," contemporaneously being diagnosed by psychoanalysis.

22. The language here has misled. It is generally taken as describing Daedalus's making the wings for his flight, with Icarus, from the labyrinth. But it is Siegfried, not Daedalus, who forges his shattered sword "anew" from iron, the "matter of the earth." (It is hard to see how the feathers and wax of Daedalus's wings could be described as "matter of the earth," and he is not making them "anew," and does not forge them.) Although "soaring" certainly suggests if not wings then the people wearing them, it also, obviously, sounds like "sword," which might be imagined as "soaring" when brandished aloft; such a usage occurs in *Finnegans Wake* (*FW* 222.22), which elsewhere (*FW* 136.34, 549.27) makes "soared" and "sored" respectively stand for a sword. As for "imperishable," practically the whole point of the Daedalus story is the perishability of his wings. Siegfried's reforged Nothung, on the other hand, is indeed supposed to be imperishable when wielded by the right hero. In *Ulysses,* Stephen will later reenact Siegfried's triumphant forging of Nothung.

23. Also "The soutane sleeve swished again as the pandybat was lifted" (*P* 50–51) and "he had heard the swish of the soutane sleeve and the crash" (*P* 52).

24. *Finnegans Wake* seems to compare itself to a reflector at *FW* 143.13: in a passage widely taken as describing someone's experience of the book, a representative "human being" ponders "the reverberration of knotcracking awes." As Clive Hart points out, "reverberration" includes Italian *riverbero* for concave mirror and Spanish *reverbero* for lantern or light; a reflector is made from a combination of both (Hart 1962a, 9).

25. See Gleason 1999, 118–20, for a consideration of Stephen's composition of the villanelle in the light of Shelley's contrast between the "original purity and force" of aesthetic inspiration and the "feeble shadow" of any resulting artistic product.

26. Compare Day (1998, 61), who also believes that the sequence is moving towards a masturbatory orgasm, but sees this as an argument against the wet dream hypothesis. For his part, Gleason sees a "bodiless sexual union" that "becomes a supplement for sex" and produces "a fantasy of

erotic release" (1999, 124), but doesn't specify whether that release is manually facilitated. Bruce Comens, noting the "resurgence of erotic stimulation" in evidence in the poem's latter half, believes that "Stephen simultaneously completes the poem and achieves orgasm" (1992, 304)—close to my reading, but it does leave me wondering what Stephen is supposed to be doing with his hands. David Weir's answer—improbable, I think—is that Stephen is masturbating during the course of composition (1996, 130–31). See also McArthur 1998, 450–51.

27. From the anonymous entry for "Cloud Chamber," in *The New Encyclopedia Britannica* 1998, 3:397.

28. Later, Joyce's notebooks were to record speculations on different kinds of other-worldly rays—"raynerves" and "Jehova rays." Wim Van Mierlo has traced these phrases to Joyce's reading in Freud's *Collected Papers,* vol. 3 *(Case Histories* [1997, 148–49]).

29. Joyce was given to describing his own thoughts in such language, speaking for instance of notes for *Ulysses* as "the languid sparks which occasionally flashed across my soul" *(L1* 154).

30. Michael Levinson discerns a similar recapitulation in the diary (1998, 43).

31. But then metempsychotically through to earlier incarnations: One voice pleads ignorance on the excuse that he was "drunk all lost life" *(FW* 515.26).

2. "A Little Cloud": A Nebular Hypothesis

1. Although one critic, Jackson I. Cope, sees Chandler as Elijah: "Chandler envisions himself as an Ur-Eliot, poet of *The Waste Land,*" thus like Elijah a "Righteous" prophet against the modern wasteland; hence his prediction that Gallaher will get married some day is actually a "prophecy" of the sort Elijah delivered against Ahab (1981, 18–19). I find this reading surreal. One, Elijah's prophecies are not primarily fortune-telling predictions but warnings about the consequences of Israel's apostasy, and his main complaint is not about anyone's marriage but, if anything, about the nation's divorce from its God. Two, neither Elijah nor Eliot can be imagined without heavy irony as calling a sunset "a shower of kindly golden dust" (73), or engaging in any of Chandler's other poetic prettifications. In fact the kind of poetry to which Chandler aspires epitomizes much of what Eliot loathed most. Three, Elijah is about as far as it is possible to imagine from Chandler's brand of timorous benignity.

2. The prospect from Chandler's office window, encompassing as it does the actions of various parties amid "grass plots and walks," seems to suggest an elevated vantage. According to Donald T. Torchiana's source (1986, 126), Chandler's building has two stories.

3. "At places on a coast there is usually a pronounced tendency for a wind to blow from the sea to the land in the morning, and from the land to the sea in the evening." (From the entry under "Meteorology" in the 1946 *Encyclopedia Britannica,* 15:346.)

4. Warren Beck (1969, 163–64) has remarked on Chandler's cloud-like drift and sense of elevation.

5. "If air is perfectly free from dust, it may be cooled far below its dew point without any condensation . . . But if smoke or salt spray from the ocean is added, rapid condensation occurs . . . Some of the ocean salts and some of the products of combustion have the quality of absorbing moisture from the air and for this reason are said to be hygroscopic. Apparently the presence of hygroscopic, or at least water-soluble, particles is essential to the condensation of moisture in the air, and such particles are called nuclei of condensation" (Blair 1943, 130). Today, incidentally, the favored meteorologist's term for these nuclei is "aerosols."

6. Sometimes lightning and thunder as well, of course, which perhaps explains why "A Little Cloud" becomes so noisy in its last pages, from the loud report of Gallaher's clap on Chandler's back *(D* 79) to the echoing roomful of screams and bawls with which the story ends.

7. A point explored in Ruoff 1969, 107–8.

8. For the *fin de siècle* and "Celtic Twilight" origins of Chandler's aestheticism, see Torchiana 1986, 131–36.

3. Distillates, Counterparts

1. With independence, Irish postboxes were changed from red to green (McHugh 1980, 411).

2. For an exploration of this theme, see Robert A. Day's analysis of a pre-*Wake* character as a collection of "objects and gestures" that circulate, assemble, and cluster about a name (1998, 8). John Paul Riquelme's study (1983) analyzes Joyce's presentation of character from the perspective of *Finnegans Wake.* Both Riquelme and Day are less convinced than I am of the existence of a coherent field behind the verbal artifice, and Day in particular gives less weight than I do to the role of the subject in integrating the objects and gestures.

3. Riquelme, inclusive page numbers, especially 54–58, 169–71. See also Kenner 1978, 15–38, for the most influential exposition of the theme.

4. The exception is Sherrill E. Grace, who defends Mrs. Kearney against a patriarchal hegemony embodied in a narrator uncritically identified with Joyce (1988, 273–81). Note: Since this argument was first made in print, Mrs. Kearney's defenders have grown; see, for instance, Leonard 1997, 133–49.

5. The process of rehabilitation was underway by the end of *Dubliners:* in "The Dead" Miss Ivors invites Gabriel to join a Gaelic "excursion" to the Aran Isles with, among others, Kathleen Kearney *(D* 188–89). Kathleen's musical career was based on her identification with the Irish Revival, to whose adherents she is evidently still an attraction.

6. In a paper presented at the 1991 James Joyce Symposium in Vancouver, British Columbia, Mary Power showed that Irish *artistes* of the period had good reason to be suspicious of entrepreneurs, who frequently found excuses to renege on contracts.

7. Because the agreement was in guineas and Holohan is paying in pounds. In addition to chiseling her, he is denying Mrs. Kearney the air of gentility that guineas long conveyed in such transactions, a gentility he has earlier found flattering enough. To a degree, the payment itself amounts to a declaration that she is no lady.

8. For the fullest treatment to date of the "mythic" consciousness of Joycean narrators, see Riquelme 1983, especially 35, 85, 105, 169.

9. Or they can vie for control. Patrick Parrinder calls the monologue of "Proteus" "a cacophony of voices, quotations, and ideolects speaking through Stephen" (1984, 133).

10. See *The Decameron,* book 1, stories 6 and 8.

11. This particular retrospective may have been begun in *Portrait,* 156, where Stephen recalls that he had "received only two pandies" during his education, "and, though these had been dealt him in the wrong, he knew that he had often escaped punishment." It may also be relevant that Stephen bears a name chosen from a passage in a Latin text, Ovid's *Metamorphoses,* describing Daedalus's flight over the sea, which neither he nor his author could have read, let alone adopted for the epigraph of this book, had not some Father Dolan or other gotten through his head the crucial

word from that passage—"*mare*"—that starts all the trouble in the pandying scene. George Orwell, who knew, maintained that boys could not be made to learn Latin and Greek without the use of the cane; later history would seem to have borne him out.

12. I here make use of certain facts about the historical Michael Cusack, a practice I think justified because Joyce confirmed the identification in notes and comments and called the citizen "Cusack" in early drafts of the episode, and because in all verifiable instances the fictional figure matches the biographical record. In 1904 Cusack was in bad health, was in fact to die of a heart condition within three years. The event was noted by Joyce, who in a letter referred to him as "old Cusack" (*L2* 210). (My main source for the biographical Cusack has been Mandle 1987.) The citizen of "Circe" is an old man: various voices refer to him as "venerable" "veteran" (*U* 12.901, 918), a "semiparalysed *doyen*" (*U* 12.557), and "The man that got away James Stephens"—a claim that, since that rescue occurred in 1866, requires him to be in his mid-fifties at least. He is clearly in poor health— cannot, indeed, cross a floor without waddling and panting (*U* 12.1783–86)—and it seems to be common knowledge that he has a bad heart. Hynes greets him with "How's the old heart, citizen?" (*U* 12.147), and that heart is soon thereafter described as thundering "rumblingly" (*U* 12.165–66); allowing for exaggeration, it appears that, along with the labored breathing (*U* 12.163–64), the heart's beating is noticeable—hardly a good sign. Cusack's hostility to English sports in general and lawn tennis in particular is registered with the reference to "shoneen games the like of lawn tennis" (*U* 12.889–90).

Incidentally, the point about Bloom's startling incivility and/or tactlessness, as contrasted with the citizen, who whatever his faults has his own grievances and his own case to make, was first broached in my *James Joyce's Metamorphoses* (Gordon 1981, 74) and has since been independently noted by Emer Nolan (1995, 96 ff), who finds other reasons for exculpating the citizen.

13. Connolly 1961, 82. See also Füger 1986, 210, for evidence that in "Sirens," the episode in which he is cuckolded, Bloom becomes identified with Malbecco, the one-eyed cuckold of *The Faerie Queene*. Some other clues pointing to the identification of antagonists: whereas in "Eumaeus" Bloom's version of the "Cyclops" exchange is that the citizen "offensively" called him "a jew," leading Bloom to respond that Christ was a Jew like himself (*U* 16.1082–85), in fact it was the other way around (*U* 12.1805–18). If we accept the common interpretation of the fight between two little boys of the next episode as a Lilliputian version of the "Cyclops" contest between Bloom and citizen, it should be significant that those boys are twins. One final note: in *Finnegans Wake* Michael Cusack, the citizen's model, joins, as "Nicholas de Cusack," with Nicholas of Cusa to propound "the coincidance of . . . contraries" (*FW* 48.34–36).

14. A connection foreshadowed, I think, at *U* 4.256–57, when Bloom, adjusting the "blind," watches Molly with his "backward eye" as she secretes her lover's letter behind him. "Backward eye" is not a bad phrase for summing up the citizen-Cyclops.

15. Kenner explains: "Paddy Dignam some time before his death assigned his insurance policy as security for a loan, and failed to complete the process by informing the company. So the insurance company, which would in the normal course of things make its payment to the new beneficiary, the moneylender [Bridgeman], may therefore . . . be constrained to pay the original beneficiary, the widow Dignam" (Kenner 1977, 389).

16. There is a Catch-22 embedded here: that Bridgeman is losing the money means that he does not deserve to. A professional sharper of the sort audiences enjoy seeing foiled would not let himself be outfoxed.

17. In *Ulysses* we see the Dignam money going for sherry and pork, and strings are being pulled to send the eldest child to a Jesuit school where Jewish students would be unwelcome. If Bridgeman is indeed Jewish, this is all almost as cruel as the conclusion of *The Merchant of Venice*.

18. As does for instance Bloom, whose provisions for Milly's future are largely tied up in an insurance policy held by the same company backing the policy Bridgeman now stands to lose (*U* 17.1855).

19. This phrase exemplifies Cunningham's diplomatic shrewdness. Literally, it denotes the neutral fact that Bloom has left his religion. The connotations, especially given the circumstances, are another matter.

20. See Adams 1967, 105. Adams assumes, naïvely I think, that although Joyce knew of this incident he was counting on the reader's not learning of it, because he wished to present Falkiner in the best possible light. This may constitute the only time when Joyce has ever been charged with going too easy on his countrymen.

21. " 'Aren't there enough words for you in English?' they asked him. 'Yes,' he replied, 'there are enough, but they aren't the right ones.' He had to make neologisms. 'For example, take the word *battlefield*. A battlefield is a field where the battle is raging. When the battle is over and the field is covered with blood, it is no longer a *battlefield*, but a *bloodfield*" (*JJ* 397).

4. The Orphic "Sirens," the Orphic *Ulysses*

1. See Hayman 1970, 88–104. See also Benstock and Benstock 1982, 10–21, and Lawrence 1981, 3–4, for useful accounts of the background and development of this approach.

2. Plato 1892, 5, 56. Compare Chaucer's *The Book of the Duchess*, lines 569–70: "Ne Orpheus, god of melodye, / Ne Dedalus with his playes slye."

3. For a survey, see Bays 1964. Prominent in Bays's treatment of the Orphic theme is Edouard Schuré's *Les grands initiés*, a book of occult lore in which Orpheus figures prominently; Joyce read it and copied passages in his notebooks (Lernout 2000–2001, 147–49).

4. Translated and quoted from E.T.A. Hoffmann's *The Magnetist*, by Bays (1964, 59).

5. Tatar 1978, 273–76.

6. Tatar 1978, 73. See also Kaplan 1975, inclusive page numbers.

7. At least this is the term I have encountered most often in my readings in the field. There are also "synergy," "telesthesia," and "hyperesthesia," along with others coined to distinguish between the sense or organ affected from afar or the way the influence is manifested. All describe distant signals registering in the organism by paranormal means.

8. See Oppenheim 1985, 142 ff, for the turn-of-the-century scientific/pseudoscientific interest in such reported phenomena and the attempts to account for them.

9. Hart 1962b, 155. (For other testimony to Joyce's interest in the occult, see Gilbert 1958, vii-viii, and Stanislaus Joyce 1958, 131–33.) Oppenheim describes such phenomena, including one remarkable, much-publicized case that made a believer of Arthur Balfour, on p. 133 and pp. 156–57. Probably the most influential promoter of cross-correspondence was Sir Arthur Conan Doyle, in his *The New Revelation*, first published in 1917.

10. Myers 1920, 1, 273. At p. xxi Myers joins "shell-hearing" and "crystal-gazing" as one of three main ways through which one "supernormally acquires information." "Crystal-gazing" is a general term for the practice of inducing trances by staring into glassy or reflective surfaces—crystal balls, of

course, but also jewels, mirrors, and pools, for instance the "pool near her [Gerty's] foot," which Bloom calls a "dark mirror" and imagines peering into, breathing on and causing to "stir" (*U* 13.1260–61). (Compare *U* 14.1045–62, where, as we will later see, Bloom goes into a trance, staring at a glassy object, a bottle; the scene is rendered as mirror-gazing.) According to an "Oxen of the Sun" memory (*U* 14.1366–71), Molly first saw Bloom after raising her head from a vessel of water.

For Joyce's familiarity with Myers' book, see Jackson and Costello 1997, 259. Frank Budgen's notes in the Richard Ellmann collection at the McFarland Library in Tulsa, Oklahoma, confirm their report.

11. Hart 1974, foldout chart between pp. 210 and 211.

12. Hart's diagram shows that the viceregal cavalcade is passing the Ormond Hotel at this time and that the action of "Sirens" begins with the barmaids watching it go by.

13. That is, forty-six times over the 8,902 words between "Begin!" (*U* 11.63) and "But wait" (*U* 11:1004), for an average of approximately once every 194 words, five times over the 2,876 words between "But hear" (*U* 11:1004) and the end, for an average of approximately once every 575 words. Another word to watch is "come," which appears twenty times before Boylan's indirectly reported climax (see below), never afterwards. "Sirens" repeatedly encourages taking the word in its sexual sense.

14. The words may be found in Gifford and Seidman 1988, 293.

15. The original wording here is "Who dares to speak of ninety-eight?"—1798, memorable year of rebellion and betrayal. Bloom updates it to his own year of crisis.

16. As Robert M. Adams notes in his catalog of "Bloom's bloopers," "Joyce has his own fun with Bloom's errors and occasionally uses them to make or conceal a point of his own" (Adams 1967, 172). The error in question is especially striking in that Bloom misreports a line that is being sung at that very moment.

17. Bloom will later be reminded of "lotion" when attempting to smell his own semen (*U* 13.1044).

18. As for "sticky," compare Bloom's thoughts that Gerty "made me do love sticky" (*U* 13.1279–80).

19. This is not the end of Molly's day with Boylan. He will have returned to her at about 5:30, when the "stoppress edition" of the *Evening Telegraph* hits the streets. At that time he will go out again, buy a copy, and return cursing the results of the Gold Cup Race (*U* 18:269–71, 423–26), though keeping enough presence of mind to magnify by a factor of ten the amount of money that—he says—he had bet on Molly's behalf. After that he and Molly will have more time together for rehearsal, punctuated by other sessions in bed probably more leisurely than the first.

20. For background on what Tatar (1978, 44) terms "a persistent tendency . . . to draw analogies between physical and psychic forces," see, besides Tatar, De Guaïta 1895, especially 87–94; "Papus" 1897, 74–77; Bays 1964, especially 191; and Oppenheim 1985, especially the chapters "Physics and Psychic Phenomena" and "A Pseudoscience." As Oppenheim notes, the word "telepathy" was coined by presumably deliberate analogy with "telegraphy," as an assertion that its action was " 'a fact in Nature' " (Oppenheim 1985, 142). Sir William Crookes, the eminent chemist and physicist whose work was critical to the discovery of X-rays, speculated, in his capacity as president of the Society for Psychical Research, that similar rays might be transmitted from one consciousness to "impinge on the ganglion of another brain" (Oppenheim 1985, 350). His name turns up repeatedly as a scientific warrant for psychic effects; we have already observed what Stephen can make out of the idea of mental "rays."

21. Finucane 1984, 180. Finucane calls this "yet another example of using contemporary science to give spiritualistic beliefs greater credibility." The original English title was *Secrets of the Future Life Unveiled.*

22. Consider this account of the search for such convergences in spiritualist activities: "Given the long-standing analogies with both electricity and magnetism, it is understandable that not a few Victorians confused the pseudoscientific theories of mesmerism with the new theories of physics publicized at the same time. In 1853 Queen Victoria was not alone in assuming that table turning was a magnetic or electrical phenomenon" (Oppenheim 1985, 219). Throughout the century and into the next, as Oppenheim documents, spiritualist and other occult phenomena were commonly accounted for in terms of electricity, electromagnetism, or magnetism, or in presumably cognate forces radiating through the ether. William Crookes, mentioned above, would like other researchers regularly monitor seances with a galvanometer" (quoted in Oppenheim 1985, 349–50).

23. See James 1950, 1:101. James attributes the origin of this widespread belief to Louis Agassiz, who remarked that "fishermen are more intelligent than farmers because they eat so much fish, which contains so much phosphorus." Apparently the venerable notion that fish food is brain food (endorsed by Bloom at U 8.821–26) traces from this observation.

24. For further examples of the book's equation of telegraphy with occult communications, see my *Notes on Issy* (Gordon 1982, 2–8). Joyce's 1924 notebook labeled VI.B.68 includes the following notation—

> telegraph
> Yawn
>   telephone
>   wireless
> Dawn
>   thought transference

—indicating that he was aware of contemporary comparisons of telepathy to telegraphy (cited in Van Mierlo 1997, 131).

25. For instance *FW* 452.08–15, in which Shaun is "tramsported" by telepathic/wireless signals coming to him from "th'other over th'ether." The parodied seance of "Cyclops," in which the voice of Paddy Dignam beams in from an otherworld supplied with modern mechanical conveniences, may be a spoof of Oliver Lodge's report, in *Raymond,* that the dead live in landscaped, fully appointed houses like those of the well-off non-defunct. For evidence that Joyce read *Raymond* and other works by Lodge, see Atherton 1974a, 266–67.

26. For the turn-of-the-century interest in Hertzian waves as a model for extrasensory conduction, see Oppenheim 1985, 378–79.

27. The Mesmeric ether-conveyed trance will be confirmed at *FW* 476.7–8, when one of the inquisitors hovering over Shaun "proxtended aloof upon the ether Mesmer's Manuum, the hand making silence." See also *FW* 360.24–25, which links a "hypnot" state with an invocation to "remesmer."

28. "After Mesmer lost control of the movement that bore his name, in France, at least, it fell into the hands of wilder visionaries who joined it with such beliefs as metempsychosis" (Oppenheim 1985, 467).

29. As this reminds us, the parallel Homeric story of Odysseus's fiery stake being driven into

Polyphemus's one eye can also conjure an ugly image of sexual intercourse. Many critics have noted the plethora of phallic references throughout this male episode.

30. See Ellmann 1972, appendix. The four "Persons" listed for the episode are "Prometheus," "No one (I)," "Ulysses," and "Galatea." Bloom obviously corresponds to Ulysses, but also, according to the Homeric story, to No one, who is embodied in the narrative voice. And if he can be involved in two distinct Persons, he can be involved in three. "Galatea" remains a puzzle because there are no women in "Cyclops," and although Polyphemus is in some stories said to have pined for a nymph of that name, there is no mention of any such figure in the citizen's life. Given my reading of the Prometheus theme—and of "Nausicaa," coming up—it is tempting to wonder whether this Galatea might be Pygmalion's, as embodied in the Gerty McDowell of the complementarily female episode following. From a different perspective, Margot Norris sees Gerty as "playing, albeit in reverse, the parts of both Pygmalion and Galatea" (Norris 1992, 178).

31. For his part, Bloom's double the citizen is doing a fair job of destroying his own liver. About their contretemps, Bloom will later recall that he gave him "one in the gizzard" (U 16.1598).

32. The sexual innuendo here is later confirmed by Molly: "he puts his thing long into my aunt Marys hairy and it turns out you put the handle in a sweepingbrush" (U 18.1386–88).

33. From which he has been exiled, according to the narrator, by the "Molly Maguires" (U 12.1314). Ahem: *Molly* Maguires.

34. Myers makes this point several times. The twins here are named Jackie (as in "Tar") and Tommy (as in "Atkins")—iconic complements.

35. To begin with, Bloom imagines the magnetized tip of his illustrative compass needle as being responsive not just to the earth's magnetic field but to "what's going on in the sun, the stars" (U 11.991)—that is, pretty much to the ends of creation. He then turns to the case of the tuning fork, vibrating in sympathy with a struck note from some distinct source, like ("Molly, he") a woman to her lover. Approaching climax, Gerty feels a "tremour" go "all over her" (U 11.695). The tuning fork introduced in "Sirens" epitomizes as well as anything the effects prominent since that episode.

36. Another (partial) concession: At such times Joyce sometimes seems to be keeping a barely plausible non-occult explanation in reserve. It has been suggested that Bloom's watch stops in sync with the Molly-Boylan get-together because Bloom's frettings about what is transpiring make him break into a sweat, which causes the soap in his pocket to become sticky and to gum up the works of the adjacent watch, which accordingly stops at the fatal hour. In "Nausicaa" Gerty is wearing perfume, and it is part of the lore of modern-day fashion magazines, anyway, that a woman wishing to make the right impression on the right man should apply perfume to the "pulse points" of wrist and throat, the idea apparently being that at moments of unusual excitement the quickened beating of her heated blood will pulsate pheromonic waves of scent toward the certain party who has elicited this reaction in her, which party will then subconsciously notice these signals, wafting his way with accelerating urgency, and respond accordingly. Gerty's face and form certainly heat up during the fireworks scene, and Bloom might conceivably be registering her correspondingly augmented scent and becoming correspondingly aroused in turn, to the point that one's curve of excitement and climax really does occur in response to the other's. If so, the effect has been largely subliminal, because Bloom isn't conscious of Gerty's perfume until later (U 12.1015–16): "Why did I smell it only now? Took its time in coming like herself, slow but sure" (U 12.1015–16). Still, note the double sense of "coming." And, given Joyce's habitual attentiveness to the mechanics of consciousness, the answer to Bloom's question here may simply be that he didn't consciously notice the perfume because at the time all of his faculties were concentrated on the senses of seeing (Gerty) and feeling (in his groin).

In any case, the fact remains that the testimony and speculation of "Nausicaa" overwhelmingly support some kind of "Orphic" explanation along the lines of hyperaesthesia, telepathy, and Mesmeric magnetism. My suspicion is that here as elsewhere Joyce wants to have it both ways.

37. "In this wireless age any owl rooster can peck up bostoons," comments someone in *Finnegans Wake* after nightfall (*FW* 489.36–90.01), and indeed the pub's radio, operating between 10 and 11 P.M., receives a range of transcontinental and transatlantic signals. In Paris, Joyce would listen to such broadcasts regularly, including programs from Ireland and America, at a time when radio dials often specified bandwidths for far-flung foreign capitals. For Joyce's radio-listening, see Connor 1993, 825–43. A BBC recording in the McFarland Library's collection, "Portrait of James Joyce," includes Maria Jolas's testimony that Joyce listened to the radio frequently, especially "to what he used to call the Transatlantic clowns over the National Broadcasting Company" from America. (Those *Finnegans Wake* "bostoons" that you can pick up are, besides Boston, the plural of Gaelic *bastún*, fool).

38. For earlier observations on Gerty and Bloom's apparent telepathy, see O'Brien 1968, 159; and Senn 1974, 277–312. See also Smith 1991, 634.

39. The suggestion was first made in *James Joyce's Metamorphoses*, 74–80, and debated during March 1998 with fellow participants on the j-joyce discussion list, to whom my thanks for helping me to clarify some of the issues raised.

40. It is true that an evidently real Gerty MacDowell does show up, at *U* 10.1205–11, in a cameo consistent with "Nausicaa." (She is also named at *U* 12.1994 and remembered at *U* 17.1847.) But, after all, men can fantasize about real women, including women they know, and given Bloom's familiarity with the Dignams, friends and neighbors of the MacDowells, it would be surprising if Bloom had not seen Gerty at some time. The most likely explanation, I think, is that, like Stephen dreaming up the temptress of his villanelle, Bloom evokes a fantasy figure based mainly on a real woman.

So again, a concession—Gerty, like the citizen, is a real physical presence, but one taken over, Orphically-telepathically-telekinetically, by Bloom, as a "projected mirage" can arise from the shimmer off of sand. As in much else, Gerty speaks for Bloom, about herself, when mooning about the message of the poem "Art thou real, my ideal?" (*U* 13.645–46).

41. See Ellmann 1972, appendix.

42. The "Technic" assigned the episode in the schema given by Joyce to Stuart Gilbert is "Tumescence, detumescence."

43. As remarked by Karen Lawrence (1981, 119). See also Ellmann 1972, 126–27; McGee 1988, 307; Kelly 1988, 33, 37; Senn 1984, 175–80; and Senn 1995, 25, for other detections of Bloomian elements in Gerty's idiom. Senn also points out that both Bloom and Gerty are leaning back against rocks.

44. The type may have had its first imperfect incarnation in the Ormond barmaids, who correspond to the Sirens of the *Odyssey* and show up when Bloom feels himself abandoned by his wife. As Lesley Higgins has observed (1997, 49), the Siren in Dante's *Purgatorio* is "crooked on her feet"—like Gerty, who, Siren-like, stays perched on a rock and moves "crookedly" in "Circe" (*U* 15.386), thus yet again mirroring the Bloom of "Nausicaa" and his "crooked" throws (*U* 13.952).

45. As Gerty herself senses when, seeing or intuiting or mind-reading the action of what she will soon call Bloom's "working" hands (*U* 11.695), she compares him to a masturbator employed by the "Congested Districts Board" (*U* 11.703). "Working" is a curious word there, one that few would likely have selected, but artisans, Prometheus for instance, also "work" with their "hands" in the act

of creation. Just before remarking those hands, Gerty avers that Bloom "could be trusted to the death, steadfast, a sterling man, a man of inflexible honour to his fingertips." "Steadfast" and "inflexible" pay tribute to Bloom's phallic rigidity here (*Finnegans Wake* includes a naughty joke about "Standfast Dick" [*FW* 210.28]), "sterling" to that too, plus his solvency, but "fingertips" is perhaps the most revealing word of the lot, being, as it is, often associated with accomplished craftsmen. (It also embeds G-E-R-T-I. In the next episode, Bloom will be called a "gert vool" [*U* 14.1482].) Thus Harry Levin, who presumably intended no innuendo, on Joyce: "he was an artist to his finger-tips" (Levin 1960, 42).

46. Galopin 1889, 97–134. For the catalog of Joyce's library, see Ellmann 1977, 97–34.

5. The Erotic Gerty, the Pornographic Gerty

1. Budgen 1967, 21; see also *JJ* 521, note.

2. *L1* 169. See Gordon 1981, 124–33, for an earlier analysis of "Penelope" as what Joyce's notes call the "odyss of Pen"—odyssey of Penelope—twice traversing the coordinates of those four cardinal points.

3. Compare Bloom in "Sirens": "Three holes all women" (*U* 11.389).

4. An argument anticipated by Richard Ellmann, who writes that "Lestrygonians" is "generated mostly out of two different attitudes towards food and sexuality" and notes some instances where Bloom's feelings about one involve similar feelings toward the other (Ellmann 1972, 74). A striking example occurs at the end, where the appearance of the carnal Boylan awakens in Bloom an appreciation for the "cream curves" (*U* 8.118) of a neoclassical building, cream and other milk products having been earlier established as food for non-carnivores.

5. See *JJ* 502–4.

6. Rabelais 1990, 181–82. In the original French, Rabelais' term here for the vagina, *comment à nom* ("I don't know what it's called"), may recall Molly's inability to find the word in the dictionary.

6. Henry's Flower

1. All following readings in the language of flowers come from Katherine Bryant's website www.cybercom.net/~klb/flowers.html, which lists the flower significations given in several handbooks published between 1853 and 1899.

2. In "Circe" (*U* 15.738–40), Martha's flower appears to have reminded Bloom of Lenehan's "Rose of Castile" gag. On the other hand, "Oxen of the Sun" (*U* 14.330–31) might be taken to nominate (as "Margerain gentle") the marigold, a midsummer flower that can be orange or yellow. For the record, in the language of flowers a large marigold signifies jealousy, a small one the message "Never despair." In *The Winter's Tale*, Perdita says about marigolds, "I think they are given / To men of middle age."

3. Although, typically, ambivalence lurks, "dominant" taking its key from "tonic," which (at *U* 11.220, 273) "Sirens" establishes, by way of the Mourne mountains, as mourning, Bloom's prevailing mood when in the throes of his dominant passion.

7. Approaching Reality in "Oxen of the Sun"

1. Before Lawrence, Kenner had rejected the notion of "a 'truth' recoverable beneath all . . . the surfaces" of the later styles (1978, 91). John Paul Riquelme reads *Ulysses* as a voyage that "departs from the mimesis of consciousness of the early episodes" (1983, 151); like Lawrence he dates the departure from "Aeolus." Jean-Michael Rabaté believes that by "Circe" any "psychological plausibility" has all but disappeared (1981, 109). In their introduction to *Post-Structuralist Joyce,* Derek Attridge and Daniel Ferrer set themselves to demonstrate "the perpetual flight of the Subject" in Joyce and his "deconstruction of representation" (1984, 10); various essays in the collection, especially those by Stephen Heath (39), André Topia (107, 110–11, 116–18, 123), and Ferrer (132–41) accordingly read *Ulysses* as affirming an anti-mimetic aesthetic. Bernard and Shari Benstock cite with approval Lawrence's statement that with "Aeolus" "the book begins to advertise its own artifice" and add that at that point "the text divides against itself" (1982, 13). Comparing Joyce to Beckett, David Hayman remarks that in both the text "tends to destroy referentiality" (Hayman in Benstock and Benstock 1982, 37). Christine van Boheemen-Saaf has Joyce teaching the reader to forego "understanding the text mimetically" (1988, 93). Colin MacCabe writes that in its middle episodes *Ulysses* "destroys the possibility of the text representing some exterior reality" (1979, 84). Patrick McGee believes that a major purpose of the parodies of the middle episodes is "to show that writing never simply mirrors the real" (1988, 70). Frances Restuccia sees the book's stylistic development as an act of progressive "literary masochism" "effected as the aggressive textuality of the latter portion of the novel . . . supersedes the excruciating mimesis of the former" (1989, 150). Brook Thomas argues that in "calling attention to himself as a manipulator of language," Joyce abandons "all pretensions to realism" (1982, 151). Wolfgang Iser cites "Oxen of the Sun" in particular as the place where language is seen to lose its grip (1974, 192). Marilyn French likewise sees it as the episode in which literary expression demonstrates its ultimate inability to convey reality (1976, 169). Many, many other critics have said much the same, at this writing most recently (again, and always) Derek Attridge: 2001, inclusive page numbers.

I think that all of these people are wrong. So, I am happy to report, does Cordell D. K. Yee, whose admirable *The World According to James Joyce* succeeds, I think, in knocking the theoretical props out from under much of what he calls this "antirealist" school of Joyceans (1997). It should be read as a companion to Geert Lernout's devastating *The French Joyce* (1990). Jefferson Hunter's brisk *How to Read Ulysses, and Why* also demurs from "recent Joycean critics who have argued against regarding *Ulysses* as a more or less reliable literary imitation of the 'real' world" (2002, 4).

2. *Pace,* as ever, Attridge, for whom "the uncontrollable properties of the material signifier" in "Sirens" undermine the episode's "history as narrative" (2001, 87).

3. Kenner, although often alert to the play of mimesis elsewhere in *Ulysses,* has repeatedly minimized its role in the middle episodes. See Kenner in Hart and Hayman 1974, especially 348–49; Kenner 1978, 91–82; Kenner 1980, 118–27. The critique has been influential: Riquelme (1983, 138–52), Rabaté (1981, 86, 199–200), Parrinder (1984, 178), and MacCabe (1979, 128–31) all cite Kenner in support of their variously anti-mimetic readings. See also Lawrence 1981, 148; Peake 1977, 263–76; Ferrer in Attridge and Ferrer 1984, 132–41; Ferrer 1988, 149–50; McGee 1988, 187; Restuccia 1989, 113; and Ziarek 1992, especially 57, 65.

4. For the remainder of this chapter, numbers in parentheses, unless otherwise indicated, will all refer to the cited line number in "Oxen of the Sun."

5. Benstock 1982, 50–51. On the other hand, Bloom is probably referring to Rudy in asking why "seemingly a healthy child" (1274) should have died in infancy.

6. He seems to have succeeded. See chapter 16.

7. Compare, for instance, "Tare and ages, what way would I be resting at all, he muttered thickly, and I tramping Dublin this while back with my share of songs and himself after me the like of a soulth or a bullawurrus?" (1018–21) with Mulligan's act in "Scylla and Charybdis": "It's what I'm telling you, master honey, it's queer and sick we were, Haines and myself, the time himself brought it in" (U 9.558–59).

8. Along with the other games enjoyed at the Dillon party, Molly and her friends, circling what the narrator calls a "grey urn" filled with water (1366–67—really a tub or bucket or some such)— have been bobbing for cherries, which explains how a "brace"—pair—should be hanging by their joined stems over her ear, having caught there when her face was submerged. (The usual reading of this "brace" as an earring is clearly incorrect: fresh-fruit jewelry was not to become fashionable, if that is the word, until Carmen Miranda; the practice of wearing only one earring did not come into vogue, and then mainly among men, until the 1980s.) Another and commoner word for this "brace" would be "bob." Bloom's memory of this first sight of Molly with a bob of cherries got from bobbing has been resurrected by Stephen's unexpected use of the homely "chance word" "bob," thus generating the whole "scene" that as "Pater" says is now before Bloom's mind. Molly's resulting evocation of "Our Lady of the Cherries" casts her, enshrined in this treasured memory, as a type of the Virgin Mary commonly commemorated as "Our Lady of" some place or attribute. (She was in fact at least a technical virgin at the time, and her birthday corresponds with the feast day of the Virgin Mary.) The language recalls Pater's semi-religious raptures about paintings, especially his famous account of Leonardo's Mona Lisa as the Eternal Female, "older than the rocks on which she sits."

9. Delivered, be it noted, by someone who was himself childless and widely known to be impotent. As for the three voices preceding, each of them in his way urging family values of a paterfamilias kind: Ruskin was impotent, Pater was homosexual, and Newman was celibate; all were childless. Like New York in the song, Joyce's irony never sleeps.

10. Yee notes that Sicily, site of the corresponding Homeric episode, etymologically signifies "privation of parents, children, or friends . . . a place of abandonment and desolation" (1997, 68).

11. Habitual as shown by Bloom's self-congratulation, after masturbating in "Nausicaa" (to which the narrator comments, "At it again?" [U 13.726]) on not having done it earlier in the bath over Martha's letter (U 13.786–87), thus so to speak saving himself for Gerty. In "Oxen of the Sun" the voice of "Junius" condemns the masturbation as "a habit," "reprehensible" enough in youth and an "opprobrium" for the middle-aged man, Bloom, to whom it has become "second nature" (930–31).

12. Sultan 1964, 284–85. See note 14 below.

13. They are: "Charley, Mary Alice, Frederick Albert (if he had lived), Mamy, Budgy (Victoria Frances), Tom, Violet Constance Louisa, darling little Bobsy (called after our famous hero of the South African war, lord Bobs of Waterford and Candahar)" (1329–34) and the newborn Mortimer Edward. The names tell us that Mr. and Mrs. Purefoy are either inordinately devoted to the British royal family or intent on appearing so. "Charlie" may recall Charles I, to royalists England's martyred monarch (said in some traditions, incidentally, to have been beheaded by one George Joyce: see Gordon 1993); Mary Alice bears the name of Victoria's third child, Alice, and her grandson's wife, the future Queen Mary; Frederick Albert combines the names of Prince Albert and the Frederick III who married Princess Victoria, daughter of Victoria and Albert, and begat Kaiser Wilhelm,

whose full name was Friedrich Wilhelm Viktor Albert; Mamy (or Mamie) is commonly a nickname for Mary (see above); Victoria Frances of course bears the name of both Queen Victoria and the princess; Violet Constance Louisa may owe part of her name to Victoria's sixth daughter, Louise. The "Lord Bobs" after whom "Little Bobsy" is named is Sir Frederick Roberts, commander in chief of the British Army. He was in a way a "hero" of the Boer War, which had however come to be unpopular with all but staunch John Bull types. Mortimer Edward's middle name is of course that of another of Victoria's offspring and the reigning king; like "Mortimer," the name chosen after the "tony relative" (U 8.367) to whom the Purefoys owe a favor and from whom they may hope for more, "Edward" is probably a gesture of obeisance to a powerful personage.

14. Frazer 1935, 7:178. See also the entries headed "Sunwise" in Opie and Tatem 1989, 383–86. Cited are several accounts of villagers of the British Isles walking sunwise (or *deshil*) three times around some special place—church, cairn, graveyard, new home—to insure good luck, sometimes chanting; P. W. Joyce documents thrice-repeated *deshil* rituals in Ireland (1903, 3:301–2), some of them, as of 1903, still current. The Arval Brethren of ancient Rome, from whom the opening chant derives, would annually circumambulate their sacred site, presumably—although I have not been able to confirm this independently—in the sunwise direction indicated by the words Joyce gives them; the ritual included the sacrifice of cattle. Taking the likeliest route from Sandymount, Bloom would have made a right, *deshil*, turn onto Holles Street from off of North Mount Street Lower, then another right turn to enter the hospital, on the right sight of the street.

15. In which regard, it would be nice to know (1) whether Bloom sets his watch to the pub clock's time of "ten to" eleven, or, mindful that such clocks are always set five minutes fast (U 8.790–91), five to eleven, and (2) whether that watch, rewound, keeps time correctly, or indeed at all, from this point on. Evidence for the negative perhaps lies in "Ithaca" 's inaccurate report that Bloom had purchased his lemon soap "thirteen hours previously" (fifteen hours would be closer to the mark), and in the absence of any mention of that watch, even during Bloom's undressing, after the "Oxen" winding. On the other hand, Bloom does finally get the time right, courtesy of the "bells in the church of Saint George," as he says goodbye to Stephen (U 17.1224–34).

16. Discussing the *deshil* theme, Senn notes that "Penelope," with "the faint incipient luster of approaching dawn," along with Molly's memories of sunny Spain and the sun-drenched day on Howth, heralds "a new turning toward the sun" (Senn 1984, 165). For other reasons to think that Bloom's "Oxen" resolution may wind up being reciprocated by his wife, see chapter 18.

17. For a recent example of a reading that on just this basis takes the chapter as an invitation "to resist the naturalization of narrative and meaning" and "dissolve . . . the relations of signifier and signified," see King 1998, 349–72.

18. Compare *The Mayor of Casterbridge*, where the prophecy of a fortune-teller comes true, thus validating Henchard's superstitious regard for old mysteries, as against Faerfae's rationalism. A book in which the prophecy turned out wrong would be a different kind of story. The same can I think be said for this episode, and for *Ulysses*, in which all of the many prophecies made will come true. (See chapter 13, note 32.) As for "Oxen" itself: In its Homeric source Tiresias's prophecy of disaster is dramatically fulfilled—the crew should have paid attention—and it is taking place in a room equipped with horn-handled utensils (144–45), which may remind us of the *Odyssey*'s stipulation that prophetic dreams come through gates of horn.

19. An association running throughout, as evidenced by Bloom's repeated confusion of Theodore Purefoy, the father, with Philip Beaufoy, the author.

20. See especially Gillet 1949, 32–46; Noon 1963, 57–125; Goldberg 1969, 66–99.

21. As Lawrence observes (Lawrence 1981, 126), Joyce's selections are predominantly "the didactic models of the essay and sermon."

22. Perhaps not all that flawed; it is, above all, a work in progress, adding, subtracting, and modifying material as the day goes on, and according to Ellmann Joyce took it "more seriously" than Stephen seems to (*JJ* 364)—more seriously, surely, than most commentators.

23. George Saintsbury and W. Peacock, whose histories of English prose were apparently Joyce's two main sources for this episode, both include a number of female authors. Nothing extrinsic prevented Joyce from including an Emily Brönte, or for that matter from continuing his chronology to include a living prose stylist like Kipling—to name two authors he admired (see *JJ* 660–61).

8. Bloom as Thomas De Quincey

1. As previously, numbers in parentheses refer to lines of "Oxen of the Sun" unless otherwise indicated.

2. *Finnegans Wake*—especially book II, chapter 2, in which for forty-eight pages a central column of text is accompanied with vocal commentary from margins and footnotes—contains many experimental approximations to the medleys, interruptions, and overlappings of real-life talk. Some of the language of the next chapter, II.3, combines such effects, produced out of the mingling voices of pub chat, with a radio voice made polyglot by the reception's tendency to wander from French station to German to Dutch and so on, often blending the languages in a staticky amalgam. A forerunner to such experiments may have been Chekhov, fond of having background dialogue implicitly comment on foreground conversation. Malcolm Bradbury's novel *The History Man* features an excursion along the same lines.

3. It is probably here that Lenehan gives the account of Throwaway's training that Bloom, on learning the correct version from the evening paper, will later dismiss as "pure buncombe" (*U* 16.1286).

4. Yes, but. "Oxen of the Sun," with its succession of dead voices, is in its way a summoning of ghosts, and, as we will see in chapter 19, one actual ghost does put in an appearance.

5. The phrase will thereafter haunt Bloom throughout the day as a synecdoche for the encounter with Boylan: see *U* 4.311, 4.444, 5.154, 10.500, 13.843, 15.306, 15.325, 15.345.

6. Or perhaps rather *On the Study of Words*, by Richard Chevenix Trench, grandfather of Haines's original: Gregory M. Downing has found many " 'Oxen' passages that substantively mirror Trench's etymological discussions," among them (on p. 160) that "currants are so called because of importation from Corinth" (Downing 1998, 48).

7. Bloom may have picked up on "currant" and reacted with sentiments registered in "Landor" 's romantically elevated diction, because of the word's private association (*U* 7.912, 15.3368) with the moment when Molly said "yes" to him. That those cherished "currants" were really goat turds is par for the Joycean course in all matters romantic.

8. Fortuitously or not, such a conjunction has been (abortively) celebrated already in the "Sirens" episode, when Bob Dollard and company begin a song, "Love and War," the concluding verse of which runs, "Since Mars lov'd Venus, Venus Mars, / Let's blend love's wounds with battle's scars" (Gifford and Seidman 1988, 292). Given what the Wife of Bath has to say about the sublunary consequences of that convergence, one can at least theorize that the glimmering hope of Bloom and his well-wishing readers that June 17 will see some kind of amatory renaissance has the stars on its side. For further testimony, celestial and otherwise, on this point, see chapters 10, 11, and 18.

9. Bloom's Bell

1. See p. 96, in chapter 7.

2. My thanks to Austin Briggs Jr. for enlightening me on this point.

3. Particularly in Kenner 1977, 382–94.

4. The vision returns in "Circe" as "the morning hours" twirling Milly's skipping rope (*U* 15.4054, 4056).

5. In "Circe," the cry of "Poldy!" is repeated by Molly's apparition as Bloom "ducks and wards off a blow" from her (*U* 15.294–96)—which blow, because she is wearing those jingling "*wristbangles*" we will soon learn about (*U* 15.318), must surely produce a (yet again, unrecorded) ringing noise. It is in this moment that Bloom makes his response of "At your service," noted earlier.

6. Hart and Knuth 1976, 24. Similarly, Harriet Blodgett argues that the "Midnight chimes from distant steeples" calling "Turn again Leopold, Lord Mayor of Dublin" (*U* 15.1364) originate in the sound of a real church bell tolling the hour, 12:15 (Blodgett 1967, 28).

10. Dublin: Sun, Moon, Stars

1. The two main programs used have been Cosmos Planetarium Simulator, Version 16.01, 1992, by Gene W. Lee, and Skymap, Version 1.2, 1992–93, by C. A. Marriott. All astronomical printouts are from the Skymap program.

2. Plotted for latitude 53.34 north, longitude 6.16 west. (Compare *U* 18.2303–4.) Times are derived by adding twenty-five minutes (for Dunsink time, in effect in 1904) to the program's base Greenwich Mean Time.

3. Facing toward the sun in the southeast, he has his back to Kingstown Harbor entrance, in the northwest. That, I think, poses a problem for the intriguing suggestion made by Stephen Whittaker and Francis X. Jordan that Mulligan can pull off his whistle trick—pretending to summon the two "strong shrill whistles" that "answer" his appeal (*U* 1.26–27)—because he has seen the steam blasts coming from the whistle of the mailboat leaving the harbor and knows that the sound will follow in about five seconds. (I also wonder just how visible such a plume of steam might be at a mile's distance.) My own guess is that there has been an earlier, unrecorded, whistle or series of whistles, and that Mulligan knows from experience about how long to wait for the next one. See Whittaker and Jordan 1995, 29–31.

4. McCarthy and Rose 1988, 37. As elsewhere in this chapter, I have relied on Knuth's maps (Hart and Knuth 1976) for compass points, in addition to latitude and longitude.

5. He is still in the building, having just exited the reading room's "dark dome" (*U* 9.1026), into what, judging from photographs, should be a relatively bright area, ringed with windows; possibly the sun is shining through one of them into his face. By the time he reaches the portico outside, his eyes have had time to adjust. Something similar happens, in reverse, in "The Sisters," where a boy coming from brightness into a dim room requires some time before he can start picking out details.

6. Later calculations for this chapter take this as the base, adding other increments according to the timetable supplied by Clive Hart (1974) in his "Wandering Rocks" entry.

7. Hart further suggests that the car is parked on the north side of the street, opposite Kernan, with its windscreen facing him.

8. See Hart 1974, 198.

9. Based on Knuth's maps, the Ormond's front runs about thirteen degrees off the east-west

axis, its right side tilting to the south. With an azimuth of 255 degrees, the sun at 3:38 is just two degrees away from being on an exact parallel. At 4:00, with an azimuth of 260, it will have shifted to a position three degrees to the north; at 4:15 six degrees; at 4:30 nine degrees.

10. In fact these Dubliners seem peculiarly aware of the moon's doings, visible or not. Apart from Mrs. Breen and Stephen, in "Ithaca" Bloom will—correctly, given the time—reflect that the moon, "invisible" as it is on the far side of the earth, is "approaching perigee" (U 17.1042–43).

11. Some of my account coincides with, and some differs from, the reading given by Gifford and Seidman 1988. Whereas they believe the star-pageant to originate with an omniscient third-person observer, I am convinced that it originates in Bloom's revery, in which memories of the night sky last seen, mingling with thoughts of family, are in turn influenced by background conversation elsewhere, registered and transformed as described in chapter 8. Other disagreements are discussed in note 16.

12. The one discrepancy is that whereas Pegasus comes after Equuleus, for Bloom it is the filly who follows the foal. But no Bloom vision would be complete without some minor muddle.

13. See the next chapter for further corroboration.

14. According to the OED, "daystar" (alternately "day-star") can designate either Venus or the sun. It has the latter meaning in "Lycidas," probably the best-known source.

15. As noted earlier, so is Mars.

16. "And the equine portent grows again, magnified in the deserted heavens, nay to heaven's own magnitude, till it looms, vast, over the house of Virgo" (U 14.1097–99)—that is, the constellation Pegasus, ascending to its apogee, is over the astrological house of Virgo. After computing this backwards and forwards I have decided that it cannot be calculated with any assurance. Pegasus is a large, sprawling constellation coextensive with another constellation, Andromeda, and might be thought of as occupying two or even more houses; an astrological house—as opposed to sign—is a highly complex variable, different for different latitudes and determined by one of many possible sets of formulae; it is unclear just what the narrative means by "over," or exactly what point in the constellation's transit is being stipulated. I suspect that the main motivation behind this part of Bloom's star-reading is that he just wants to get Molly's "Virgo" in there somehow. Gifford and Seidman are surely wrong in taking this as an account of the zodiacal sign Virgo's descent in the sky as Pegasus ascends. Signs and houses, although they bear corresponding names, are astrologically distinct. Nor does it make sense to have Pegasus suddenly "arise . . . among the Pleiades," because both have been westering, at the same pace and distance apart, all night.

17. Molly, born September 8, is a Virgo; as noted above Bloom is a Taurus. The presentation of Milly and Molly as a pair of horses may have to do with the fact that Milly is a Gemini—the twins— and that her constellation is now prominent in the sky; also contributing is a chain of associations including Lynch's "Phyllis," a young woman, and Lenehan's "filly," both under more or less simultaneous discussion.

18. The same word seems to be used in the same sense at U 1.181–82: "They halted, looking towards the blunt cape of Bray head that lay on the water like the snout of a sleeping whale." In actuality the view "towards" Bray head, about seven miles to the south, is blocked by another land mass.

19. As always, there are other things going on, notably a child being sung and rocked—rockabyed—to sleep.

20. According to The James Joyce Archive, Joyce added the Muta-Juva dialogue in mid-1938, so he could have known the sky for a March morning of that year. (I think he originally planned to set

Finnegans Wake in the future, overran his target date, and as with his premonitions of World War I in *Ulysses* took advantage of the opportunity to play retroactive prophet.) The passage about the "rugaby moon," on the other hand, first appeared in April 1926. To foresee this Joyce would have had to make some calculations, or, more likely, to have consulted one of the astrologers he occasionally saw. (See Costello 1993, 318; and Wescott 1990, 101).

11. Bloom's Birth Star

1. *Pace* Gifford and Seidman (1988, 70), who raise the Taurus possibility but consider it to be counterbalanced by what they see as the suggestion that, as "watercarrier" at *U* 17.183, Bloom may share Joyce's sign of Aquarius.

2. It went by this name in Joyce's time. An 1898 volume (Clerke et al. 1898, 485) refers to it as "a very remarkable star, sometimes called the 'Blaze Star.' " Mr. Michael Poxon, of the website *Handbook of Binocular Astronomy* (freespace.virgin.net/m.poxon/hba-home.htm) informs me that it was so named by the nineteenth-century astronomer Sir John Herschel. The reason for the name is probably to be found in the observation by one astronomer of the period that it "blazed forth suddenly" (Smith and Chambers 1881, 445).

3. "The first documented outburst of T CrB [T. Corona Borealis] took place on the night of 12 May 1866 . . . Its greatest [magnitude] (circa 2.0) was reached on the same night and the star began to decline rapidly, becoming invisible to the naked eye in about eight days." (My translation, from the Italian, of an entry in website *Ottica De Maria,* Internet address www.otticademaria.it/Astronomia/Estate/C_CrB/c_crb.html.) Astronomy webmaster Jack Horkheimer confirms that, in a pattern repeated by its 1946 reappearance (for which see footnote 6 below), the star "quickly [dimmed] back to its normal invisible-to-the-naked-eye brightness." (Internet address www.jackstargazer. com, for website *Star Gazer.*) One recent guide reports that it reached a maximum magnitude of 2.0 on the first night, thus surpassing the 2.2 of the constellation's brightest star, then "began to fade rapidly" (Burnham 1978 2:708–9).

4. Although even in this case it may be noted that Bloom automatically translates "periodical" into "annual," and goes on to confirm that when one of his bends is over Doran is sober "for the rest of the year" (*U* 8.595–98).

5. Horkheimer (www.jackstargazer.com) reports that by the end of the night of May 12 "it was actually brighter than the brightest star in the Crown, Alphecca." See also the citation from Burnham in footnote 3 above.

6. Public allegorizing too: in America, much was made of the fact that it appeared just one year after the end of the Civil War; in France, one astronomer, incorrectly thinking himself the first to discover it, named it "Pax," in the forlorn hope that it would usher in an age of peace. I obtained this information from Horkheimer (see note 3 above) and the *Mes Etoiles* website (mesetoiles. fr./couronnebor.htm), respectively, on the Internet. For the superstitious, it may be of interest that T. Corona Borealis reappeared on February 9, 1946, not quite a year after the end of World War II in Europe.

7. The phrase "after incalculable eons of peregrination," I suggest, is this chapter's equivalent of "after a myriad metamorphoses of symbol."

Incidentally, it seems a good bet that in having Stephen assign a dramatic celestial event to Bloom's and Shakespeare's years of birth, Joyce was mindful that his own birth, in 1882, occurred in

282 / NOTES TO PAGES 142–49

the year of the Great September Comet, the brightest comet to appear between 1769 (which saw the births of Napoleon and Wellington, a coincidence noted in *Finnegans Wake*) and 1997.

8. Stephen uses the word because the nova in question was visible during the day. The "Oxen" voice is speaking of Venus as "harbinger of the daystar," which, because Venus is proverbially the morning star, would normally denote the sun. But this Venus "metamorphoses" into Aldebaran, the alpha star of Taurus, the constellation that was indeed in its very near vicinity at sunrise of June 17 (the "Oxen" passage has it rising "among the Pleiades," which are right next to Taurus), as it would have been on June 16 as well. I am far from sure, but the sense would seem to be that Venus is thus the "harbinger" of a star, the nova, which in its blazing brightness will temporarily resemble or rival or conjoin with Aldebaran. Complicating these speculations is the fact that Aldebaran is here situated on Taurus's "forehead," whereas the location usually assigned it is the left eye. But then, the two spots are close—could, with a minimal allowance, be considered the same spot—and Joyce had reasons for wanting it to be the forehead.

9. Not in Joyce's lifetime, that is. Nineteen eighty-five was to see the canonization of Leopold Mandic—Saint Leopold, from then on—a member of the Capuchin order who spent most of his life in Padua and was there when Joyce made his brief visit. He was renowned for the power of his faith, which was all the more striking by contrast with his dwarfish, enfeebled person. His feast day is May 12. That is because his birthday was May 12, 1866. All of which, I have to say, I find intriguing, but probably a coincidence.

12. Plotinus, Spencer Again, and the Proliferant Continuances of "Oxen of the Sun"

1. The assumption behind Crotthers' suggestion that the birth of "swineheaded" and "doghaired" offspring is caused by an "arrest of embryonic development at some stage antecedent to the human" (988–91). (As before, all parenthetical line numbers refer to "Oxen of the Sun," unless otherwise specified.) Joyce, who as I have earlier suggested may have something like this doctrine in mind when the Stephen of *Portrait* compares Lynch to a reptile, will make much of it in *Finnegans Wake*. It was a commonplace of Joyce's day—most fully presented, perhaps, in Spengler's *The Decline of the West*—that all civilizations passed through a natural cycle, from primitive infancy to a golden age of maturity to the senescence of decadence, analogous to the stages of human life. Joyce noted the prevalence of such conceptions in one of his 1912 Padua examination essays. (See *JJP* 19.)

2. As Joyce put it in an early essay, "in the history of words there is much that indicates the history of men" (*CW* 28).

3. Mommsen 1957, 1:288. As the foremost turn-of-the-century historian of the Roman Empire, Mommsen seems a likely source for Joyce's knowledge of this period.

4. Such sentiments reflect not just Bloom's private concern about his own family line. Public alarm about declining birth rates were much in the news in the war years, especially in France, where it was feared that they signaled a weakening of national vigor. Similar anxieties had been behind the campaigns of Caesar Augustus and later emperors to encourage large monogamous families. In Ireland, depopulated since the Famine, the prolific and the patriotic were sometimes rhetorically linked, a connection that may have something to do with the feeling in "Cyclops" that Bloom's failure to produce more children, and especially a surviving male heir, is not only unmanly but anti-Irish, as well as with this episode's jeremiads against contraception.

5. In an episode where national sterility equals a wasteland and propagation a cloudburst, con-

doms and other forms of birth control are invariably described as raingear, keeping out the wet (see 771–98).

6. As earlier remarked, such passages also confirm Purefoy's subordination to the earthly authority centered in the Castle.

7. These events are numerically coordinated with biblical chronology, a paragraph to a century: see my *James Joyce's Metamorphoses* (1981, 87–89).

8. Not such an original idea: In *The Planets*, Gustav Holst had done much the same two years earlier. An earlier exercise along the same lines is James Thomson's "A Walk Abroad" (Haining 1975, 165–75).

9. Given the omnipresent fatherhood theme, this identification probably owes something to the tradition that Odysseus was the son of Hermes, the Greek Mercury. Stephen, whose problematic identity as Bloom's spiritual son we are sometimes encouraged to contemplate, has the wide-brimmed hat and staff (as well as the curious learning and the wandering ways) associated with Hermes-Mercury.

10. Notwithstanding this introduction, Hermes-Mercury is the only planet whose name, as far as I can make out, is not plausibly signaled by the text of the episode. That Joyce was attending to such things seems indicated by the not-a-coincidence expression "after many *marches* environing in divers lands and sometime *venery*" (139–40; my italics). Earth and, along with his consort Juno (1134), Jupiter (slumming as Thor, the "hammerhurler," and see note 12 below), Saturn ("Cronion"—Chronus), Uranus *("coelum"*—Caelus), and Neptune ("pissedon"—Poseidon) are also sounded, as of course are sun, moon, stars, and Milky Way.

11. The traditional male symbol ♂ derives from the astrological sign for Mars's shield and spear.

12. Although Jupiter is not named here, in "Eumaeus" this juncture will be remembered as the "visitation of Jupiter Pluvius" *(U* 16.41).

13. This would be a typical kind of Joyce tip-off, especially in "Oxen of the Sun." In fact every one of the authors mentioned in Joyce's letter to Frank Budgen *(L1* 139–40) seems to have been incorporated into its text. I list the names in the order Joyce gave them. Sallust—"sallies" (804); Tacitus—"tickets" (462); Mandeville—"mandement" (137); Malory—"malady" (39); Taylor—"tailtickler" (575); Hooker —"hook" (1552); Milton—"minion" (185); Burton—"batten" (393); Browne—"brown" (480); Bunyan—"bunions" (1425); Pepys—"peep" (1547); Evelyn—"Eve" (298); Defoe—"deflowering" (344); Swift—"swift" (91); Steele—"stealeth" (261); Addison—"adenoids" (1244); Sterne—"stain" (985); Landor—"languor" (199); Pater—"paternal" (1058); Newman—"no man" (396). Besides this, almost all the authors not named in Joyce's letter but generally agreed to contribute their voices (the one exception seems to be Carlyle, unclubbable as always) are similarly named, as follows: Goldsmith—"goldsmith" (286); Chesterfield (Philip Stanhope)—"wanhope" (105); Dickens—"Dixon" (125); Lamb—"Lamb" (1580); Le Fanu—"Le Fécondateur" (778); De Quincey—"quinsy" (1425); Burke—"Burke's!" (1391); Walpole—"ywimpled" (81); Junius—"genius" (1119); Macaulay—"Malachi's" (524; see Halper 1973, 44, for Joyce's later equation of "Malachi" with Macaulay); Ruskin—"muskin" (676). Other authors are present as well, including the five most important for *Ulysses:* "anon" (891), "Moses" (247), "homer" (1418), "will" "shake" "spear" (201, 1326, 129), and "James" "Augustine" "rejoiced" (1548, 299, 883).

14. Saturn's multicolored rings ("a veil of what do you call it gossamer . . . flows about her starborn flesh and loose it streams, emerald, sapphire, mauve and heliotrope, sustained on currents of

the cold interstellar wind, winding, coiling, simply swirling" [1104–7]) and Jupiter's red spot ("it blazes, Alpha, a ruby and triangled sign upon the forehead of Taurus" [1108–9]) will be glimpsed from a distance, after we have passed into the Uranus orbit, as part of a general retrospective turn. Compare *Finnegans Wake*, where Jupiter twice appears simultaneously as god and as planet, identifiable by its red spot—once at *FW* 605.05–13, and once more at *FW* 582.28–83.03, where a rotund father-figure, his "juniper arx" heaving, displays a "Redspot" on "his browband." Likewise for Saturn, which also twice appears in simultaneously mythical and astronomical get-up: at *FW* 415.07–19 as a dancing father "soturning around," surrounded by a retinue in turn described as "the Little Newbuddies that ring his panch," and at *FW* 494.09–12, where a highly anthropomorphized picture of the solar system includes "Satarn's serpent ring system."

15. Starting at line 905, in a sequence that seems to begin with an overlapping of Saturn overtones—another father-figure, famous ("I am the murderer of Samuel Childs" [1017]) for eating his children—we hear of "patron" (905), "prince" (906), Molly's father the "gallant major" (916), Bloom as "censor of morals" (921), Bloom's former boss (926), "the Sublime Porte" (943), a royal commission (947–48), the king (961), Aristotle (975), God (1009), and, twice, "father" (957, 1033–34). (We also learn from Mulligan that "the supremest object of desire" is "a nice clean old man" [999–1000]). The second mention of "father" helps send Bloom off on a revery (1038–77) centered first on memories of his own father, Rudolph, at "the paternal ingle" (1050), then on thoughts about how he "is himself paternal" (1062).

16. Daniel Weiss has noted that the line "Calf covers of pissedon green" "unconsciously recalls the sacred oxen of Poseidon" (Weiss 1956, 6).

17. But at this writing seems on the verge of losing its planet status.

18. See Ball 1893. The word "wanderer" is used at least twice (pp. 307, 315) to designate comets; page 328 refers to their "wanderings." (The term is first used of both planets and comets, to distinguish them from fixed stars.) As with the calculations outlined in chapter 10, *The Story of the Heavens* is Bloom's main source of astronomical lore. That Joyce at least looked into it is indicated by the accurate description of its contents (*U* 10.526–28) and the borrowings from it. For instance, "Ithaca" at 17.2017 adopts Ball's statement that returning comets are "suncompelled"—in Ball's own words (p. 322) "attracted by the sun."

19. William Hutchings discerns a similar biographical narrative behind the fourth chapter of *Portrait* and draws a comparison to "Oxen of the Sun" (1978, 339–45).

20. Coming just after the first nine paragraphs, if each of the opening three groups of three chants (beginning "Deshil," "Send us," and "Hoopsa," respectively) is counted as a separate paragraph, as they clearly are in the Rosenbach manuscript and the 1961 Random House edition. The Gabler edition used in this book seems conflicted on the issue: each of the three groups concludes with a line break, signaling its separation from the next group of three, but none of them is indented. The edition's textual notes leave me confused about the reasons for this rendering. For other objections to what Carol Shloss calls the edition's "mistaken decision to print dialogue flush left with the margin," see, besides Shloss herself (1988, 66–85, especially p. 73), Kenner 1988, 17. Kenner addresses the numerological implications of the opening (now non-) paragraphs and describes the decision to remove them, based on a supposed "lost document," as "a flimsy basis for tampering." *D'accord.*

21. Compare *Finnegans Wake*, where a similarly expiring figure is invited to "Slip on your ropen color and draw the noosebag on your head" (*FW* 377.08–9).

13. Approaching Reality in "Circe"

1. For a contemporary account of these affiliated conditions, see Gowers 1907.

2. My main source for this paragraph has been Thornton 1976.

3. For the length of this chapter, all parenthetical citations not specifying episode number are to "Circe."

4. "Every one knows that a hypnotised subject is easily hallucinated" (Myers 1920, 1:179).

5. Compare "Circe," where one of Bloom's hallucinatory extravaganzas, lasting over six hundred lines, is sandwiched between two sentences spoken, probably without pause, one after the other (1353–1958).

6. Susan Kurjiaka observes that "Bloom almost hypnotizes himself" in the "Calypso" scene, in one of several instances revealing his susceptibility to hypnotic and "hypnagogic" states (Kurjiaka 1989, 53).

7. In which connection it is worth noting that, during the "De Quincey" vision reviewed in chapter 8, Bloom was in "a region where grey twilight ever descends" (*U* 14.1080–81).

8. For some pertinent present-day accounts of the condition, see Lishman 1987, 221–23; Persinger and Makarec 1987 (especially 181); Glaser 1970, 328–33; Lewis et al. 1984, 1585; Greenberg, Hochberg, and Murray 1984, 1588; and alphabetic entries under "Epilepsy" in Becker 1986. For earlier accounts, see De Watteville 1887, 731–42; and Mayo 1851, 87–121.

9. Which opens with a "deafmute idiot . . . shaken in Saint Vitus' dance" (14–15). Saint Vitus is the patron saint of epileptics.

10. That Stephen had two shots in short order is confirmed by Bloom's "Circe" reflection, about his drunken state, that the "Second drink does it. Once is a dose" (639). Given the imminence of the pub's closing, Stephen would not have had time to dilute these drinks even if he had wanted to. In fact he was, as we said in my college days, chugging it—never a good idea, and certainly not for that drink, in his state.

11. Vogt 1981, 337. Mixed with water, absinthe became milky or, poetically, "opalescent."

12. From Delahaye and Noël 1999, 36. My thanks to David Earle for making this picture available to me.

13. Corelli 1890, 122. Corelli's accounts of the absintheur's visions—of "glittering bacchantes, nude nymphs in a dance of hell, flashing torrents and dazzling mountain-peaks, of storm and terror, of lightning and rain, of horses galloping, of flags flying, of armies marching, of haste and uproar and confusion and death!" (1890, 20), along with merry-go-round, whirling planets, even a cancan show—repeatedly recall the wilder flights of "Circe."

14. Thus Bloom's explanation, in "Ithaca," of Stephen's later collapse, that it results from "inanition," "exertion," and "certain chemical compounds of varying degrees of adulteration and alcoholic strength" (*U* 17.37–38): the unadulterated absinthe on top of all that beer.

15. Accounts of absinthe-induced hallucinations especially pertinent to "Circe" may be found in Magnan 1876, 37, 41; Vogt and Montagne 1982, 1022; and Vogt 1981, 339.

16. See for instance the description of "*l'épilepsie absinthique*" in the "*Absinthisme*" entry of the 1886 edition of *La Grande Encyclopédie* 1:152. See also Magnan 1876, 25–26; Magnan 1893, 5–7, 28, 37; Boyce 1893, 1097–98; Atwater et al. 1903, 2:24. See also Vogt and Montagne 1982, 1023; and Vogt 1981, 338. Corelli also remarks that absinthe can produce "giddiness, swooning, and fits of delirium which resemble strong epilepsy" (1890, 339).

17. To facilitate which, perhaps, both have also been rendered relatively insusceptible to the more carnal lures surrounding them. Joyce's note "Absinthe weakens potency (debility)" (Herring 1972, 397) demonstrates familiarity with the widespread belief—partly responsible for its being banned in France—that absinthe reduced sexual desire. So much for Stephen; for his part, Bloom, as we have noted, is in a state of "indifference due to masturbation" (*L1* 148).

18. Which helps answer John Paul Riquelme's observation that the hallucinations of "Circe" begin before either Stephen or Bloom appears (see Riquelme 1983, 141). Yes, just as the Gerty-derived idiom of "Nausicaa" begins before Gerty (or Bloom) is introduced. From *Dubliners* on, Joycean narrative typically both emanates from some central character and operates with enough autonomy to keep going when that character is offstage. "Circe" derives not from one but from two characters by virtue of the fact that both are currently prone to the same kinds of distortion of reality.

19. Quoted by Pound in an article published in June 1922. See Read 1967, 198. Interestingly, Joyce's early draft for the "Cyclops" episode has Bloom in an open-air market looking at gutted fish and imagining them as hanged martyrs, just before experiencing the multiple martyrings of that episode (Herring 1977, 154). The final version includes only a mention of his "sloping around by Pill lane and Greek street with his cod's eye counting up all the guts of the fish" (*U* 13.213–14), along with a mock-heroic catalogue of the market, fish included (*U* 13.68–117). Though it would be asking a lot, Joyce may have expected a reader familiar with Dublin to have seen the impressions recorded during Bloom's itinerary as contributing to some of the episode's distortions.

20. For a convincing account of the origins of this focus in the theories of Romantic epistemology and aesthetics, see McGrath 1986, especially 264, 268.

21. My thanks to my colleague John Anthony for playing this piece for me on the piano.

22. Eleanor Selfridge-Field, commenting on the antiquarianism of Marcello's psalms, observes of the composition Stephen is playing that it incorporates both "a chant of the Spanish Jews and Homer's Hymn to Ceres" (Selfridge-Field 1988, 208; see also Selfridge-Field 1990, 24), and cites Marcello's statement that it had been transposed from the "hypolydian mode" to the "hypophrygian" (Selfridge-Field 1988, 215). Compare Stephen's remark on the piece (2087–93).

23. A variety of possible resinous ingredients of both perfume and hair preparations are listed in Poucher 1936, 1:288–91, 316–19, 247, and 2:374–99; and Rimmel 1845, 260.

24. The return of this famous passage from Thomas Moore's orientalist melodrama *Lalla Rookh* is doubtless also facilitated by the "oriental" music in the background. See Kershner 1998, 288–89.

25. See Kelly 1988, 59.

26. For a more thoroughly phantasmagoric example, see chapter 15.

27. And of course other details introduced in "Circe," probably or definitely non-hallucinated, are also confirmed in the pages to follow. Stephen still has a torn jacket (noted in "Circe" at 4271–72), a hurting hand, a soapsuddy handkerchief. He is remembered to have been unconscious and to have been helped out of a fix by Corny Kelleher. At the end of "Circe" he was covered with shavings, and at the beginning of "Eumaeus" he still is. Bloom still has his money, which he will duly return in an amount consistent with the "Circe" calculations.

So: if "Circe" just recycles or reshuffles the material of the previous episodes, what is all this? Precycling? Preshuffling? I suggest that instead the obvious conclusion is that *Ulysses* is continuously drawing material from a preexistent virtual field of memory and minutiae, that each episode elicits a different selection from this field, and that "Circe," including its hallucinations, is one of these episodes.

28. Although, as noted in the next chapter, Bloom has very briefly remembered the mezuzah that Virag, remembered just as "poor papa's father," used to touch.

29. For instance, "In the college he had made his first communion and eaten slim jim out of his cricketcap" (P 93)—the second detail was recorded in the original Clongowes narrative, the first was not. This is a variant of the "mnemonic flashback pattern" catalogued in Cohn 1978, 37–38.

30. A point first made in Hart and Knuth 1976, 29, who remark that Bloom in general seems to have been literally following in Stephen's footsteps.

31. In the process, surely, giving voice to the Bloom who misses Milly's presence in his home. The Blooms are undergoing what is today called "empty nest syndrome."

32. See Brandabur 1971, 47–48. For its part, *Ulysses* contains several prophecies, and all of them prove to be true. Mr. Deasy and Myles Crawford both predict World War I; publican Larry O'Rourke and a drinker in Burke's both predict the outcome of the Russo-Japanese War; as I have noted the "Defoe" voice of "Oxen of the Sun" predicts both the fire that breaks out at the end of the episode and the sex of the Purefoy newborn; Bloom inadvertently predicts the winner of the Gold Cup; Stephen has predicted *Ulysses* (and begun writing *Dubliners: U* 7.922); both Stephen and Bloom have had prophetic dreams the night before that, in their different ways, pan out or seem likely to pan out (for Stephen's, see 3929–31; for Bloom's, see chapter 18).

33. Although not by much. In "Hades" (*U* 6.741–42) Bloom knows that "*Habeas corpus*" means that somebody "has the body." As for "*carneficem*," as we will see later, Bloom's knowledge of Ponchielli's *La Gioconda* has probably familiarized him with the Italian "*carnefice.*"

34. Christy L. Burns makes much the same point in remarking on how Joyce's onomatopoeic effects "extend . . . away from phonetic realism toward an emphasis on how the ear bends a sound toward its relevant message"—for instance the "Haltyaltyaltyall" (181) of bicycle bells, heard by Bloom as a signal to stop (Burns 2000, 39). See Senn 1995, 102, for an account of stages of one Bloomian perception, registered in the narrative, as they move from one act of attention to another before reaching the final recognition.

14. "Circe" Again: Thirty-two Anomalies

1. Unless otherwise indicated, all parenthetical citations are to "Circe."

2. The expression "ring off" comes from the time when telephone operators were signaled to break a connection by rotating the crank used to call them up. MacHugh apparently does not do this. There is no ring-off "whirr," and he never says goodbye. It would be extraordinarily rude—the 1904 equivalent of slamming the phone down—to ring off someone after a curt "Come across yourself." For the mechanics of the procedure, see the "Telephone" entry of the 1911 *Encyclopedia Britannica* (vol. 25, especially p. 551) and quotations under "ring" (inflexional forms) 10.d of the *OED*. Eventually, of course, ringing off was to be replaced by the "automatic telephone receiver" of the kind that Bloom envisions installing in Flowerville (*U* 17.1525), that is, a receiver that automatically breaks the connection when hung up. In the *OED* entry just cited, an 1899 issue of *The Electrician* says of this innovation, "Ringing off is avoided, as this is performed automatically by replacing the receiver on the hook." Evidently, five years later it still had yet to reach Dublin.

3. It takes Bloom, who departs with the promise that he will be "Back in no time" (*U* 7.436), 221 lines (from *U* 7.435 to *U* 7.656) to leave the newspaper office, go around to the nearby quayside auction room, greet Keyes and negotiate with him about changes in the advertisement, and phone back

to the office. On the other hand, if we count from the moment when MacHugh tells him to come back, it takes him 334 lines (*U* 7.629 to *U* 7.963) just to make the (shorter, because not completed) return trip, going at a pace that has him "breathless" and "puffing." Normally, of course, textual length is no reliable index of clock time. But in "Aeolus" it is, more or less, because "Aeolus," especially in the sequence in question, is mainly talk, and talk can be timed. Further, it just so happens that this sequence contains the one *Ulysses* passage that Joyce, acting out O'Molloy's rendition of Taylor's speech, recorded himself, thus giving us an idea, surely, of how long he thought that speech should take. The entire sequence, from the moment MacHugh tells Bloom to "come across" to the moment Bloom shows up, is 2,650 words long, of which 1,639 are dialogue, sometimes punctuated with dramatic pauses, dramatic gestures, lulls for musings and cigarette-lightings, and so on. Joyce's recording, which comes to 463 of those 2,650 words, lasts just over four minutes. Take it as a guide to the entire sequence, read that sequence as a dramatic production, and I guarantee that you will not make it in anything like under ten minutes—and even ten minutes would require Bloom to move at a rate of no more than a foot a second, or about a mile and a half an hour. (Try it.) And he is in a hurry. On the other hand, if Bloom were finally to get the hint at the moment when MacHugh closes the telephone room door (*U* 7.908), thus shutting off all sounds of conversation, and if he were to start his sprint then, the timing of his appearance, fifty-four lines later (*U* 7.962), becomes entirely plausible.

4. And then adds, looking at Bloom, "Well, nearly all of us" (*U* 9.261). Bloom is one of the few people in his circle who has probably never heard the sound of Dodd's voice, a fact that may account for the preposterous thieves' argot (1922–23) coming from Dodd in a previous Bloom hallucination; anyone else would have known that he does not really sound like that. This language is consistent with Bloom's belief that Dodd is a "dirty" (*U* 8.1159) operator, underhanded if not underworldish.

5. Joyce's note: "Costello, big head" (Herring 1972, 222).

6. Earlier in the episode, Bloom has come close to rehearsing it, during a moment of Othello-like jealousy. Exorcising, as he thinks, Boylan, he says, "Go, go, go, I conjure you" (2725).

7. The continuation of this turn operates along the same principles. Briefly, Zoe's reference to marriage and widowers (3833) summons up a mainly Bloomian vision of the widow Dignam, confected out of the morning funeral and his later visit to her home. (Stephen contributes the "pen chivvying her brood of cygnets," doubtless emblematic of the "Swan of Avon," that appeared in his Shakespeare theory [*U* 9.160–61].) That word and that visit had produced some grim thoughts ("Strange name. [That is, "Scottish Widows"] Takes it for granted we're going to pop off first" [*U* 13.1228]) discernible behind Shakespeare's semicoherent epileptic rant "Weda seca whokilla farst" (3853), from the *Hamlet* line "None wed the second but who killed the first," spoken by a man playing a widow. The theme is female exploitation, or worse, of men, which Stephen says is the story of Shakespeare, who accordingly turns into Martin Cunningham, supposed to be Shakespeare's dead ringer and famously run ragged by an intemperate wife. But the only still-extant widower in *Ulysses* is Simon Dedalus, the "Noisy selfwilled man" (*U* 874) whose habitual obstreperousness rings through this Shakespeare's "*paralytic rage.*"

8. Concession: hearing one of the bells, Stephen probably could not have heard the other one, about a half-mile away, nor can I see how he could have made the connection. This is one association that does seem to come from elsewhere. Still, the basic conception, of "two bells . . . twang[ing] in diphthong" (*U* 3.127) is Stephen's.

9. Bloom in "Lotus-eaters," thinking of Edward VII: "Talk: as if that would mend matters" (*U* 5.876–77).

10. A complication here, similar to the one about Reuben J. Dodd's Jewishness: the real-life Lyster was not a Quaker. Still, *Ulysses* makes him one. Joyce was either in error or had reasons of his own.

11. Although both probably do reflect Bloom's take on Stephen's presence: the helmet of this stage direction, and the waistcoat, cane, and lambkin of the next (4966–67), are most likely prompted by Stephen's hat, waistcoat, ashplant, and handkerchief. (Stephen had been unable to locate that handkerchief at *U* 3.498, probably because Mulligan, after using it to wipe his razor, had thrust it back in a different pocket. Bloom will find it for him in "Eumaeus.") The point is that Stephen's mind, that is the image-forming faculty that has been manufacturing such hallucinations through- out the episode, is nowhere in evidence here.

12. Three of four, like most of the non-"Circe" examples given below, come from "Wandering Rocks," as do a disproportionate number of similar items appearing in the most frenzied passages at episode's end. This occurrence does not seem accidental. Of the preceding episodes, "Wandering Rocks" is the one not dominated by any center of consciousness, although different minds are fore- grounded at different points. It is as if, lacking any one center of psychic gravity, it was less able than the others to hold onto its material.

13. He had originally imagined them as midwives. The change to cocklepickers—and the ac- companying change of their midwife's bag to a cocklepicker's bag—probably arises from fusion or confusion with the cocklepickers who arrived on the scene shortly afterward (*U* 4.342).

14. Sometimes these roots are difficult indeed to detect. Why, as one example, does Blazes Boy- lan come out with the nonsensical "Blazes Kate!" during Bloom's hallucination of him (3750)? Here, *Finnegans Wake* supplies a helpful hint when one of the washerwomen, in a dismissive mood, says, "O, blazerskate!" (*FW* 200.04). A check with McHugh's *Annotations* gives us "blatherskate" (alter- nately "blatherskeit"), Anglo-Irish for "nonsense." So: is anyone, during the time occupied by Boylan's hallucinatory appearance, expressing the opinion that someone or something is nonsense? We cannot be sure, but the only background conversation is being carried on by Lynch, who is much given to such expressions, especially about the sort of thing, palm-reading, his companion is demon- strating. I suggest that the hallucinatory equivalent of dream-logic is at work here, that Bloom hears Lynch's "Blatherskeit," for obvious reasons transforms the first two syllables into "Blazes," then does the best he can to make the expression make sense by adding "Kate." He may also be influ- enced by the presence of Kitty Ricketts, who sometimes goes by the name of Kate.

15. Via "blue fuse," a World War I term for the long fuse of an exploding shell. Also, Egan is rolling and smoking "gunpowder cigarettes"—*Ulysses*-era cigarette tobacco was mixed with gun- powder to facilitate the burn—whose "loose tobaccoshreds" then ignite.

15. "Circe" Yet Again: An Operatic Finale

1. The transformation scenes of Christmas pantomimes clearly helped inspire the special effects on show in "Circe." So too did the surreal metamorphoses that characterized the early cinema. See, especially, Briggs 1989, who cites a number of strikingly "Circe"-like transformations from the movies of the time and points out passages in Joyce's notes for the episode that appear to be tran- scriptions of such scenes. For the animated films of the period, see Crafton 1982; for an incisive re- view of how such films influenced Joyce's transformation scenes, especially in "Circe," see Buchan 1998. Again: I believe that Joyce's main advance over this tradition was that unlike (in his assess- ment) Flaubert, he always presents his transformations as being generated by a particular con- sciousness in particular circumstances.

2. As before, all parenthetical references, unless otherwise specified, are to "Circe."

3. The rain came as the unexpected break in a long drought; therefore no one was prepared with galoshes or any other raingear (U 14.1442); therefore the brothel's recent customers have been entering with wet shoes, leaving footprints.

4. Described as a "gilt mirror." Compare the stage directions for Exiles: "Over the mantelpiece a giltframed glass" (E 15).

5. This feature is not specified in the initial inventory. See lines 4016–17 and my commentary, below.

6. Bowers 1972, 677.

7. Around 1980, at the Musical Museum of Deansboro, New York. The museum has since gone out of business and sold off its collection.

8. Like much else in this episode, the metamorphosis of Lynch's poker recalls the stage effects popular in turn-of-the-century theatre. In his Victorian Spectacular Theatre, 1880–1910 (1981, 115–16), Michael R. Booth describes Henry Irving's production of Faust, in which the swords of Faust and Mephistopheles were made to glow with electricity and send a "blue fire" between them. Joyce may be remembering some such spectacle in the stage directions for Finnegans Wake ii.1, in which Shaun/Chuff's sword flashes like lightning, "light likening" (FW 222.22–23).

9. Among Joyce's contemporaries, Conrad, Wilde, and Doyle are given to gas-jet atmospherics. Especially pertinent, considering what we have seen of Stephen's and Bloom's states, is Havelock Ellis's 1898 essay "Mescal: A New Artificial Paradise" (Ellis 1975, 180), which describes the effects of gaslight as seen by someone under the influence of mescaline: "The gas jet (an ordinary flickering burner) seemed to burn with great brilliance, sending out waves of light, which expanded and contracted in an enormously exaggerated manner. I was even more impressed by the shadows, which were in all directions heightened by flushes of red, green, and especially violet. The whole room, with its white-washed but not very white ceiling, thus became vivid and beautiful." By contrast, the "subdued and steady electric light" of another room yields nothing nearly so vivid or dynamic.

10. See note 37 to chapter 4.

11. Which as it happens complains about a camp counselor who, not wanting his campers to be "sissies," "reads to us from something called Ulysses." My thanks to Sebastian Knowles for pointing this out.

12. Just before writing this paragraph, when I was playing a recording of the music to remind myself of how it went, my (at the time) nine-year-old daughter ran into the room and began doing exactly that.

13. "Ithaca," lines 36–42: "The collapse which Bloom ascribed to gastric inanition and certain chemical compounds of varying degrees of adulteration and alcoholic strength [Stephen's lethal beer-and-absinthe one-two], accelerated by mental exertion and the velocity of rapid circular motion in a relaxing atmosphere [the whirling La Gioconda dance], Stephen attributed to the reapparition of a matutinal cloud (perceived by both from two different points of observations, Sandycove and Dublin) at first no bigger than a woman's hand." That is, Bloom blames Stephen's collapse, which will occur a few minutes after the scene under review, on drinking and whirling, whereas Stephen remembers himself as having been affected by a change in the weather. As remarked in chapter 7, there has been thundery weather around since the middle of the episode before "Circe." For the initial association between a small cloud—here imagined as the origin of one of the evening's thunderclouds—and Stephen's mother, see U 1.247–79; the passage supplies much of the material

for the "Circe" confrontation between Stephen and his mother. For a fuller treatment of this part of the subject, see chapter 18.

16. Haines's Hallucination

1. As mentioned earlier, I am convinced by Kenner's argument that *U* 14.1010–37 is an account not of Haines's showing up at the hospital but of Mulligan's story of his appearance at George Moore's soirée. See Kenner 1980, 115.

2. According to Atherton, one of Joyce's sources for this story was Thomas Hardy's poem "Panthera," in which Jesus' father, the Panthera of the title, winds up as one of his son's crucifixioners (Atherton 1955, 24).

3. The envisioned vampire of Stephen's poem is "pale"; Gerty has earlier marked Bloom's "pale" face (*U* 4.397, 13.415).

4. Vampires were a common theme in the *Grand Guignol* and other sensationalistic entertainments of the time. See, for the fun of it, Anne Rice's *Interview with the Vampire*, which features a fantasy based on one such Paris show (Rice 1977, 217–27). Stephen's "Proteus" scenario of a vampire who "comes . . . through storm his eyes, his bat sails bloodying the sea, mouth to her mouth's kiss" (*U* 3.397–98) has much in common with Dracula's entrance in the Stoker novel.

5. For innuendoes of homosexual tastes in Haines and his set, see *U* 9.1210–12, 15.4704–6.

6. See the foldout graph between pages 210 and 211 of Hart (1974).

7. Or later: both hang around the same neighborhood for the rest of the day.

8. For other Bloom testimony on the incident, see *U* 16.95–97, 249–51, 1868–71. In the last of these, Bloom warns Stephen not to trust Mulligan—again, a strange thing to say if the two have just been in a brawl.

17. "Ithaca" as the Letter *C*

1. Both capitalized and lower case. The count for the eighteen episodes of the book is as follows: (1) "Telemachus": 690 *c*'s out of 41,848 characters = 1 in 60.65; (2) "Nestor": 391 out of 25,917 = 1 in 66.28; (3) "Proteus": 567 out of 33,686 = 1 in 59.41; (4) "Calypso": 567 out of 33,4364 = 1 in 60.61; (5) "Lotus Eaters": 664 out of 36,812 = 1 in 55.43; (6) "Hades": 1,022 out of 63,362 = 1 in 62.00; (7) "Aeolus": 1,038 out of 59,710 = 1 in 57.52; (8) "Lestrygonians": 1,230 out of 73,642 = 1 in 59.87; (9) "Scylla and Charybdis": 1,108 out of 70,804 = 1 in 63.9; (10) "Wandering Rocks": 1,429 out of 75,652 = 1 in 52.94; (11) "Sirens": 1,230 out of 73,781 = 1 in 59.98; (12) "Cyclops": 2,301 out of 122,692 = 1 in 53.32; (13) "Nausicaa": 1,685 out of 92,179 = 1 in 54.71; (14) "Oxen of the Sun": 2,337 out of 115,896 = 1 in 49.59; (15) "Circe": 4,860 out of 250,542 = 1 in 51.53; (16) "Eumaeus": 2,774 out of 131,418 = 1 in 47.37; (17) "Ithaca": 4,278 out of 151,637 = 1 in 35.45; (18) "Penelope": 1,727 out of 120,700 = 1 in 69.89. I reached the totals for each chapter by having my word processor program replace the *c*'s with *cx*'s, then subtracting the original character count from the new count.

2. Other features of the Odysseus-and-the-bow story run throughout. Some examples follow:

Stretching/stringing the bow:
"they crossed both the circus before George's church diametrically, the chord in any circle being less than the arc which it subtends" (*U* 17.8–10).

"Under a row of five coiled spring housebells a curvilinear rope, stretched between two holdfasts" (*U* 17.150–51).

"he had excelled in his stable and protracted execution of the half lever movement on the parallel bars" (*U* 17.521–23).

"she sustained her blond hair for him to ribbon it for her (cf neckarching cat)" (*U* 17.896–97).

Archery—target:

"concentric circles of waterrings" (*U* 17.899).

"miniature mechanical orreries" (*U* 17.573–74)—concentric circles in three dimensions

"observing through a rondel of bossed glass . . . pedestrians, quadrupeds, veloci-pedes, vehicles, passing slowly, quickly, evenly, round and round and round the rim of a round and round precipitous globe" (*U* 17.498–502).

The shot through the row of axes:

"the odour inhaled corresponded to other odours inhaled of other ungual fragments, picked and lacerated by Master Bloom . . . each night in the act of brief genuflection and nocturnal prayer" (*U* 17.1493–96).

Toxon—Greek for "bow":

"the toxin aforesaid" (*U* 17.631).

"narcotic toxin" (*U* 17.1918–19).

3. These circles will later hover above his head as he drifts off to sleep—will, that is, correspond to the "one sole unique advertisement to cause passers to stop in wonder . . . reduced to its simplest and most efficient terms," which "habitually" forms the subject of his "final meditation" (*U* 17.1769–72). "Advertisement" comes from *ad-vert*, to turn toward, which is what Stephen and Bloom do, toward the reflection of the lamp projecting those circles, prior to launching their "trajectories" (*U* 17.1171–92).

4. One familiar to the young Joyce: his early aesthetic notes contain the sentence "Pornographic and cinematographic images act like those stimuli which produce a reflex action of the nerves through channels which are independent of esthetic perception" (Scholes and Kain 1965, 96).

5. Which, as Bloom fully understands (*U* 12.1147–48, 13.1122–24), is mainly the business of "rep-etition," or of what Pavlov was teaching modern advertising's pioneers to call "reinforcement." Re-inforcement is simply a matter of incrementally establishing and then strengthening a conditioned reflex arc. The subject who has absorbed a thousand messages associating "Coca" with "Cola" and five hundred messages associating "Pepsi" with "Cola" is correspondingly likelier to reach for the first. Bloom advances this formula—it is what he calls "the whole secret" (*U* 12.1148)—with the con-viction of someone in on one of the most commercially exploitable discoveries of his time.

6. For instance Tennyson, in *In Memoriam*, describes Arthur Hallam as "master bowman" among debating Cambridge undergraduates who, when the others could only send their arrows "slackly from the string" or at best hit "an outer ring," would always "cleave the mark." In *Portrait* (where an intemperate thought rebounding on its thinker becomes a "shaft of thought" coming "back to its bowstring" [*P* 193]), Lynch answers Stephen's aesthetic epigrams with "Bullseye" (*P* 212)! As the Tennyson passage may remind us, the comparison occurs fairly frequently in Homer.

7. Some of Joyce's working notes to "Eumaeus" and "Ithaca" suggest a continuing interest in the subject. The *Scribbledehobble* notebook entry for "Ithaca" includes the passage "plexus: psyche: li-bido: neural paths" (Connolly 1961, 161).

8. Some representative passages from Mosso: "Fatigue is a chemical process. . . . muscular exertion increases the quantity of oxygen absorbed and of carbonic acid eliminated by man" (1904, 104). And: "In the same manner as the bacteria, the cells of our body—those of the brain, for instance—give off noxious substances, and the more intense are the vital processes of the brain the more abundant are the surroundings amidst which they live, and, if one may so express it, soil the blood which, after having laved the brain, is to irrigate the nerves and cells of other parts of the body" (1904, 118). For other contemporary testimony on what is variously termed "decomposition products," "disassociations of various substances," "effete material," "carbonaceous matter," and *substances réductrices* of fatigue that "clog and poison" muscles and nerves, see also Mosso 1904, 120; Amar 1920, 212–13; Baines 1918, 18; and Ioteyko 1925, 22. For a useful survey of medical doctrine on the subject during Joyce's day, see Rabinbach 1990, especially chapter 5, "The Laws of the Human Motor," and chapter 6, "Mental Fatigue, Neurasthenia, and Civilization." See also the "Muscle and Nerve" entry in volume 19 of the 11th *Encyclopedia Britannica*, in which the by-products of fatigue are referred to as "excreta."

9. From Joyce's notes to "Circe": "depleted nerve centers" (Connolly 1961, 121).

10. And a defining symptom of locomotor ataxy, the neural disease that Joyce assigned to "Circe," was what were invariably called "lightning pains." See Osler 1917, 915.

11. As suggested by Joyce's notes to the episode, there is probably a mathematical application as well:

"Eucl space no total curvature of spine (Milly)
Lobatschewsky const. tot. curv. neg
Riemann " " " pos." (Herring 1972, 474)

It may or may not be also pertinent that, in the most famous formula of the century, C stands for the speed of light.

12. Joyce's notes to "Ithaca" include the sentence "0 produces ∞" (Herring 1972, 456). (See also Whittaker and Jordan 1995, 33, for their suggestion that the "arc of urine" coming from Stephen and Bloom "is concentric with . . . the sphere of the firmament.") Considering, incidentally, that Penelope was a famous weaver, we may hypothesize that the standard back-and-forth, in-and-out movement of a weaver's shuttle would, viewed from the side, trace a chain of ∞s. (Considering, also, that the whole point of Penelope's shuttle was that its work was never ended, it may occur to us that ∞ was the right symbol for her in at least one other sense.) Molly's number is eight—her chapter, for instance, has eight sentences—and ∞ is 8 lying (like Molly) on its side. It is also probably not accidental that an 8 is traced by the common hands-curving-inward-then-outward sign for the full female figure. (See *U* 10.564.) On page 293 of *Finnegans Wake*, ALP's pubic triangle is plotted by the partial intersection of two circles, making for a sideways-8 outline.

13. Roy Gottfried's study of Joyce's attention to "the physical object of the book," especially "those signs that are themselves the material product of a mechanical process," above all the forms of the letters themselves, has yielded a number of arresting insights (Gottfried 1995, especially 3, 4, 13, 15, 30). Gottfried also detects the word "see" in the letter C (1995, 59, 174). For other examples of Joyce's highlighting of the alphabet's "iconicity," see Füger 1997, 60–80. *Finnegans Wake*, of course, contains multiple examples. As I have observed elsewhere, in "Ithaca" Bloom's and Stephen's parallel urinations spell out Y visually (*U* 17.1194) and S auditatively (*U* 17.1197), by way of introducing us to someone whose monologue begins and ends with the word "yes." (The vowel is "suppressed,"

as in Bloom's "cryptogram" of the same episode.) Finally, it may be noted that César Abin's carica-
ture of Joyce was, at Joyce's specification, based on the outline of a question mark (Jolas 1998, 14).

14. Quoted from Crary 1990, 72.

18. Passport to Eternity

1. The muse, whatever else she is, is a woman. Introduced in the parallel "Calypso," Molly's
first utterance is "Mn" (U 4.57)—as in "Mnemonsyne."

2. Riquelme 1983, 142–46. See also Davenport 1987, 86.

3. Homer 1963, xi, 84–89. Subsequent references will be cited in the text by episode and line
number.

4. For an informative review of Phillips's career, including Ulysses, and Joyce's familiarity with
it, see Kershner 1976, 194–201.

5. As Kershner points out, Stanislaus Joyce listed Phillips as one of the writers on the Ulysses
theme whom his brother had studied (1976, 196). Indeed, James Joyce seems to have been following
Phillips's career as early as 1899 (1976, 194).

6. Phillips reduces the narrative of the Odyssey to a prologue on Olympus, an opening and closing scene set in Ithaca, and the episodes of Odysseus's departure from Calypso and his descent into
Hades. Like "Circe," the Hades scene occurs before the resolution and is the longest and most sen-
sational in the work.

7. Basic 1986, 112–13. Rather than taking "Woodshadows" as pure poetry-conditioned projection, however, I would hypothesize that the outer fringes of the cloud have begun casting scattered
patches of shadow reminiscent of the checkered shade of forests, so that the line in question results
from a synthesis of perception and paradigm rather than the imposition of one on the other. In "Nausicaa" Bloom, looking at the horizon, is not sure whether he is seeing "nightclouds" or trees (U
13.1077–78).

8. "Fergus now" is muttered, according to the directions, "thickly with prolonged vowels" (U
15.4934), a slurring that might plausibly produce something sounding like "Ferguson."

9. In "Circe" (U 15.3067–69), Bloom becomes a slave of the ruby ring.

10. It is a good bet he will have Sinbad dreams in his sleep, that for instance the citizen will appear as a man-eating giant, a Cyclops. In fact Bloom's day is in process of being transformed into an
(oriental) odyssey before the book ends. Because Bloom habitually makes himself the hero of such
stories (U 17.1755–56), he is well along toward the role assigned him by Joyce's title.

11. Burton 1934, 2:1326. See also Yared 2000, 157, who confirms that as of the beginning stages of
Finnegans Wake Joyce had marked Burton's note that Zabadiah's name "derives from Zubdah, cream
or fresh butter, on account of her plumpness and freshness." "Plump" is a word associated with
Molly. It is unlikely, incidentally, that Stephen has ever seen a real creamfruit.

12. Compare U 15.295–330, 3087–3113 with Burton 1934, 2:1287–88. Jessamine is an ingredient of
Molly's perfume.

13. As Robert Adams discovered (Adams 1967, 80–81), the "Tinbad" and "Whinbad" of Bloom's
nodding-off soliloquy were in fact features of the Arabian Nights pantomimes of the time. In fact the
odds are that most if not all of the "Sinbad" variants recorded at U 17.2322–26 are being really, audi-
bly enunciated by Bloom.

14. At FW 199.11–27, ALP is described as having brought her bedridden husband a breakfast of,

among other things, eggs, tea or coffee, and toast. She has gotten dressed up and made up for the occasion, though not, it seems, in a harem outfit. If one looks for links to the *Ulysses* story, it is at least suggestive that this breakfast includes "blooms of fisk" (*FW* 199.15–16).

19. The Mysterious Man in the Macintosh: A Prize *Titbits* Story by Mr. James Joyce

1. See, especially, Damon 1948, 220; Gilbert 1958, 170–73; Lyons 1959, 138–39; Raleigh 1959, 59–62; Duffy 1965, 183–85; Crosman 1968, 128–36; Begnal 1972, 565–68; French 1976, 186; De Vore 1979, 347–50.

2. Adams 1967, 218, 103; see also Adams 1974, 102–3; and Kermode 1979, 49–73.

3. Herring 1987, 83. Italics in original. N.B.: "to mystify Bloom and thus the reader." "Thus"? Because Bloom is confused about "parallax," we readers are duty-bound never to look it up? In any case, Herring takes the opposite position in his 1984 essay "Joyce *et le fantôme à la gabardine*" (1984).

4. A bit of a muddle here: Ellmann's M'Intosh note refers the reader to a page in Herbert Gorman's biography of Joyce that does not, in any edition consulted, contain the quotation cited. Instead, it is to be found in Ellmann's notes, dated June 1954 and on file at the McFarland Library at the University of Tulsa, from an interview with Joyce's friend Claud Sykes: "He used to ask everybody, who was the man in the mackintosh?" According to the note, Sykes's memory of this is from 1918.

5. Kelleher 1956, 8. See also John Noel Turner 1997, 94, 109.

6. See also Weiss 1956; Lennon 1958; Mason 1955; Kelleher 1956, 1–9; and Turner 1997, 83–112.

7. Of some definite candidates who have been proposed—Mr. Duffy of "A Painful Case," James Clarence Mangan, Leopold Bloom himself, James Joyce himself, the Holy Ghost, Theoclymenos (a shadowy figure in the *Odyssey*), Wetherup (a shadowy figure in *Ulysses*, about whom nothing is known except that he used to make remarks about food), and Bloom's grandfather Virag—the first five, not being grieving widowers, can be eliminated. Evidence on the last three is too insubstantial to fit any profile.

8. Molly's memory concurs: "his [Bloom's] father must have been a bit queer to go and poison himself after her still poor man I suppose he felt lost" (*U* 18.1061–62). Note also Bloom's thoughts in "Hades": "Last time I was here was Mrs Sinico's funeral. Poor papa too. The love that kills" (*U* 6.996–99). Given the Sinico context, Rudolph is clearly being remembered here as an example of someone who died for "the love that kills."

9. Although the coroner's verdict of "death by misadventure" might have been enough to gain his admittance, had Bloom *fils* insisted on the point. After all, Rudolph seems to be buried in a proper Ennis cemetery. So perhaps he has a genuine grievance against his son for not fulfilling his deathbed wish, and has shown up, like Hamlet Senior on his second visit, to see to the completion of unfinished business.

10. According to Costello 1993, 132, the Joyces had a family plot in Glasnevin.

11. See Olive Anderson, especially her reference (1987, 232) to "the belief (so often noted by folklorists) that the ghost of a suicide was restless and apt to wander." *Hamlet* itself testifies to the proverbial restlessness of the ghosts of murder victims. In *Portrait* the young Stephen imagines his room as haunted by the ghosts of murderers, and in "The Dead" Gabriel half-envisions the ghost of Michael Furey, dead for love of Gretta, standing, unrequited, outside the hotel.

12. Also that Margaret "thought she saw her in the brown habit in which she was buried" (*JJ* 133). Paddy Dignam is also buried in a brown habit. I'm not sure what such a "habit" would look

like, but M'Intosh's macintosh is brown. Like the mirror in Mrs. Dedalus's deathroom, incidentally (*U* 9.221), Mrs. Joyce's mirror was immediately covered, according to Costello, out of fear that the soul "might be carried away by the ghost of the dead, said to linger about the house until the funeral" (Costello 1993, 210). In *Ulysses* the room also has a "deathcandle" (*U* 127), supposed to frighten away ghosts. (Compare *Finnegans Wake* 295.3–7.)

13. Of which there is one instance in *Ulysses:* the "brief sharp unforeseen heard loud lone crack emitted by the insentient material of a strainveined timber table" that Bloom hears but cannot account for (*U* 17.2059–62). This is the first of the three "enigma"s that round off Bloom's day, the second one being "Who was M'Intosh?"

14. According to Peter Haining's entertaining *A Dictionary of Ghost Lore* (1984, 125), the proper term for "a tangible spirit form wearing clothes" is "materialization." Distinctive dress has long figured in popular accounts of ghost-sightings such as the American folk song "Long Black Veil." In *Portrait,* the ghost supposed to haunt Clongowes—who like scores of cases cited by Myers first appears at the exact moment of his faraway death—is identified by his "white cloak" (*P* 19) (see also note 12 above). The many ghosts of *Finnegans Wake* often come appareled: the "googoo goosth" who terrifies Kate, for instance, is wearing "his honeymoon trim" (*FW* 557.06–8). According to Haining, the word "revenant" designates spirits who "are always fully dressed in the garments they wore in life" (Haining 1984, 164).

15. The remainder of his diet may reinforce this picture. In "Wandering Rocks" (*U* 10.1272) he is seen eating "dry bread" and probably for that reason is labeled "Bartle the Bread" (*U* 14.1550) later. No one has identified "Bartle," but if the epithet is meant as a word-play on "barley bread" then it would accord more or less with M'Intosh's "Wandering Rocks" appearance, because dry bread is proverbially the fare of the destitute and barley bread is proverbially a staple of the lower orders. As the coarsest of meals barley was also supposed to be the heartiest, a belief that doubtless contributed, well into Joyce's time, to the widespread prescription of barley water for invalids. Be it noted also that before offering the blood sacrifice to the shades of Hades, Odysseus pours out libations, all sprinkled with barley (*Odyssey* 11.29–31). Finally, given "Bartle the Bread," it seems at least a suggestive coincidence that the character Bartley, in Synge's *Riders to the Sea*—which Joyce knew well, probably by heart—is discovered to have died by a woman hurrying to "give him his bit of bread."

16. This association between beef tea and revival, miraculous or medicinal, was around, apparently, from the start. The brand name Bovril was coined as an amalgam of Latin *Bovum* and "Vril," the life-sustaining elixir of Bulwer Lytton's 1871 science fiction novel *The Coming Race*. (*Finnegans Wake* apparently alludes to both book and substance at 246.11–12.) The *Evening Telegraph* of May 4, 1904, features an ad for Bovril as the most "sustaining of all food-beverages . . . a splendid protection against the inclemencies of the weather, and the most valuable aid of the doctor in convalescence." See also Jones 1959, 59, for a reproduction of an 1894 ad in which a rival brand of beef tea is shown bringing someone back from the edge of death. As such productions make clear, the idea was that beef tea distilled the essence of beef cattle, long held to be the most nourishing of foods. A similar idea, surely, adheres to the cattle's blood fed to the dead of the *Odyssey;* indeed Bloom seems to assume as much in the passage from *U* 8.729–30, quoted above.

17. "Now their [ghosts'] liberties have been greatly extended; they can go anywhere, they can manifest themselves in scores of ways . . . besides being able to do a great many things that human beings can't do, they can now do a great many things that human beings can do."—L. P. Hartley, quoted in Sullivan 1978, 1. For illustrations of Hartley's words, see Cox and Gilbert 1986. The collec-

tion includes many examples of ghosts who eat, drink, appear during daylight, and so forth. See also Finucane 1984, who notes (p. 149) that "Most apparitions recorded in our collections are quite 'normal' in appearance, voice and general behaviour."

18. See Fussel 1975, 122, for Edmund Blunden's representative account of a ghostly enemy officer of World War I, who, wearing a macintosh, shows up behind English lines. The *OED* entry for "Macintosh" includes this quotation from the July 1900 *Quarterly Review:* "The bodies of officers having been buried in macintoshes had not so disappeared."

19. I base this statement on one assumption, that Ellen Bloom was no more than forty years old when she gave birth to Leopold. That granted, the rest follows. Between sixteen and forty when Bloom was born, she would have been between ten and forty-three years younger than her husband, who was a "septuagenerian" in 1886 (*U* 18.1892), therefore between fifty and fifty-nine in 1866, the year of Bloom's birth. Other indications tend, I think, to the conclusion that the age gap was very wide: Rudolph is invariably remembered as an aged figure, and in 1866 first-time pregnancies after the age of forty were rare and cause for alarm.

20. The hostile narrator of "Cyclops," playing alliteratively on the name, remembers Rudolph Bloom as a "robbing bagman" (*U* 12.1581). According to the *OED*, a "bagman" is, definition two, a tramp (like Dusty Rhodes), and, definition three, a traveling salesman, the "bag" being derived from definition one, someone who carries a bag, such as the "case of bright trinketware" once carried by Rudolph Bloom (*U* 14.1052).

21. Therefore, like Rudolph, a grieving widower, the most prominent in Homer. Joyce's Buffalo notes read—

> Antikleia dies of grief (suicide)
> Laertes goes to country (Herring 1977, 15)—

suggesting, I think, that Laertes' retreat is something of a parallel mortification, even a substitute for suicide.

22. Homer 1950, 237, 375, 373, 248. All references are to Butcher and Lang, the translation usually employed by Joyce (Homer 1950). Joyce's notes for the "Ithaca" episode include about a dozen references to the sequence in Butcher and Lang, book 24, in which Odysseus deceives Laertes and then reveals his true identity, including the note "Laert. ashes on head" from the translation's "With both his hands he [Laertes] clutched the dust and ashes and showered them on his head, with ceaseless groaning." (See Herring 1972, 463.) From the same source, a note to "Oxen of the Sun," appearing among phrases used during the M'Intosh appearance in that episode, reads "down with the dust" (1972, 248), an accurate description of Laertes when first spotted by Odysseus. In Butler's translation, Laertes "filled both hands with the dust from off the ground and poured it over his grey head" (Homer 1968, 369). "Dust from off the ground": how distant, really, is that phrase from "Dusty Rhodes"?

23. Besides the inquest's finding of "Death by misadventure" (*U* 6.364) and Martin Cunningham's judgment of "Temporary insanity" (*U* 6.330), there is Bloom's apprehension in "Ithaca" that he might follow his father's course by committing suicide from "an aberration of the light of reason" (*U* 17.1766–67), and Molly's assessment that Rudolph must have been "a bit queer" (*U* 18.1861).

24. Rose and O'Hanlon 1989, 43. The editors note the echo of the "Hades" phrase in the "Oxen of the Sun" passage.

25. On "Pop," see Hayman 1990, 29, 108–16, 130–38.

26. Mr. John Smurthwaite, in the course of taking issue with the argument presented in this chapter, notes that Rudolph Bloom has already shown up, in "Circe," *in propria persona* (U 15.248–79), and suggests that this does not square with his separate reappearance, in the same episode, as M'Intosh. I would answer that such a double turn would be nothing exceptional for this costume-show of an episode, in which for instance Mulligan alone is recognizable, under a variety of different names and outfits, in four distinct appearances. (From e-mail and postal correspondence with John Smurthwaite.)

27. The Rosenbach manuscript of *Ulysses* shows that at one point M'Intosh was introduced as a "fellow" rather than as a "galoot," the word that appears in both Gabler and Random House editions (see also Joyce 1984, 1:222), and he is in fact later referred to as "fellow" (U 6.891). "Old fellow" (see U 1.156) is a slang term for "father," one applied to Rudolph (at U 12.1580). As for the later "galoot," it derives from the Hebrew *galut*, for *exile*—a word that certainly applies to Rudolph's life (see U 17.1907–8).

28. The Linati list is as follows: Ulysses, Elpenor, Ajax, Agamemnon, Hercules, Eriphyle, Sisyphus, Orion, Laertes etc., Prometheus, Cerberus, Tiresias, Hades, Proserpina, Telemachus, Antinoos (from Ellmann 1972, diagram between pp. 187 and 188). With the help of Gilbert's earlier schema, almost all these figures can be linked to their respective Dubliners, as follows:

"Ulysses"—Bloom.

"Elpenor"—Dignam (identified by Gilbert 1958).

"Ajax"—John Henry Menton (Gilbert).

"Agamemnon"—Parnell (Gilbert).

"Hercules"—Daniel O'Connell (Gilbert).

"Eriphyle," killed by her son, whom she then haunts (the story is partially recorded in Joyce's notes: see Herring 1972, 278)—Mrs. Dedalus, according to Mulligan's version and Stephen's guilt.

"Sisyphus"—Martin Cunningham (Gilbert).

"Orion," in Homer's Hades driving beasts across the fields of asphodel—the drover encountered on the way to Glasnevin (U 6.385–91), goading the cattle toward the river and "killing day." We have earlier seen (in chapter 8) how in "Oxen of the Sun" Bloom will imaginatively revive, indeed constellate, this figure as an agent of death.

"Laertes etc." Well?

"Prometheus"—Jesus Christ, displaying his Sacred Heart like Prometheus his liver, as pondered by Bloom: "Would birds come then and peck ..." (U 6.957); also see note 29 below.

"Cerberus"—Father Coffey (Gilbert).

"Tiresias"—aside from Laertes, the one puzzle of the list. My candidate is Reuben J. Dodd, who like Tiresias is bent over with age, walks with a cane—depictions of Tiresias always include a walking-stick—and is forever telling people what they don't want to hear.

"Hades"—John O'Connell (Gilbert).

"Proserpina"—Mrs. John O'Connell, prodigiously fertile in the fields of death (U 6.746–52).

"Telemachus"—Stephen.

"Antinoos"—Boylan.

29. For Prometheus:

> Here Tityos, Earth's giant son, lies sprawling
> Over nine acres, with a monstrous vulture
> Gnawing, with crooked beak, vitals and liver
> That grows as they are eaten . . .
> —Virgil 1951, 164

As remarked in the previous note, the "Hades" analogue to Prometheus/Tityos is the image of Jesus displaying the Sacred Heart, envisioned by Bloom as being pecked at by birds. Amid Joyce's notes listing Homeric and Virgilian "Hades" personae there appears the line "Tityos (sacred heart)" (Herring 1977, 29).

30. From Joyce's notes to "Hades," recorded in Rose and O'Hanlon 1989, 35:

> Descent into Hell
> Orpheus, Pollux, Theseus
> Herakles, Aeneas

31. "On the slow weedy waterway he had floated on his raft coastward over Ireland drawn by a haulage rope past beds of reeds, over slime, mudchoked bottles, carrion dogs" (U 6.443–44).

32. "Crowded on the spit of land silent shapes appeared, white, sorrowful, holding out calm hands, knelt in grief, pointing. Fragments of shapes, hewn. In white silence: appealing" (U 6.459–61).

Compare:

> To the bank come thronging
> Mothers and men, bodies of great-souled heroes,
> Their life-time over . . .
> " . . . There they stand, a host, imploring
> To be taken over first. Their hands, in longing,
> Reach out for the farther shore.
> —Virgil 1951, 154

33. . . . No bird Could fly above it safely, with the vapor
Pouring from the black gulf (the Greeks have named it
Avernus, or A-Ornos, meaning birdless)
—Virgil 1951, 152

In Rose and O'Hanlon 1989, 35, Joyce translates "Averne" as "birdless": his note gives the Greek spelling for the word.

34. Compare

> There are two portals,
> Twin gates of Sleep, one made of horn, where easy

Release is given true shades, the other gleaming
White ivory, whereby the false dreams issue
To the upper air.
—Virgil 1951, 175

For other echoes of the *Aeneid* in "Hades," see Schork 1997, 128–29.

35. For earlier discussion of "Circe" as an alternate "Hades," see the previous chapter.

36. The same Thomas Burke mentioned earlier, author of a story featuring a macintosh-wearing ghost.

37. The exceptions to this generalization tend to prove the rule. William Brayden, editor of the *Freeman's Journal*, Mr. O'Madden Burke (compare his appearance in "A Mother," in *Dubliners*), and Sir Frederick Falkiner all routinely carry umbrellas for ornamental reasons. Similarly, Cashel . . . Farrell, Dublin's mad pedestrian, always carries his "stickumbrellandustcoat." The umbrella carried by one of the women Stephen sees on the shore becomes, in his "Parable of the Plums," a symptom of old-maidish timidity *(U* 7.937–39). The "raincaped watch" of "Circe" *(U* 15.674) likely began their shift after the weather turned.

38. As he puts it, "it runs in our family" *(U* 15.2783). That is why he carries around his "heirloom," the shriveled potato, so dry that it will, according to the theory, suck up the excess moisture in the air, thus reducing the main environmental cause of rheumatism and similar conditions. According to Bloom, it is because he surrendered that potato that he has since suffered an attack of sciatica *(U* 15.2794–96). As for "runs in our family": The only person in *Ulysses* beside M'Intosh seen wearing a macintosh is the apparition of Lipoti Virag, Bloom's grandfather and Rudolph's father *(U* 15.2306–7). When an affliction runs in the family, might we not expect the standard remedies—for instance a potato, for instance a raincoat—to do so as well?

20. Seeing Things in *Finnegans Wake*

1. Laughlin 1934, 160. Other passages from the same source relevant to Joyce's own case: "The patient first sees smoke in front of the eye, which appears suddenly after the loss of one eye. The trouble can disappear for hours, or even whole days, when the patient is distracted by gay emotions and is in good health. He later sees black objects floating which disappear as the sight is lost . . . Still later a candle-light produces a rainbow. After this, pain is felt as if the eyeball were splitting; it becomes immovable, loses its black color and is curded" (148). "As given by the patient, the symptoms were fiery and prismatic spectra; misty indistinct vision, may be able to distinguish objects only on one side; may have pain across forehead which increases. It is often found after rheumatic symptoms as pains in the teeth and head" (151).

2. From a representation of such an operation in Fox 1904, 250.

3. All parenthetical citations are to *Finnegans Wake*.

4. See chapter 14, 181–83.

5. Quoted in Garvin 1976, 108. Joseph Holloway also remarked on the young Joyce's "weird penetrating eyes" (quoted in Stephenson and Waters 1999–2000, 173).

6. Especially when he has "caught at" the "calamum" (302.15–16): "calamus," a writer's reed, "coolaman," an aborigine learning to write, and, because writing replaces and mimics talk, "mum" and "mumming."

7. See first citation in the *OED* entry.

8. My thanks, again, to Austin Briggs Jr. for first pointing this out to me.

9. Poincaré, on the nebular hypothesis: "In spite of the objections which have been urged against it, in spite of the discoveries which astronomers have made and which would indeed astonish Laplace himself, it is always standing the strain, and it is the hypothesis which best explains the facts." I found this quotation on the *Blackmask Online* website but have been unable to locate the original passage. Other Poincaré statements, however, are consistent with it: see Poincaré 1911, 82, and the review of his thinking on the subject in Brush 1996, 122–33. On Joyce and Poincaré, see Mackey 1999, 58.

References

Primary Sources

Berrone, Louis, ed. 1977. *James Joyce in Padua.* New York: Random House.
Ellmann, Richard, ed. 1966. *Letters of James Joyce.* Vols. 2, 3. New York: Viking Press.
——. 1975. *Selected Letters of James Joyce.* New York: Viking Press.
——. 1982. *James Joyce.* New York: Oxford Univ. Press.
Gilbert, Stuart, ed. 1966. *Letters of James Joyce.* Vol. 1. New York: Viking Press.
Joyce, James. 1961. *Exiles.* New York: Viking Press.
——. 1963. *Stephen Hero.* Edited by Theodore Spencer. New York: New Directions.
——. 1964. *A Portrait of the Artist as a Young Man.* Edited by Chester G. Anderson and Richard Ellmann. New York: Viking Press.
——. 1965. *Finnegans Wake.* New York: Viking Press.
——. 1967. *"Dubliners": Text, Criticism, and Notes.* Edited by Robert Scholes in consultation with Richard Ellmann. New York: Viking Press.
——. 1984. *Ulysses: A Critical and Synoptic Edition.* Prepared by Hans Walter Gabler with Wolfhard Steppe and Claus Melchior. New York: Vintage Books.
——. 1986. *Ulysses: The Corrected Text.* Edited by Hans Walter Gabler with Wolfhard Steppe and Claus Melchior. New York: Vintage Books.
——. 1987. *Collected Poems.* New York: Viking Press.
Mason, Ellsworth, and Richard Ellmann, eds. 1959. *The Critical Writings of James Joyce.* New York: Viking Press.

Secondary Sources

Adams, Robert M. 1967. *Surface and Symbol: The Consistency of James Joyce's* Ulysses. New York: Oxford Univ. Press.
——. 1974. "Hades." In *James Joyce's* Ulysses: *Critical Essays,* edited by Clive Hart and David Hayman, 91–114. Berkeley: Univ. of California Press.
Amar, Jules. 1920. *The Human Motor, or The Scientific Foundations of Labour and Industry.* London: George Routledge and Sons.
Anderson, Margaret. 1990. "James Joyce in Paris." In *James Joyce: Interviews and Recollections,* edited by E. H. Mikhail, 133–36. London: Macmillan.

Anderson, Olive. 1987. *Suicide in Victorian and Edwardian England.* Oxford, U.K.: Clarendon Press.

Atherton, J. S. 1955. *"Finnegans Wake:* The 'Gist of the Pantomime.' " *Accent* 15: 14–26.

———. 1974a. *The Books at the Wake.* Mamaroneck, N.Y.: Paul P. Appel.

———. 1974b. "Oxen of the Sun." In *James Joyce's* Ulysses: *Critical Essays,* edited by Clive Hart and David Hayman, 313–39. Berkeley: Univ. of California Press.

Attridge, Derek. 2001. *Joyce Effects: On Language, Theory, and History.* Cambridge, U.K.: Cambridge Univ. Press.

Attridge, Derek, and Daniel Ferrer. 1984. "Introduction: Highly Continental Enevements." In *Post-Structuralist Joyce: Essays from the French,* edited by Derek Attridge and Daniel Ferrer, 1–13. Cambridge, U.K.: Cambridge Univ. Press.

Atwater, W. O., John S. Billings, H. P. Bowditch, R. H. Chittenden, and W. H. Welch. 1903. *Physiological Aspects of the Liquor Problem.* 2 vols. Boston: Houghton Mifflin.

Baines, Arthur E. 1918. *Electro-Pathology and Therapeutics.* London: Ewart, Seymour, and Co.

Ball, Robert. 1893. *The Story of the Heavens.* London: Cassell and Co.

Basic, Sonja. 1986. "Transparent or Opaque? The Reader of *Ulysses* Between Involvement and Distanciation." In *International Perspectives on James Joyce,* edited by Gottlieb Gaiser, 106–31. Troy, N.Y.: Whiston Publishing.

Bays, Gwendolyn. 1964. *The Orphic Vision: Seer Poets from Novalis to Rimbaud.* Lincoln: Univ. of Nebraska Press.

Beck, Warren. 1969. *Joyce's Dubliners: Substance, Vision, and Art.* Durham, N.C.: Duke Univ. Press.

Becker, E. Lovell, ed. 1986. *International Dictionary of Medicine and Biology.* New York: John Wiley and Sons.

Begnal, Michael H. 1972. "The Mystery Man of *Ulysses.*" *Journal of Modern Literature* 10: 565–68.

Benstock, Bernard. 1982. "On the Nature of Evidence in *Ulysses.*" In *James Joyce: An International Perspective,* edited by Suheil Badi Bushrui and Bernard Benstock, 46–64. Totowa, N.J.: Barnes and Noble.

Benstock, Bernard, and Shari Benstock. 1982. "The Benstock Principle." In *The Seventh of Joyce,* edited by Bernard Benstock, 10–22. Bloomington: Univ. of Indiana Press.

Bickerton, Derek. 1968. "James Joyce and the Development of Interior Monologue." *Essays in Criticism* 18: 32–46.

Binet, Alfred. 1894. *The Psychic Life of Micro-Organisms: A Study in Experimental Psychology.* Translated by Thomas McCormack. Chicago: Open Court Publishing Co.

Blair, Thomas A. 1943. *Weather Elements: A Text in Elementary Meteorology.* New York: Prentice-Hall.

Blodgett, Harriet. 1967. "Joyce's Time Mind in *Ulysses:* A New Emphasis." *James Joyce Quarterly* 5: 22–29.

Boheemen-Saaf, Christine van. 1988. "Joyce, Derrida, and the Discourse of 'the Other.' "

In *James Joyce: The Augmented Ninth*, edited by Bernard Benstock, 88–102. Syracuse, N.Y.: Syracuse Univ. Press.

Booth, Michael R. 1981. *Victorian Spectacular Theatre, 1880–1910*. Boston: Routledge and Kegan Paul.

Bowen, Zack. 1967. " 'The Bronzegold Sirensong': A Musical Analysis of the Sirens Episode in James Joyce's *Ulysses*." In *Literary Monographs*, no. 1, edited by Eric Rothstein and Thomas K. Dunseath, 255–98. Madison: Univ. of Wisconsin Press.

Bowers, Q. David. 1972. *Encyclopedia of Automatic Musical Instruments*. Vestal, N.Y.: Vestal Press.

Boyce, Rupert. 1893. "The Seat of Origin and Paths of Conduction of the Fits in Absinthe Epilepsy." *British Medical Journal*, Nov. 18, 1097–98.

Brandabur, Edward. 1971. *A Scrupulous Meanness: A Study of Joyce's Early Work*. Urbana: Univ. of Illinois Press.

Briggs, Austin Jr. 1989. " 'Roll Away the Reel World, the Reel World': 'Circe' and Cinema." In *Coping with Joyce: Essays from the Copenhagen Symposium*, edited by Morris Beja and Shari Benstock, 145–57. Columbus: Ohio State Univ. Press.

Brush, Stephen G. 1996. *Nebulous Earth: The Origin of the Solar System and the Core of the Earth from Laplace to Jeffreys*. Cambridge, U.K.: Cambridge Univ. Press.

Buchan, Suzanne. 1998. "Graphic and Literary Metamorphosis: Animation Technique and James Joyce's *Ulysses*." *Animation Journal*, Fall, 21–34.

Budgen, Frank. 1967. *James Joyce and the Making of Ulysses*. Bloomington: Indiana Univ. Press.

Burnham, Robert Jr. 1978. *Burnham's Celestial Handbook: An Observer's Guide to the Universe Beyond the Solar System*. New York: Dover Publications.

Burns, Christy L. 2000. *Gestural Politics: Stereotype and Parody in Joyce*. Albany: State Univ. of New York Press.

Burton, Richard F. 1934. *The Book of the Thousand Nights and a Night*. 6 vols. New York: Heritage Press.

Chaucer, Geoffrey. 1987. *The Book of the Duchess*. In *The Riverside Chaucer*, edited by Larry D. Benson, 329–46. Boston: Houghton Mifflin.

Clerke, Agnes M., A. Fowler, and J. Ellard Gore. 1898. *Astronomy*. New York: D. Appleton.

Cohn, Dorrit. 1978. *Transparent Minds*. Princeton, N.J.: Princeton Univ. Press.

Comens, Bruce. 1992. "Narrative Nets and Lyric Flights in Joyce's *A Portrait*." *James Joyce Quarterly* 29: 297–314.

Connolly, Thomas. 1961. *James Joyce's Scribbledehobble: The Ur-Workbook for Finnegans Wake*. Evanston, Ill.: Northwestern Univ. Press.

Connor, James A. 1993. "Radio Free Joyce: *Wake* Language and the Experience of Radio." *James Joyce Quarterly* 31: 825–44.

Cope, Jackson I. 1981. *Joyce's Cities: Archaeologies of the Soul*. Baltimore, Md.: Johns Hopkins Univ. Press.

Corelli, Marie. 1890. *Wormwood*. New York: H. M. Caldwell.

Costello, Peter. 1993. *James Joyce: The Years of Growth, 1882–1915*. New York: Pantheon.

Cox, Michael, and R. A. Gilbert. 1986. *The Oxford Book of English Ghost Stories*. New York: Oxford Univ. Press.

Crafton, Donald. 1982. *Before Mickey: The Animated Film, 1893–1928*. Cambridge, Mass.: MIT Press.

Crary, Jonathan. 1990. *Techniques of the Observer: On Vision and Modernity in the Nineteenth Century*. Cambridge, Mass.: MIT Press.

Crosman, Robert. 1968. " 'Who Was M'Intosh?' " *James Joyce Quarterly* 6: 128–36.

Damon, S. Foster. 1948. "The Odyssey in Dublin." In *James Joyce: Two Decades of Criticism*, edited by Seon Givens, 203–42. New York: Vanguard Press.

Darwin, Charles. 1888. *The Descent of Man and Selection in Relation to Sex*. 2 vols. London: John Albermarle.

Davenport, Guy. 1987. "The Scholar as Critic." In *Every Force Evolves a Form*, 84–98. San Francisco: North Point Press.

Dawson, Hugh J. 1988. "Thomas MacGreevy and Joyce." *James Joyce Quarterly* 25: 305–22.

Day, Robert A. 1998. "The Villanelle Perplex: Reading Joyce." In *Critical Essays on James Joyce's* A Portrait of the Artist as a Young Man, edited by Philip Brady and James F. Carens, 52–67. New York: C. K. Hall and Co.

Deane, Vincent, Daniel Ferrer, and Geert Lernout, eds. 2001. *James Joyce: The* Finnegans Wake *Notebooks at Buffalo: Notebooks 6.B.6 and VI.B.10*. Turnhout, Belgium: Brepols Publishers.

De Guaïta, Stanislas. 1895. *Au seuil du mystere*. Paris: Chaumel.

Delahaye, Marie-Claude, and Benoît Noël. 1999. *L'absinthe: muse des peintres*. Paris: Les edition de l'Amateur.

Devlin, Kimberly J. 2002. *James Joyce's "Fraudstuff."* Gainesville: Univ. Press of Florida.

De Vore, Lynn. 1979. "A Final Note on M'Intosh." *James Joyce Quarterly* 16: 347–50.

De Watteville, A. 1887. "Sleep and Its Counterfeits." *Fortnightly Review* 47: 732–42.

Dickens, Charles. 1908. *A Child's History of England*. London: T. Nelson.

———. 1986. *The Posthumous Papers of the Pickwick Club*. Oxford: Clarendon Press.

Downing, Gregory M. 1998. "Richard Chevenix Trench and Joyce's Historical Study of Words." *Joyce Studies Annual*, 37–68

Duffy, John J. 1965. "The Painful Case of M'Intosh." *Studies in Short Fiction* 2: 183–85.

Ellis, Havelock. 1975. "Mescal: A New Artificial Paradise." In *The Hashish Club: An Anthology of Drug Literature*, edited by Peter Haining, 175–89. London: Peter Owen.

Ellmann, Richard. 1972. *Ulysses on the Liffey*. New York: Oxford Univ. Press.

———. 1977. *The Consciousness of Joyce*. New York: Oxford Univ. Press.

Encyclopedia Britannica. 1946. Chicago: Encyclopedia Britannica, Inc.

Ferrer, Daniel. 1984. "Circe, Regret and Regression." In *Post-Structuralist Joyce: Essays from the French*, edited by Derek Attridge and Daniel Ferrer, 127–44. Cambridge, U.K.: Cambridge Univ. Press.

———. 1988. "Characters in *Ulysses*: 'The featureful perfection of imperfection.' " In

James Joyce: The Augmented Ninth, edited by Bernard Benstock, 148–51. Syracuse, N.Y.: Syracuse Univ. Press.

Feshbach, Sidney. 1998. "A Slow and Dark Birth: A Study of the Organization." In *Critical Essays on James Joyce's* A Portrait of the Artist as a Young Man, edited by Philip Brady and James F. Carens, 130–41. New York, C. K. Hall and Co.

Finucane, R. C. 1984. *Appearances of the Dead: A Cultural History of Ghosts*. Buffalo, N.Y.: Prometheus Books.

Foster, Edward. 1886. *The Arabian Nights' Entertainment*. New York: D. Appleton.

Fox, L. Webster. 1904. *Diseases of the Eye*. New York: D. Appleton.

Franklyn, Julian. 1967. *Shield and Crest*. London: MacGibbon and Kee.

Frazer, James George. 1935. *The Golden Bough: A Study in Magic and Religion*. 12 vols. New York: Macmillan.

French, Marilyn. 1976. *The Book as World: James Joyce's* Ulysses. Cambridge, Mass.: Harvard Univ. Press.

Füger, Wilhelm. 1986. "Bloom's Other Eye." *James Joyce Quarterly* 23: 209–17.

———. 1997. "Scriptsigns: Variants and Cultural Contexts of Iconicity in Joyce." *Joyce Studies Annual*, 60–80.

Fussel, Paul. 1975. *The Great War and Modern Memory*. New York: Oxford Univ. Press.

Gabler, Hans Walter. 1998. "The Genesis of *A Portrait of the Artist as a Young Man*." In *Critical Essays on James Joyce's* A Portrait of the Artist as a Young Man, edited by Philip Brady and James F. Carens, 83–12. New York: G. K. Hall.

Galopin, Augustin. 1889. *Le parfum de la femme*. Paris: E. Dentu.

Garvin, John. 1976. *James Joyce's Disunited Kingdom and the Irish Dimension*. Dublin: Gill and Macmillan.

Gifford, Don, with Robert J. Seidman. 1988. Ulysses *Annotated: Notes for James Joyce's* Ulysses. Berkeley: Univ. of California Press.

Gilbert, Stuart. 1958. *James Joyce's* Ulysses. New York: Vintage Books.

Gillet, Louis. 1949. "Stèle pour James Joyce." In *A James Joyce Yearbook*, edited by Maria Jolas, 32–46. Paris: Transition Press.

Glaser, Gilbert H. 1970. "Epilepsy and Disorders of Perception." *Research Publications: Association for Research in Nervous and Mental Disease* 48: 318–33.

Glasheen, Adaline. 1954. "*Finnegans Wake* and the Girls from Boston, Mass." *Hudson Review* 7: 89–96.

Gleason, Paul. 1999. "Dante, Joyce, Beckett, and the Use of Memory in the Process of Literary Creation." *Joyce Studies Annual*, 104–42.

Gottfried, Roy. 1995. *Joyce's Iritis and the Irritated Text: The Dislexic* Ulysses. Gainesville: Univ. Press of Florida.

———. 2002. *Joyce's Comic Portrait*. Gainesville: Univ. Press of Florida.

Goldberg, S. L. 1969. *The Classical Temper: A Study of James Joyce's* Ulysses. New York: Barnes and Noble.

Goodavage, Joseph F. 1968. *Write Your Own Horoscope*. New York: Signet.

Gordon, John. 1981. *James Joyce's Metamorphoses*. Dublin: Gill and Macmillan.

———. 1982. *Notes on Issy*. Colchester, U.K.: A Wake Newslitter Press.

———. 1986. Finnegans Wake: *A Plot Summary*. Syracuse, N.Y.: Syracuse Univ. Press.

———. 1993. "Royal Losers." *Joyce Studies Annual*, 213–16.

Gorrio, Tobia [Arrigo Boito]. 1996. *Libretto for* La Gioconda. Translated by Walter Duclous. New York: Ricordi.

Gowers, William R. 1907. *The Borderland of Epilepsy*. London: J. and A. Churchill.

Grace, Sherrill E. 1988. "Rediscovering Mrs. Kearney: An Other Reading of 'A Mother.' " In *James Joyce: The Augmented Ninth*, edited by Bernard Benstock, 273–81. Syracuse, N.Y.: Syracuse Univ. Press.

Greenberg, Donna B., Fred H. Hochberg, George B. Murray. 1984. "The Theme of Death in Complex Partial Seizures." *American Journal of Psychiatry* 141 (Dec.): 1587–89.

Gutherie, W.K.C. 1966. *Orpheus and Greek Religion*. New York: W. W. Norton.

Haining, Peter, ed. 1975. *The Hashish Club: An Anthology of Drug Literature*. London: Peter Owen.

———. 1984. *A Dictionary of Ghost Lore*. Englewood Cliffs, N.J.: Prentice-Hall.

Halper, Nathan. 1973. "Malachi Again." *A Wake Newslitter* 10: 44.

Hampson, R. G. 1994. "Toft's Cumbersome Whirligig: Hallucinations, Theatricality, and Mnemotechnic in V.A.19 and the First Edition Text of 'Circe.' " In *Reading Joyce's "Circe,"* edited by Andrew Gibson, 143–78. Amsterdam, The Netherlands: Rodopi.

Hart, Clive. 1962a. "Explications, for the Greeter Glossary of Code." *A Wake Newslitter* 1 (Mar.): 3–9.

———. 1962b. *Structure and Motif in* Finnegans Wake. London: Faber and Faber.

———. 1974. "Wandering Rocks." In *James Joyce's* Ulysses: *Critical Essays*, edited by Clive Hart and David Hayman, 181–216. Berkeley: Univ. of California Press.

———. 2002. "Chiastic Patterns in 'Wandering Rocks.' " In *Joyce's Wandering Rocks, European Joyce Studies*, vol. 12, edited by Andrew Gibson and Steven Morrison, 17–26. Amsterdam, The Netherlands: Rodopi.

Hart, Clive, and Leo Knuth. 1976. *A Topographical Guide to James Joyce's* Ulysses. Colchester, U.K.: Wake Newslitter Press.

Hayman, David. 1970. Ulysses: *The Mechanics of Meaning*. Englewood Cliffs, N.J.: Prentice-Hall.

———. 1974. "Cyclops." In *James Joyce's* Ulysses: *Critical Essays*, edited by Clive Hart and David Hayman, 243–76. Berkeley: Univ. of California Press.

———. 1978. *A Facsimile of Buffalo Notebooks VI.B.9-VI.B.12*. New York: Garland Press.

———. 1982. "Joyce → Beckett/Joyce." In *The Seventh of Joyce*, edited by Bernard Benstock, 37–43. Bloomington: Indiana Univ. Press.

———. 1990. *The Wake in Transit*. Ithaca, N.Y.: Cornell Univ. Press.

Heath, Stephen. 1984. "Ambiviolences: Notes for Reading Joyce." In *Post-Structuralist Joyce: Essays from the French*, edited by Derek Attridge and Daniel Ferrer, 31–68. Cambridge, U.K.: Cambridge Univ. Press.

Herring, Phillip. 1972. *Joyce's* Ulysses *Notesheets in the British Museum.* Charlottesville: Univ. of Virginia Press.

———, ed. 1977. *Joyce's Notes and Early Drafts for* Ulysses: *Selections from the Buffalo Collection.* Charlottesville: Univ. of Virginia Press.

———. 1984. "Joyce et le fanôme à la gabardine." *Europe: revue littéraire mensuelle,* 657–58, 25–29.

———. 1987. *Joyce's Uncertainty Principle.* Princeton, N.J.: Princeton Univ. Press.

Higgins, Lesley. 1997. " 'Lovely Seaside Girls' or 'Sweet Murderers of Men': Fatal Women in *Ulysses.*" In *Gender in Joyce,* edited by Jolanta W. Wawrzycka and Marlena G. Corcoran, 47–61. Gainesville: Univ. Press of Florida.

Hitchens, Christopher. 2000. "Lord Trouble." *New York Review of Books,* 11 Sept., 26–28.

Homer. 1950. *The Odyssey.* Translated by S. H. Butcher and A. Lang. New York: Modern Library.

———. 1963. *The Odyssey.* Translated by Robert Fitzgerald. New York: Doubleday.

———. 1968. *The Odyssey.* Translated by Samuel Butler. New York: AMS Press.

Hunter, Jefferson. 2002. *How to Read* Ulysses, *and Why.* New York: Peter Lang.

Hutchings, William. 1978. "Ontogenesis/Phylogenesis: The Pattern of Historical Development in Chapter 4 of *A Portrait.*" *James Joyce Quarterly* 15: 339–45.

Ioteyko, Josefa. 1925. *La Fatigue.* Paris: Flammarion.

Iser, Wolfgang. 1974. *The Implied Reader: Patterns of Communication in Prose Fiction from Bunyan to Beckett.* Baltimore, Md.: Johns Hopkins Univ. Press.

Jackson, John Wyse, and Peter Costello. 1997. *John Stanislaus Joyce: The Voluminous Life and Genius of James Joyce's Father.* New York: St. Martin's Press.

James, William. 1950. *Principles of Psychology.* 2 vols. New York: Dover Press.

Jeans, James Hopwood. 1946. "Cosmogony." *Encyclopedia Britannica,* 6:488–93. Chicago: Encyclopedia Britannica, Inc.

Jolas, Eugene. 1998. "Remembering James Joyce." *Modernism/Modernity* 5: 2–29.

Jones, Edgar F. 1959. *Those Were the Good Old Days.* New York: Simon and Schuster.

Joyce, P. W. 1903. *A Social History of Ireland.* London: Longmans, Green and Co.

Joyce, Stanislaus. 1950. *Recollections of James Joyce.* Translated by Ellsworth Mason. New York: New York James Joyce Society.

———. 1958. *My Brother's Keeper: James Joyce's Early Years.* New York: Viking Press.

Kaplan, Fred. 1975. *Dickens and Mesmerism: The Hidden Springs of Fiction.* Princeton, N.J.: Princeton Univ. Press.

Kelleher, John V. 1956. "Notes on *Finnegans Wake* and *Ulysses.*" *Analyst* 10: 1–9.

Kelly, Dermot. 1988. *Narrative Strategies in Joyce's* Ulysses. Ann Arbor, Mich.: UMI Research Press.

Kenner, Hugh. 1956. *Dublin's Joyce.* Boston: Beacon Press.

———. 1977. "The Rhetoric of Silence." *James Joyce Quarterly* 14: 382–94.

———. 1978. *Joyce's Voices.* Berkeley: Univ. of California Press.

———. 1980. *Ulysses.* London: George Allen and Unwin.

————. 1988. "Reflections on the Gabler Era." *James Joyce Quarterly* 26: 11–20.

Kermode, Frank. 1979. *"The Genesis of Secrecy: On the Interpretations of Narrative.* Cambridge, Mass.: Harvard Univ. Press.

Kershner, R. Brandon. 1976. "Joyce and Stephen Phillips' *Ulysses.*" *James Joyce Quarterly* 13: 194–201.

————. 1998. "*Ulysses* and the Orient." *James Joyce Quarterly* 35: 273–96.

King, Mary C. 1998. "Hermeneutics of Suspicion: Nativism, Nationalism, and the Language Question in 'Oxen of the Sun.' " *James Joyce Quarterly* 35: 349–72.

Kurjiaka, Susan. 1989. "The Hypnagogic State in *Ulysses.*" *Mount Olive Review* 3: 50–58.

La Grande Encyclopédie: Inventaire Raisonné des Sciences, des Lettres et des Arts. 1886. Paris: H. Lamirault.

Laughlin, Robert Clark. 1934. "Glaucoma: A Historical Essay." *Bulletin of the Institute of the History of Medicine* 2/3: 141–63.

Lawrence, Karen. 1980. " 'Aeolus': Interruption and Inventory." *James Joyce Quarterly* 17: 389–405.

————. 1981. *The Odyssey of Style in* Ulysses. Princeton, N.J.: Princeton Univ. Press.

Lennon, Michael J. 1958. "The End of the 'Oxen of the Sun.' " *Analyst* 15: 14–16.

Leonard, Garry. 1997. "The Masquerade of Gender: Mrs. Kearney and the 'Moral Umbrella' of Mr. O'Madden Burke." In *Gender in Joyce,* edited by Jolanta W. Wawrzycka and Marlena G. Corcoran, 139–49. Gainesville: Univ. Press of Florida.

Lernout, Geert. 1990. *The French Joyce.* Ann Arbor: Univ. of Michigan Press.

————. 2000–2001. "Richard Wagner's *Tristan und Isolte* in the Genesis of *Finnegans Wake.*" *James Joyce Quarterly* 38: 143–55.

Levin, Harry. 1960. *James Joyce: A Critical Introduction.* Norfolk, Conn.: New Directions.

Levinson, Michael. 1998. "Stephen's Diary, the Shape of Life." In *Critical Essays on James Joyce's* A Portrait of the Artist as a Young Man, edited by Philip Brady and James F. Carens, 36–51. New York: C. K. Hall and Co.

Lewis, Dorothy Otnow, Marilyn Feldman, Margo Greene, and Yvonne Martinez-Mustardo. 1984. "Psychomotor Epileptic Symptoms in Six Patients with Bipolar Mood Disorders." *American Journal of Psychiatry* 141: 1583–86.

Lishman, William Allyn. 1987. *Organic Psychiatry: The Psychological Consequences of Cerebral Disorder.* Oxford, U.K.: Blackwell Scientific Publications.

Lodge, Oliver J. 1916. *Raymond, or Life and Death, with Examples of the Evidence for Survival of Memory and Affection after Death.* New York: George H. Doran.

Lyons, John O. 1959. "The Man in the Macintosh." *A James Joyce Miscellany, Second Series,* edited by Marvin Magalener, 138–39. Carbondale: Southern Illinois Univ. Press.

MacCabe, Colin. 1979. *James Joyce and the Revolution of the Word.* New York: Barnes and Noble.

Mackey, Peter. 1999. *Chaos Theory and James Joyce.* Gainesville: Univ. Press of Florida.

Magalener, Marvin, and Richard M. Kain. 1956. *Joyce: The Man, the Work, the Reputation.* New York: New York Univ. Press.

Magnan, V. 1876. *On Alcoholism: The Various Forms of Alcoholic Delirium and Their Treatment.* Translated by W. S. Greenfield. London: H. K. Lewis.

————. 1893. *Recherches sur les centres nerveux: Alcoolisme, folie des héréditaires dégenerés paralysie génerale, médecine légale.* Paris: Libraire de L'Académie de Médecine.

Mandle, W. F. 1987. *The Gaelic Athletic Association and Irish Nationalist Politics, 1884–1924.* Dublin: Gill and Macmillan.

Mason, Ellsworth. 1955. "The Oxen of the Sun." *Analyst* 10: 10–18.

Mayo, Herbert. 1851. *On the Truths Contained in Popular Superstitions, with an Account of Mesmerism.* Edinburgh, Scotland: Blackwood.

McArthur, Murray. 1998. "The Origin of the Work of Art in *Portrait* V." In *Images of Joyce,* edited by Clive Hart, C. George Sandulescu, Bonnie K. Scott, and Fritz Senn, 2:450–64. Gerrards Cross, U.K.: Colin Smythe.

McBride, Margaret. 1996. "*Finnegans Wake:* The Issue of Issy's Schizophrenia." *Joyce Studies Annual,* 145–75.

McCarthy, Jack, with Danis Rose. 1988. *Joyce's Dublin: A Walking Guide to* Ulysses. Dublin: Wolfhound Press.

McGee, Patrick. 1988. *Paperspace: Style as Ideology in Joyce's* Ulysses. Lincoln: Univ. of Nebraska Press.

McGrath, F. C. 1986. "Laughing in His Sleeve: The Sources of Stephen's Aesthetics." *James Joyce Quarterly* 23: 259–75.

McHugh, Roland. 1980. *Annotations to* Finnegans Wake. Baltimore, Md.: Johns Hopkins Univ. Press.

Milton, John. 1977. *Paradise Lost.* In *Complete Poems and Major Prose,* edited by Merritt Y. Hughes. New York: Odyssey Press.

Mommsen, Theodor. 1957. *The History of Rome.* 5 vols. Glencoe, Ill.: Free Press.

Mosso, Angelo. 1904. *Fatigue.* Translated by Margaret Drummond and W. B. Drummond. London: Swan Sonnenschein and Co.

Myers, Frederic W. H. 1920. *Human Personality and Its Survival of Bodily Death.* 2 vols. London: Longmans, Green and Co.

The New Encyclopedia Britannica. 1998. Chicago: Encyclopedia Britannica, Inc.

Nolan, Emer. 1995. *James Joyce and Nationalism.* London: Routledge.

Norris, Margot. 1992. *Joyce's Web: The Social Unraveling of Modernism.* Austin: Univ. of Texas Press.

Noon, William T. 1963. *Joyce and Aquinas.* New Haven, Conn.: Yale Univ. Press.

Nugel, Bernfried. 2000–2001. "James Joyce, Mastersinger: Echoes and Resonances of Richard Wagner's *Die Meistersinger von Nurnberg* in *A Portrait of the Artist as a Young Man.*" *James Joyce Quarterly* 38: 45–61.

O'Brien, Darcy. 1968. *The Conscience of James Joyce.* Princeton, N.J.: Princeton Univ. Press.

O'Grady, Thomas B. 1991. "Little Chandler's Song of Experience." *James Joyce Quarterly* 28: 399–405.

Opie, Iona, and Moira Tatem. 1989. *A Dictionary of Superstitions.* New York: Oxford Univ. Press.

Oppenheim, Janet. 1985. *The Other World: Spiritualism and Psychical Research in England, 1815–1914*. Cambridge, U.K.: Cambridge Univ. Press.

———. 1991. *Shattered Nerves: Doctors, Patients, and Depression in Victorian England*. New York: Oxford Univ. Press.

Osler, William. 1917. *The Principles and Practice of Medicine, Designed for the Use of Practitioners and Students of Medicine*. London: D. Appleton and Co.

"Papus." 1897. *La magie et l'hypnose recueil de faits et experiences justifiant et prouvant les enseignements de l'occultisme*. Paris: Chamuel.

Parrinder, Patrick. 1984. *James Joyce*. Cambridge, U.K.: Cambridge Univ. Press.

Peake, Charles. 1977. *James Joyce: The Citizen and the Artist*. Stanford, Calif.: Stanford Univ. Press.

Percy, Thomas. 1966. *Reliques of Ancient Poetry, Consisting of Old Heroic Ballads, Songs, and Other Pieces of Our Earlier Poets, Together with Some Few of Later Date*. 3 vols. New York: Dover.

Perera, Charles A. 1949. *May's Manual of the Diseases of the Eye for Students and General Practitioners*. Baltimore, Md.: Williams and Wilkins.

Persinger, Michael A., and Katherine Makarec. 1987. "Temporal Lobe Epileptic Signs and Correlative Behaviors Displayed by Normal Populations." *Journal of General Psychology* 114: 179–95.

Phillips, Stephen. 1902. Ulysses: *A Drama in a Prologue and Three Acts*. London: John Lane.

Plato. 1892. "Laws." *The Dialogues of Plato*. Translated by Benjamin Jowett. London: Dover Publications.

Plotinus. 1956. *The Six Enneads*. Translated by Stephen MacKenna and B. S. Page. New York: Pantheon Books.

Poincaré, Henri. 1911. *Leçons sur les hypothèses cosmogoniques professés à la Sorbonne*. Paris: Librairie Scientifique A. Hermann et Fils.

———. 1952. *Science and Method*. Translated by Francis Maitland, New York: Dover.

Poucher, William A. 1936. *Perfumes, Cosmetics, and Soaps*. 3 vols. New York: D. Van Nostrand Co.

Power, Arthur. 1974. *Conversations with James Joyce*. Chicago: Univ. of Chicago Press.

Power, Mary. 1981. "The Discovery of *Ruby*." *James Joyce Quarterly* 18: 115–21.

Rabaté, Jean-Michael. 1981. *James Joyce, Authorized Reader*. Baltimore, Md.: Johns Hopkins Univ. Press.

Rabinbach, Anson. 1990. *The Human Motor: Energy, Fatigue, and the Origins of Modernity*. New York: Basic Books.

Rabelais, François. 1990. *Gargantua and Pantagruel*. Translated by Burton Raffel. New York: W. W. Norton.

Raleigh, John Henry. 1977. *The Chronicle of Leopold and Molly Bloom: Ulysses as Narrative*. Berkeley: Univ. of California Press.

———. 1959. "Who Was M'Intosh?" *James Joyce Review* 3: 59–62.

Read, Forrest, ed. 1967. *Pound/Joyce: The Letters of Ezra Pound to James Joyce, with Pound's Essay on Joyce*. New York: New Directions.

Restuccia, Frances. 1989. *Joyce and the Law of the Father.* New Haven, Conn.: Yale Univ. Press.

Ribot, Theodule. 1873. *English Psychology.* London: Henry S. King and Co.

———. 1906. *Essay on the Creative Imagination.* Translated by Albert Baron. London: Kegan Paul.

———. 1977. "Diseases of Memory." In *Significant Contributions to the History of Psychology, 1750–1920,* edited by Daniel N. Robinson, 3–205. Washington, D.C.: Univ. Publications of America.

Rice, Anne. 1977. *Interview with the Vampire.* New York: Ballantine Books.

Riffaterre, Hermine B. 1970. *L'orphisme dans la poesie romantique: Themes et style surnaturaliste.* Paris: A. G. Niset.

Rimmel, Eugene. 1845. *The Book of Perfumes.* London: Chapman and Hall.

Riquelme, John Paul. 1983. *Teller and Tale in Joyce's Fiction: Oscillating Perspectives.* Baltimore, Md.: Johns Hopkins Univ. Press.

Rose, Danis, and John O'Hanlon. 1989. *James Joyce: The Lost Notebook: New Evidence on the Genesis of Ulysses.* Edinburgh, Scotland: Split Pea Press.

Ruoff, James. 1969. "A Little Cloud." In *James Joyce's Dubliners: A Critical Handbook,* edited by James R. Baker and Thomas F. Staley, 107–20. Belmont, Calif.: Wadsworth.

Scholes, Robert, and Richard M. Kain. 1965. *The Workshop of Daedalus: James Joyce and the Raw Materials for A Portrait of the Artist as a Young Man.* Evanston, Ill.: Northwestern Univ. Press.

Schork, R. J. 1997. *Latin and Roman Culture in Joyce.* Gainesville: Univ. Press of Florida.

Selfridge-Field, Eleanor. 1988. "Marcello's Music: Repertory vs. Reputation." In *Benedetto Marcello: La sua opera e il suo tempo,* edited by Claudio Madricardo and Franco Rossi, 205–22. Florence: Olschki.

———. 1990. *The Music of Benedetto and Alessandro Marcello: A Thematic Catalogue.* Oxford, U.K.: Clarendon Press.

Senn, Fritz. 1974. "Nausicaa." In *James Joyce's Ulysses: Critical Essays,* edited by Clive Hart and David Hayman, 277–312. Berkeley: Univ. of California Press.

———. 1984. *Joyce's Disclocutions: Essays on Reading as Transition.* Edited by John Paul Riquelme. Baltimore, Md.: Johns Hopkins Univ. Press.

———. 1995. *Inductive Scrutinies: Focus on Joyce.* Edited by Christine O'Neill. Baltimore, Md.: Johns Hopkins Univ. Press.

Shloss, Carol. 1988. "Review of G. George Sandulescu and Clive Hart, *Assessing the 1984 Ulysses.*" *James Joyce Quarterly* 25: 395–401.

Smith, Craig. 1991. "Twilight in Dublin: A Look at Joyce's 'Nausicaa.' " *James Joyce Quarterly* 28: 631–35.

Smith, William Henry, and George F. Chambers. 1881. *A Cycle of Celestial Objects.* Oxford, U.K.: Clarendon Press.

Spencer, Herbert. 1916. *First Principles.* New York: D. Appleton and Co.

Stephenson, Paul, and Margie Waters. 1999–2000. "We Two and the Lost Angel: The Cousins." *James Joyce Quarterly* 37: 167–72.

Sullivan, Jack. 1978. *Elegant Nightmares: The English Ghost Story from LeFanu to Blackwood.* Athens: Ohio Univ. Press.

Sultan, Stanley. 1964. *The Argument of* Ulysses. Columbus: Ohio State Univ. Press.

Tatar, Maria M. 1978. *Spellbound: Studies on Mesmerism and Literature.* Princeton, N.J.: Princeton Univ. Press.

Thomas, Brook. 1982. *James Joyce's* Ulysses: *A Book of Many Happy Returns.* Baton Rouge: Louisiana State Univ. Press.

Thornton, E. M. 1976. *Hypnotism, Hysteria, and Epilepsy: An Historical Synthesis.* London: William Heinemann Medical Books.

Topia, André. 1984. "The Matrix and the Echo: Intertextuality in *Ulysses.*" In *Post-Structuralist Joyce: Essays from the French,* edited by Derek Attridge and Daniel Ferrer, 103–26. Cambridge, U.K.: Cambridge Univ. Press.

Torchiana, Donald T. 1986. *Backgrounds for Joyce's Dubliners.* Boston: Allen and Unwin.

Turner, John Noel. 1997. "Commentary on the Closing of 'Oxen of the Sun.' " *James Joyce Quarterly* 35: 83–112.

Turner, Jonathan H. 1985. *Herbert Spencer: A Renewed Appreciation.* Beverly Hills, Calif.: Sage Publications.

Van Mierlo, Wim. 1997. "The Freudful Couchmare Revisited: Contextualizing Joyce and the New Psychology." *Joyce Studies Annual,* 114–53.

Virgil. 1951. *The Aeneid.* Translated by Rolfe Humphries. New York: Scribners.

Vogt, Donald D. 1981, "Absinthium: A Nineteenth-Century Drug of Abuse." *Journal of Ethnopharmacology* 4: 337–42.

Vogt, Donald D., and Michael Montagne. 1982. "Absinthe: Behind the Emerald Mask." *International Journal of the Addictions* 17: 1015–29.

Walzl, Florence. 1982. "A Book of Signs and Symbols: The Protagonist." In *The Seventh of Joyce,* edited by Bernard Benstock, 117–23. Bloomington: Univ. of Indiana Press.

Weir, David. 1996. *James Joyce and the Art of Mediation.* Ann Arbor: Univ. of Michigan Press.

Weiss, Daniel. 1956. "The End of the 'Oxen of the Sun.' " *The Analyst* 9 (Mar.): 1–16.

Wescott, Glenway. 1990. "At Lloyd Morris's Party." In *James Joyce: Interviews and Recollections,* edited by E. H. Mikhail, 100–101. New York: Macmillan.

Whittaker, Stephen, and Francis X. Jordan. 1995. "The Three Whistles and the Aesthetic of Mediation: Modern Physics and Platonic Metaphysics in Joyce's *Ulysses.*" *James Joyce Quarterly* 33: 27–48.

Wodehouse, P. G. 1930. *Very Good, Jeeves.* Garden City, N.Y.: Doubleday, Doran and Co.

Yared, Aida. 2000. "Joyce's Sources: Sir Richard F. Burton's *Terminal Essay in* Finnegans Wake." *Joyce Studies Annual,* 124–66.

Yee, Cordell. 1997. *The Word According to James Joyce: Reconstructing Representation.* Cranbury, N.J.: Associated Univ. Press.

Ziarek, Ewa. 1992. " 'Circe': Joyce's Argumentum ad Feminam." *James Joyce Quarterly* 30: 51–68.

Index

Italic page number denotes illustration.

315

astronomical/astrological references
(*cont.*)
and Bloom, 230; to constellations,
111, 114, 124–25, 132–34, 280nn. 11,
12, 14, 18; dawn, June 17, 114, *133;*
Dublin sky, *137;* Equuleus rising,
132; in *Finnegans Wake,* 137; journey
of discovery, 151–53; mid-morning
constellations, *125;* to moon, 127–28,
131, 280n. 10; night sky of "Ithaca,"
135; in "Oxen of the Sun," 140, 283n.
8; Pegasus rising, *133;* pinpointing
Bloom's birth date, 114, 132, 134,
138–42, 281nn. 1, 3; to sunshine,
122–29. *See also* Blaze Star
astronomical journey of discovery,
151–53
Atherton, J. S., 99, 205
Attridge, Derek, 275nn. 1, 2
authoring, 51–52, 102–3, 106
autogenetic principles, 88

Bain, Alexander, xiii, 13
Barnacle, Nora, 86–87, 231, 233–34, 236,
256
Basic, Sonja, 229
Bath of the Nymph (print), 76, 77
Beck, Warren, 266n. 4
Bello Cohen (fictional character), 226
Ben Dollard (fictional character), 63, 129,
180, 278n. 8
Benstock, Bernard, 275n. 1
Benstock, Shari, 275n. 1
Bergson, Henri, 221
Berman, Louis, 8
Bernard, Claude, 221
Biblical journey of discovery, 150–51,
283n. 7
Bickerton, Derek, 41–42
binary oppositions, 2, 264n. 13

Binet, Alfred, 12
biogenetic law, 7, 14, 143–44, 282n. 1
biographical journey of discovery,
153–55
Biran, Maine de, 221
Blaze Star, 114, 138–42, 281nn. 2, 3, 5, 6
Blodgett, Harriet, 279n. 6
Bloom. *See* Leopold Bloom (fictional
character)
"blue fuse," 194–95, 289n. 15
Bob Cowley (fictional character), 62, 180
Bob Doran (fictional character), 139
Boheemen-Saaf, Christine van, 275n. 1
Bohr, Niels, 9
"bostoons," 72, 273n. 37
boustrophedonic labyrinth, 83, 86–87
Bovril, 242, 296n. 16
Bowen, Zack, 56
Bridgeman (fictional character), 50–51,
268nn. 15, 16, 269n. 17
Bridie Kelly (fictional character), 77
Brother Michael (fictional character),
24–25
Brünhilde (fictional character), 23
Budgen, Frank, xi–xii, 143, 200, 283n. 13
Bunyan voice, 95, 102, 151
Burke voice, 96, 152, 154
Burns, Christy L., 264n. 13, 287n. 34

C (letter), 212–13, 220, 222, 291n. 1. *See
also* arc theme; curves
"Calypso" (Joyce): bells ringing in,
118–19; evidence of Bloom's
epilepsy in, 285n. 6; links recalled in
De Quincey phase, 111–12, 113
"Camp Granada" (Sherman song), 201,
290n. 11
canal bargeman, 247, 299n. 31
Captain O'Shea, 48
cardinal points, 76, 274n. 2

"Scylla and Charybdis" (Joyce) (*cont.*)
lantern in, 199; literary style of, 90;
on method of reading, 106; question
about word all men know, 223;
recasting of Shakespeare, 228;
Stephen clinging to Shakespeare, 94,
107; Stephen's description of
cuckoldry, 80
Seidman, Robert J., 280n. 11
self-definition/self-negation, 46–54
Selfridge-Field, Eleanor, 286n. 22
Senn, Fritz, 273n. 43, 277n. 16
sensory stimuli. *See* smells that evoke
memories; sounds affecting
characters; stimuli to
visions/hallucinations; words
evoking memories
1798, 64, 270n. 15
sex: attitudes toward food and, 274n. 4;
Bloom's attitude toward, 80;
Bloom's thoughts about, 76–77;
description of in *Portrait of the Artist*,
20–21; music/synchronicity and,
59–60, 61, 63–67; neo-Platonists view
of, 144. *See also* masturbation
Seymour Bushe (as fictional character),
172–73
Shakespeare, William: birth star of,
141–42, 281–82n. 7; on fatherhood,
102; references to works of, 167,
171; reflection of in mirror, 32,
181–83, 187, 192, 228, 256,
288n. 7; Stephen's fixation on,
94, 107
Shaun (fictional character): address to
school girls, xiv, xv; astronomical
references and, 135–36; interview
with reporter, 40–41; key signature
dispels his uncertainties, 258;
recognizes shape of lozenge, 256;
scrutiny of, 31–32; self-definition/

self-negation of characters, 46; use of
telepathy, 69
Shem (fictional character), 46, 205,
250–51, 254–56
Sheridan voice, 96, 152
Sherrington, Sir Charles, xiii, 214, 215
Sicily, 276n. 10
Siegfried (fictional character), 23, 265n.
22
Simon Dedalus (fictional character), 11,
264n. 11; as candidate for M'Intosh
identity, 239–40; in dance of death
scene, 185; identification with
Orpheus, 56–57; in Shakespearean
portrait scene, 288n. 7; use of Orphic
phenomenon, 59–60; view of
Mulligan, 211
Sinbad (fictional character), 232–36
"Sirens" (Joyce): active principle of, 92;
Bob Cowley's song, 180; Boylan-
Molly affair in, 79; Boylan's time of
arrival at Molly's, 181; chronology
of, 61–62, 270n. 12; connection
between love/Mars/Venus, 278n. 7;
destabilizing psychic intensity in,
192; dropping of blinds in, 199;
events at Dolphin's Barn in, 83–85;
identification of Bloom in, 268n. 13;
introduction of arranger, 74–75;
jingling sound in, 116–17; musical
language of, 90; narrative of, 275n. 2;
Ormond barmaids of, 273n. 44;
Orphic dimension in, 58–75, 168;
references to sunlight in, 129–30;
130; split-screen montage effect, 55;
as temptation to sentimentality, 106
Sir Robert Ball (as fictional character), 9,
264n. 6, 284n. 18
Sir Thomas Brown voice, 95
"Sisters, The" (Joyce), 32, 42, 232, 279n.
5. *See also Dubliners* (Joyce)